This is the most detailed, sophisticated, and comprehensive treatment of autonomy currently available. Moreover it argues for a quite different conception of autonomy from that found in the philosophical literature.

Professor Berofsky claims that the idea of autonomy as origination in the self is a seductive but ultimately illusory one. The only serious way of approaching the subject is to pay due attention to psychology and its emphasis on liberation from the disabling effects of physiological and psychological afflictions. A sustained critique of concepts such as moral autonomy, self-realization, ideal autonomy, and identification is offered. The author replaces these with an alternative model that focuses on vital, competent, and unencumbered engagement in the world.

Liberation from self

Liberation from self

A theory of personal autonomy

Bernard Berofsky

Columbia University

CAMBRIDGE
UNIVERSITY PRESS

Published by the Press Syndicate of the University of Cambridge
The Pitt Building, Trumpington Street, Cambridge CB2 1RP
40 West 20th Street, New York, NY 10011-4211, USA
10 Stamford Road, Oakleigh, Melbourne 3166, Australia

First published 1995

Printed in the United States of America

Library of Congress Cataloging-in-Publication Data
Berofsky, Bernard.
Liberation from self : a theory of personal autonomy / Bernard
Berofsky.
p.   cm.
Includes bibliographical references and index.
ISBN 0-521-48045-0 (hc)
1. Self (Philosophy)   2. Free will and determinism.   I. Title.
BD450.B438   1995
128–dc20   95-11441
                                                        CIP

A catalog record for this book is available from the British Library.

ISBN 0-521-48045-0 Hardback

To my mother

Contents

Liberation from self

1
Introduction

Acts of God are not acts of God. They are sudden, unexpected, natural occurrences with a significant impact on human affairs. It is, therefore, not incoherent to contend, as I do, that autonomous agents are not individuals whose actions and decisions are self-directed. I hasten to add that this negative conclusion about autonomy is not just fallout from the rejection of the very project of theorizing about the self. It is rather a result which is forced on us by the convergence of a variety of considerations, including powerful intuitions about particular cases.

Taking etymology seriously, we begin, like everyone else, with the assumption that autonomy is self-direction and embark on a search for the difference between self and other. When William Blier, a member of David Koresh's cult, acquiesced in his own suicide, he was acting from motives, values, and beliefs that were inculcated from without in a way which made him a virtual paradigm of heteronomy. Although Blier's action was inspired by motives that were in a sense his, that were among other things accessible to him in the unique way any person knows her own mental states, we rightly hesitate to describe his behavior as self-directed. His submission to another person – Koresh – was as complete as is possible for a human creature. As we continue the search for a precise understanding of self-origination, we shall eventually come to realize that the assumption that autonomy is either self-origination *or* self-direction, useful as it has been, must, like Wittgenstein's ladder, be abandoned.

It is a truism that early environments can greatly narrow a person's mode of thinking, range of experience, or vision, so as to limit severely the range of feasible options. What the individual then needs is the expansion of his horizons and the capacity to respond rationally, openly, and flexibly to his current environment. I will argue that autonomy is essentially constituted by the manner in which an agent is engaged in her world rather than the metaphysical origin of her motivations. If we say of a person who finds meaning in an activity he has hitherto been unable to appreciate that he is now really expressing his true nature, we are just redescribing this open relation to the world in a misleading metaphysical

The project which culminated in this book began while I was a Fulbright Research Fellow at the Hebrew University of Jerusalem in 1988. I wish to thank the United States–Israel Educational Foundation for providing this opportunity for me.

way. When the self is absorbed in the other, there is potentiality for a form of delight unfettered by a fear of inauthenticity and enriched by a flow of activity that is both spontaneous, yet governed by its own internal logic. When this potentiality is realized, we tend to speak of self-realization as if we are offering an explanation, when in truth we are producing a metaphor.

Critics of the view that freedom is the liberty of indifference are fond of observing that our freedom is not threatened by the need to subordinate ourselves to the rules of mathematics and logic. We do not feel that we would have greater freedom (at least of a worthwhile sort) if we retained the ability to withhold judgment in the face of deductively conclusive evidence. I believe that we should feel similarly unafraid by the correlative need to subordinate ourselves to the other areas of life in which we act and find our satisfactions. In this way, autonomy is achieved.

As living things, we essentially strive and act. Through our activities, whether they be baseball or meditation, we find our satisfactions and our fulfillments. A mathematician is delighted to be able to *see* a complex proof; a cyclist is delighted to *see* the results of a regimen prescribed by those more experienced in this sport; a scientist is delighted to *see* the results of his experiment, confident that his adherence to established procedures confers reliability on these results. None bemoans the loss of freedom occasioned by the inability to reject these outcomes or regards the significance of the enterprise as compromised for this reason. To be sure, one may wish to retain the freedom to abandon any enterprise; but whether or not one is a mathematician, there is something perverse in wanting the freedom to reject a theorem one knows to be true.

A person who is given negative freedom, that is, freedom from interference in her affairs by others, will have attained a perfectly useless state if she lacks intelligence, skills, knowledge, and emotional health, traits I shall summarily call "positive freedom." Even if she has desires, she may flail about aimlessly, futilely trying to achieve some of her goals. And the goals themselves may be unfulfilling, shallow, even self-destructive. If she wishes any sort of fulfillment, she will certainly need relevant knowledge and skills. She may not want to be a mathematician, musician, or cyclist. But if she does, she must submit herself to the rules that are operative in these dominions and acquire knowledge of established results. And if she wishes to forge radical change, she must still acquire the discipline needed to understand and use the methodology and techniques against some of which she may wish to rebel. The demands of rationality, discipline, knowledge, and independence will assuage worries about subordination to unworthy ideals, to dictators, and to unruly mobs. The engagement with the world of which I speak constitutes autonomy only for beings possessed of both competence and individuality.

Autonomous persons must be independent, not just from the pernicious influence of others, but from the pernicious influence of their own earlier lives. For that robust engagement with the world is possible only for persons who have liberated themselves from the disabling effects of physiological and psychological afflictions. We are all limited and, perhaps, our lives are completely determined. But there are crucial differences in the manner in which our earlier life bears on our later life. The possibly deterministic process that has brought us to our current state may have an independence and authenticity depending on the character of *current* interactions. The autonomy of a sculptor is grounded in knowledge of the craft, its techniques, its history, its standards, in his openness, and in his ability to respond to relevant inputs, his work as it has so far evolved, his own responses to that work, and relevant features of the world such as the manner of his involvement in professional life. If these elements are in place, we do not require in addition a radical rupture with the past.

On the other hand, when we have formed and retained an irrational belief that is rendered immune from learning through experience, when we respond to the world in a cognitive style that is prone to produce distortion, when our experience is filtered through subjective principles designed to reinforce prejudices which serve a defensive function, we have failed to transcend our origins in a way that bears on our capacity to establish an autonomous connection to the world.

In order to characterize impediments to autonomy, therefore, we must turn to psychology for a deeper understanding of the ways these barriers can form. It is striking to observe that this is done by very few philosophers who are interested in autonomy.[1]

We would rightly look askance at a work in the philosophy of physics that contained no physics. We not only demand that speculations about the content and implications of actual physical theories be informed by scientific data; but we also don't suppose that much insight is gained from purely conceptual inquiries into the general nature of laws, theories, and experiment. Philosophers do not dictate to scientists; so they must be attuned to scientific developments in order to test their views about the general character of laws and theories in light of the actual practice and results of scientific theorizing and experimentation.

Yet most philosophers who address the issue of personal autonomy ignore psychology in spite of the centrality of the notion of autonomy in certain theoretical approaches and most evidently in the domains of developmental and clinical psychology. Thus, there would be reason for philosophical interest in psychological work on autonomy whether or not the tack I have taken, which naturally accords a central place to psychology in virtue of the pivotal role of the concept of liberation, is viable.

This conclusion may appear naive to those who discern a variety of fundamentally distinct projects within the philosophical literature, each one attempting to appropriate *the* idea of autonomy, when in truth a different idea is associated with each project. For why should one suppose that a detailed knowledge of psychology is relevant to all these projects?

One should not. But the rub is that those projects which ignore psychology are fatally flawed in ways that will be detailed in this book.

The psychologically driven notion I will be elaborating originates from reflection on the manner in which we pass from totally dependent creatures to ones who are more or less equipped to operate independently and responsibly. Given the varying degrees with which human beings succeed at this transition, we may seek to formulate a humanly realizable goal of realistic autonomy or characterize a scale and a range on that scale such that people falling within that range can be counted as having achieved a normal degree of autonomy.[2]

But those worried by the specter of determinism may see these differences as superficial. For whether one falls within or without the normal range on the autonomy scale, the agent is in any event just a construction out of the forces of heredity and environment and cannot, therefore, count as an original source of action or value. Yet rather than despairing altogether of the project of defining autonomy, these pessimistically inclined philosophers are often tempted instead to focus on the very state we cannot attain. If, in light of the encumbrances imposed by nature and nurture, none of us can be ideally autonomous, we can at least understand what a divine-like realization would be.

But if we are to dwell with envy upon this idea and begrudge the human condition for acting as an absolute barrier to our participation in this ideal, we must see the idea as both intelligible and desirable and we shall see that there are deep problems on both scores. Ultimately, I reject both the coherence and the relevance of this ideal and insist upon a more realistic conception which concedes the genuine impact on us of the contingencies of genetic endowment and upbringing. Evidently, we can conceive of beings with greater powers and autonomy than we have. But the biological and psychological limitations under which we operate do not preclude the construction of an account of our autonomy which need not be viewed as a pale substitute of "the real thing."

If admirers of ideal autonomy believe that *none* of us is autonomous, Kant thought that, regardless of our situation in the world, we must *all* be autonomous. The most striking contrast with the notion to be embraced in this book is the conception of autonomy as a metaphysical condition, not admitting of degrees. On this account, autonomy is like Sartre's freedom, a fate we cannot escape, rather than an achievement some of us fail to realize. It is a condition shared by all equally.

All what? Kant regarded autonomy as a property of the wills of all rational selves. As a rational self or agent (self-cum-actor), I can lose neither this property nor, since its possession is an either-or matter, even a portion of it. This view of us permitted Kant to draw, from the self's rationality, the remarkable conclusion that we are all necessarily bound by the moral law. How?

A moral agent is one who submits himself to moral principles. But if I retain the freedom not to be a mathematician or a cyclist, I can liberate myself from bondage to the constraints of these activities. Why should I not then opt out of morality and free myself from *this* sort of slavery? And since morality often conflicts with self-interest, there is a pressing argument on behalf of this option. I may be disadvantaged without knowledge of mathematics or, in more limited contexts, the ability to ride a bike; but I would surely be at an *advantage* if I could disavow principles which often enjoin me to sacrifice my interests.

Theories which locate the ground of moral principles in contingent human interests and concerns, according to Kant, permit this bizarre freedom to reject morality because they fail to appreciate the distinctive force of moral principles. If, for example, I follow moral rules because I believe them to be divinely inspired, my interest in the rules is merely extrinsic. Obedience is a means to secure God's approval. The burden of morality is then contingent on my interest in His approval. Given the nature of morality, it follows that my act, though in accordance with morality, has no moral worth.

How then can a *rational* being be moved by a moral principle in such a way as to confer moral worth on that being? He must respect the principle as such and not be bound to it via an extrinsic interest, such as the desire for salvation. Kant's ingenious solution to this problem is well-known: If the principle is not extrinsic, it must have been created by the person, that is, the rational being, himself. I am bound by moral principles because they originate in me, that is, in my reason. Morality is possible only if we are autonomous, only if we have, through our reason, created the very laws which bind us. The conception of freedom as submission to law merges with the idea of autonomy as self-governance. We are governed by laws we create or laws which derive from the necessity of our natures. We have then this magnificent union of morality, rationality, and autonomy.

All facets of Kant's moral theory have undergone thorough and oftimes devastating criticism. For example, the inability of the abstract formalism embodied in the categorical imperative to sustain a specific morality has been frequently documented. In general, efforts to derive morality from rationality have been assailed by many in ways I find highly convincing.[3] I shall, therefore, restrict myself to an evaluation of some important, contemporary, Kantian-inspired efforts to produce a derivation along these lines. My conclusion will be that these efforts fail and consequently that autonomous agents, in spite of their rationality, need not regard themselves as under the domination of morality. I shall in fact adopt a stronger position, that autonomous agents need not be driven by any values, moral or nonmoral, if the manner by which one is moved by values requires the introduction of principles for the evaluation of the worth of motives that might generate action.

In spite of the general repudiation of Kant's views in ethics, he continues to exert an enormous and relatively unchallenged authority in contemporary thinking about autonomy. There is a tendency among many simply to identify the general notion of autonomy with the Kantian notion of moral autonomy, as if an alternative to Kant's views is unthinkable. His conclusions are often treated as if they were articles of faith, assumptions thinking persons need not bother to reevaluate. D. T. Meyers (1987) begins an article on the subject with the sentence: "People are personally autonomous when their conduct is morally permissible and is not dictated by any technical rule, and when they are doing what they, as individuals, want to do" (619). Never again in this article is the connection of autonomy to moral permissibility raised as an issue. Yet Meyers apparently supposes that lip service must be paid to the alleged intimacy of these two ideas, an intimacy Kant at least argued for.

The abandonment of moral autonomy through a critique of doctrines which attempt to capitalize on the fact that autonomous agents are rational may be judged premature. If morality cannot be eked out of rationality, the fault may lie in Kant's overly narrow conception of rationality or the sterility of his moral universalism. On the one hand Kant saw the deliberating agent as an individual confronting moral dilemmas alone, reflecting without benefit of the membership each one of us has in a community whose language, values, and practices have shaped us and have determined the character of the issues we face. To the extent that Kant acknowledges an extraindividual component, it turns out to be a species-wide one – rationality – and we have again bypassed that intermediary between the individual and the species, to wit, the community and its traditions.

The relocation of the deliberating subject in a space which acknowledges the individual's essential participation in a community meets with profoundly different responses. If individual identities cannot be extricated from the social meanings which shape them, perhaps moral deliberation is viable only against a background of shared commitments, shaped by a common tradition. The direction of this neo-Aristotelian communitarianism is then the deflation of autonomy, for the latter is an inherently individual notion. An agent qua autonomous sets himself apart from his group, even if he rejoins it after a personal assessment. Complete immersion in a group is reversion to tribal society, whose structure is antithetical to individual autonomy.

The more interesting response for our purposes, then, comprehends the retention of autonomy as a value, based perhaps upon the failure of communitarianism to take seriously the actual predicament of individuals who both live in many disparate communities and participate as well in a global environment which expands our awareness of life styles and ideology. Taught to prize tolerance in the sphere of belief and practice, we are constantly bombarded with data which enrich our options. And it is not as if we needed to move beyond our geographic borders to find controversies which forge deep moral divisions.

These remarks about communitarianism hardly count as even a first stab at a serious critique of one source of the challenge to the value of individual autonomy. Moreover, how do we address the fact that our "particularity can never be simply left behind or obliterated. The notion of escaping from it into a realm of entirely universal maxims which belong to man as such . . . is an illusion" (MacIntyre 1981: 205–6)?

It is undeniable that deliberation proceeds in a context whose meanings are determined from without and whose agent is embedded in a cultural matrix that is provided rather than chosen. Yet when assumptions and unspoken values are rendered explicit, the mature and informed agent whose cultural heritage happens also to include the Enlightenment and the Liberal tradition will be sensitive to the absence of consensus and the arbitrary character of appeals to tradition. Since, as we have insisted, an autonomous deliberator must be rational, can we yet appeal to that element, understood in an unKantian manner, in an effort to forge a morality that will appeal to or even bind autonomous agents irrespective of their particular and varying traditions?

The contractarian tradition provides an affirmative answer. If reason begins as a tool to be used by perfectly selfish utility maximizers, it can become the basis for a bona fide commitment to morality once the individual recognizes the personal advantages of a social contract which limits each person's freedom for the benefit of all. But a detailed examination of David Gauthier's sophisticated efforts to effect this derivation leads to the conclusion that, if my reason begins as a tool of my passions, it remains forever that. So we look elsewhere for philosophies which purport to show how agents, whose individual natures are intimately bound up with the particular group of which they are a part, can transcend their particularities by a rational process which can lead to the universal validation of moral principles.

If autonomous agents qua autonomous must be rational, they must as agents engage in the practice of argumentation, a practice which, as Jürgen Habermas insists, embodies normative presuppositions. One of these presuppositions is a procedural principle which specifies conditions for the resolution of practical disputes in a way that is acceptable to all participants. The principle's universal validity is grounded in a feature common to all groups of rational agents, to wit, the use of discourse as a social mechanism to resolve disputes and restore consensus. Thus, Habermas acknowledges the social nature of the individual without abandoning the quest for universal validity in ethics. Autonomy remains a component of the moral life insofar as the reflections of individual persons are not automatically constrained by the context of particular community and tradition. They are, however, constrained formally by a context common to all groups for "there is no form of sociocultural life that is not at least implicitly geared to maintaining communicative action by means of argument" (Habermas 1990: 100). Since the moral skeptic "cannot drop out of the communicative practice of everyday life" (Habermas

1990: 101), the autonomous agent who rejects morality would presumably have "to take refuge in suicide or serious mental illness" (Habermas 1990: 100). I believe that autonomy is a value – although it may not be the supreme value – and will argue, pace Habermas, that a value-free autonomous agent does not necessarily face this desultory choice.

If the model of the autonomous agent is different from that of the moral agent, we face the question of the relative merits of these models. We do not burden ourselves with the *assumption* that autonomy is supremely valuable, but rather attempt to discover, after the analysis is complete, just how valuable it is. Although the account is immune from the gender-based critiques of autonomy such as Carol Gilligan's, I do conclude that certain communitarian values are incompatible with autonomy and are forced, therefore, to reject *autonomism*,[4] the idea that all value ultimately rests on autonomy as a foundation.

In advancing the claim that autonomous agents need not be motivated in part by an evaluation of the moral *or* nonmoral worth of the motives inclining them to action, I am reacting against another reversion to Kantianism, the view, still quite prevalent, that autonomy is linked to higher-order evaluation, a view which is itself linked to the idea that the self is more likely to be located on the reflective rather than the motivationally primitive level. In opting for the significance of identification with certain motives, its advocates disregard the self-deceptive and rationalizing character this often assumes. But even the demand that the identification be "rational" will not, I argue, save the doctrine. There is often little reason to think that second-order reservations about first-order desires are closer to the core of the person than those desires themselves or that they fail to derive from sources external to the self. In fact, the paradigm case of heteronomy for David Shapiro is the rigid individual, one whose life is saturated by principles. In his case, the principles are internal voices, rigidly applied to situations, and estranging him from his own feelings and motivations. The principles are not informed by independent data and adjusted accordingly, and the individual is incapable of spontaneity. In order to achieve autonomy, he must shed these encumbrances to allow the sort of open engagement with his world I earlier described.

In defending my account of autonomy, I will not simply be offering it as one among many. For if my critique of Kantian-based accounts is sound, the underpinnings of at least one opposing view, to wit, the identification of autonomy with moral autonomy, will have been withdrawn. And since I will argue for the incoherence of the notion of ideal autonomy, its rejection will be similarly based on difficulties inherent in the doctrine. And if identification accounts fail because they rest on faulty accounts of the self, we will, I believe, be driven in the direction of the idea I hope to elaborate, to wit, that the conception of autonomy as liberation is not just one conception among several viable ones, each meeting different desiderata, but is rather the one idea of personal autonomy that survives conceptual and empirical scrutiny.

As we begin to explore alternative conceptions, it would be helpful to identify a core meaning, that is, a condition which makes an account an account of autonomy, and not some other notion. Yet it would be misleading to suggest that there is a sharp line between X and a theory of X, as if philosophers share a common "concept" of autonomy and differ on the "nature" of the state picked out by that concept. Why should matters be less murky here than in other philosophical domains? Yet, although philosophers construct differing theories for very different purposes, we can find in the political roots of the term some sort of thread that loosely ties discussions of autonomy together.

The Greeks applied the term "auto nomos" to a city-state which was not under the control of another city-state. Autonomy denoted independence and the ability to govern oneself without outside domination. And, of course, this is the way we use the term today. It is essentially a synonym for "political independence." We then expand this idea to rule out those polities which are in chaos and, in spite of their independence, unable to govern themselves at all. Since "self-rule" implies "rule," we see then the need to add some sort of competence condition to the independence requirement.

In the sphere of personal autonomy, we analogously demand independence (of the right sort) from another *person*. And the demand for minimally effective rule over ourselves dictates the further requirement of rationality. For, in order to effect self-rule, we must be in possession of principles which permit critical scrutiny of the diverse issues which arise during our lives. Although we enter adulthood with values and attitudes derived in large part from others, a failure to submit these matters to continuing scrutiny invalidates the claim to *self*-governance, for the individual thereby remains indistinct from the group. In addition, since a commitment to rationality is the best overall means to secure one's objectives, the scrutiny of an irrational deliberator is likely to result in frustration and ineffectiveness.

I will qualify this conclusion by arguing that there are special cases in which the power to reject reason can be of great personal value. Great achievements, for example, have often been effected by individuals who are irrationally tenacious, yet whose irrationality in these special circumstances does not undermine their autonomy. Thus, although I sever the link between autonomy and morality, the connection between autonomy and basic rationality is upheld.

It would be tidy at this point to proclaim that an account is an account of autonomy only if it incorporates the conditions of independence and minimal rationality. And the very situation of the subject matter does indeed make it impossible practically at least to challenge the inclusion of independence. In the case of rationality, however, there are philosophers who baldly proclaim its irrelevance to autonomy (Crocker 1980: 36–43). And Robert Nozick (1981: 354) complains that, since an ideally autonomous being can be under no constraints, she would not be bound by "the demands of rationality" either. I will be constrained, then, to argue for the inclusion of rationality, understood as at least instrumental rationality. The defense rests on our status as essentially purposive beings, agents groping about for ways to effect our short- and long-term goals, utterly lost without rationality as a tool – among others – to this end, as well as to the absolutely essential end of establishing our very independence. An ideally autonomous agent might require the power to reject reason; but the idea of such an agent is anyway incoherent.

Our purposiveness calls on certain capacities, to set priorities, formulate long-term goals, subordinate certain interests for the sake of goals deemed more important, anticipate actions to promote these goals, and reflect on the extent to which success has been attained. These capacities depend not only upon rationality, but also upon an internal coherence lacking in extreme cases such as multiple personality, severe psychosis, and perhaps, split brains. So a third condition of autonomy, linked, like rationality, to the political requirement of minimally effective rule, must be added: personal integrity. An individual must have some internal coherence or unity before we can even broach the subject of his autonomy. It is, for example, difficult to understand what the autonomy of Smith can consist of if Smith is a multiple personality, dramatically and uncontrollably shifting from one persona to the next throughout his life.

The soundness of identifying these as components of the core notion is attested to by the implicit adoption of them by conceptions as disparate as Kant's and mine. I am autonomous for Kant insofar as I create the laws which govern me. I am not, therefore, dependent on others; indeed an attachment to others through some desire or need on my part undermines the autonomous status of the rule under which I place myself.

With respect to rationality, it may sound unfair, in light of the enormous differences between Kant's conception and others, including the one toward which I am favorably disposed, to regard the umbrella term "rationality" as covering a single general idea. Yet one of the principal differences among competing conceptions of rationality, including Kant's, is that of strength. "Rationality" is not straightforwardly ambiguous. It is rather that Kant's account is not "rich" or "thick" enough for the purposes.

The only prima facie problematic condition is the third, personal integrity. Since, for Kant, autonomy is a characteristic of the will qua rational, that is, shorn of the nonrational motivations that are normally accessible to consciousness and experiential scrutiny, personal integrity would be irrelevant to Kantian autonomy if it is a feature of the phenomenal self, if, that is, it concerns the internal harmony or coherence of psychological elements like thoughts and desires. Rejecting the noumenal self, I do indeed conceive of personal integrity as the integration of psychological elements. Yet surely Kant thought of the rational self as a fundamental unity no matter the character of its metaphysical trappings. He agrees, therefore, that, whatever the subject of autonomy is, it must possess a fundamental unity. In abandoning Kant's doctrine of the noumenal self, I am changing the locus of the person or self, but am retaining the idea that a disintegrated self cannot be autonomous.

Armed with these minimal conditions, we will be able to detect the errors of those who have confused various bona fide human ideals with that of autonomy. For once we equip our independent, rational, and integrated agent with freedom and knowledge, her key tools, we will find no convincing argument that she must then go on to embody other, distinct ideals such as flourishing, morality, or self-expression. In point of fact, the proposal to construe autonomy in one of these ways runs afoul of the possibility that a fully competent adult can autonomously reject any of them! To put it in less question-begging language, I can construct no sound case for the heteronomy of a rational, fully competent, independent, and emotionally mature adult, who deliberately and knowingly rejects any or all of these ideals. A rejection of liberation – as I understand it – is, on the other hand, essentially a reversion to dependence, the very antithesis of autonomy.

The orientation and concerns of psychologists and psychoanalysts are different from those of philosophers. The latter, neither burdened nor illumined by the presence of competing theoretical structures, often rich in detail, are prone to predicate autonomy of persons or human beings, whereas psychologists are apt to take liberties by distorting the "ordinary meaning" of the term in the service of an overall theoretical goal. Thus, Heinz Hartmann, who coined the term "ego autonomy" in 1939, was concerned to restore an authority Freud had originally assigned to the ego prior to the formation of his structural theory. In Freud's earlier writings, the ego is postulated as a system of the mind which is sometimes dominant in a sphere of behavior. Since the ego is associated with the sense of self, behavior under its control may be said to be self-determined. After several theoretical alterations, the structural theory emerged and with it, the apparent demise of ego autonomy in the face of domination by the instincts of the id. Freud announces his agreement with Groddeck that "what we call our ego behaves essentially *passively* in life" and that "we are lived by unknown and *uncontrollable* forces" (Mausner 1990: 7). I say "apparent" because there are, at the same time, contrasting claims, such as Freud's identification of the aim of analytic therapy: "analysis does not set out to abolish the possibility of morbid reactions, but to give the patient's ego *freedom to choose* one way or the other" (Mausner 1990: 8). Hartmann wanted to stress again the ego's independence from the id, that is, its capacity for synthetic functioning in a conflict-free zone distinct from those of its activities which serve the function of defense against the id instincts.

Other psychoanalysts, most notably David Rapaport (1951; 1953; 1958), picked up on this theme. The ego can emerge as an independent entity in part by converting responses which were originally designed to protect the id into the building blocks of an autonomous system. The ego can have its *own* motives and operate according to its *own* rules. Its autonomy is grounded as well in its independence from the environment along with its capacity to delay and modify response both to sensory and to drive stimulation.

A pressing theoretical question which naturally arose in regard to these developments in psychoanalytic theory concerns the relation between the construct of ego autonomy and the pretheoretical concept of autonomy as attributed to a person. If, as the self psychologists say, the ego is not the self, then the connection may well be tenuous. Shapiro has advanced this charge, contending that the model of ego autonomy is at best a model of self-regulation rather than self-direction. Through incorporating the idea of "automatic internal controls, detours, and modifications of the drives and needs themselves," thus transforming action "from an essentially blind and immediate motor discharge to the effective instrument of modulated and reality-attuned needs" (1970: 332), the theory assimilates autonomy to the condition of a self-regulating mechanism, such as a thermostat or any device with the internal capacity to restore itself to equilibrium in the face of environmental changes. But that is a far cry from the idea of action as consciously chosen after a process of deliberation. Shapiro has chastised Freudian theory in general for its failure to include a volitional component in a theory of action. He would reinstate a component of "folk psychology" against the revisionary approach of the followers of Freud. Almost all human action, even neurotic action, is voluntary, he insists. There are unconscious needs; however, they "will not affect action directly, but only insofar as they affect the various stages of those volitional processes and the conscious motives and choices that are their outcome" (1970: 341).

If the richness of the history of the concept of autonomy in psychological and psychoanalytical theorizing fails to convince philosophers of the relevance of psychological work to their interests, the identification of autonomy as the goal of therapy by Freud at one stage and by others from different schools of therapy ought at least to perk the curiosity of the philosopher as to the connection between the psychological and the philosophical notions. Since my intention at this point is simply to draw attention to this possibly rich source of insights, I shall not elaborate further on psychological history or current trends. Nor in fact will this book present these details, for that is a project in its own right. I have rather tried to avail myself of relevant psychological work in the account as it unfolds.

Part of the explanation that the theoretical literature is ignored is that the concept of autonomy is invoked primarily by psychoanalytic writers and many philosophers look upon this approach with disdain. The course I have chosen is, therefore, a risky one even though I do not anticipate that future investigations will necessitate a major overhaul of the views advanced here. Moreover, I have tried to be noncommittal at key points. For example, in Chapter 8, when efforts are made to characterize the manner in which our past acts as a barrier to autonomy, I canvas a variety of competing approaches in order to produce a formulation general enough to encompass the entire gamut of major theoretical views.

Thus, I shall construct the outlines of a theory of autonomy as liberation. Although it will not be possible to address all facets of this construction in sufficient detail, my case rests as well on a repudiation of other accounts whose failures I will document. It also rests on the soundness of a metaphysical shift I will urge. Only when we begin to see the futility of the initially seductive idea that the quest for autonomous action or decision is the quest for action or decision whose origination can be authenticated metaphysically will we be able to reorient our thinking and look instead at action or decision whose authentication rests upon the agent's link to the world.

One of the principal sources of confusion to a reader of the historical and contemporary literature is the absence of any clear demarcation between freedom and autonomy. One man's autonomy is another woman's freedom and vice-versa. Although my aim is not clarification of the extant literature, I will at least begin with a description of the way I propose to distinguish these ideas. After defending an account of freedom of action in terms of power in Chapter 3, I formulate a conception of agent or positive freedom in terms of the fundamental internal requirements central to any human endeavor. Such traits as intelligence, knowledge, and basic physical skills, for example, are essential or highly useful to the satisfaction of a wide range of activities and decisions, including long-term commitments. They enhance our freedom of action or power, although free agents may or may not possess the freedom to do and decide to do what is (deeply) important to them. These skills are not just important in terms of the enhancement of power, but also because they permit an individual to regulate his activities and decisions critically and independently, that is, autonomously. Yet the capacities which expand a person's powers do not automatically confer greater self-direction in his life. A slave may have powers and skills he is nonetheless unable to use in ways he might choose. Or a disciple may use his powers to discern and act on the wishes of his leader. Since positive freedom is only necessary for these sorts of independence, we move on to the other dimensions of autonomy.

In deference to the tenacity of the belief that autonomous agents are necessarily guided by evaluations of the worth or value of the objects of their desire, I devote Chapter 5 to the construction of a more precise formulation of this view (the Evaluation Conception) and contrast it with one which characterizes values in terms of the objects of a hypothetical choice. The latter position (the Motivation Conception) permits us to locate both the self and the values of the self on the primary motivational level, that is, the first-order will as oriented toward action.

The role and value of rationality are addressed in Chapter 6 as a preliminary to the effort to construct a defense of the Evaluation Conception by deriving this account of value from the rationality we expect of an autonomous person. This chapter also contains an analysis of procedural independence, a key ingredient of autonomy. And, in light of the incoherence or irrelevance of ideal conceptions of autonomy, we are forced to confront the impact of contingency on the autonomy of ordinary mortals.

The Motivation Conception is ultimately vindicated by the failure, demonstrated in Chapter 7, to derive the Evaluation Conception from the assumption of rationality. A portrait of an autonomous agent is constructed, one in which spontaneity, vitality, and competence, rather than reflective evaluation, become the cornerstones. I argue that this person is not necessarily impoverished by the absence of evaluation. He has self-esteem and ideals, sustains a gamut of human emotions (so long as the moral component of these emotions is purged), enters relations like love and friendship, and has the capacity for those virtues that do not implicate moral evaluation, for example, courage.

The resistance to this picture of a modified Nietzschean Übermensch that survives an appreciation of the fact that it is not being *advocated for adoption* – one might in the end opt for morality – derives, I suspect, from adherence to a utopian psychology which renders us more deeply moral than the facts dictate. Emboldened by the extent of bad or irrelevant scientific psychology, philosophers have engaged in a great deal of armchair psychology (e.g., much of so-called moral psychology), far more than they would have permitted themselves in the area of physics. And we come out "smelling like roses." If I am guilty of the same crime, at least I can hope to make the picture a little less lopsided.

The core of this new conception of autonomy, objectivity, is explained in Chapter 8. A person with this trait is open to the world as it is and is capable of adjusting his responses appropriately. He is, therefore, minimally burdened by cognitive styles that are prone to produce distortion, significant limitations of intelligence, memory, or perceptual powers, and backward-directed psychological states, that is, unreliably formed, yet causally active mental states which are resistant to rational review.

In Chapter 9 we discover that no viable conception of the self can play the role of author of the decisions and actions of an autonomous agent as we now understand that idea, that is, as one whose decisions are made under conditions of freedom, knowledge, rationality, independence, objectivity, and personal integrity. The reason is that it is impossible to formulate a prima facie plausible account of the self according to which the self fails to be the author of *heteronomous* decisions and actions.

A highly qualified endorsement of the value of autonomy is made in Chapter 10. Extreme views, that it is always valuable to expand the scope of autonomy, that nothing is valuable unless autonomy is a component, that all communities of autonomous agents are better than all basically heteronomous communities, are rejected. The value of autonomy is explained and preserved from the challenges posed by the feminist critique of C. Gilligan.

2
Freedom and autonomy

This book is about autonomy. In the next three chapters a conception of freedom will be defended according to which autonomy is different from, but dependent upon, freedom. I want first to summarize, without argument or elaboration, the results about freedom so that I can contrast freedom with autonomy and thereby introduce the basic ideas about the latter which guide my thinking.

Positive freedom and autonomy

Positive freedom is comprised of a set of personal traits which are essential or highly useful to the satisfaction of a wide range of activities and decisions, both short- and long-term. It encompasses relevant knowledge, including self-knowledge, and a variety of intellectual and physical competences. (Among intellectual competences, I include capacities for memory, perception, calculation, reasoning, information processing, and the elimination of irrational and inconsistent belief sets.) A free agent is free of debilitating physical infirmities, addictions, and severe stress. (I count a certain level of emotional health as a separate condition of autonomy. The details are presented in Chapters 8 and 9. Personal integrity, including the absence of conditions like severe psychosis, multiple personality, and split brains, is regarded as a *condition* of positive freedom rather than one of its *elements*.) Free agents may or may not possess the freedom to do and decide to do what is (deeply) important to them.

This brief characterization of positive freedom has been at least superficially value-neutral. Intelligence is a good thing; but its possession tells us nothing about the moral qualities of the agent. It can be used for good or for evil. What Isaiah Berlin (1958) had in mind by positive freedom, however, is only superficially neutral. He condemned various historic conceptions of freedom, most notably the self-realization doctrines of idealism, for evolving into apologetics for totalitarian systems through the assumption that only members of the elite ruling class, who recognize the intrinsically social nature of the self, are able to determine the way in which each of us can achieve realization through the assumption of our proper social roles. Similarly, those conceptions of the self according to which certain components are "higher" or "more truly a part of the self" readily lent themselves to integration into an oppressive social system in which the state took on the role of "representing" the better part of the individual in a struggle against the darker forces within.

Berlin's legitimate fears led him to opt for negative freedom, the absence of interference by others, as the sole legitimate form for society to countenance. Later we will identify serious problems distinguishing positive from negative freedom. Moreover, theorists who follow Berlin and attempt to formulate a comprehensive philosophy of the state based on negative freedom alone have faced severe limits.[1] Yet if we follow Berlin and shift our focus to the nature of external interference, we are thereby presumably relieved of the burden of elucidating the character of self-determination. Whatever the latter is, it plays no role in an account of (negative) freedom.

This conclusion may be premature.[2] Whatever one's views on these matters, however, we seem to be compelled to take a stance on the doctrines which disturbed Berlin if we want to know what autonomy is. Autonomy is *self*-regulation; hence one needs a concept of self or one chucks the concept of autonomy. Autonomy is independence; but that is the lack of dependence on the other and so again one must know the difference between the self and the other.

The problem is aggravated by the fact that the self-other distinction is not just the distinction between one person and another, but includes as well the distinction within the person or the body between self and nonself, at least for those who would regard things like the capillaries in one's feet or desires one would prefer not to possess as outside the self.

So even if positive freedom is best conceived not as a charged notion, autonomy is. We may object to the blatant imposition of values onto a metaphysical topic by those who identify the self with the higher and the nonself with the lower; but we are forced at least to distinguish the self from the nonself. And if we then go on to *advocate* the promotion of autonomy, as most who write on the subject do, the following example will show how we might well be forced into a position close to the one feared by Berlin.

The state's right to force children to receive a minimal level of public education would typically be defended by appeal to the consideration that even a rudimentary education promotes positive freedom, that is, the development of basic skills, fundamental information, critical intelligence. But when the Amish complain that their community can provide all that is needed in these regards, given their life style, the standard rebuttal is that it is important to provide children with the tools for a variety of life styles because those who choose to reject the religion of their parents will otherwise be at a serious disadvantage. The Amish rebuttal is that, since their life style is divinely prescribed, the state should not encourage the promotion of alternative ones.

At this point the Amish position may well be bolstered by the addition of a metaphysical argument. The Catholic version of this argument is represented by St. Thomas Aquinas whose theory of the self or soul incorporates the idea that its natural leaning is to the good. Through our wills, we are by nature inclined toward the good which completes ourselves. Although knowledge of God is each man's final end, he may fail to see this if he is subject to the pressure of the passions or the allure of sense. In applying a doctrine of this sort, the Amish might point to the seductive character of education, that is, its tendency to turn a child toward the *natural world* rather than God and, therefore, away from his *natural end*. What may look at one level as a clash of values, therefore, turns out to be a debate about the nature of the soul or self. Secular education is evil not directly because it promotes immorality, but rather because it perverts human nature. Even if education provides skills and information, these tools will not be useful to and will actually detract from the flourishing of the *real* person.

There is at this point no way to avoid a confrontation between conceptions of the self and, indirectly therefore, views on autonomy. The above controversy engages a naturalistic with a theological view of the self. There are other controversies concerning the extent to which self-realization is *socially* (rather than theologically) defined *and*, perhaps, the characterization of the ideal society in which realization is possible.

It is interesting, therefore, to compare the Thomist or the Amish conception of self-realization with a social version such as T. H. Green's (1885–8). For if secular education is antithetical to the individual's struggle to realize himself in God, it is absolutely essential to the individual's struggle to realize the common good. Accordingly, Green, unimpressed by worries about interfering with the alleged right of parents to refuse to send their children to school, devoted himself to the struggle *for* mandatory education for grade-schoolers in England.[3] Since the individual good can only be realized through the common good, we must accept limits on negative freedom. "Thus to the grown man bred to civil liberty in a society which has learnt to make nature its instrument, there is no self-enjoyment in the mere consciousness of freedom as exemption from external control, no sense of an object in which he can satisfy himself having been obtained" (Rodman, 1964: 89).

Society must, therefore, forbid interference with functions and institutions essential to the individual's ability to foster the common good.

Green was well aware of the extent to which actual societies fail to be vehicles of individual self-realization; yet he insisted that, in the system of social relations created by individuals through their self-seeking consciousness, the individual's consciousness of the absolutely desirable

finds a content or object which has been constituted or brought into being by that consciousness itself as working through generations of men. . . . Interests are thus supplied to the man . . . in satisfying which he is conscious of attaining a true good, a good contributory to the perfection of himself and his kind. (Rodman, 1964: 81)

Green, then, shared with the Liberals of his day a faith in the common man's inherent goodness and his potentiality for moral advancement and civic virtue. The state can promote this flourishing by various steps, such as an improvement in the material conditions of existence, but it need not, in light of the nature of individuals, enforce virtue. Since goodness is supposed naturally to emerge once the fetters are removed, it was at times frustrating for Green to observe so many intransigent individuals refusing to enter the stage of liberation predicted by his theory. Rodman describes Green's reaction.

When Green realized that better material conditions did not of themselves bring an immediate end to the chronic drunkenness that had become an opiate for the miseries of the Industrial Revolution, he turned to the ideas of compulsory temperance legislation; and it was here that he came nearest to violating his own guiding principle that the state could not enforce virtue. (1964: 29)

If autonomy is *self*-realization, we must decide whether the self is directed to God or the common good. And this metaphysical stance may well affect our views on social practices and institutions. It may also call forth the condemnation of those who, like Berlin, see these views as apologetics for illicit interference in the lives of others.

We shall eventually see, however, that autonomy is *not* self-realization or flourishing. Since autonomy is prima facie self-*direction*, we must address the nature of the self. But even if my self is naturally impelled toward the general good, I can autonomously deny that aspect of my nature so long as *that* decision has its origin in the self. There are *internal* conflicts and we sometimes opt for one aspect of our nature over another. Can Green show that we are so simple that, if we choose to reject society – and people in fact, in one way or another, do – the basis of that decision must be external to the self? If we look at Green's efforts to ground a social conception of the good upon "human nature," we see that he is hard pressed to find purely metaphysical premises from which it follows that *no* agent can find, *within* the recesses of her individual self, alongside communal urges, an impulse to solitude, radical self-reliance, or outright antisocial behavior.

The religious version would have analogous difficulties showing that, even if the most fulfilling life is in God, each instance in which a thoughtful person has rejected such a life is one in which the motivation is extrinsic, that is, the forces leading to this decision originate outside the self.

It is undeniable that individuals form their ideals, values, and self-conception in interaction with society. The fundamental social nature of the self has been eloquently elaborated by a host of philosophers and social theorists. Hordes of contemporary thinkers view the social formation of the individual and the reciprocal character of relations of recognition, which are essential to the emergence of a sense of individuality, as absolute barriers to a process of desocialization which preserves the integrity of the person. For example, Habermas believes that "individuals acquire and sustain their identity by appropriating traditions, belonging to social groups, and taking part in socializing interactions" (1990: 102) such that withdrawal from these processes means "regressing to the monadic isolation of strategic action, or schizophrenia and suicide" (102) and incorporates in his conception of autonomy the principle that "the free actualization of the personality of one individual depends on the actualization of freedom for all" (1990: 207).

It is worth observing on Green's behalf that there are powerful social motives within all of us. Sometimes, as in the case of patriotism, they take a political cast. We would have as hard a time proving that these motives are all unnatural as we have contended Green would have proving that a recluse cannot lead a truly satisfying or natural life. Support for the underlying point of view as it is presented in Habermas raises questions that are, at this point, too ill-defined to admit of a defensible answer.

Thus, if we *were* talking about self-realization – and Green *is* – we would have to confront the formidable task of determining which of two incompatible drives truly represents the self and the temptation facilely to resort to expulsion from self as an adjudicating device. And we would have to render more precise the constraints on self-realization imposed by the social embedding of the individual as well as his sense of his individuality.

But again, *we* are not talking about self-realization. A characterization of autonomy as *self-direction*, then, will not in itself determine whether the life of a saint, a civil servant, or a hobo is *per se* the most autonomous. We cannot a priori preclude the possibility of an individual with conflicting proclivities autonomously deciding for or against these lives. Now these results *do* bear to some extent on the policy question. For if we militantly contend that metaphysics is not on the side of religion, then the educational disadvantages suffered by one deprived of a decent secular education make the person less free. We have no reason to believe that one equipped with a knowledge of science must use that knowledge on behalf of goals and pursuits which do not really reflect *her* underlying nature. She then lacks the tools a critically competent citizen needs to get along in the world and to make independent decisions. In ways I will later elaborate, her autonomy is diminished. So Amish children *are* less free and autonomous than others.

If autonomy should be universally cultivated, then in social policy I come down on the side of Green, but not because of a view about the intrinsically social character of the self. I simply acknowledge with him the importance of the basic tools education provides to enrich life's possibilities and to expand the range of viable life styles, professions, and goals.

So *if* all values are to be subordinated to that of autonomy, I am committed to a view about public policy Berlin and others might regard as intrusive. But I do *not* affirm this antecedent for it is not evident, as some philosophers – for example, Haworth (1986) – have supposed, that autonomy is the basis of all other values. (I discuss the value of autonomy in Chapter 10.)

In fact, even if it were that foundational, there would still be a real issue here. Suppose we concede that Amish children are less autonomous and suppose we concede that, for similar reasons, their elders are, too. So the life style is chosen basically out of ignorance and narrowness. Heteronomous adults transmit their heteronomy from one generation to the next. If we then *impose* public education on this group, possibly in violation of their freedom of religion, we are compelling them to be free and autonomous. We are treating them like children, restricting their freedom now so as to enhance it for the future. If a parent has an *obligation* to do this for the sake of his child, does not society at least have a *right* to do this for the sake of its citizens?

Note, first, that the issue is not one of safety. The Amish are not endangering themselves or others in any obvious sense. Their religion does not demand sacrifices, and so on. They are rather denying themselves, through ignorance, of the benefits of an autonomous life. Just as we would regard it as an intrusion to *force* a friend to take a course or undertake therapy so that he can improve his life (even though it is *not* an *illicit* intrusion to push him away from an oncoming car), so it is an intrusion to force an adult member of the religion to do likewise. Even so, there still remains the issue of his right to transmit this disability to his progeny.

The limited point I want to make is that, even if autonomy is a foundational value, the right of society to force its promotion upon its members when that conflicts with the right of religious expression and the right parents have to determine (within limits) the manner of development of their children is not self-evident.

Given that positive freedom is comprised of traits like intelligence, basic skills, and knowledge, it is clear that autonomy is different; the capacities which expand a person's powers do not automatically confer greater self-direction in his life. Intelligence is nice to have; but if, like Joseph Goebbels, I use it to discern better the wishes of my master, my autonomy is hardly enhanced. The fundamental discrepancy between the notions can be highlighted by examining a person who chooses unfreedom or slavery.

The case can be described locally or globally. The global example would be the disciple who submits himself totally to the whim of another, the guru, out of some freely chosen goal, say, to achieve enlightenment. The local example is that of a person who chooses not to act on one of his own desires; he prefers to be rendered unable to do so. The alcoholic who knows he will experience weakness as he begins his phase of total withdrawal requests restraints which he knows he will desperately work against as the urge to consume alcohol takes over. He displays autonomy as he arranges for the limitations on his liberty.

The significance of these cases for us is that neither an alcoholic nor a disciple or, for that matter, a slave surrenders positive freedom! Generally speaking, negative freedom is forfeited. In all cases an environment is entered in which external restrictions upon freedom of action are dramatically increased. The alcoholic will be frustrated when he seeks a drink, and the slave will be prevented from escaping. But both retain knowledge, skills, intelligence, rationality, and emotional stability. (Of course, in special cases, a person *may* surrender his freedom as well. The disciple may become a psychological cripple, unable to return to a normal life. Or a master may force a slave to undergo crippling brain surgery.)

Whether a person freely enters one of these states or is forced to do so, his autonomy is compromised once he is in this state and that clinches the case for distinguishing positive freedom from autonomy.

Might the heteronomy of the slave simply *be* his lack of negative freedom? Imagine, however, a person forced into slavery who struggles his entire life against this condition, does everything he can to defy his master and thwart his wishes, and tries unsuccessfully to satisfy his own desires, including the desire to escape. Although this slave suffers from the loss of negative freedom, he retains a great deal of autonomy. His decisions are entirely his own and, were the world less unyielding, he would be a model of perfect freedom. From an internal perspective, he is a fully self-determined agent; but he happens to be trapped in an environment which denies him the resources he needs. He is, like Leonardo, trying to build devices like flying machines when the available information and technology are inadequate. We don't fault Leonardo's autonomy because he is ahead of his time. Why should we fault the autonomy of the independent slave? Later in this chapter, I will defend a distinction between pure autonomy and proficiency which will permit us to acknowledge the autonomy of the frustrated slave, while conceding the absence of a closely related feature, to wit, the ability to translate decisions, autonomously arrived at, into action.

Autonomy, romantic self-expression, and flourishing

Given our understanding of the difference between autonomy and freedom, we are now in a better position to distinguish autonomy from other ideals. For it has been confused not just with freedom, but also with what I will call *romantic self-expression* and also with *flourishing*.

We have seen that the idea of self-determination requires a distinction between self and other and, therefore, generates controversies about the boundaries of the self. Many theorists extend the "other" to facets of body *and* mind. For these theorists, therefore, an agent's choice can be heteronomous because it is exercised under the dominating influence of external forces comprised of her own (?) desires. The typical example is the unwilling addict. We will soon consider objections to the way particular theories draw this line. There are three ways of undertaking this critique: (1) We may argue that there is a line; but it should be drawn in a different way; (2) We may deny for metaphysical reasons that there is a line; (3) We may deny for ethical reasons that a line should be drawn.

By *romantic self-expression*, I refer to the third point of view. One who rejects addictive behavior as an instance of self-expression does not deny the identification of autonomy with self-expression. She simply demands a critical attitude toward this idea of self-expression. One should be able to formulate a cogent theory of the self according to which the addictive desires of an unwilling addict are outside the self and one can then understand why this addict is heteronomous. The second line of attack finds no feasible way of defending any such critical attitude. The defender of *romantic* self-expression, on the other hand, objects to the very project of drawing lines. Life should be lived to its fullest. Ideally, all desires should receive expression, for every distinctive mode of satisfaction enhances the richness of human existence. Of course, this view is incoherent. But one smitten by this Dionysian ideal will find the fact of conflicts of desire and the dangers of uncritical self-expression tragedies which will have to be resisted in some way or another. Some will abandon prudence out of the need to taste all. Others will move in the direction of enlightened self-interest or prudential egoism. The key point is that romantic self-expression is not autonomy for one may autonomously reject it, as indeed most of us do. More generally, self-*government* is different from self-*realization*.[4] I can choose not to realize or to develop some aspect I find "in there." This distinction is clearer if the self-realization is romantic because proponents of this position do not object on metaphysical grounds that a portion of the self is not being allowed expression. Their objection is ethical in nature. The more interesting distinction, therefore, is between autonomy and what I will call *metaphysical egalitarianism*. Instead of the worry that some valuable experience will be missed by the quashing of desire, there is the more intellectual worry that some experience will be ejected from the self without sufficient reason. There are two paths a metaphysical egalitarian might take. She may use this position to ground the ethical view of romantic self-expression: Everything *should* receive expression for everything *is* a part of me. We face again all the difficulties of the romantic point of view. It is incompatible with any viable notion of self-control and, hence, self-government. We happen to be too complex to allow expression to all desires and at the same time to be able to gain a handle on our lives. If there really is no viable way of denying ownership of some desire which conflicts with everything (else) I hold dear, which I desperately wish to be rid of, and which has been introduced into my psyche by a malevolent neurosurgeon without regard for its integration with the other elements within that psyche, then we must simply conclude that autonomy and self-expression do not coincide. The more plausible version of metaphysical egalitarianism, then, permits autonomous decisions to reject or suppress elements of the self just so long as the decision itself originates in the self.

There are moderate versions of romantic self-expression and metaphysical egalitarianism which deserve to be mentioned. Although it is foolish to allow every last impulse, no matter how silly, dangerous, or immoral, its right to be expressed, one may argue that every human being should develop all her fundamental potentialities – physical, intellectual, social, aesthetic, moral, and spiritual – as best as she can. The metaphysical egalitarian sees all of these dimensions as internal to the self, whereas the advocate of romantic self-expression is at least convinced of the importance of developing each component. Yet here again, why can't one autonomously choose to suppress not just a desire, but an entire dimension of human flourishing?

Evidently, a blind person who desperately wishes to see is unable to express his deepest desires and is thereby less autonomous and less proficient.[5] But I had a blind teacher of Indian religion, Dr. Subhodh Chandra Roy, who reported that he rejected an opportunity to have his sight restored by a safe operation. He may have had fears, perhaps unconscious ones, but I have no specific reason to doubt his word that he just had no strong desire to see.[6] He did express the fear that he would be distracted from his religious quest by what he knew would be a new and overpowering connection to the world. Almost everyone would be prepared to pay this or a similar price. But Dr. Roy was not; and I cannot say he was less autonomous as a consequence. (He was certainly less proficient at many things *he* wanted to do, but he was even prepared to pay this price.) If he was irrational, it was not evident. He just had a very different set of preference rankings from the rest of us and suffered from idiosyncrasy, not heteronomy.

What about ignorance? Since the absence of relevant information diminishes our autonomy, wasn't Dr. Roy less autonomous by dint of his failure to know what it is like to see? (He was blind from birth.) And suppose that he would indeed have conceded his error had he undergone the operation and come to experience the miracle of sight. On these suppositions, he was heteronomous. But suppose that after the initial excitement and novelty had worn off, Dr. Roy would have come eventually to conclude that the ugliness he now was forced to confront so vividly combined with all the new distractions in his religious life were too high a price, as he had initially feared. We can only count him heteronomous now by imposing a conception of human flourishing at which he would balk.

By refusing the operation, Dr. Roy refused to develop an aspect of himself which others have developed into some of the noblest expressions of the human spirit. He can neither create, nor understand, nor appreciate a universal form of communication. He cuts himself off as well from the natural delights of the visual world. In suppressing a natural dimension of human existence which is a source of great value to all who share in it, Dr. Roy is knowingly stifling the realization of a potentiality which is as much a part of his nature as it is a part of that of any sighted person.

Although we have raised a question about the extent to which this particular decision was fully informed, the issue may be pressed by considering clear examples of asceticism or celibacy, as practiced for religious reasons. Certainly in some of these cases, the people both know what they are doing and *can* appreciate what they turn their back on. If we cannot explain all such examples on the basis of ignorance or neuroticism of an appropriate sort, we shall have again to suppose that a self-chosen agent can choose to suppress a part of the self.

I hope in this work to specify the conditions of autonomy. It is too early, therefore, to say that Dr. Roy's decision was autonomous. But that he rejected a part of himself does not preclude the internal generation of a decision made with all relevant information. If his decision is autonomous – and I shall eventually argue that it is – then autonomy is not constituted by fulfillment of potential or realization of self. Indeed, a more general point of view to be found in these pages is the rejection of any value-laden account of autonomy according to which our conception of autonomy is derived from a conception of the good life. Even if a life in which all our potentialities are developed is in that respect fuller or more worthwhile, it does not follow that autonomy requires such a life.

Moderate metaphysical egalitarianism remains a plausible position in spite of these conclusions about autonomy. That one may autonomously reject an entire dimension of our selves does not evidently imply that that dimension is expelled from self. I can reject a part of myself.

There are several distinct conceptions of flourishing. Although a person whose ambitions are frustrated is not flourishing, we may decide that a person who is satisfying all his ambitions is not, as well. We may say that Dr. Roy is not as flourishing as he might because he has suppressed a fundamental source of value. But since I have designated the ideal according to which this result obtains as (moderate) romantic self-expression, I shall use the word "flourishing" to designate an ideal according to which it depends not just on the fulfillment, but also on the depth and breadth of desire. This ideal is more explicitly value-laden for it demands not just the satisfaction of desires actually present in the agent, but also the creation of new desires to supplement the possibly meager supply that is available. We supposed above that Dr. Roy had a minimal desire – and perhaps at an earlier age a quite strong desire – to see. Moreover, he would have appreciated sight had he acquired it. He just had other desires and concerns whose development resulted in the long run in the formation of an apathetic or even hostile attitude toward the removal of this infirmity. Although he is not flourishing as much as others, he is better off on this score than a woman we will call Laura, whom Christine Swanton (1992) describes:

The origin of the desires of a woman with severely limited horizons, for example, may owe little to exploitation, repression, manipulation, and other standard "alien" influences. And yet those desires may be severely restricted by the narrow environment in which she finds herself. She may have had parents neglectful of her intellectual development, or have been brought up in conditions of poverty, ignorance, prejudice, vice, and a host of environmental circumstances that limit and distort her attitudes and aspirations, and her view about her roles. (134)

No matter how hard she tries, Laura cannot fathom what others see in classical music, urban excitement, diverse friends, higher education, travel, and so on. She is perfectly content as is, perpetuating her parents' mode of existence and transmitting their prejudices and narrow aspirations.

Laura is not autonomous because she is not independent, and she may well be deficient in rationality. I shall develop these themes in later chapters. But there are persons who lead very simple lives who *are* independent and not irrational. They have chosen their way of life because they cannot appreciate the diverse fruits of civilization and culture. They are content, but narrow. They raise issues about the concept of autonomy we will later address. I want simply at this point to draw a tentative distinction between autonomy and flourishing insofar as the failure to flourish of a rational, independent version of Laura does not clearly tell against her autonomy. I shall return to this issue in Chapter 9.

Autonomy, proficiency, competence, and strength of will

Earlier, I said that a noncomplacent slave would be autonomous if he exercised independent critical competence in relation to important decisions. Yet we do think autonomy requires a certain degree of effectiveness. When we look at the child's development toward autonomy, we see her as increasing in the capacity to achieve mastery over the environment.[7] Although some of this competence pertains to decision making, much of it pertains to action. An agent, like our noncomplacent slave, who is forever frustrated by the inability to translate his goals into action is not a paradigm of autonomy. I propose that we then distinguish *pure autonomy* or *autonomy of choice* from *proficiency*. An autonomous agent's decisions are entirely her own, even if, by virtue of the lack of negative freedom or certain elements of positive freedom (skills, knowledge, etc.), she is ineffective in achieving her goals. A proficient agent need not be autonomous and an autonomous agent need not be proficient. Since our focus is so often on action, the term "autonomy" is frequently used to mean what we are calling "proficiency."

Autonomy of choice is different from the *freedom to make decisions*. Although our discussion of freedom will focus upon freedom as it pertains to action, I shall apply the results to decision. We can have or lack the power to act in a certain way *or* to make a certain decision; we can, in fact, have freedom of action *or* decision in *any* sense.[8] Just as we can be free to perform an act in the sense that it was reasonable to expect us to have performed it in those circumstances, so we can be free in the same sense to make a certain decision. Just as there is negative freedom of action, so can there be negative freedom of decision. I can interfere with your decision-making ability by a drug, for example. Positive freedom of decision would be constituted by the same sorts of elements, for example, intelligence and knowledge, except that skills and abilities of a physical nature are evidently more useful to the enactment of most decisions than to the bare making of them.

So one can have the freedom to decide without autonomous choice. Intelligence, knowledge, relevant skills, and awareness of all relevant alternatives can exist alongside the abandonment of independence.

If I submit myself to a guru or fall into the hands of a slaveholder, I may say that I now lack the freedom to make my own decisions. I have argued that it is more accurate to say that I have given up or lost my autonomy unless my guru has actually disrupted the decision-making process (through drugs, surgery, brainwashing, misinformation, or induced psychosis). More conventional constraints, of course – the guru's goons – apply to my proficiency, not my autonomy of choice. The goons interfere with my (negative) freedom and, therefore, my proficiency.

But freedom of decision is closer to autonomy than freedom of action for there is an important difference here between action and decision. The example of the rebellious slave is one of autonomy of choice combined with the absence of proficiency grounded in the absence of negative freedom. The rebellious slave uses his freedom of decision on behalf of his autonomy. So he easily has autonomy without freedom of action. But if his master now limits his freedom of decision (through drugs, surgery, brainwashing, misinformation, induced psychosis), he will also undermine his autonomy. His decisions will no longer be generated from within. So freedom of decision is a necessary, but not sufficient condition of autonomy. Moreover, restrictions on action can have an independent effect on the decision-making process in that the attractiveness of a prospect can be dependent on information about the means and consequences of its realization.

Both *autonomy* and *proficiency* should be distinguished from *competence*, a term used by some as the key analysands of autonomy.[9] Competence is actually positive freedom characterized functionally. An agent with intelligence, rationality, relevant skills and the like is clearly competent to take on decision-making tasks.

But a competent person may not be disposed to use her skills. She may display deep irrationality or perhaps total dependence on others. She has the makings of an autonomous individual, but is not autonomous. She knows better; but for one reason or another has not matured in a way which would permit her to use her gifts to make wise or independent decisions. She is intelligent, but cannot think for herself. She may think she is independent, but impartial observers know she is a victim of self-deception. She is simply taking over the opinions of authority figures, perhaps because she wants the basic decisions regarding her life to be made by another.

Although competence is then not sufficient for autonomy, it is, at a certain level, necessary. For an autonomous agent is at least one who makes independent decisions; she is one who, on the basis of the cumulative weight of her own experience, establishes her own values, rules, and goals as she confronts the ones she has inherited from the authority figures of her childhood. This ongoing process can be counted as successful only if the person is equipped with the appropriate intellectual tools and skills to permit a proper review and evaluation. Whether a person takes over intact her intellectual and moral legacy or seeks to formulate radically new commitments and values, one who lacks critical skills will be unable to count the result her own.

Although irrationality may be an emotional rather than an intellectual failing, rationality does presuppose a level of critical competence. A critically incompetent person cannot be rational for, even if he is disposed to evaluate his principles and values, he will do so in an illogical or muddled manner. There are, of course, many manners and degrees of incompetence. Those which are so severe as to jeopardize the person's ability to achieve his own objectives interfere directly with his proficiency. Those which interfere with the integrity of the decision-making process may interfere with his autonomy of choice.

In a particular situation, is there any more autonomy an agent blessed with autonomy of choice and proficiency can want? Perhaps. For should an agent make an autonomous decision and possess both the competence and the negative freedom to enact this decision, he may find that he lacks the strength of motivation required to actuate the decision. After careful reflection, he unambiguously endorses a particular undertaking; his practical reason has concluded that a certain action is clearly the best thing to do in the circumstances and he reports in full honesty that he intends to do it. Yet he finds that he just does not want to do it or that his desire is too weak to offset a countervailing desire. His will is too weak to effect the promptings of practical reason and he is unable to rectify this deficiency; he lacks *strength of rational will.*

Strength of desire, interpreted in a certain way, can be confused with strength of will. I might have a very weak desire to visit my mother, but be able nonetheless, in virtue of a strong will, to bring myself to do it. If we construe desire as but one type of motivation, then since the will must be moved by something or other, it would be better to identify strength of will with strength of motivation.[10]

The clearest examples of weakness of rational will are cases of addiction or compulsion. But not all instances of weakness result from the presence of an overwhelming competing urge. An infirm will is a constituent of various character traits and moods such as anomie, melancholia, world-weariness, lethargy, dispiritedness, sloth, and depression. (At the other end of the spectrum, we find people with boundless enthusiasm and energy, who are temperamentally disposed to plunge into projects, both significant and profound, as if their life were at stake.) When it is difficult to assimilate these traits to addiction by the identification of a specific motive that is competing with the one endorsed by practical reason, the potential exists for a profound schism within the self. For if an agent's motivational impotence is a general trait, not triggered by a local failing, such as a specific urge or passion, yet his intellect is sufficiently intact so as to submit rational deliverances to the will, there will be a massive discrepancy between the intellect and the will. He rarely does what he recognizes he should do.

Philosophers have challenged the possibility of such extremes through a defense of *motivational internalism*, the doctrine that, since motivational force is intrinsic to practical reason, complete bifurcations of intellect and will are unintelligible. Versions of this thesis differ, depending upon divergent interpretations of each side of the equation. With respect to intellect, R can be *a* reason for me to do A; R can be *one of the reasons that bear on* my decision to do A; R can be *the reason* on the basis of which I have decided that A is the overall best thing to do. On the side of will, R can have some or decisive motivational strength.

Since we are concerned about a possible breakdown between autonomous decision and will, we need only worry about the case in which an agent has made a decisive judgment that a course of action is the overall best one in the circumstances. Now, the version of the internalist view according to which this decision must be motivationally effective would preclude the possibility of autonomy of choice combined with weakness of rational will. Once a proficient agent knows what the best thing to do is, he will do it. But this doctrine, which rules out weakness of will, is utterly implausible. Even if the judgment of practical reason in itself incorporates a tendency to perform the endorsed action, this tendency can be stifled by a competing appetite.

Thus, even if the weaker version of internalism, according to which practical reason implicates (possibly weak) desire is sustained, we still can have a failure of will. It appears then that we must add strength of rational will as a separate component of *full autonomy*.

In assuming that the proficiency of an agent who has made an autonomous decision does not confer full autonomy on that agent, we are implicitly distinguishing the freedom to act on the decision (proficiency) from the strength of will required for execution. Yet the distinction blurs when we consider that strength of will can be sapped by breakdowns of negative freedom. I may induce weakness of rational will in you by injecting you with heroin, thereby forcing you to abjure a prompting that is in accord with a decision you have just arrived at autonomously. Since you now lack proficiency, there is no need to refer to weakness of will as a separate ground of your heteronomy. To be sure, not all instances of a weak will arise from external interference. Yet we shall want to characterize positive freedom broadly enough to encompass more than just physical and intellectual skills. Breakdowns of an emotional, characterological, or psychological nature can also affect positive freedom. Addicts and depressed persons are generally unfree, but the unfreedom is not negative. Perhaps, then, we can make do with the notion of proficiency alone.

This conclusion receives additional support once we realize that weakness of rational will is far less common than we may ordinarily suppose. If we take seriously the thought that one suffering from this state is *unable* to will a certain action or lacks the strength of motivation that is *required* to will this action, we can see that there are many conditions which only approximate weakness of rational will. For it is often hard, but not impossible, to muster the requisite strength of will. Although we may decide that a seriously depressed person is unable to will certain actions, surely many of those suffering from less extreme conditions, for example, world-weariness or lethargy, are capable of action and may well be blamed in certain contexts for failing to put forth the effort that would be sufficient. This distinction between inability and weakness is crucial for we excuse those suffering from compulsion or addiction and regard those suffering from weakness of will as potential candidates for blame.

We can thus explain many instances of the breakdown of autonomy that implicate the will in terms of the absence of freedom or power, a more careful analysis of which will be provided in the next two chapters. Yet individuals who are burdened with powerful temptations, dark moods, or character defects which render ordinary tasks formidable do fall short of an ideal. If we were to describe an ideally autonomous agent, as I will in Chapter 6, we shall want to think of him as possessed of a psychological structure that creates a perfect mesh between intellect and will. The dictates of practical reason receive an enthusiastic and unchallenged response as they wend their way through the motivational nexus toward the will. An agent who fails to possess this perfect harmony would surely prefer to have it and would, therefore, lack autonomy to the extent that he was unable to effect it.

There are people who believe, typically for religious reasons, that life should incorporate a struggle, not only against certain forces of nature and society, but against one's own imperfections as well. The ideal just formulated, therefore, would not be viewed by these persons as appropriate for human beings. Although this may be so, the perspective from which this point of view issues is not one which holds autonomy in high regard. If the harmony of intellect and will is not an ideal for all, if autonomy is not an ideal for all, it does not follow that harmony is not an essential ingredient in ideal autonomy.

Although an individual action of an ordinary person may be fully autonomous, only an ideally autonomous agent performs just fully autonomous actions. Yet it is important to recognize that many people have virtually full autonomy in many spheres. Even if they face temptation, conflict, ennuie, fears, and enervating physical and emotional conditions, they do not suffer from a serious defect of will and can be expected to execute the decisions they have autonomously arrived at.

Dispositional, occurrent, social, and scope of autonomy

We must also be careful to distinguish *dispositional* from *occurrent autonomy* (Young 1986). An individual decision may be reached autonomously although the agent is generally not autonomous. For example, he may be incapable of pursuing long-range goals because he is impulsive, easily distracted, emotionally distraught, or suffering from any of a variety of disorders which limit his ability to sustain a project. We may add to this breakdown of dispositional autonomy the failure to be generally inclined to occurrent autonomy, whether or not the person is capable of extended pursuits. Thus, an individual episode of autonomy does not an autonomous agent make. (Conversely, a generally autonomous agent may [will] on occasion act heteronomously.)

The absence of self-fragmentation is clearly a condition of dispositional autonomy, but less so of occurrent autonomy. My self must have some integrity permitting me to recognize in the near future projects begun now and the extent to which they have been realized, to formulate plans for the furtherance of the project, and to make revisions in light of changing circumstances and modifications in *my* desires and concerns. Methodologically, it may be preferable to define occurrent autonomy first. Once we know what an autonomous decision is and what sort of integration of the self is required to underwrite the viability of long-range projects, we should be able to define dispositional autonomy. Yet it is important to remember that dispositional autonomy is the notion the friend of value has in mind when he insists that, although an autonomous decision may not implicate values (in a serious way), a truly autonomous agent must be alert to the occasions on which values do indeed bear on his deliberations.

Many of these thoughts show also that it is sensible to think of autonomy as a matter of degree. Relative to the decisions I actually make, I may be disposed always, often, sometimes, or never to make them autonomously. I may be autonomous in certain domains of my life and not in others. The concept of *sphere of autonomy* is thus particularly helpful given that dispositional autonomy tends to be distributed unevenly within an individual. Mature, healthy individuals, disposed to and capable of independent judgment and displays of confident action in certain spheres will, in other departments of life, lack the required tools or may even act like children. Since freedom is a matter of degree, so is autonomy. I may increase my power and, therefore, my critical capacities by increasing my information base, my logical acumen, or certain skills. Children grow into independent adults and so become more and more autonomous. We lose sight of these truisms when we talk about the conditions of autonomy. But there will be occasions on which we shall have to be reminded of these elementary facts.

Yet often, when we wish to know how autonomous a person is, we are not inquiring about either her occurrent or her dispositional autonomy. For, although a person may make all her decisions autonomously, in which case all her decisions belong to one of her spheres of autonomy, the spheres themselves may be very narrow. If she is a serf, a slave, or a member of a religious commune, she may not deliberate about much at all. She never reflects on matters such as her profession, marital status, or social class, restricting her decision-making activity to the most mundane matters. Let us say that her *scope of autonomy* is not, therefore, *extensive*.

The extent of an agent's scope of autonomy is a value-laden matter since the narrowness of the range of matters that enter into the deliberations of this woman cannot be characterized quantitatively. Not only does she make all her decisions autonomously; it may also be the case that she makes many decisions (about meals, about the clothes she will wear, etc.). The narrowness of her scope of autonomy is rather grounded in the *insignificance* of the sorts of matters about which she is autonomous.

Autonomy of scope is a property of an individual and must, therefore, be distinguished from *social autonomy*, to which it is related. A *group* of persons has social autonomy with respect to a certain sphere if the members of that group are given the right and the opportunity to make decisions about matters in that sphere. Since an individual may fail or be unable to exercise this right, his individual autonomy is not increased in extent in spite of this addition to his group's social autonomy.

Since a society must provide the opportunity to exercise these rights, the capacity for social autonomy is a function of advances in knowledge and technology. Societies now have the power to grant its members social autonomy in medical matters to an extent undreamed of only decades ago. And since autonomy is highly prized in Western societies, advances in technology have gone hand in hand with the conferral of these individual rights. Thus, decisions about life and death, formerly made by the medical community, are now made routinely by individual patients or their families.

The transmission of authority to the individual is, of course, a mixed blessing. For one thing, the burden can be emotionally devastating. Since a person might well not want to have it, a question arises as to the possibility of autonomously rejecting the enhancement of autonomy. (I have allowed that a person can autonomously choose slavery.) The issue of the value of autonomy, including scope of autonomy, will be addressed in Chapter 10.

It is by now a philosophical truism that voluntary actions are not necessarily actions resulting from a self-conscious act of choice arising out of a deliberative process. Agents undertake projects which incorporate deliberate physical actions many of which are not preceded by occurrent acts of choice. Yet these actions are fully voluntary; the agent acts for reasons she is prepared to advance in defense of the actions and she is willing to take responsibility for the action and some of its consequences. Since autonomy can be absent or manifest in these deliberate, voluntary actions, it would be a mistake to restrict the range of the concept of (occurrent or dispositional) autonomy to explicit choices. This is an important extension of the concept for it permits us to apply it on the basis of the mode of interaction between the agent and her world. I shall later argue that this wider understanding of the idea is fully justified, and that a truly autonomous agent is rightly understood as a liberated person, engaged with her situation in an open and creative way.

So, although positive freedom does not imply autonomy, autonomy presupposes a certain amount of positive freedom. We turn now to freedom.

3
Freedom of action

In a sense, we are all free to run four-minute miles. There is no law against it; we all have access to tracks, shorts, and running shoes; we will be neither ostracized nor beaten by our neighbors in the event that we are about to succeed. Insofar as no one is interfering with us, we possess negative freedom. As desirable as this condition is, its shortcomings as a complete account of freedom are conspicuous when we consider how unfair it would be to blame an octogenarian for her failure to reach this goal in spite of her best efforts. In another sense of freedom, positive freedom, the deficiency is internal. In virtue of her inability to run a four-minute mile, she lacks positive freedom to do so and is consequently blameless. With respect to our context, she lacks an essential tool for a display of autonomy as proficiency. We turn first to the idea of ability that is appealed to here.

Ability

Let us begin inside the skin. In one important sense of "free," to be free to do something, one must be able to do it. Since differences of ability have a lot to do with internal differences among human beings, we may try to characterize ability as an internal state. We pick out this state by a variety of descriptions; my ability to jump 3 feet into the air would *be* the ability to jump 15 feet were I on the moon. Here perhaps we have one ability described in different ways. But in the movie *The Hustler*, Eddie Felsen (Paul Newman) learns that, in virtue of being extraordinarily talented at pool, he also has the *distinct* ability to play billiards. It is not just that he learns that a set of subjunctive conditionals different from those he instantiates when playing pool apply to him. For that is true of our jumper. It is rather that ability is in part a pragmatic concept and, since we regard pool and billiards as distinct games, we regard Felsen as possessed of distinct abilities. Of course we suppose that an internal state grounds these conditionals and one set of internal states can be associated with several sets of conditionals. But it would be a mistake then to identify ability with the internal state, for these pragmatic considerations show that the concept of ability is more fine-grained than one based strictly on internal states.

If we wish to know about the structural features associated with an ability, we may wish to draw important distinctions among the state which constitutes physical ability, the state which constitutes the relevant propositional knowledge, and perhaps the state which comprises psychological requirements, for example, the absence of phobias and other debilitating afflictions. (At this stage, of course, the best we can do is to fix the reference of the internal states by these environmentally based characterizations.)

The cognitive component of ability is important. Boris Becker may not be able to defeat Ivan Lendl unless he believes he can. And if I have the physical capacity to perform each component action of a series which constitutes the creation of a Stealth Bomber, but do not have a clue as to what to do with the huge pile of metal in front of me, I do not have the ability to build a Stealth Bomber. These considerations require us to qualify the conclusion about the individuation of ability. If Felsen had never heard of billiards, and had to be shown what to do, we might still think that he *revealed* that he had ability at billiards when he performed so well the first time. But if a Stealth Bomber emerges after 8 months of detailed instructions at the level of the most primitive operations – hammering, screwing, soldering, tightening, and so on, in the absence of any functional knowledge concerning any parts or the whole, I can hardly be credited with having had this ability prior to the beginning of the operation. Thus, the importance of information relative to skill varies with the nature and complexity of the task.

Some comments about the propositional knowledge necessary for ability. There are problems in describing an internal state as knowledge. For one thing, if knowledge includes truth and justification, it must be more than a state of the brain. Whatever relevant state of the brain obtains, it counts as an epistemic component of the ordinary concept of ability only if the truth and justification conditions obtain. (The same point can be made for belief; Walter's internal state counts as the belief that water is wet according to the prevailing opinion only if Walter stands in an appropriate relation to H_2O.)

We do not in any case need to suppose that the specific beliefs required for an ability are knowledge for the beliefs need not be justified or held rationally. If Becker believes truly that Lendl has a harder time returning serve from the backhand side, it does not matter that the belief is groundless or based on poor evidence. Nor does the causal route of acquisition matter. And although, in this case, truth might matter, suppose that Becker believes that he can defeat Lendl tomorrow because he holds the false belief that he can defeat Lendl anywhere, anytime. Suppose as well that the bloated belief is necessary to the ability to defeat Lendl on that occasion if Becker can play with sufficient confidence only when he feeds upon grandiose and deluded self-conceptions. We must often deceive ourselves to achieve difficult goals. Thus, although the irrelevance of the truth value of a belief normally implies the irrelevance of the belief, there are special cases in which neither justification nor truth is strictly relevant to ability.

Suppose now that Becker, his confidence shaken, believes he will lose, plays poorly as a consequence, but wins on a fluke. The question raised by this sort of case is whether the ability to do something follows from having done it. In one sense of "can," "*P* does *A*" entails "*P* can do *A*" and it is tempting to move then to "*P* is able to do *A*." This temptation is at the basis of those once-in-a-lifetime abilities such as Joe Dimaggio's having hit safely in 56 consecutive games. It is a temptation that is best avoided. One reason is that abilities would then be multiplied ad infinitum: I have the ability to type the number "6" with my big toe while singing the "Marseillaise" after having spent three weeks in a cheap hotel in Calgary. If the concept of ability is to have a significant psychological use, it will have to be far more severely restricted.

This is not to rule out *all* uniquely manifested abilities. Sports records and other human achievements are clearly superior candidates for the status of abilities than concocted ones such as the one just mentioned. Part of the reason for this, of course, is that we are only interested in certain sorts of achievements and in certain levels of description of those achievements. (Since anyone who can run the four-minute mile can do so wearing purple shorts, we are not interested in the finer level of description.) Since one of the important uses of the concept of ability is to make comparisons among human beings, we are not interested in many of the vast number of things we all can do, for example, bend our index finger. (On the other hand, since another use of the concept is scientific, an anatomist or a physiologist will be interested in some common human abilities.)

If this sensible suggestion to restrict severely the descriptions which are candidates for ability types is taken, then the role of the concept of ability becomes more complex in the context of discussions of freedom. For any action type can, given the context, become significant in a variety of ways. I may be under an obligation to perform that bizarre act involving typing and singing. (Suppose the action is required by some television game show in order for me to win money I need so that my mother can undergo an operation.) To be sure, the performance of this bizarre act depends upon more conventional abilities and those may be the ones we regard as relevant. But it is beginning to appear that freedom demands a notion of "can" more general than ability. After all, I may be free to perform this bizarre act and my failure to do so under these morally significant circumstances will ground a judgment of blameworthiness in spite of the absence of an "ability" to perform that act. And in performing this act, I can display my autonomy and my proficiency. Further grounds are supplied by the following consideration.

The environment is relevant not only to the nature of the ability, but also to the relative difficulty of exhibiting it. Some abilities are easy to display; others are very difficult. In one sense, an ability needs to be manifested just once in order for its owner to be said to have it (as a type, to be sure). Dimaggio hit safely in 56 straight games just once even though he was in his prime long after the event. So some abilities cannot even be exercised when the agent is under coercion: if Dimaggio had had to repeat on pain of execution, even during his prime, he would most likely have failed to do so. He was not free to exercise one of his abilities, although no clear impediment could be identified.

Abilities as tokens

One way of dealing with this conceptual misfortune is to take context seriously. If our concern is freedom in relation to a particular action, decision, or agent-in-a-situation, the context is automatically taken into account. Since situations and opportunities change, the ability (as a type) to do A may then be present in one situation and not in another. Becker can play tennis, but he cannot play tennis now (because he has no racket, is sleeping, etc.). These token abilities or powers make a lot more sense in philosophically interesting contexts; for example, in spite of Becker's (type) ability, one would not blame him for failing to win a match because his racket is strung with piano wire. Also, type abilities may be next to impossible to display even if one is given carte blanche with respect to the environment. Dimaggio can hit safely in 56 straight games; but one would not blame him for failing to repeat on demand even if failure carries terrible consequences. And our practical interest in restricting type abilities is inapplicable to token abilities. We may not want to count running a four-minute mile in purple shorts or typing the number "6" with my big toe while singing . . . as abilities; but in a given situation, I may have or lack the power to do these things. These considerations apply as well when we reflect on the requirements for autonomy or proficiency. For the presence of type abilities may be irrelevant or inapplicable to specific contexts in which we would deny autonomous choice or proficiency.[1]

Although type ability, linking agents to action types during extended periods of time, appears to ignore context, in practice, judgments of type ability are ambiguous, varying in meaning depending on *context*, determined by our willingness to acknowledge possibilities remote from the actual. We are all capable of suicide, says the psychologist. We can all be brought to the brink if conditions are right. Often, the term "capacity" is used to reflect this difference. So we all have the capacity, but the ability is contingent on circumstances which bring us closer to realization. In "She almost committed suicide; but she was finally unable to bring herself to do it," we are using a strong sense of "ability" in which little deviation from the actual is allowed. It is this narrower, stronger sense which is invoked when we hesitate to ascribe the ability to commit suicide to a nonsuicidal person just because he would do it if he had an irresistible desire to do so. In "All experienced mountain climbers possess the ability to climb Mount Everest," on the other hand, a great deal of deviation from the actual is being permitted.

I have observed that one central role for the concept of ability is the identification of people who differ from the majority. This fact explains another component of the notion. "When someone is able to do something that very few normal persons have the ability to do, that person's ability is consistent with only infrequent success" (Benson 1987a: 333). Even extraordinary ability is compatible with occasional lapses of judgment. Since we want some people to be considered good at darts, we do not require perfect judgment, whereas, in the case of pedestrian abilities such as bending one's index finger, even a single failure signals a lapse of ability. Abilities which set a person well apart from the norm, for example, the ability to climb Mount Everest, are compatible with *frequent* failures under conditions in which no fault can be found with opportunity conditions or effort. The climber can be fully able (in the type sense) to do what turned out to be causally impossible to do. And this is the principal reason the token notion of ability is the one that is relevant to freedom. When opportunity conditions cannot be faulted, we would not otherwise know on what basis to withhold blame directed against an outstanding dart shooter who happens to miss in spite of maximal effort.

For power, it does not matter where precisely the explanation of the failure lies, with opportunity conditions or skill. If I am in a situation in which I fail to do something I desperately want to do in spite of supreme efforts and in light of the fact that success would be causally impossible, I am in one way or another "disabled."

We are obliged to turn then to token ability. It may be true that there was another occasion on which Dimaggio could have accomplished that feat, but failed to. What are the truth conditions of such an assertion?

A traditional answer given by those who would attempt to reconcile freedom and determinism is that one has a (token) ability if and only if its exercise would follow upon the presence of the desire to exercise it or perhaps upon an effort to do it. Advocates tout as the merits of this proposal its reduction of the notion of power to a nonmodal base and the consequent use of the hypothetical analysis of ability in defense of compatibilism. We would sometimes have the power to act otherwise in a deterministic world for sometimes we would have acted otherwise if only we had wanted to.

If desire is not identified with motivation in general, there is no good reason to analyze ability in terms of it. For I can just as easily display ability by acting on a sense of duty as by acting on desire. But ability is exhibited when a person sets out intentionally to act, even if the act is unmotivated. (And if action requires motivation, the motivation is irrelevant here.) To acknowledge the fundamentally conative character of ability, it is then preferable to propose that a person P in a situation S has the (token) ability to do A in S if and only if all that need happen for P to do A is that he set out intentionally (try, choose) to do it.

Among the numerous objections to this and other versions of the hypothetical analysis of ability is the failure to acknowledge explicit presuppositions of intentional action or motivational potentiality. The analysis of ability applies only to agents who are conscious, language users, and possessed of minimal emotional and intellectual maturity. For such persons are intuitively the sorts of creatures who are potentially eligible to undertake intentional action. Without this proviso, we have to say that a poker player who is in a coma, but is propped at a table with other players and cards, has the power to play poker now. For he would play poker now if he were to set out to. (See Berofsky 1987: 74–9.) Even though there is something intrinsically different between two comatose persons only one of whom plays poker, without a notion of token ability we would have to ground the inappropriateness of blaming a comatose person for failing to join us in a game of poker in a way other than by citing his inability to play.

The appending of these explicit presuppositions has been deemed a victory for the incompatibilist. It amounts not only to the abandonment of a purely hypothetical analysis; in addition, the presuppositions themselves, for example, language possession, may require analysis in terms of ability. Thus, a person who can read a book is a person who has linguistic abilities, and so on. The belief that compatibilism can be defended by an analysis of ability in which modal terminology is reduced entirely to conditional forms is undermined. We concede this much to the incompatibilist.[2]

Successful action requires the cooperation of the world. I have the ability to do A if the conditions of success are present even though I would be unable to restore some of them were they absent. Hence, I am unable to do A only if a condition of A is absent and I cannot bring that condition about. (The "cannot" here is, of course, that of token ability. It is not enough just to have the type ability for I may lack the power to display this ability in the circumstances. Also, I may have the power to bring about a relevant condition of A and consequently be [token] able to do A; yet this power may be too idiosyncratic to be reflected in a general ability; the power in question, for example, may be the power to type the number "6" with my big toe while singing the "Marseillaise". . . .)

On Sunday, Fred, a fairly good golfer, makes his first hole in one. The world on that day was unusually cooperative. Now we have challenged the relevance of the notion of type ability to freedom on the grounds that type ability has little to do with moral responsibility or autonomy. In this case, since Fred performed this feat, he displayed the token ability to do it. If token ability is the morally relevant idea, then we should be prepared to submit Fred's action to moral scrutiny. But how can Fred be held morally praiseworthy or blameworthy for an action over which he has so little control? Even if Fred needed the money he would win in the tournament for an operation to save the life of his mother, we could not blame him for missing a hole in one – the only way to win the tournament – had he failed.

We can only ask Fred to try. Yes, had he failed, he would not have been culpable – he cannot bring the world into line. But that does not mean that he was not morally required to make that hole in one on Sunday. For on that special occasion, whether or not anyone knew it beforehand, he came to learn that he did indeed have the power and might have been derelict for failing to exercise it. On that occasion, what he is required to do – try – coincides with success.

An agent who has the power to do something morally good is not always blameworthy for failing to do so. In this case, for example, the extreme improbability of a hole in one may fairly enter Fred's calculations, and he may decide to drop out of the tournament on Saturday and seek other means of acquiring the money for his mother's operation. Moreover, had he stayed, we would not prior to the shot affirm that he is obliged to be successful. The key point is that the failure to do what one has the power to do raises the possibility of one's moral liability, whereas the absence of the token ability exonerates one from liability and renders displays of autonomy or proficiency impossible *even when one has the type ability*.

Suppose that I am paralyzed and consequently unable to move my legs. Yet I would move my legs if I set out intentionally to do so for my efforts would inspire a brilliant neurosurgeon to perform an operation which would restore my ability to walk. My inability to walk *now* is predicated on my inability to bring about the requisite conditions *now*. But I will be able to walk next week for I can bring that about. We, thus, need to provide temporal qualifiers in two places.

P has token ability at t_n to do A in situation S at t_{n+1} if and only if (a) either all the conditions of P's doing A in S at t_{n+1} except P's setting out intentionally to do so are present at t_n or P can at t_n bring any such conditions about and (b) P can at t_n set out intentionally to do A in S at t_{n+1}.

The inability to produce an analysis of power which reduces power to a nonmodal base is upsetting only to those compatibilists, among whom I do not count myself, who rest their position on hypothetical analyses of ability. I have argued elsewhere that an alternative strategy is preferable, that the compatibilist position may be grounded in the fact that nomic necessity does not entail the absence of power (Berofsky 1987). We may, therefore, concede the demise of purely hypothetical analyses of power without abandoning the very notion of power, essential to key contexts in which freedom or responsibility are at stake. (If I am wrong and determinism is true, then we lack the token ability to perform any actions we do not in fact perform.)

Other difficulties for the analysis have been cited (Chisholm 1964). If I am able to play Bach's second Partita, but am afflicted with stage fright, I will fail to perform the piece just because I am trying to do so. This difficulty is only apparent for it depends on a failure to identify actions specifically enough. Although I am able to play-Bach's-second-Partita-in-the-privacy-of-my-practice-room, I am unable to play-Bach's-second-Partita-before-an-audience, and the analysis accords with these facts.

With respect to some actions I am able to perform, success is contingent on a sustained or prodigious effort. If I am incapable of producing an effort of suitable dimensions, I lack the ability. To accommodate this consideration, we revise the analysis accordingly:

P has token ability at t_n to do A in situation S at t_{n+1} if and only if (a) there is a dimension of effort E such that E is necessary for P to do A at t_{n+1}, (b) P can at t_n exert E in S at t_{n+1} and (c) P can at t_n bring about all the conditions of P's doing A in S at t_{n+1} (other than effort) that are not present.

The analysis contains a feature we want, to wit, it entails that P would do A if he were to exert maximal effort. It also contains a feature we definitely do not want, to wit, it is utterly trivial. It says basically that a person has a token ability to do A if he can do all that is needed to do A.

We can do a little to rectify the triviality. I have talked about the internal states a person is in when he possesses a type or token ability and have supposed that there is an internal physical and/or psychological difference between two persons, only one of whom has a certain ability. Of course, the actual identification in physiological terms of these inner states is anything but trivial; however, the analysis of the concept of ability would not and could not produce these descriptions. We can nonetheless observe that this state explains the behavior that constitutes displays of the ability. Consequently, the concept of ability is different from the concept of religious affiliation or legal right. The latter notions involve relations to a community and permit the possibility that two persons who are physically and psychologically identical differ in these respects. We incorporate this idea in the following way:

P has token ability at t_n to do A in situation S at t_{n+1} if and only if there is an internal physical and/or psychological state PS and there is a dimension of effort E which is necessary for P to do A at t_{n+1} such that P is in PS and PS explains the fact that (a) P can at t_n exert E in S at t_{n+1} and (b) P can at t_n bring about all the conditions of P's doing A in S at t_{n+1} (other than effort) that are not present.

This is, to be sure, not a monumental departure from triviality. The analysis characterizes token ability in terms of an internal state conferring the power to exert a potentially successful effort. But power ("can") remains a primitive idea for, in light of the consideration that a person *cannot* do something if any condition of its being done, including effort, is absent and the person *cannot* bring that condition about, we again concede the failure of purely hypothetical analyses. Instead of futilely trying to analyze power reductively, then, we should concentrate our efforts, as has been done in the previous section of this chapter, on clarification of truth conditions.

If an agent displays the power to do A when she does A, she displays this power when she does A unintentionally. For she would not have been able to do A at all had the above analysans not been true of her. She would not have been in *PS* and would consequently not have been able to try to do A. And, although she did not try to do A, she could not have done A without this capacity.

Are there not certain things we can do – closing our eyes, for example – about which we do not say that we try to do them? And are there not certain things we do – a graceful tango, for example – only when we do not try to do them? Here, I invoke Chisholm (1964), who observes that, in all these sorts of cases, there is something *else X* I can try to do such that I will succeed at the original task by trying to do X. (I can try to look the way I do when I'm asleep; I can try to do whatever I try to do when I succeed at dancing a graceful tango.) In fact, the analysis already incorporates this modification for it is not assumed that E is an effort specifically on behalf of A. The effort must be necessary for P to do A; but it might be an effort to do something else B such that, in doing B, the agent does A.

Positive and negative freedom

Whatever the conditions of (type) ability are, since successful performance depends on the person as well as the environment, a variety of options is open to the frustrated agent. Since one can improve one's abilities by changing one's environment, one can either move to a new environment or modify the existing one. We often expect social policy to promote the expansion of options in such a way as to avoid the extreme step embodied in the former alternative. Third, we can work to change our inner states.

The interplay between intrinsic and extrinsic factors is the primary reason no clear distinction between positive and negative freedom can be made. The same environmental condition can be regarded as a grand opportunity by one person, shrugged off by another as a mild annoyance, and treated by a third as an absolute barrier. The sight of a snake will induce Sam to dash out to the garden in hot pursuit, make Harry a bit uncomfortable about continuing his gardening chores, and will be thought by Frank as exonerating him from any responsibility to go into the garden. And the same internal conditions will constitute an ability in one environment and not in another as is illustrated by the example of the dependence upon gravity of the ability to jump a certain height.

So the removal of social and legal barriers, for example, to achieve racial equality, may be regarded as inconsequential so long as the skills for taking advantage of new opportunities are absent. And the attainment of parity of ability may be regarded as inconsequential if a pervasive pattern of discrimination persists.

Furthermore, since one and the same internal factor can be called either positive or negative, the latter distinction is quite arbitrary. Is intelligence a component of positive freedom or is stupidity a barrier to action and, therefore, a component of negative freedom? There may be no way to provide a general characterization of the distinction between positive internal states required for an action and internal states which would count as barriers to some action were they present.

Strictly, since stupidity is a condition not induced by personal intervention, it cannot diminish negative freedom. This fact illustrates the insufficiency of negative freedom to freedom as it concerns us. Moreover, it behooves a proponent of negative freedom at least to define the boundaries of the sort of freedom which concerns him. If he wants to say that stupidity is a form of *incapacity*, and genuine unfreedom arises only when there is *restraint*, he owes us an account of the difference. But Lawrence Crocker (1980: 11–15) has convincingly shown that there is no principled way of drawing this distinction.

There are contexts which appear to render the distinction between positive and negative freedom more precise. Later, we shall shift our interest to the freedom of agents rather than their actions or even their wills. Since the question requires us to formulate the general conditions of free agency, we are obliged to look at inner capacities and environmental circumstances divorced from particular contexts. What promotes an agent's freedom? What in general is the best sort of environment and the best internal makeup for the flourishing of this good? From an internal point of view, there are a variety of cognitive, emotional, and character traits which a person must possess if he is to be (positively) free and, since freedom is essential to autonomy, autonomous. We will in fact find it impossible in specifying the conditions of agent freedom to abandon reference to some sort of distinction between traits of the agent which are invariant to environment – so-called positive freedom – and environmental circumstances which limit the agent's power to express these traits – so-called negative freedom.

Further advantages related to the positive-negative distinction flow from the decision to treat freedom as token ability. Freedom of action is at least a dyadic relation; it relates agents to action types. But, in acknowledging that freedom of action, like ability, is best interpreted as a token notion, we have narrowed the issue even further. An agent is free in context c_1 to perform an A-type action and is not free in context c_2 to perform an A-type action. If freedom is here constituted by power or token ability, then interferences or preventing conditions can be treated, not as *terms* of the freedom relation, but as *reasons* which determine whether or not the person is free. That is, Sam is free to go in the garden *because* he is not afraid of snakes, and Frank is not free to do likewise *because* he is. And the difference emerges when we observe what each does if he wants to go into the garden.

Gerald MacCallum (1967) specifically rejects this suggestion, insisting that freedom is a triadic relation involving an agent, preventing conditions, and actions. He says that the understanding of a sentence like "Smith is free *to* leave the country *because* there are no restrictions on his leaving" (1967: 316)[3] requires an understanding of the "range of obstacles or constraints from which Smith had been claimed to be free" (317). This would be true *if* freedom were triadic. But the above analysis of power explains how we do not need to have this understanding, how we can instead treat preventing conditions as grounds for denying freedom. For we know that, whatever the range of potential obstacles, if Smith leaves the country at will, then there were no obstacles and he was free-to-do-so simpliciter.

Another advantage of my approach to token ability is that it collapses negative and positive freedom, or ability and opportunity. It is J. L. Austin's (1961b) all-in sense of "can." To be able in this sense is to be assured that all conditions are go, and any further inquiry into differences among enabling conditions is a frill. The analysis cannot, therefore, falter on failures to clarify the difference between inner and outer, or positive and negative. That result, in virtue of the inherent unclarity of these distinctions, is welcome.

On MacCallum's account, advocates of negative freedom may sensibly be regarded not as championing a certain type of freedom, but rather as concentrating upon one term of the relation, preventing conditions, for example, legal restrictions, social pressures, and personal circumstances. They worry, therefore, about the introduction of coercive measures which increase unfreedom. Advocates of positive freedom, on the other hand, attend to the sorts of things an agent can or cannot *do* and worry instead, therefore, about the absence of internal conditions which could enhance freedom. Of course, MacCallum is not wedded to a positive-negative distinction either. The theory incorporates the idea of preventing conditions, but does not per se specify a way of sorting these conditions out.

It is important to realize that MacCallum's suggestion has to do with the logical form of freedom judgments and not with their truth conditions. If the suggestion is adopted, we are still faced with the formidable task of deciding when a factor turns into a condition preventing an agent from performing a certain action.

Looking more closely at environmental restraints, the ones proponents of negative freedom tend to concentrate upon, we find a variety of types of influences. There are, beyond physical constraints, social, psychological, and legal ones as well, even though these are generally weaker than the physical. So we must acknowledge degrees of constraint.[4] There are other dimensions along which constraints vary. Manipulation is different from coercion not just because coercion is stronger; a bank robber coerces the teller, but a mother might dominate her child more effectively by manipulation. Legal constraints may be quite weak and some may feel that, strictly, the term denotes a complex of laws and psychological reactions to law such that the constraint is per se the psychological reaction. A law of which a person is ignorant is not inhibiting; the real limitation on the person derives from the fear or the aversion to the consequences of law violation. We must also relativize the constraint to the character of the action being constrained. The most significant distinction in this regard is that of action in contrast to decision to act. Many things I cannot do I can at least choose, try, or decide to do. So we distinguish freedom of action from freedom of will or, in MacCallum's scheme, add acts of will as possible values in the range of the action variable.

Next, we contrast the external option-limiting factors from the internal ones. Internal barriers may be classified under aversions (compulsions, obsessions, addictions, phobias), ignorance, and a variety of intellectual and emotional incompetences. (Among intellectual incompetences, there are cognitive failures of memory, perception, calculation, and reasoning, including limitations on information processing capacity, irrational and inconsistent belief sets, the use of nonrational simplification procedures, defense mechanisms to protect self-esteem which also distort data, compartmentalization,[5] nontransitivity of preference, and more. Emotional disabilities [or conditions which place one under a serious emotional disadvantage] encompass psychosis, character disorders, psychopathy, severe stress, childhood, split brain, multiple personality, and more.) There are, of course, other illuminating classificatory systems; we may, for example, try to isolate those factors which sap the will from those which pertain to a defect of skill that thwarts a fully committed agent.

This list of intellectual and emotional barriers to freedom highlights again the arbitrary character of the distinction between positive and negative freedom. For this list comprises the very conditions entering (in positive form) accounts of positive freedom.

Another classificatory issue concerns the status of emotional competence. It is undeniable that many emotional conditions are barriers to token ability and, hence, freedom. Since I view freedom as a necessary condition of autonomy, I appear to be excluding emotional health from a list of the *elements* of autonomy, counting it rather a *condition* of autonomy. Yet as we delve into the subject, we will find that a key component of autonomy is what I call objectivity, a condition that is intimately linked to emotional health. The manner of counting or locating elements is trivial; an autonomous agent needs relevant freedom and, consequently, the absence of emotional barriers. The specific character of these barriers is spelled out in the discussion of autonomy, but I mention this here to prevent unnecessary confusion.

Each barrier may then be classified in terms of strength. But now we face an important decision. If the maximum strength of some obstacle makes it impossible to perform a certain action, rendering the freedom *to* act nil, what shall we do about the overwhelming majority of cases in which we act under constraints of varying degrees of strength? What does our fledgling theory of freedom say about this?

Valuational conceptions of freedom

I have spelled out some benefits of an account of freedom of action in terms of token ability or power. Yet we cannot simply identify freedom with token ability. For it is undeniable that ascriptions of freedom are often withheld even when the presence of pure power is conceded. In his heavyweight championship fight with Rocky Marciano, Joe Louis did not fall to the canvas when he did "of his own free will" or "freely" just because he could have held out a few more seconds through a Herculean effort of which he was barely capable. It is clear then that the token ability to do A does not entail that, if one does A, one does so *freely*. But given that we are not even inclined to say that Louis was "*free to* remain standing," in spite of the fact that he was able to do so through an effort of titanic proportions, we may be tempted at this point to shift to the following, very different analysis of freedom. We address the issues raised by the fact that constraints come in different strengths by regarding an agent as unfree to do A when the forces against which he is struggling are so powerful that it would be unreasonable to require that he expend the energy or strength to overcome them. (See Kaufman 1962; Audi 1974; and Greenspan 1987.)

Instead of viewing this account as denying that freedom is power, we may rather see it as a proposed *analysis* of power. Our earlier failure to produce a satisfactory reductive analysis of power or token ability may then be explained in terms of the fact that the ascription of power is really a sort of valuational judgment. The possession of this primitive modal property by an agent is no more than the reasonableness of a certain *expectation* or *response* of others to the agent's circumstances. Often when we say "He could not have done otherwise," we are saying something like "It would be unreasonable to demand (retrospectively) the expenditure of energy (or the creation of fear or anxiety or the like) that would have been required for him to have done it." Since moral and valuational matters bear on the reasonableness of a demand, "can" itself turns out to be a normative notion. When a task becomes so difficult and there are no urgent reasons to insist that it be done, we allow "He cannot do it" to remain unchallenged. So instead of supposing that token ability is a metaphysical given our analyses of freedom must accommodate, we suppose instead that issues calling for an evaluation rather than a discovery are to be found at what had been supposed to be a fundamental level of fact.

Proponents of this shift sometimes tout its potential to cut through the interminable debates about free will. They herald this insight as the key to the solution to the free will problem unavailable to those who narrowly focus upon the metaphysical.[6] If, say, the ascription of power is tantamount to a value judgment, then an incompatibilist might be wrong to suppose that determination automatically entails unfreedom. Since the valuational premise might be independent of the assumption of determination, it is conceivable that freedom (as power) is not ruled out by determination.

An incompatibilist would surely balk, specifically at the context-dependence of "can" as it is construed on the valuational point of view. "Ralph just could not bring himself to ask for a raise" might fetch universal assent at the water cooler. But when Ralph reports his failure of will to his starving son, it would be quite appropriate for his child to charge "You really could have done it." If there is no single standard of reasonableness, there is no fact of the matter about Ralph's power and, whatever the incompatibilist supposes is ruled out in a deterministic world, it is surely something which does not vary as a function of differing standards of reasonableness.

The incompatibilist contends that, if it is causally impossible to do something, it is unreasonable to expect someone to do it (unless the person controls the causal conditions themselves). So "valuational power" *presupposes* power as causal possibility. Since determinism implies that no unactualized possibilities are causally possible, the incompatibilist concludes that, under determinism, no one has even the valuational power to perform an action he failed to perform. The incompatibilist can thereby co-opt the value-laden notion of freedom. (It is common to observe that the ascription of power to a human being is typically more than the ascription of a causal possibility. Indetermination guarantees certain causal possibilities, for example, that my finger moves. But I may be unable to move it at will; I may lack control over its movements for they may occur randomly and may never occur when I set out to perform them. Although this result shows that power is *more than* causal possibility in the important cases, it does not show that the richer notion of power does not also, like valuational power, presuppose causal possibility. So the case against incompatibilism is still found wanting.)

Although there is undeniably a valuational sense of the term "free," the identification of freedom with valuational power is not the breakthrough some had hoped for. For example, people often do what it is unreasonable to expect them to do. If, in the doing of A, an agent rises above expectations, she clearly displays the power to do A. But since it was unreasonable to expect her to have acted that way, we will have to say that she did what she was not free to do! We will have to say that she lacked valuational power, and we now see that that notion is in the end an oxymoron. If I do something, I have the power to do it (even if, like the case of a hole in one, I cannot repeat and I cannot be said to have displayed "the ability to make holes in one"). So, if powers exist, their presence is not dependent upon normative matters. Yet in affirming someone's freedom or even in saying that someone can do something, we are often, as the proponents of this valuational sense insist, doing something other than affirming the presence of this power. We must then acknowledge distinct senses of "free" and in this spirit propose the following definition of one of these senses:

P is free$_v$ to do A if and only if it is reasonable to expect P to do whatever is necessary for him to do A.

As noted earlier, freedom$_v$ is unclear in a pivotal way. Reasonableness is relative to a standard. Even if there are external constraints on personal judgments of reasonableness, the normative dimension of the notion creates doubts about the possibility of universal standards. It is unreasonable to ask someone to do something he cannot do; but it is also unreasonable to expect someone to do what is immoral or supererogatory.

Although we might try to argue for universal moral standards, there are independent difficulties in applying freedom$_v$ to the core contexts in which freedom is linked to moral responsibility or autonomy. In determining whether it is unreasonable to expect an agent to act in a certain way, we must, in virtue of the normative dimension of reasonableness, take into account her responsibilities, the commitments she has made, and a variety of other morally relevant considerations. If two persons are in a situation calling for a display of unusual bravery on behalf of a worthy end, it may be reasonable to demand this undertaking only of the one who had earlier promised to do so. Thus, the conclusion that an agent is unfree$_v$ is relevant to exoneration from moral responsibility if only as the result of these analytic connections. This result has some unfortunate consequences.

Note first the oddity of saying that a person is not free to act bravely just because she has not promised to do so and the further oddity of saying, in the event that she does perform this supererogatory act, that she did not act bravely of her own free will or she did something she was not free to do. Given that we should dispense praise on the agent who kept her promise, must we then withhold praise from the agent who went beyond the call of duty?

By parity of reasoning, we do not regard a person's autonomy as undermined when she acts in a way it is not reasonable to expect her to act. Since supererogatory acts can evidently be autonomous, they would have to be performed by people who are free in a sense other than this valuational one.

An effort to promote freedom$_v$ as the relevant one in these contexts may be grounded on the traditional compatibilist identification of unfreedom with coercion. For it is indeed plausible to construe coercion as a normative notion. (See Nozick 1969; Audi 1974; and Greenspan 1978, 1987.) So if freedom is the absence of coercion, freedom must be a value-laden notion.

But freedom cannot be identified with the absence of coercion *if* we wish to view freedom as essential to moral responsibility. For it is clear that a person who submits to a threat under coercion may be liable for so submitting if it is very important that he not submit, his office or position requires that he not submit, he has promised not to submit, and/or he believes the coercive force will cease (well) before it becomes literally impossible to hold out. An agent is not necessarily off the hook just because he was coerced.

Our principle concern is autonomy, however, and coercion may be incompatible with it. For autonomy centrally encompasses procedural independence, a condition prima facie absent under coercion. (Independence is discussed in Chapter 6.) Yet coercion is just one way of becoming dependent on another – manipulation, hypnosis, and self-induced subordination are others – and but one way of sometimes becoming unfree. We would be multiplying senses unnecessarily should we identify (a different sense of) freedom for each distinct pathway.[7]

Thus, although we often have freedom$_v$ in mind, the upshot of the current discussion is that we need to postulate a sense of freedom, call it freedom$_p$ which identifies it with power or token ability, understood in a way which resists its reduction to normative or valuational notions. It is perhaps ironical that this conclusion is grounded in part on the significance of moral contexts to many discussions of freedom. The very fact that we have moral praise and blame in mind when we ascribe freedom indicates that we have something other than the reasonableness of behavior in mind. Again, we praise people who act "unreasonably"; and, although we usually do not blame people if we think it is not reasonable to expect them to have acted differently, we adjust our judgments of reasonableness on the basis of the moral features of the situation unless the agent literally could not do otherwise, that is, unless he was not free$_p$ to do otherwise.

If freedom$_p$ understood in this way is a viable notion, we appear to be in a position to explain the difference between compulsion and weakness of will, a difference whose significance is grounded in the fact that blame is appropriate only for the latter condition. A person who experiences weakness of will maintains the freedom$_p$ to resist temptation and thereby remains accountable. Matters are not that simple, however, for a person who is compelled from within or from without may also retain the freedom$_p$ to do otherwise. Most judgments of compulsion or coercion do not demand the literal impossibility of the coerced action. In most cases, then, the distinction turns on the truth of freedom$_v$ judgments. Was it reasonable to expect the person to combat the powerful forces acting on him? It does not follow from this alone that the distinction between compulsion and weakness of will varies as a function of differing standards of reasonableness. For there may not be differing standards in the sense of "justified standards." We sometimes condemn the lax standards of groups who permit their members to absolve themselves from responsibility by appeals to their "inability."

Although the above considerations should dash expectations for a single, value-laden notion of freedom of action, it is conceivable that a valuational conception of *agent* freedom is defensible. Susan Wolf's (1980,

1990) account is particularly germane for it challenges the role my account has assigned to power. Since she regards freedom, when it is a condition of moral responsibility, as the ability to understand and act in accordance with the right, a person who lacks the power to do the wrong thing will count as free.

But no one can seriously affirm that the "moral compulsive," lacking the power to do evil, is *free to* do evil. Nor is Wolf just echoing the hierarchical view that, in the absence of any internal conflict, she acts *freely*. Wolf is talking about the freedom of an agent, not the freedom of an agent in relation to an action type or token, and we, therefore, reserve discussion of her views until the next chapter.

I have said little in defense of the nonnormative status of power or token ability. There do appear to be clear cases. If a man is falling from a window, can we really suppose that, in saying that he cannot reverse direction, we are just talking about the reasonableness of an expectation? Surely, that reasonableness rests on the nature of things.

I believe, as I indicated earlier, that the incompatibilist has a nonnormative idea in mind when he worries that determinism reduces one's power to the actual. The agent is, in these metaphysical circumstances, not free to do otherwise and is consequently absolved of moral responsibility. But hierarchical theorists and others who believe that the concept of freedom relevant to judgments of responsibility is willingness, harmony, or having what one (deeply, really) wants, rather than power, may feel that value is important to the *relevant* conception of freedom. They will be unperturbed by the previous remarks designed to show that the incompatibilist conception of *power* is a factual one. The incompatibilist worry is misguided, they believe, because power (or control or avoidability) is per se irrelevant to responsibility and the worst determinism does is to negate power (Frankfurt 1971, 1975). I shall argue against this view in the next chapter.

Since moral responsibility in contrast with freedom *is* an explicitly value-laden concept, it is evidently easier to make a case that valuational matters bear more directly on the prima facie conflict between determination and moral responsibility. Aristotle (1931: 1965) believed that nothing excuses matricide if the act is voluntary. In a similar vein, J. L. Austin (1961a) noted that "I did it inadvertently" may do as an excuse for treading on the snail, but not for treading on the baby. Some acts are so terrible that excuses for them ought to be much harder to come by. We must take greater precautions to prevent them and are culpable if we fail to do so. Yet Aristotle requires at least that the act of matricide be voluntary and Austin would have had to admit that it is *possible* to have an excuse for treading on the baby. So a wedge exists, permitting an incompatibilist to find that even heinous acts may be excused when the agent is appropriately deficient and, he would contend, determination is a sufficient deficiency.

If the cited deficiencies of freedom$_v$ require its replacement, we have yet to establish that its successor should be freedom$_p$ rather than a third alternative.

The hierarchical theory

A hierarchical theorist interprets free action (call this sense freedom$_h$) as the absence of dissonance across volitional levels.[8]

Whereas we have tacitly supposed that both freedom$_v$ and freedom$_p$ are the freedom of an agent to perform an action type in a particular context (freedom *of* action), the hierarchical theorist insists that freedom$_h$ is the analysis of freedom as a characteristic of a particular action. Since freedom$_h$ is different from freedom of action, the hierarchical theorist can allow that a person who succumbs to temptation may be able (free) to act differently although he does not act freely$_h$, that is, willingly.

Consider then a case in which a powerful coercive force is imposed from without. Abner, a guard who is forced to reveal secrets after the infliction of lengthy and painful torture, surely does not succumb freely. This result may indeed be in accordance with the hierarchical theory, but *only* if Abner is more dismayed at his having revealed the secrets than he is pleased that he is finally free of the suffering he was undergoing. We must on the theory consider which of Abner's desires he endorses or identifies with (more). But the reason that Abner acted unfreely is not the hierarchical one – that he confronted an internal struggle between the endorsed desire to resist and the victorious fear of continued pain – but rather that he tried very hard to do something and failed. Although Abner fails to resolve a conflict in a way that he finds satisfactory, imagine a mountain climber, Alice, who fails in spite of a single-minded and maximal effort. There is a struggle in this case too; the opposition is, however, not her own desires, but rather the forces of nature. Psychologically, there is no ambivalence. Alice is, to be sure, not free to climb the mountain, just as, perhaps, Abner is not free to keep the secrets. The problem for the hierarchical theorist is that neither Abner nor Alice capitulates *freely* although the latter experiences no internal dissonance. Perhaps then dissonance is not that important to freedom.

We might well add another sense of freedom, freedom$_d$, characterizing action not performed under duress which is abnormal relative to various standards, such as those which obtain in interpersonal transactions. Suppose, for example, that Abner is (1) more pleased that he is finally free of the suffering he was undergoing than he is dismayed at his having revealed the secrets and (2) blameworthy for having succumbed to this pressure in virtue of his promise to keep the secret combined with the devastating consequences of the revelation. Since Abner performed the action of disclosure, it follows that he was free$_p$ to do it and we may also suppose that, if he could have held out a bit longer, he was free$_p$ to retain the secrets. And since he really should have tried harder to refrain, he was also free$_v$. And with respect to the freedom *of* the disclosure, it was free$_h$ because he ultimately endorsed the desire which moved him to act. But Abner is not free$_d$. Thus, one may lack freedom$_d$ even though one possesses all the other freedoms.

Although we would normally excuse a person who reveals secrets under lengthy and painful torture, we would increase our expectations of Abner if we learn that he was aware of the potential dangers, he promised not to talk, he knew that revelation would result in enormous suffering, he could have held out a little longer, and he had reason to believe help was on the way. But if he literally could not do otherwise, if he lacked freedom$_p$, we have no choice but to regard him as unfree$_v$.

The senses of freedom so far mentioned are:

1. P is free$_v$ to do A if and only if it is reasonable to expect P to do whatever is necessary for him to do A.
2. P is free$_p$ to do A if and only if P has the power or token ability to do A (understood as a metaphysical condition, not reducible to normative notions).
3. P does A freely$_h$ if and only if P endorses the motive which leads him to do A.
4. P does A freely$_d$ if and only if P's doing of A does not occur under abnormal duress.

Freedom$_v$ does not necessarily coincide with freedom$_h$. Indeed, one of the principal objections to Frankfurt's view is that it fails to handle cases of weakness of will, in many of which the agent has freedom$_v$, but lacks freedom$_h$. For a person who regretfully succumbs to temptation may well be subject to the charge that he ought not to, that he should have resisted it. It is reasonable to expect that someone would have tried harder if a great deal is at stake. Yet the interlevel dissonance requires us to say that the agent lacked freedom$_h$.

More specifically, consider Albert, who fails to quit smoking in spite of valiant efforts. In light of health considerations and the jeopardy continued smoking poses for his family, Albert may be free in all senses specified so far *except* freedom$_h$. It is difficult to quit, but it is not impossible and he really should. He is even free$_d$ since the duress he would experience is not abnormal in the circumstances. Thus, the mere dissonance between first and second levels is relatively unimportant to Albert's overall freedom.

Arthur, who defeated the nicotine demon under similar circumstances may also be free$_p$ and free$_v$. For he might have continued to smoke and is in a situation similar to Albert's, that is, one which contains a moral imperative to quit. Yet Arthur, unlike Albert, does not constitute a clear case against the hierarchical theory because he is not clearly unfree$_h$. Yes, he struggled; however, since his better self won, his action is in accordance with the aspects of his nature he most identifies with, even if the *path* to action was turbulent. Internal dissonance does not imply the absence of conflict, for conflict may be present on or between levels; it rather implies that the result fails to accord with the agent's *highest*-order volitions (Frankfurt) or perhaps the agent's deepest values (Watson).[9]

The matter is, as we shall see later, more complex. In spite of Arthur's judgment that he should not continue to smoke, combined with the success of that resolution, it does not follow that Arthur's action is in accordance with his deepest values. I shall argue in Chapter 5 that the hierarchical theorist has confused "height" with "depth." A second-order judgment, that is, one directed at one's primary will, need not represent a facet of the total person that is closer to the core than the primary will itself. There are many cases in which we cannot help but continue to identify ourselves with that primary will, where the identification is gleaned not from a second-order judgment, but rather noncognitive components of the self, for example, desires and feelings. So although Arthur's judgment that he should stop smoking coincides with his behavior, it does not follow that Arthur is free of serious dissonance. For he may continue to identify himself as a smoker. He may have identified himself with the heroes in 1940s movies, the macho types who always got the women in the end as they deftly flicked the cigarette from between their lips before the inevitable and suggestive fadeout. He now is depressed and feels uncommitted to any former projects. His actions are stilted and half-hearted and his dreams reveal a preoccupation with different facets of smoking.

Thus, the difficulties for the hierarchical theory already cited will be augmented later as we look more closely at its conception of identification. We have, then, failed so far to identify a sense of freedom that should replace power or token ability as the core of the notion I am seeking.

Knowledge and freedom

Knowledge is a component of positive freedom essentially in virtue of its central role in enabling agents to act purposively and to make intelligent and effective decisions. In certain contexts, for example, Locke's man in the locked room, the man is unfree to leave whether or not he knows the room is locked. This is so because the information would not constitute an enabling condition. Information is important when it can make a difference. So if the man has lockpicking tools, his ability then *is* a function of his knowledge of their use.

Should the room, unbeknownst to the man, be unlocked, he retains the ability to leave. He is at liberty to leave for he would leave if he were to try to do so. Note, though, that he is neither free$_v$ to leave nor blameworthy for failing to do so even if he stays just because he wants to. If morality requires the agent to leave in these circumstances, the man would be less than moral in virtue of a character flaw revealed by the absence of a desire to leave; but he would still not be morally blameworthy for the specific failure in this case, to wit, the failure to leave the locked room. Nonculpable ignorance, as Aristotle saw, excuses. The same may be said of his freedom of will. The deception may make him unfree$_v$ and blameless even though he remains free$_p$ because he retains the bare power to decide to leave. Monumental, nonculpable ignorance can obviously absolve an agent from responsibility for a result even in a case in which the ignorance does not preclude the agent's power to bring the result about.

Thus, although ignorance about our abilities does not typically affect them, the ignorance can bear on our freedom in other senses. We are not denying the importance of the distinction between the two types of ignorance: lack of know-how interferes with ability and, *therefore*, freedom; lack of insight into ability leaves the ability intact, but interferes with other sorts of freedom.

Suppose that the man would prefer to leave the room and stays only because he believes he has no choice. So he is the agent of another's will, one at variance with his own. Although he is not strictly coerced, the manner of operation, the results, and the moral features of this situation are quite similar to a case of coercion. It is also a case in which the victim's autonomy is restricted for his actions are in an important sense not being determined by his own wishes.

It is crucial to distinguish the disability induced by the ignorance from the disability induced by the manner by which the man acquired the misinformation. His subjection to the will of another is a consequence not of his ignorance, but rather of the manipulation through deception by another person. And evidently this manipulation can succeed without imparting misinformation. An authority figure may impose himself on me by inducing me to believe *truths* about which I have not been given an opportunity to form independent judgments. I am no less heteronomous for acting on these truths than for acting on falsehoods, except that my proficiency is enhanced by the possession of genuine information.

A person who acts from ignorance not brought on in a manipulative manner will not feel used, will not be an instrument of another's will, and will not, therefore, in any clear sense, be heteronomous. To be sure, innocently induced ignorance is a defect of the person suffering from the ignorance which *can* obviously inhibit his ability to make intelligent decisions and act successfully once those decisions are made. This failing, which is a limitation on positive freedom, can also interfere with one's autonomy of choice. If the knowledge I lack is knowledge concerning my own motivations, then part of my incapacity may well be a failure to see that I am greatly dependent upon another person, that I am actually relinquishing my autonomy and submitting to the will of another. This is not to say that I am being manipulated by the other person. The problem may be entirely mine. For some deep-seated reason, I may be unaware that I regard this other person as a powerful authority figure whose casual suggestions register in me as commands. So the freedom impaired by my ignorance in this sort of case also has an adverse effect on my autonomy.

Duress

Although a person acting from an irresistible impulse lacks freedom$_p$ and, therefore, freedom$_v$, the vast majority of cases of duress or conflict are ones in which an obstacle or exigency does not constitute an absolute barrier to some action. In these cases, an agent may do what he wants because he wants to do it, thereby becoming a clear-cut candidate for freedom, but one of several factors apparently reduces or eliminates his freedom. The person would prefer not to be in the situation because the action makes him unhappy for one of a variety of reasons: either (a) he must act contrary to another, possibly strong, desire (he wants the boat, but does not want to part with the rent money) or (b) he would be better off not to have to make a choice even though he wants to do the action he does rather than the available alternatives (he prefers to surrender his money than sacrifice his life) or (c) he resents some feature of the situation (he recognizes that he is being manipulated, but can see no viable way out) or (d) he must act immorally to satisfy the desire (he needs the money, but does not want to cheat the man to get it).

Most choices require us to surrender something of value. Unfreedom in any sense cannot be contrasted with the absence of sacrifice. I freely choose to purchase a boat even though it costs me *something*, money I could have used for something else, for example, a new Porsche. We move closer to serious duress if we suppose the money is required for a needed item, food, rent, clothing, medical services, my life or the lives of my loved ones. Although it may sometimes be implausible to say that I *cannot* sacrifice a needed item for a frill, I may nonetheless be free$_p$ to do so. So "I have no choice but to use the money for food" expresses my unfreedom$_v$: I cannot reasonably be expected to act otherwise.

I would not choose to enter certain choice situations, in particular, those in which the choice available to me does not permit me to improve my lot and may result in its being worsened. This happens when my life is threatened unless I hand over my wallet. I come off worse than I was prior to the threat no matter what I do. Yet this feature does not explain why I feel that I am not free to do other than hand over my wallet. For if I happen to be a guest of my well-meaning, but unsophisticated employer in a restaurant I realize is very bad, I may be perfectly free to choose from among the dreary choices on the menu. That I cannot extricate myself from the situation makes me unfree to leave the restaurant, not unfree to choose the fillet of pseudo-Dover sole. That I mind submitting to the threat does not explain the feeling that the act of surrendering the money is unfree. For I also mind having to eat in the restaurant, but do not regard the act of ordering the sole as unfree. To be sure, there is the additional feeling of resentment in the case of the theft, but that does not suffice for the loss of freedom. I sometimes resent a street person for approaching me for money, yet remain free to refuse him money. (In the latter case, there may be something like the uncomfortable feeling one has when one refuses certain charitable requests, and this is a milder form of the feeling of coercion. But I am not coerced because the penalty, the uncomfortable feeling or the realization that I am not very charitable, is tolerable.) Even if I give him the money, I may mind and even resent his behavior. I may feel exploited because of the manner in which a standing disposition or character trait of mine has been activated by someone who wants to use me. But I am not and do not feel literally coerced.

The matter of need seems crucial. I need my life; I do not need the sole. Nor do I need to feel like a compassionate human being or to be free of uncomfortable feelings. So I am free to turn the street person away and to reject the sole. And my feeling that the street person's behavior is somewhat coercive rests in part on the fact that my desire to think of myself as compassionate is strong. In all these cases, I may lack the freedom$_v$ to reject my needs, whether or not I have the freedom$_p$ to do so. Indeed, one can lack freedom$_p$ and, therefore, freedom$_v$ in those more desirable situations in which one is made an offer one cannot refuse. I may feel coerced to accept the million dollars and the Lamborghini. Although, should I find no fault with my will, I would have freedom$_h$, I might lack freedom in all other senses to reject the offer. The distinction between character and action should be invoked to explain why we may regard a person who can be coerced by such incentives as possessed of distorted values even when we cannot blame him for responding as he does. His character is not laudable; but, given his unfreedom$_p$, we cannot invoke a *further* charge of blameworthiness for succumbing to these urges. (See Berofsky 1987: chs. 3, 4.)

Our subject is freedom, not threats. A lot has been written about the difference between threats and offers; but the matter is not crucial for us since a person may lack freedom when he accepts an offer (he cannot refuse) and may possess freedom when he succumbs to a threat. (We may think a person cowardly and immoral for agreeing to blow up Omaha on pain of being kicked in the groin.) The previous reference to need, then, pertains to conditions of freedom, not conditions under which one is under a threat. I can be unfree to abandon my needs whether or not the danger arises from a threat. I am not free to remain at the bottom of my pool until I drown even though no one is threatening me. The relation between freedom and needs will be taken up again shortly.

I shall not seek here to specify more carefully the conditions of freedom$_v$ or moral responsibility. I have in general upheld the significance of power, including knowledge, yet conceded, in terms of usage, the ubiquitousness of freedom$_v$ in most contexts. Frequency is, however, a minor virtue. Perhaps freedom$_d$ is invoked as often as any other; but in the absence of context, such as is provided by a concern with moral responsibility or autonomy, little of philosophical interest may be gleaned from such statistical data.

4
Agent freedom

Advocates of valuational freedom are reacting against the idea that ascriptions of freedom to a human being are just ascriptions of the capacity to engage in unfettered or unimpeded activity or the absence of sufficient causes. Freedom has a moral as well as a metaphysical dimension. If we ignore the former, there would be no difference between the freedom of a human agent and the freedom of a fly or an electron. Freedom is that state which enables its bearer to be guided through life by values; it permits the agent to embody in action moral and nonmoral values, thereby sanctioning third party judgments of the agent's worth and responsibility for those actions.[1] Although the absence of impediments or the availability of adequate opportunity may be a necessary condition for any being to achieve this state, there are also conditions internal to the agent, including those which set creatures with values apart from others. Although I upheld the centrality of a nonvaluational conception of freedom of action in the last chapter, we will have to look more closely at the claims made on behalf of this normative component for the case of free *agency*.

This project – the definition of free agency – is complicated by the fact that the same internal change can either enhance or diminish freedom depending upon the environment and the same external change can either enhance or diminish freedom depending upon internal capacities. That snake in the garden had very different effects on Sam, Frank, and Harry. Conversely, a face lift might enhance one's freedom in a society which prizes youth and diminish it in one which venerates age. We were able to bypass this distinction for the case of freedom of action since any instance of free (token) action, according to the definition, presupposes that all internal and external requirements are satisfied.

Clearly, some internal factors are relatively invariant to internal and external context. Intelligence is almost always freedom-enhancing and psychosis almost always freedom-reducing. So if we construe the project of defining agent freedom, abstractly considered, as the formulation of conditions agents should meet prior to their immersion in society, we look to these components of positive freedom to define the heart of this concept. A person with intelligence, rationality, skills, and talents may or may not be lucky when he is thrust into the world. But he at least possesses the tools he can utilize on behalf of the ends he might wish to promote should his society afford him the opportunity to do so.

We might then simply identify agent freedom with positive freedom and, in the end, that is indeed what we do. But we reach this conclusion by discovering the obstacles in the way of an account of agent freedom formulated by extrapolation from the idea of freedom of action, which has already been clarified.

Agent freedom and freedom of action

Is there any conception of freedom which can be carried over to the context of agent freedom? All the senses hitherto identified are oriented to particular situations. An agent is free$_p$ to do (or will) otherwise in S and may then be free$_v$ and morally responsible even though she is not free$_d$. But in situation T, everything might be different for the same agent. If we believe that some people are more free than others, is our task then to define conditions under which as many of an agent's actions and decisions will be free in some or all of the already specified ways?

But if the sheer number of free token actions and choices is the crucial factor, consider an individual (we shall suppose is highly intelligent, skilled, and emotionally stable) who is forced to spend his life in front of a television set in order that he can play mock games the real versions of which are played by the actual contestants on game shows. He may be able to make enormous numbers of free choices, that is to say, strategies for (mock) victory. It might be said that this person's unfreedom is constituted by the monumental narrowing of options imposed by his environment. Although (possibly) possessed of a high degree of positive freedom, he suffers an extraordinary amount of negative freedom. But in what sense is this true in light of the *number* of free actions he is permitted?

In answering these questions, we must be careful not to invoke moral considerations for we do not want just to *suppose* that freedom can only be used on behalf of good or noble ends. If the TV watcher's life has little value, that says nothing per se about the extent of his freedom, at least without further argument.

Joel Feinberg (1980) presents a portrait of one Martin Chuzzlewit, who has a single overriding and utterly trivial desire in life. Although he lacks the ability to obtain anything else – his ineptitude is vast – he achieves his goal and is completely content. If we imagine that our TV watcher is Martin Chuzzlewit, then we cannot fault his freedom on the grounds of a failure to control all important aspects of his life. For, insofar as the activity he has no choice but to pursue is happily the only one he deems satisfying, he exercises complete control in that narrow area that is all that matters to him. And he may achieve this goal without calling significantly upon his intelligence, skill, and emotional stability. (We suppose that he does not care that his strategies or answers are often wrong; he just loves the thrill of the contest.) In light of our sensitivity to the distinction between the nature of freedom and its value, is there any relevant way we can deploy *our* frustration at either the emptiness of Chuzzlewit's life or his failure to utilize his capacities?

Relativistic conceptions of agent freedom

The question that cases like Martin Chuzzlewit force us to confront is the possible relativity of freedom. We may attempt to count this man unfree in two different ways. We may, for example, ignore his strange psychological constitution as well as his (normal) biological constitution, including his needs, interests, desires, and values. We count him unfree then in virtue of the extraordinary limitation in the *range* of options available to him, whether or not he is or should be interested in taking advantage of them. Freedom under this alternative is *not* relativized to individual desires, needs, interests, or values; his unfreedom is grounded in a failure to be able to do very much rather than a failure to satisfy or fulfill these elements. That he is free to do all that he wishes tells us only that he is content, not that he is "really" free.

This approach fails to avoid relativity, however. Since Chuzzlewit makes an unlimited number of free choices, we judge him unfree because of the small number of option *types* available to him. But we have no way of classifying options without a tacit reference to human nature. Even if *Jeopardy* permits him to choose from 4,000 categories of questions, the range of his choices remains extremely narrow. And that observation depends on the fact that normal human beings, including Chuzzlewit, have a variety of capacities – intellectual, physical, social, moral, aesthetic, and spiritual – of which he is exercising a portion of but one. My cat does not lack freedom in virtue of her inability to appreciate Miro, read Molière, and support World Vision; cats don't have the relevant capacities. Although we ignore the individual differences among human beings or between Chuzzlewit and others, we are still relativizing Chuzzlewit's unfreedom to his inability to exercise those fundamental human capacities which are atrophied by a life devoted to TV watching. If Chuzzlewit needs human companionship, even if he fails consciously to acknowledge it, his unfreedom is constituted by the specific inability to fulfill this innate need.

A more drastic sort of relativization would characterize freedom in terms of the *individual's* desires or interests. Freedom then becomes the freedom to do what we (most) want to do. This is the approach a variant of which is taken by the hierarchical theory when it denies freedom to those who are not content with, who would prefer not to have, their own desires, whether these desires are grounded in common human drives or are utterly idiosyncratic. Feinberg rejects this position. He contrasts Martin Chuzzlewit with Tom Pinch, a man with enormous powers, but totally frustrated by the fact that the only thing that matters to him is unavailable. Pinch's *freedom*, claims Feinberg is not affected by the unfortunate distribution of options, only his *contentment*. Or imagine an absolute monarch who becomes so bored with a life in which no effort is required to achieve whatever he wants that his desires eventually dissipate. He goes through the motions of living, but cares about nothing. His condition is pitiable; but he has lost no freedom.

We have contrasted two sorts of relativization – to common human needs or capacities and to individual desires or interests. Without any sort of relativization, we would have to count Chuzzlewit's freedom as diminished should his society ban the disembowelment of toads. For it would then be irrelevant to cite either the fact that humans are not as such driven to perform this sort of act or the fact that Chuzzlewit just happens not to be interested in this sort of undertaking.

The adoption of a definition of freedom as the freedom to pursue our needs or innate drives is a way of acknowledging that interference with the food supply is, relative to the facts of human nature, more damaging to human freedom than the ban on toad disembowelment (even if the latter limits everyone's freedom$_p$ and a few people's freedom$_p$ to do what they want to do).

Correlatively, this notion helps us in part to identify the amount of freedom *in a given society*. A society which restricts freedom of access to food and shelter, which imposes limits on freedom of assembly and religion, which disallows a free press and the free flow of information has less freedom than one in which these restrictions are absent.

Some of these limits on freedom do not strictly concern needs. When our project is a definition of "social freedom," however, we must liberalize our account. For a free society must permit agents to have extensive control over their lives, a control which is not possible without the provision of conditions which are essential to most human activities or to many deemed important by substantial numbers of persons, whether or not these activities are grounded in innate drives or fundamental needs.

A more accurate accounting of social freedom would grade restrictions. Governments which order the killing of masses of civilians or prevent the distribution of food to certain groups for political reasons limit freedom more seriously than those which interfere with sexual needs, for the latter are not life-threatening. We then turn to freedom of speech, assembly, access to information, for these freedoms are crucial to the pursuit of virtually any life, of any set of commitments. Freedom of religion would be of lesser importance for a significant number of persons would not be adversely affected, at least directly, by restrictions in this domain.

We can make finer distinctions, but our project is not a definition of social freedom. *Our* context is individual freedom and autonomy. Although we seek a general definition of freedom and autonomy, we seek one applicable to individuals and, in that context, we cannot ride rough-shod over individual differences. A society which bans religion has significantly less freedom than one which permits all forms of religious expression. But the village atheist couldn't care less.

Joseph Raz makes a point in a different context which can be used in support of a sharp distinction between these two projects, social and individual freedom. He distinguishes needs from desires, contending that it is good to satisfy biological needs even if the person does not want to because their fulfillment is a precondition of the ability to pursue new goals and that ability is valuable whether or not it is wanted. But he also insists that one can sometimes do a *greater* harm by satisfying a person's needs. For the person may have critical goals, ones which permeate his life, which militate against fulfillment of certain needs. Although one's *self-interest* is always adversely affected by the frustration of biological needs, in unusual cases, one's *well-being* may be thereby enhanced.

"A person who undergoes great deprivations in order to bring medical help to the victims of an epidemic is sacrificing his interest in favor of that of others, but his life is no less successful, rewarding or accomplished because of that" (1986: 296).

This self-sacrificing individual who brings medical aid to others rejects the superiority of his own personal interests for the sake of a goal he deems more valuable. Accordingly, the threat to block the only route to the epidemic victims would be a greater threat to his freedom than the threat to deprive him of food. A definition of freedom formulated to capture the social sense, therefore, would be of no use to describe the freedom of this person. We must look to the individual agent's goals to determine what is important and the diversity of human nature makes even a reference to biological needs restricting in this regard.

Raz's example is of interest not just because it poses a sharp distinction between social and individual freedom. It also undermines the conception of freedom as the freedom to fulfill one's species-based capacities. Our capacity to formulate goals which transcend and even conflict with our humanity calls for a liberalization of this account of freedom.

In Chapter 2, I distinguished autonomy from both flourishing and self-expression, insisting on the right of an individual to reject an entire domain of human potentiality without abandoning his autonomy. So long as Dr. Roy's decision to remain blind was informed, rational, and independent, it was also autonomous, even though it was a decision to repudiate a natural human capacity.[2] If autonomy presupposes freedom, this result reinforces the above example of Raz's. Dr. Roy is not free to do a lot of things normal humans can do; but his well-being, dependent as it is on *his* personal (rational, informed, independent) choice to pursue a life of religious devotion, may well be secure.

If in response we revert to the other sort of relativization, construing freedom as the freedom to do what one wants to do, we shall be confusing freedom with contentment, a possible candidate for the *value*, not the *nature* of freedom. Two equally free agents can differ enormously in terms of frustration and contentment, depending upon the contingencies of social arrangements, the law, and psychological and physical realities. A musician devoted to the study of contemporary composition would lead a far more frustrating life than a beer lover in a society which permits only Gabrieli to be played, but any beer to be drunk. A commitment to view the musician as free as the beer drinker does not preclude us from acknowledging an important difference between the two by saying in addition that the beer drinker is far more free *to do what he wishes to do* than the musician.

Clearly, a rational social policy will encourage as much freedom as possible, relative to other fundamental social goals. So we might even expand our conception of external or negative freedom to require that options be widened unless there is sufficient social justification for refusing to do so. It should not be a difficult matter, barring a preposterous set of assumptions, to suppose that the imposition of barriers to the performance of any composer except Gabrieli is arbitrary. But I will not adumbrate further on this for, as I have said, this book is not about the political dimension of freedom.

We ought then to construe variations in the distribution of options as relevant to the *value* of the freedom we have or lack. A society which permits musicians to play only the music of Gabrieli, but encourages diversity in the selection of beer and toothpaste, is inferior to one which permits complete latitude in the manner of musical expression, but demands that everyone use Budweiser and Crest (see Berofsky 1987: 68). But we cannot draw any definite conclusions about the distribution of agent freedom in the two societies.

Raz himself sees the noble individual he describes as prepared to sacrifice his interests not for certain desires, even core desires, but rather for his well-being. The freedom to pursue one's well-being is different insofar as well-being, according to Raz, is the achievement of *valuable* goals derived from the social forms available to the agent. A person cannot be well off, according to this view, if his deepest desires are satisfied and he is completely content, should those desires be unsavory.

We now have three sorts of candidates for the relativization of freedom, therefore. Accordingly, if relativization to need and to desire are both rejected, we may still think of freedom as other than pure power for it may turn out to be the freedom to pursue *valuable* goals. Wolf's account – freedom as the ability to recognize and be moved by the Right – is another variant of this idea.

A central question of this book concerns the extent to which a fully free, autonomous agent must be motivated by concerns which are (objectively) valuable or which are so judged by the agent. Can he be driven neither by a concern for morality nor indeed by desires on which he has conferred the status of values? In order not to prejudge this question, we must reject, as a matter of strategy, loaded conceptions of freedom like those of Raz and Wolf. We may ultimately be forced to concede the impossibility of a metaphysically free and autonomous agent who is also value free in some significant sense; but that will be the result of this inquiry, not its starting point.

I, therefore, choose not to restrict the notion of freedom to the freedom to do what we want to do, the freedom to do what we need to do, or the freedom to pursue (worthwhile) goals. (A detailed defense of the exclusion of the third sort of relativization is provided at the end of this chapter.) Thus, an agent's freedom *is* enhanced by the enactment of legislation permitting anyone to disembowel toads. If freedom were the only social value – and it is not – society should allow for an indefinite diversity in fundamental goals, including ones that are independent of or even antithetical to biological interests. More is better.

We may wish to insist that there at least be relativization to *possible* human desires or goals. It is balmy, for example, to campaign for legislation permitting ice hockey to be played on the planet Mercury. And there may be acts that can be performed which no human being would ever wish to perform. But a more serious difficulty confronts this nonrelativistic conception of agent freedom. If Bill can do all that Jill can do and Bill can do one thing Jill cannot do, then Bill clearly has more freedom than Jill on this conception. But we are nonetheless unable to produce either an absolute or a comparative general definition of agent freedom. For it is unclear what we should say about other sorts of cases in light of two important stultifying constraints.

First, let us recall that Chuzzlewit can do an enormous number of things and, without any constraints on type formation, an enormous number of types of things. If we wish to say either that Chuzzlewit is unfree or that he has very little freedom just because there is so much he cannot do, we cannot be bemoaning the numerical limitations on him. In fact, on certain theories of action, he will be able to do an infinite number of things, in which case, even though a normal human being can do all that Chuzzlewit can do and a great deal more, he will not be able to do a greater *number* of things. So agent freedom does not depend on the quantity of actions in our power.

If, then, we turn to variety, but are unable to take into account either the importance or value of the actions to the agents as individuals or as human beings, how would we compare Chuzzlewit to one who cannot participate in all the game shows available to him, but is instead permitted to paint, read, walk in the garden, work at his job, and talk to his friends? Our theory cannot say why Genghis Khan, who never had the opportunity to watch TV, is more free than Martin Chuzzlewit. And given the value-laden character of scope of autonomy, we have no theoretical basis on which to ground Chuzzlewit's lack of this trait. The effort to generate an account of free agency out of the account of free action has failed.

Agent freedom as positive freedom

One of the conclusions drawn so far is that the value of positive freedom is a function of social and psychological factors, so that under special circumstances, for example, those of Martin Chuzzlewit, positive freedom neither enhances nor detracts from the ability of the agent to achieve what is important to him. Chuzzlewit happens not to need whatever skills and rationality he may possess in order to play these TV games. Thus, in very special circumstances, the traits commonly identified as positive freedom are insignificant. So if the world were very different, if, for example, God gave us all we wished for on a silver platter, we would come to regard our intelligence, our capacity to process information, our emotional stability, and our logical acumen as vestigial. They would lose their entitlement to the label "positive freedom" for they would in no way enhance our freedom in any sense: They do not help us to perform more or better actions.

Of course, one can always describe a world in which traits that are generally useful turn out to be liabilities – intelligent or highly skilled people are berated by the shortsighted masses or penalized by a jealous sovereign. Any social or legal restriction can enhance the ability of some people to achieve their objectives – masochists, prison guards, people who use incarceration as a means to relieve guilt or remove themselves from the demands of society. And in a world in which almost everybody falls into one of these groups, these social or legal "restrictions" would lose their claim to the label "negative freedom."

Yet one cannot deny the existence of such fundamental internal requirements, as health, intelligence, and a reasonable level of emotional stability, for virtually any human endeavor in almost any set of circumstances we are likely to confront. We call intelligence a component of positive *freedom* not because it invariably enhances freedom of action, but rather because it contributes in a central way to most of the projects we set out upon. And even in a world in which God gives us all we desire, we would still need positive freedom if we wish to be autonomous. For we must still assess our situation in order to decide what it is that we want even though we need not take into account factors relevant to our proficiency at achieving the objectives we choose – God guarantees that we will be proficient. Positive freedom would be irrelevant if God enters these deliberations in order to ensure a desirable outcome; but in so doing, God also ensures a heteronomous decision. If the agent retains his autonomy or independence, he will need knowledge, rationality, and the other components of positive freedom.

Also, even if a person chooses a life bereft of long-term commitments, preferring to adjust his goals in light of new opportunities and changes of personal perspective, it is impossible to be free without the *capacity* for long-term commitments. Even this person may be guided by a long-range policy: he prefers spontaneity; he does not wish ever to sacrifice a chance for fresh experiences in order to fulfill a past commitment. No matter how frequently a person vacillates, changes his mind, or fails to look beyond the immediate situation, the *inability* to take on moderately long-term obligations would be disabling even to his current life style. For example, one component of this ability, the awareness of the waxing and waning of opportunities, of the success or failure of even a mini project, in general of duration and one's evolution therein, provides a person who lives for the moment with the minimal tools for more extended commitments.

Impulsive persons, of whom psychopaths are an extreme sort, are characterized in part by a tendency to be moved by the whim of the moment rather than by a concern for extended projects. They become infatuated quickly, lose interest, and then shower their affection on a new object of curiosity, ad indefinitum, failing thereby to coordinate their attractions with ongoing projects and concerns which provide the basic sustenance for normal persons. Shapiro observes:

When the content of a whim or impulse fails to be modified by stable aims or enriched and modulated by associative and affective connections in such an integrative process, that content remains primitive and bare, and, failing to be anchored in stable interests, it tends to shift erratically. (1965: 142)

The impulsive fails to be driven by a genuine interest in the object for his attenuated attention span does not permit him to savor, learn about, and study the connections to other things of those momentary objects of strong attraction. These temporary immersions, although intense, enable the impulsive to prize some elements of the object, but he will be uninterested in features which require an extended and somewhat detached relationship to elicit. Only a person who is capable of appreciating the distinctive satisfaction of long-term projects and extended commitments will be able to acquire a deeper understanding of the objects and persons around him. In the absence of this sustained interest, the impulsive fails to be able to utilize critical and emotional resources to test hypotheses, suspend judgment, explore relationships, and revise earlier conclusions in the light of new experience.

Although the dangers of impulsiveness are evident – those who act in haste often repent in leisure – one particular impairment, the reduction of freedom and autonomy, is especially relevant. For the impulsive personality is less likely to understand the nature of the objects to which he directs his attention and is less likely, therefore, to have relevant knowledge.

To be sure, we may not be interested in components of positive freedom unless they bear on our actual desires. Just as Tom Pinch is able or free to do many things he does not care to do, so he may know how to do many things he lacks a desire to do. And the impulsive may object that, even if his perspective on things is highly limited, thereby rendering him prone to significant ignorance, he knows what he needs to know for his limited concerns. Since we are seeking a general account of human freedom, not one geared to specific types of agents, we look to those basic physical, psychological, and intellectual conditions which are likely to enhance in general the options open to us. Thus, it is more important for freedom that we be able to move our limbs than our ears, even though some strange people might prefer the specific freedom to move their ears. The ability to move arms and legs provides us with enormously expanded powers, unlike the ability to move our ears. And if one objects that an increase in the sheer number of options – and who knows how to count actions anyway? – is often insignificant, he must be reminded that we have decided to distinguish the nature of freedom from its value.

So we reaffirm the earlier conception of positive freedom as comprised, from the internal point of view, of a set of traits which are essential or highly useful to the satisfaction of a wide range of activities and decisions, including long-term commitments. These traits almost always enhance our token abilities or powers, although free agents may or may not possess the freedom to do and decide to do what is (deeply) important to them or what is simply important.

With respect to the particular response of the impulsive, we agree in part that the more significant deficiency is not the specific ignorance his orientation encourages, but rather the general proneness to misunderstanding, of which ignorance is a consequence. The impulsive approaches the world in a way which inhibits an understanding and appreciation of that world as it actually is. (This epistemic limitation is, of course, not the impulsive's only emotional deficit.) In Chapters 8 and 9, I shall place this component at the center of my account of autonomy.

If we ignore even the most important desires of an agent in the definition of positive freedom, can we also ignore the very elements which give freedom, in the sense in which it is the subject of our inquiry, its significance? Why be free unless we can use our powers to transform the world according to our values? Are we not distinguished from other creatures possessed of powers not just by the range and sophistication of these powers, but also by our awareness of their significance for the world and for ourselves? For the world, we see these capacities as enabling their bearer to make improvements, and for the bearer, we see them as opportunities to reveal to the world his moral nature and to receive the appropriate response of that world to the manner with which these gifts are used. Do we not need values almost as much as food and rest? If we regard an agent as (negatively) unfree because his environment fails to fulfill some basic need, ought we not regard an agent bereft of values as similarly deprived? Must we not construe positive freedom as a value-laden concept, as several philosophers have recently urged, or can we rest content with the gloss offered above in which freedom is conceived as a purely metaphysical or psychological condition whose principal *function* may perhaps be the securing of our values?

These questions can be answered only if we expand upon this account of human freedom. I have offered a provisional list of internal traits which would be generally useful to secure an agent's goals, whatever they may be. Construed as basically enhancing an agent's powers, they do not yet include a reference to certain higher-level skills some philosophers identify with autonomy. These skills are important because they permit an individual to regulate his activities and decisions critically and independently.[3] As I said earlier, slaves are not free even though they may possess an enormous amount of positive freedom. They may be mentally and physically healthy, informed, and rational. They may also have a great deal of freedom of action, the ability and opportunity to do an enormous variety of things. They have powers and skills *they are nonetheless unable to use in ways they might choose.* At some basic level, they do not choose their own lives. Some things they must do whether or not they want to; and even if they want to please their master and derivatively acquire the desires of their master, they lack independence. In some sense not yet adequately clarified, their goals are not self-determined. Perhaps, as we transform this account of positive freedom into the fuller ideal of autonomy, the role of values will become clearer. We will perhaps be able to discern the importance to a self-determining agent of values he may then realize through the skills constituting his positive freedom.

Freedom of decision

A musician dedicated to the study of contemporary music has autonomy even if he lives in an oppressive society in which only the music of Gabrieli is permitted to be played. His failure to be able to act on his choice – his lack of freedom of action – is a failure of proficiency, not autonomy. Yet this is naive insofar as an informed and rational agent would be aware of the possibilities of acting on his decision and would, accordingly, take these possibilities into account as he forms his decisions.

We might, however, in an effort to retain a sharp distinction between autonomy and proficiency, attempt to bracket the specific information regarding the capacity of that agent to act on his choice, where such capacity is a function both of ability and opportunity, of positive and negative freedom. One might imagine this agent behind a veil of limited ignorance so long as it is possible to pry apart the knowledge required to make a rational decision from the knowledge of the agent's proficiency, that is, his power (ability plus opportunity) to convert the decision into action.

This agent's ignorance of the probability that an action will bring about a goal, however, adversely affects the very viability of formulating a preference ordering among his goals. For information as to the ways to reach a certain goal may be bound up with information as to whether or not the goal will be satisfactory; the means may be so onerous that they offset the satisfaction of attaining the end. Thus, ignorance in this regard affects the wisdom of a decision in such a way as to reduce freedom and, therefore, autonomy.

In the fundamental sense of "rational," an agent's rationality is relative to his information such that information detrimental to a decision, but unavailable to an agent, does not reduce the rationality of his decision. The issue, however, is not the agent's rationality, but rather his autonomy. And just as we earlier observed that power rests on abilities which include relevant true beliefs, many of them concerning knowledge how, so here we must acknowledge that an agent's *autonomy of choice* depends on the amount of relevant information available to him. Knowledge plays an important role in both freedom of action as well as autonomous choice.

There is, therefore, no sharp line between autonomy and proficiency. There is good reason to look askance at an alleged case of perfect autonomy and total lack of proficiency. A person who really has neither information nor relevant skills pertaining to the realization of his goals is lacking the means necessary for an intelligent evaluation of those goals. There is good reason for the common transition found in the literature from autonomous choice to proficiency. That is, of course, not to deny the obvious difference between the two notions – although related, they are also distinct.

A radical limitation of options can ultimately affect autonomy by interfering with freedom of choice. Even when an agent is not disadvantaged by ignorance, a totally stultifying environment can eventually take its toll on his decision-making capacities. Indeed, the very knowledge that an action is impossible can render an agent incapable of deciding to perform it. Whether or not that is a logical truth, it is enough for our purposes that it just be a causal truth.

Thus, if our TV watcher – call him Guzzlewit for, unlike Chuzzlewit, he is miserable in his new life – had been unwillingly thrust into this position after having led a normal life, he would still be completely proficient at achieving the limited ends available to him. Eventually, however, when he is fully convinced that he must acquiesce in the catastrophic loss of negative freedom he has suffered, he may well become *unable* even to choose from options other than those few he can act upon, perhaps because his strength of will has been sapped and he is now motivationally crippled.

Earlier, I rejected a definition of freedom which relativizes freedom to human needs or innate drives. A person may autonomously choose to frustrate her own needs or sacrifice her own interests on behalf of a goal she has autonomously selected. This goal gives her life purpose even if it threatens that very life. Had Chuzzlewit independently and rationally selected his life, and had he done so with all relevant information and in a sober and emotionally mature frame of mind, he would have done so autonomously.[4] The reasons we find this possibility incredibly remote are those which explain our feeling that, in spite of his contentment, Chuzzlewit is a pitiable creature. He lacks scope of autonomy *now* whether or not *at an earlier time* he autonomously chose to enter this state.

Thus, limitations on freedom count as limitations on dispositional autonomy only if the actions in question might reflect possible choices of the agent. My autonomy is not adversely affected by my not being free to disembowel toads. Restrictions on freedom can, however, adversely affect my scope of autonomy even when these restrictions are of no personal moment to the agent, just as Chuzzlewit's autonomy is diminished by his inability to make decisions about matters of significance, in spite of his indifference to these circumstances.

An autonomous agent, then, uses his freedom to ensure that his decisions are his own, that they are, in a sense which requires further explication, "internally generated." He, thus, engages his critical powers, in other words, his freedom, here conceived as a tool for critical judgment. If he autonomously chooses to become a slave, he loses his autonomy in spite of the character of its origin. Freedom is a capacity comprised of a variety of internal traits, and autonomy is the critical use of these traits on behalf of independent choice.

We must now provide defense for the claim, assumed throughout the previous discussion, that agent freedom should not be relativized to value.

Freedom and value

Absolute versus relative conceptions of value

People's values differ. If my freedom requires that my choices be guided by values, does it suffice that the values which are efficacious are mine, no matter how idiosyncratic, ill-conceived, or immoral they are? Or must they be objective in the sense that their status as values is not dependent on their being the objects of desire of any person or persons or even the objects of desires that would arise in some person under certain ideal conditions? If objectivity is required, my adoption of the wrong values would automatically render me unfree.[5]

A serious advantage of the demand for genuine or objective values is that we are then in a position to explain the failings of the child, the person with a deprived upbringing, and the mental defective. For we are able to account for the intuitively plausible judgment that people suffering from these deficits lack freedom in terms of the fact that none is able to guide his or her life by those values which actually apply to prevailing circumstances. None of these persons is sufficiently sensitive to *the* relevant values or, if sensitive, sufficiently adept at evaluating courses of action in terms of them. Moreover, since the acknowledgment of certain values is not a sufficient safeguard against weakness of will, the objective interpretation is able to account for certain forms of immorality – a free agent, one who, on this account, recognizes that certain actions are wrong, may nonetheless succumb to temptation and be morally blameworthy for so doing.

But the freedom and moral blameworthiness of the agent who experiences weakness of will depend upon his acknowledgment of a failure to abide by values he accepts. How, then, can the advocate of the objective interpretation account for more serious forms of immorality, in particular, ones which involve the very rejection of values most of us hold dear? When Himmler recommends that his troops immunize themselves from feelings of compassion, an obedient follower will end up failing to appreciate the norms which really apply and proceed to act accordingly, that is, monstrously. Are we then constrained to place him in that group of children and deprived adults? Failing to acknowledge relevant values, he, too, lacks freedom and, therefore, blameworthiness. But surely not *all* persons who reject the values that are objectively grounded are unfree and consequently morally blameless.

To be sure, some unfree persons are morally responsible. But Abner, who succumbed under great, but not overwhelming duress to torture and revealed secrets he had promised to keep in the knowledge that such revelations would have disastrous consequences, is very different from the follower of Himmler. Why should we think of the latter as unfree? He is not faced with Abner's conflict. The follower of Himmler is depraved; but not all depravity is deprivation.

The difference between the morally depraved follower of Himmler – call him MD – and a morally deprived child in the Hitler Jugend – call him HJ – is clear enough in general terms. HJ was provided authorities, information and misinformation, modes of thought, a variety of carefully selected materials for absorption, and generally, experiences, at a point in time when he lacked the rational capacity, knowledge, and maturity to screen these stimuli in a discriminating way (see Philips 1987). To be sure, *all* early education is *partly* indoctrination; but we expect education in a democratic society to adhere to certain canons of respect for children which require educators to submit as much as possible to rules of evidence and to train youngsters to be independent, to develop and use their own critical judgment in the hope that they will develop into autonomous adults. Thus, the range of permissible views and behavior to which children are exposed must be significantly wider than it is among HJ's comrades.

As HJ grows up, we may initially excuse his uncivilized behavior on the grounds that he is not responsible for the distorted moral and nonmoral beliefs he acquired at a time he lacked the capacity for evaluation and on the basis of which his behavior is not unreasonable. We may not *continue* to excuse him if we believe that his critical faculties are developing in such a way that exposure to new experiences renders reevaluation both possible and reasonable to expect even for one as initially distorted as he. As reflection on guilt for war crimes demonstrates, it is no easy matter to decide in a real case whether someone's background is *so* distorted and his adult development *so* thwarted that we cannot (retrospectively) have expected such a reevaluation.

So MD's guilt is based either on his not having been indoctrinated as a youth into the Nazi cause or, having been so indoctrinated, his maturation's not having been so protective or distorted. And should he be guilty on these counts, he will be so judged in virtue of the possession of capacities for decency which also confer freedom upon him.

If we want to count some bad people as free, yet preserve the idea that anyone, regardless of her moral views, will want to appreciate the values *she* accepts and be competent in assessing their applicability and in revealing her character through action, relativization is the obvious course of action. If we discard the objective dimension, we will then permit those with odious values to be free. People with conflicting value systems may all be free to express *their* values and *their* characters.[6]

Do we then lack an explanation of the diminished freedom of the child or the adult with a deprived background? For example, we cannot always explain diminished freedom in terms of diminished power or control. Perhaps the severely retarded are literally unable to do many things normal people can do. But the problem with children and those with unfortunate backgrounds is that they fail to exercise *intelligent* control over the many things they are fully able to do. They act in inappropriate and harmful ways – often just like immoral people – because, as immature or stunted, they are incapable of guiding themselves by the standards accepted by normal adults.

But we need not revert to the objective interpretation with its attendant difficulties in order to account for the unfreedom of children and those with deprived upbringings. Their deviance constitutes unfreedom not on the basis of the unacceptability of their standards or their relative inability to appreciate the norms objectively governing their conduct, but rather on the understandable state of their ignorance. An adult who has suffered an impoverished childhood may have been deprived of the potential for independent judgment so that her moral reasoning, perhaps weak or distorted, is as good as we can expect.

Support for this suggestion may be gleaned from reflection on the following example. Imagine a commune whose members are taught that all human beings are equal and in which respect for each member of the human race is fostered. But these values are inculcated in a totally autocratic way. Not only are children introduced to materials which promote respect for all the diverse peoples of the world. They are also subjected to the most advanced forms of behavior modification on behalf of this end. They are denied access to books and other materials which might pervert these values. Censorship of all forms of art is practiced, and persons who question the value of universal equality and dignity mysteriously vanish.

A clever student may detect the deep inconsistency of a system which promotes universal respect through methods which deny it to the supposed beneficiaries of the system. No matter. Even if a student acquires a rather distorted conception of equality, the fact that his values are more or less ones we too adopt does not make him any more free than a brainwashed Nazi. We can account for the deprived upbringing of a member of this state by pointing to the arrested development of his critical capacities rather than the content of his ideals.

Thus, the greater freedom of the normal adult is not grounded in his greater valuational insight (evil people can be free), nor in his greater ability to effect values already adopted (a child may be free to effect her limited set of values), but rather in the possession of a range of *valuationally neutral* critical powers, that is, components of positive freedom, construed functionally in terms of their role in critical assessment.

Since the development of these powers is incomplete in children and arrested in others, we have a simple explanation of unfreedom in both cases. There is no need, therefore, to ground the unfreedom of the child in her diminished ability to express her nature or her values. For if we are prepared to describe the child's self in terms appropriate to the child, we may view the child as expressing her (childlike) self as fully as an adult is expressing her very different (adult) self. It is, of course, reasonable to deny all children freedom, but not freedom as self-expression. For some children may be capable of expressing their selves-in-formation. But, barring prodigies, no child will possess mature critical powers – rationality, logical acumen, information processing capacity. And it is on that basis that they are unfree.

S. Wolf's view of valuational freedom

A person achieves freedom, according to Wolf, when she aligns herself with reason and morality. Wolf collapses the nature and value of freedom by characterizing freedom as the proper relation to objective rightness. She, therefore, adopts the objective interpretation, but renders herself immune from the objection that this interpretation does not permit evil people to be held blameworthy. For she rejects the view that permits MD to count as blameless on the grounds that he is not in fact living the moral life. She can count MD as free so long as he possesses the *ability* to (1) recognize the moral reasons he failed to recognize (1980: 164) and (2) appreciate the world for what it is (1990: 62).

So as blameworthy, MD must at least be *able* to do the right thing. But she denies that the power to do wrong is essential to freedom for, if that were so, then, since freedom is desirable, the addition of the power to do wrong to one already in perfect alignment should enhance the value of the state, but it does not. If we compare the agent in perfect alignment with one who can do wrong, but always chooses not to, we will find that they act for identical reasons and that the potentially evil person is not more free, but instead more burdened, specifically by temptation.

Consider a test case. Alicia has received an admirable upbringing. She has internalized the values she has been taught through an open process of questioning and rational discussion. Her values track the Good to the extent that this is objectively possible. Alicia finds to her dismay that she is developing powerful impulses to abandon the moral and nonmoral values she acknowledges to be correct. She finds herself identifying with these selfish and wicked impulses, while at the same time condemning the error of her potential ways. She has been taught that it is sometimes acceptable to act selfishly and to devote some of her time and energy to the promotion of her own talents and interests even when this time and energy could have been used to serve altruistic enterprises. But her selfish interests in this case are not benign; they involve gratuitous harm to others and have no redeeming quality other than Alicia's personal gratification. Alicia recognizes that her personal gratification is a reason to satisfy her selfish desires; but she also sees that it is overridden by the harm she would inflict on others. Although her struggle is a constant one, in the end she does not veer from the path of duty. She acts rightly and responsibly, but feels that life is passing her by as she presses on to do her duty at the expense of what matters most to her. She is further frustrated by the realization that she *is* doing what is overall the best thing to do – for in her special circumstances that does not coincide with the most preferred course of action.

So Alicia is moved by the right because it is right and, as Wolf notes, is accordingly deserving of moral praise. Wolf also insists that this praise need not be withdrawn were we to discover that Alicia's struggle fails to be genuine. So if moral tribute accrues, it is not on the basis of the ability to act immorally; if Alicia does the right thing for the right reasons, it does not matter that she lacks the freedom$_p$ to do otherwise. We might just deny that Alicia is free in any sense and ground the dispensation of praise on the basis of admiration for her virtue and the action flowing therefrom along with the moral credit due her for earlier efforts to attain this state.[7] But Wolf does not take this tack and rather formulates a conception of freedom which Alicia satisfies.

Given that Alicia possesses both negative and positive freedom, I do not disagree with Wolf that Alicia possesses agent freedom (although she may be unfree in a variety of senses to act contrary to reason). I do not even wish to take issue with Wolf's contention that Alicia would be free even if she were unable to do the wrong thing. What I specifically object to is the blanket proviso which dictates that the freedom of *everyone* is the specific freedom to do the right thing. For *if* we are going to relativize freedom at all – and I have argued that we should not – we should instead relativize freedom to one's deepest desires or to that which one most cares about on reflection. Unless Wolf can make the case that we all must care most about morality or the Right, the case of Alicia indicates the arbitrariness of selecting the dimension of objective value over personal value. We admire Anne Frank for her idealism, not for her psychological insight, when she proclaimed that "I still believe that people are really good at heart" (1952: 237). By what right does Wolf preclude by analysis Alicia's lack of freedom to pursue what is most important to her just because it is antithetical to morality?

Alicia is a good person, but why say she is free on the basis of what she views as her *enslavement* to morality? Moreover, the assumption that freedom is self-expression will not generate this result; Alicia is unable to express her deepest self, the aspect of her being she would, if she could, display to the world as the manifestation of her individuality. She is frustrated, ambivalent, and unfulfilled. Her reason tells her that *overall* she is behaving rationally; she has chosen the best course of action, all things considered. But her appetitive nature, with which she identifies, could not care less.

This criticism does depend on the assumption that Alicia meets Wolf's own test for freedom, that her submission to morality is grounded in her recognition of the wrongness of the self-centered option. Can this assumption be sustained as Alicia withdraws from wholehearted participation in the enterprise of morality? All habits have sustaining power permitting them to survive with some strength the demise of their rationale. It is one thing to act in the right way because one realizes that the action is right, regardless of the origin of this realization; it is another to adhere to the dictates of morality out of force of habit or a concern to avoid the uncomfortable feeling of acting in a novel way, a way one's parents once disapproved of. As morality loses its significance for Alicia, what hold can it continue to have over her other than the force of habit or various extrinsic considerations such as the fear of parental reprimand?

To answer these questions satisfactorily, we must understand what is involved in recognizing that an action is right and what is involved in acting because of this recognition. With respect to the former, if Alicia was a paradigmatic case of a moral agent before her transformation, what would make us believe that she no longer recognizes that the realization of her fantasies would be wrong? Yet in light of her disengagement from morality, what motivating force can the recognition of rightness or wrongness as such command?

Although it is often difficult to sort out motivations in a situation in which there are multiple reasons for action, the case that Alicia *cannot* continue to respond to morality is weak. First of all, we note that the recognition that an action is wrong is neither necessary nor sufficient for forbearance for anyone; we simply require of Alicia then that her recognition of wrongness be causally relevant to the forbearance. Given that Alicia had been sufficiently rational to respond to moral reasoning before her transformation, why is it so difficult to believe that she is open to moral reasoning now?

But if the indulgence of her sinful urges is more important than morality to Alicia, why does Alicia continue to follow the dictates of morality? What explains this allegiance other than force of habit?

We have now changed the question. If we want to know why Alicia eschews malevolent behavior, the answer is that she realizes it is wrong (and she has been trained in a certain way). So she is a moral agent. If we want to know why she does not act on her highest value, self-realization in the form of wicked behavior, the answer is the same as would be given in any other case of a discrepancy between motivation and valuation. Either Alicia is just like an unwilling addict, drawn irresistibly to act contrary to her deepest values, or she suffers from weakness of will, that is, her deepest wishes are not as strong as her moral motivations. In permitting a discrepancy between valuational and motivational scales, as virtually all theories do, we automatically permit the possibility of Alicia. If Alicia is suffering from weakness of will rather than compulsion, then, although I would count her free   she is not a slave to morality – I do not do so because she happens to be responding to the Right.[8]

Alicia presents a difficult case for one like Wolf, who defends a conception of freedom as rational action combined with a conception of reason as the faculty for apprehending the Right. Alicia's actions appear to be responsible, right, and rational on Wolf's conception of rationality.

If we sever freedom from morality in this way, how can we explain why only free agents deserve praise and blame? A valuational conception of freedom at least provides the connecting link. That Wilbur has the token ability to give me ten dollars does not explain why his failure is morally culpable, but that Wilbur has the ability to do the right thing does explain why his failure is morally culpable. If freedom is instead construed as the capacity for robust, independent self-activity – as is the case on our account of positive freedom – we will apparently not be able to explain why such agents deserve credit or merit blame.

"Able to X" is an extensional context. If I can hit a home run in a major league ballpark, I can do that of which Babe Ruth did 714 in his lifetime. So if Wilbur owes me ten dollars, then his ability to return it is the ability to do the right thing. But "that Wilbur failed to act on his ability to X explains the fact that Wilbur deserves to be blamed" is an intensional context. If X is *doing the right thing*, the sentence is true; if X is *giving me ten dollars*, it is false. People deserve blame only if they misbehave. Wolf is certainly right that the link between freedom and responsibility implicates the notion of the ability to do the right thing. But that we are interested in certain freedoms because they are relevant to the assignment of praise and blame does not imply that freedom itself must be characterized in value-laden terms. A doctor is interested in sickness because he wants to treat sick people. There is a conceptual link between sickness and treatment – only sick people should be treated. But the concept of illness may well be characterizable independently of the concept of treatment. Analogously, even though only free actions deserve to be praised or blamed, freedom as such need not receive a normative definition. In that way, we are also in a position to explain why some free actions merit neither praise nor blame.

Critical competence

I reiterate the conviction that freedom is a value-neutral notion, functionally described as critical competence, a cluster of tools an agent in a supportive environment is able to use to translate his values into decisions and actions and to reveal to the world his moral character. Although I have found no good reason to characterize freedom in terms of the ends for the sake of which a moral agent would utilize his freedom, preferring instead to conceive of freedom neutrally and to permit free agents a wide variety of ends from which to choose, the feeling that values must enter into the discussion in a more intimate way dies hard.

Let me underscore the virtual unanimity on the question of the importance to freedom or autonomy of the possession of a value system. For Gary Watson (1975), the person must determine whether the objectives are good or desirable. For Graham Nerlich, "it is mainly in the conflict between the (motivational and valuational) systems, and in the continuing victory of our values, that our true autonomy lies" (1989: 20). Haworth too contends that a deliberator needs to know if his preferences are consistent with his principles and values (1986: 37).

Other things being equal, therefore, an agent is more autonomous on all these accounts to the extent he considers whether his preferences clash with his values. It appears then that Haworth, Benson, Nerlich, Watson, Wolf, and Dworkin all agree on the crucial place of values in the life of a free (Watson, Benson, Wolf) or autonomous (Haworth, Dworkin, Nerlich) agent.[9] In order to evaluate this claim, we turn next to an explicit discussion of the concept of value.

5
Values and the self

Having pressed for a value-neutral account of freedom, I cannot but be impressed by the insistent demand for a central role for the notion of value or evaluation, if not in the analysis of freedom, then perhaps in that of autonomy of choice. (By definition, scope of autonomy implicates values, but that is not the notion we are currently trying to understand.) Even relativistic interpretations inevitably require that free or autonomous agents be essentially concerned to realize their values, no matter how silly, odious, or bizarre. There is no way to deal satisfactorily with this deeply ingrained view without a careful attempt to understand the nature of value and evaluation.

Values and desires

Even if we are sympathetic with the notion of objective value, it is clear that a person can have values that are not aligned with objective value; a person can be immoral, for example. Our project, then, concerns the difference between an individual's desires and *her* values.

We might describe this task as a search for the factor that forces a distinction between the two notions. For example, desires come in varying strengths. But since we certainly want to accommodate the thought that one state of affairs or goal is more highly valued or prized than another, we are not forced to distinguish and do not yet comprehend the difference between a strong desire for some goal and the placing of great value on that goal.

Similarly, just as we can desire a state of affairs either for its own sake or as a means to a distinct end, so can we regard a state of affairs as having intrinsic or instrumental value. Indeed, since "value" in this discussion will be used to mean "intrinsic value," then the relevant desires will be directed to objects or states of affairs desired for their own sake. In this respect, then, there is no difference between desires and values.

Nor is the difference to be found in the relative effectiveness of desires and values. I can fail to act on my desires, and I can fail to display my values.

Although many desires would appear to be too trivial or fleeting to count as candidates for values, we cannot infer just from the content of a desire that it cannot attain the status Mt. Everest had for Hillary. Perhaps there are a priori limits on what sorts of things can be values for human beings; but we have not as yet laid down those limits, and given the enormous diversity within our species, we should be very careful about how this is done.

One a priori consideration, however, is the degree of generality of the content of the desire. For, although people have found great value in and have organized their lives around quite specific goals – the conquest of Mt. Everest, the acquisition of the Holy Grail – we are not inclined to count the climbing of Mt. Everest a value even for Hillary. We would instead seek a more generalized form of this quest, for example, adventure, conquest, danger, so that the specific goal can be subsumed under ideals and traits of character which are realized in other pursuits of the agent. Hillary devoted enormous time and energy to the Everest climb, even after it was successfully completed, but a value is supposed to pervade a variety of facets of our lives even if not all that pervades is a value. This is especially true in light of the preponderance of traits of character, which are inherently general, in lists of values. Chastity, compassion, patriotism, and dedication to family, are ways of being that are central in the lives of those committed to them.

As interesting as this fact is, I regard it as peripheral in the context. I am more interested in the act of placing a value on something than in the less inclusive act of adopting something as a value. One can value a value and one can value traits, projects, relationships, and ideals which are too specific to be ordinarily characterized as values. Ahab's overriding ambition may have reflected a variety of values; however, since he placed such importance on his special quest, only pedantry prevents us from counting the capture of that white whale as one of his values. Henceforth, "value" will be used in this extended sense embodied in the phrase "placing a value upon." Our values are the things we regard as important or care deeply about. As yet, however, we have not discovered the difference between values in this sense and (strong) desires.

The single, most powerful reason that forces a bifurcation between desire and value is internal conflict. In the act of condemning our own inclinations or desires, no matter how strong, we find ourselves under a rational constraint to replace the description of our state of mind as both wanting to do A and not wanting to do A with an intelligible alternative.

As powerful as this reason is, it is not decisive. For the introduction of the notion of value is not the only conceivable way to restore coherence. In Frankfurt's early formulations of the hierarchical theory, for example, he disambiguated the conflicted mind in terms of the objects of desire rather than by replacing one of the desires with a different sort of intentional state. I want to do A, but I do not want to have the desire to do A. It was for this very reason that Watson (1975) objected to Frankfurt's conception of unfreedom as a simple clash of *desires* (in which the desire to do A wins out). Frankfurt's characterization of the second-order desires which may conflict with the desires which move us to act afforded them no special status beyond their higher-order position, that is, their having as objects first-order desires. If Watson is right, then, we have to look beyond the fact of conflict per se, in order to characterize the distinctive elements of those conflicts that do not simply pit one desire against another. But if in certain cases the opposition to a desire is rather a value, we have yet to understand the ground of that depiction.

Whether or not the fact of conflict requires the introduction of a notion that is conceptually distinct from desire, we can draw one important moral from the attitude toward conflict we sometimes take. In repudiating a desire in the face of its possibly irresistible strength, we implicitly draw a distinction between value and intensity of desire; to place a value on A is not simply to detect a strong urge for A. Thus, we can see why a whim for Häagen Dazs macadamia brittle ice cream, to which I succumb in spite of a painful awareness of the consequences, hardly generates a value. Nor does the intense desire to kick a chair I accidentally bumped into.

Although a straightforward identification of strong desires with values is unacceptable, it may be possible nonetheless to analyze values in terms of desires or to treat values as a subset of desires. It may be argued that, although my desires may not be aligned with objective value, I cannot value a state of affairs unless I want to bring it into existence. For example, sometimes conflicts between desires can be resolved by critical reflection, by, say, the discovery of new information. I may desire an outcome which I later discover to be unsatisfying or too costly. If, consequently, the strength of the desire diminishes, then the conflict may be eliminated. Perhaps then we can *identify* an agent's values with her strongest knowledgeable desires. On this account, if I possess all relevant information about the options available to me, my values will *be* my strongest desires.

This position is an instance of *reductionism about values*. A state of affairs has objective value or worth only if the possession of this "property" – objective value – does not follow from facts about the actual desires of people or the desires a person would have under certain ideal conditions. A reductionist views values either as desires that fulfill certain conditions or as the desires a person would have under certain conditions. With respect to either set of conditions, the reductionist demands both that there be no reference to objective value and that, should the conditions include intentional states, the objects of the intentional states will not themselves be objective value. The point of the latter qualification is that, even though we are trying to capture the notion of individual value, someone might wish to think of this as a relation to objective value. We shall later call this alternative to reductionism the Evaluation Conception of value. On this latter interpretation, an individual who is misaligned may nonetheless *believe* that a certain state of affairs is worthwhile. A reductionist about values will not characterize values in terms of such beliefs.

If we do not introduce a distinction between personal and objective value, our moral vision will prevent us from accepting the reductionist thesis. For even a desire that satisfies constraints such as cognitive saturation will sometimes be judged by a morally sensitive person as worthless or senseless.

Richard Kraut describes a person who chooses to punish himself out of a sense of guilt (1994: 40–1). He renounces his own good or well-being by spending his life at a boring and insignificant job. Since he is doing what he most wants to do, his well-being cannot be characterized in terms of desire satisfaction.

Kraut's distinction is reminiscent of that of Raz (Chapter 4). But since Raz's example of a person who sacrifices his own interests for the sake of epidemic victims is an example of one whose goals are worthwhile, we tend to overlook the more bizarre possibilities that force a distinction between personal value and objective value. For it is undeniable that we sometimes place value on senseless or masochistic ends, that is, ends that have no objective value.

A reductionist about values need not believe that the notion of value can be defined in nonnormative terms. The view that values are the strongest knowledgeable desires is reductionist, but knowledge may well be a normative notion. (In fact, according to many, belief, too, is ultimately normative.)

An effort to resuscitate the *deflationary* position (i.e., the view that values are essentially just strong desires) might be advanced by an appeal to the alleged irrelevance of information. On the reductionist version according to which values are strong, informed desires, Peter, an executive for whom all that matters is the number of rungs on the ladder of success he manages to climb, would be deemed not to count success in the corporate world as a value should he find that life at the top is far more empty and shallow than he had supposed. Perhaps Peter would never have begun the climb had he known better, but how can one deny that the driving force that has mobilized his energies all these years has not represented a value for him? He might have had different values, but that is a different story.

We can rebut the extreme position if we can find a nonintrusive way of distinguishing the surface values of a person from his "real" values. The most plausible example would be one in which a person's freedom of decision is abruptly quashed by the action of an external party which, through its great power, introduces a desire into the psyche of another person, without the knowledge or acquiescence of the affected person and without regard for that person's actual desires, needs, interests, and values. Through hypnotic suggestion, perhaps, Calvin just finds that he now has an overpowering urge to take up mountain climbing, and he begins at that point to devote all his energies to that end.

I have no decisive rebuttal to the deflationary theorist who is prepared to bite the bullet and say of Calvin that mountain climbing is now one of his values. Of course, considering the way this desire arose, it may turn out that the desire is difficult to sustain in light of Calvin's other desires and his current life style. (Suppose he is afraid of heights and trapped in Nebraska.) If the desire is badly supported (see White 1991: 201), its strength may be sapped by Calvin's efforts to maintain other interests and desires that conflict with mountain climbing. Alternatively, this desire may not receive much positive support from Calvin's other desires, but it may not seriously conflict with his current set. Or, as in a conversion experience, Calvin may be induced by the force of this new love to modify his current situation so as to restore equilibrium with mountain climbing as the new motivational core. We can then at least say against the deflationary position that a desire cannot be deemed a value unless it takes hold of the person in a reasonably significant way. (Thus, that whim for Häagen Dazs, or that urge to kick a chair, no matter how intense, are not values.) Desires, even if they happen to be very specific in content, must be reflected in other dimensions of the person's being, his affective, conative, and intellectual life.

The extent to which a concern permeates the many facets of a person's life is, however, a poor criterion by which to determine just how valuable the matter is. Clearly, the sheer *amount* of time, energy, thought, and concern is irrelevant. We devote a lot of time and worry to dreary tasks. People with dull jobs may have to spend much of their existence attending to matters of little moment, while realizing their values only in their daydreams. The prospect of realizing their values is crowded out by petty concerns or even by a preoccupation with the quest for food and shelter.

Yet values are more than mere daydreams. Since we would at least expect efforts at realization were they possible, we can in addition presume indirect effects on behavior, avowal, will, thought, and emotion. This diffusion of values is in fact guaranteed in a minimal way by the very concept of desire, for a desire is a state that is paradigmatically expressed in all these realms. Now, the suggestion that values take hold of a person in a way that is more significant – to rule out desires like the desire to kick the chair – is, to be sure, vague. But the specific issue that concerns me here is whether reasonable significance can be characterized in a way that is compatible with reductionism about values. Since the view of value that I ultimately wish to challenge lies at the opposite end of the spectrum from the deflationary view, I am not concerned to refute the latter. My target, the Evaluation Conception of value, rather demands *further* conditions on value beyond those any plausible reductionist theory provides. According to this view, it is not enough to count a desire as a value should the agent be fully informed and should the agent adopt the value under conditions of dispassionate reflection. The Evaluation Conception demands in addition that the agent view the realization of the valued state of affairs as genuinely worthwhile. Since I am less concerned about the deflationary attitude which says that the reductionist's conditions are not *necessary* rather than the Evaluation Conception's worry that they are collectively not *sufficient*, I will attempt to formulate a plausible reductionist conception that is rich enough to confront the Evaluation Conception.

From what perspective can a plausible set of constraints on the conversion of desires into values be formulated? I begin with the thought that a minimally rational agent (MRA) who values a state of affairs {S} would choose to realize S if she had the freedom$_p$ (power) and no positive reason not to do so. Certain constraints flow from this perspective. For example, an MRA would prefer that desires be informed for, without information, there is a real chance that whatever grounds she has for pursuing {S} are bogus: the realization of {S} may be unsatisfying or worthless. In demanding relevant knowledge about {S}, an MRA is avoiding needless frustration and the expenditure of wasted time and energy. Second, the choice to realize {S} must be made dispassionately. An MRA must reflect carefully and intensively on all relevant considerations. She should also not be under the sway of a powerful emotion, passion, or intense mood which has the potential to cloud her vision and steer deliberations along lines which would be repudiated under more sober reflection. Also, although conceding that values change, we want them to have a certain stability; we want them not to be subject to frequent mood shifts. This requirement serves then to ensure that values, as David Gauthier puts it, are stable under experience and reflection. (The deflationary theorist is likely to remind us that the insistence upon informed, dispassionate, and stable choice entails that there are many persons who go through life caring about many things they do not strictly value and valuing things they would not honestly characterize as important to them. Although this is true, we must again remind ourselves of our current indifference to the deflationary end of the spectrum.)

There is a prima facie problem with the requirement of dispassionateness. If a person is inclined to be charitable often, but only when he is confronted with graphic evidence of the needs of others, we would apparently have to conclude that charity is not one of his values. For when he is dispassionate, he is not moved to be charitable. But surely, this stance underrepresents his commitment to the value of charity, displayed in numerous acts of generosity induced by pictures of the pitiful condition of the potential recipients of his generosity. A dispassionate stance may be appropriate in a court of law, where we seek impartiality and justice. But why should we suppose that this stance is also the proper one for an agent to take when he is reflecting on whether to realize some desired state of affairs?

We may certainly concede that the value of charity to this man is not as great as it is to one wholeheartedly committed to charitable enterprises without the constant goad of an external impetus. More importantly, the dispassionateness condition may not actually be violated in the original example. For the emotions that are ruled out by this requirement are not any strong emotions, but rather ones that are prone to "cloud one's vision and steer one's deliberations along lines which would be repudiated under more sober reflection." Compassion may or may not cloud one's vision. If the sight of starving children induces this man to turn over all his rent money to Oxfam and he later regrets this act, he is indeed too volatile to satisfy the dispassionateness condition. But if sober reflection does not induce regret, then his emotion-laden act may well count as dispassionate. Moreover, the value of charity is more significantly revealed in the choice of a life incorporating this virtue. Even if this man is incapable of a charitable impulse unless goaded by appropriate pictorial and verbal displays, he may be perfectly capable of a dispassionate selection of this virtue as one that guides his life at appropriate points.

Alternatively, this hypothetical dispassionate choice may be a rejection of charitability in spite of this man's tendency to succumb to graphic appeals to his emotions. He "wears his heart on his sleeve" and is undertaking psychotherapy in the hope it will cure him of this "weakness." We shall see later that the conclusion that charity is not one of his values may be true, but its establishment requires further substantiation.

Dispassionateness then is certainly not emotional frigidity. Some emotions are calm, not prone to distort, and lack volatility. Although we are concerned about turbulence in this context, we do not address this concern by demanding that these choices be made only by one with ice water in his veins. That would certainly distort the picture, requiring us falsely to deny that compassion is a value to one whose emotional disability prevents him from endorsing what is indeed important to him just because the endorsement must be dispensed during an emotionless state.

The requirement of freedom enables us to deal with cases in which an agent possesses values she is unable to choose to realize. If I have a neurotic fear of attachment I am desperately attempting to eradicate, the value of human relationships for me may not be revealed in a hypothetical choice situation, even if I am informed, dispassionate, and stable. For the neurotic fear may impel me to choose isolation. Decisions made under its sway may not be dismissed by invoking the requirement of dispassionateness for this fear may not have the volatility or transience of dark moods and strong emotions. Fear is, to be sure, a strong emotion; however, it is not panic and, in directing one's behavior, it is not necessarily clouding one's vision or one's understanding. It is unreasonable, as I said previously, to demand that these choices be made by one bereft of all emotion; so how would one distinguish fear from, say, love, a strong, behavior-directing emotion which, in its extreme form, can also cloud vision?

We would not anyway want to rule out from the emotional state of value-determining choices *all* fears. Placing my head in the mouth of a rabid lion is not a value to me because intensive reflection, which includes vivid contemplation of the prospect accompanied by an anticipatory aversive reaction, induces me to reject this activity.

We need a criterion to mark off neurotic fears in addition to strong moods and passions which are potentially distorting. My fear of human involvement and my fear of being eaten by a rabid lion are both choice-inhibiting, although I value only the former of these feared states of affairs. A distinction can be made in terms of freedom. The neurotic who really wants to be rid of her disorder is not free to display the value of personal relationships in this choice situation, whereas I would not choose to place my head in Leo's mouth even if I could.[1]

It is worth observing that the neurotic would display the value of human relationships in other behavior, for example, her regular therapy sessions, or in emotional reactions, which are often better guides to one's values than actual choices in nonideal situations of this sort. That personal attachments are of value to this person is reflected in her disappointment at a failure to change and in resentment directed to her therapist. This is not to say that emotional components are irrelevant should the choice be made under ideal conditions. Evidently, a free, informed, healthy choice to pursue a life filled with close personal attachments would be reflected on both the conative and the affective levels. We would anticipate the formation of certain specific kinds of desires as well as their associated emotions. To want to cultivate a close friendship with Rudy is in part to be disappointed by obstacles placed in the path, proud that one has persevered to remove these obstacles, and pleased by progress toward this end. (These are elements of the constraint of reasonably significant permeation.)

The dispute between the reductionist about values and the Evaluation Conception of values can be formulated in the language of utility theory. The reductionist proposes constraints on desire or preference – for example, I have proposed that it be informed and dispassionate – which would permit the identification of value with utility, rendering value, therefore, a *measure* of preference rather than a *standard* by which to judge it.[2]

Gauthier believes that the identification of value with utility requires that preference be considered, that is, stable under adequate experience and reflection and revealed in behavioral and attitudinal manifestations which cohere with one another (1986: 28).

Consider an academic who proclaims the pursuit of scholarship as his deepest value. Yet his scholarly output is meager and of poor quality in spite of his gifts and the amount of time he spends on his work. Only his friends and colleagues realize that he actually cares far more about his family. He takes great delight in his wife and children even though, in order to nourish his self-deception, he spends an inordinate amount of time going through the motions of research.

This example reveals again the insignificance of the sheer amount of time someone devotes to some matter. It also illustrates the familiar fact that honest expressions of preference may be belied by actual behavior or by emotional manifestations, so that we must be careful about the way preferences are actually determined. We shall later in this chapter explore further the ramifications of self-deception. The point I wish now to stress is that, at choice points, the academic has opted for family over scholarship. In order to stay with his family, he decided to forego an opportunity to spend a semester in Rome where he could have examined manuscripts crucial to his research. He spends money on his daughter's education at the expense of books for his research, and so on.

Although the divergence between behavior and avowal renders the academic's preference unconsidered in Gauthier's terms, I would still want to count some cases of this sort as ones which reveal an agent's values. There may be reasons, for example, the pressures exerted by peers, which explain the academic's inability to acknowledge his "real" values, but in at least *this* case (like the woman who fears attachment), those are revealed in behavior, not in attitude or verbal reports. Another example, to be described more fully in the next chapter, is that of Frithjof Bergmann, who came eventually to acknowledge that his past behavior had indeed been in accordance with his deepest values in spite of his earlier failure to recognize this fact.[3]

But if the importance of these choice points is that they reveal the academic's preferences, have we not returned to the view that values are just informed, dispassionate, and stable preferences? What then is the difference between the academic's choice of family and my nightly choice of grilled trout?

In thinking about the daily decision to have grilled trout, we think about a confined decision: What shall I eat? This decision must be made by most of us, whether or not food is important to the one making the decision. Grilled trout is not a value because the value of food is limited for most people. That is the reason that value can be ascertained only when we make choices across categories. Trout takes on greater significance if I choose it over my daughter's education or the quality of my next book. Thus, an accurate picture of a person's values would have to be determined from *hypothetical* decisions among a wide range of options. In each decision-making situation, the agent makes an informed and dispassionate choice from options he has the power to act on.

The motivation conception of value

I have formulated a specific version of reductionism about values, based upon a set of constraints on desire that would be adopted by a free and minimally rational agent who is given the opportunity to choose to realize the desired state of affairs. Call this the Motivation Conception of value. The current formulation is vague in several ways. If a person is not actively pursuing a professed goal, it is not clear what we should demand of him to count this professed goal a value. After all, he has other concerns and ambitions. Not all values are overarching.

Thus, it might foster precision to rank values, as we rank desires or preferences. After all, some values are more important than others. And if values are to be derived from preferences, the task should not be intrinsically more difficult. Talk would then shift from X's being a value to X's being more valuable to a person than Y. We might then reintroduce the nonrelative language by selecting as values those which are high on the relative scale. The refusal to act on behalf of an espoused goal under a variety of conditions may reveal that one is deluding others and possibly oneself. But if we can shift to a comparative language, we will not have to make such an either-or decision.

I have defined values in terms of choice rather than desire or preference. We could alternatively design a set of questions which tell us a person's *preferences* under a variety of hypothetical circumstances. If we can also determine what this agent would *choose* under the same set of hypothetical circumstances, we might discover that the results do not precisely coincide with those concerning preference. When the agent is aware that his preferences are really to be enacted, he backs off a bit. There are alternative ways of describing the phenomena. We may, of course, decide to redescribe his preferences to restore the match, thereby refusing to countenance the possibility of discrepancy. Otherwise, we must look for explanations. In any event, if a person is prepared to sacrifice little in the way of his personal ambitions and comforts when confronted with possible actions which he believes would have some chance of promoting global justice, we certainly have a right to conclude that his desire for justice is just not strong enough to be counted a value.[4] This result is in accordance with the Motivation Conception.

Consider the familiar example of the unwilling addict again. He chooses drugs (intentionally) because his desire for drugs is overwhelming. Does he prefer drugs to abstinence? Well, to call him "unwilling" is to say he prefers not to *be* a drug addict. Does it follow that, in a concrete choice situation, he prefers not to take the drugs? If so, the concept of preference is doing no work on the first-order level of explanation of action: he chooses to take drugs because he has an overwhelming desire to take drugs. So another tack is to shift the object of preference from the act to the choice. He wants and chooses drugs; but he prefers not to have this want or he prefers not to have made this choice.

On this approach, the concept of first-order preference reduces to the comparative concept of desire. What we prefer is what we most want. In order to have a preference different from the strongest desire, one must count as objects of desire and preference the *having* of the desires themselves.

Since decision theory has coopted the notion of preference, representing it by utility functions, it imposes rationality constraints. Thus, if I am rational, I am not permitted both to prefer A to B and to prefer B to A. Although decision theory does not prohibit *wanting* A more than B along with *wanting* B more than A, it would sound just as odd for an agent to report her conflict of desires in this way. She can want A and she can want B, knowing that she cannot have both; she can have reasons for *preferring* A to B and reasons for *preferring* B to A; but the request to learn which she wants more is a request to make an "all things considered judgment," one which is no longer relativized to reasons. If I prefer the wood-to-wood join of Helmstetter cue sticks to the join of Huebler cue sticks, yet like the inlaid butts of Hueblers more than the Helmstetter butts, it does not follow that I both want a Huebler more than a Helmstetter and want a Helmstetter more than a Huebler. We have no reason to insist on two comparative notions on the first-order level. (If anything, ordinary language sanctions *preference*, not *desire*, as relative to reasons.)

If we, therefore, wish to see whether a person's values can be determined from his first-order life, we are obliged to look either at his desires or his choices. We need not worry about a third possibility.

When an agent makes a choice under (relatively) ideal conditions, it is still *that* agent making the choice. In describing the agent under ideal conditions, therefore, we are *not* describing an ideal agent. Insofar as the legitimacy of counterfactual conditionals about individuals are conceded, it cannot strain this idea to permit examples in which individuals are posited as choosing under unrealized conditions of full informativeness, dispassionateness, stability, and freedom. I mention this to forestall objections from those who remind us that individuals never adopt values in a vacuum, that values are always context-relative, where the context inevitably includes an environment and a set of traditions relative to which the acceptance or rejection of a potential value makes sense. The individuals we are talking about are as immersed in a tradition as they happen in fact to be, and they are making their choices as members of the group or culture to which they happen in fact to belong.

These reflections help somewhat to render the hypothetical choice situation more determinate. For since a particular individual is supposed to be participating in deliberation, the decision to realize a particular desire is made relative to his other desires. There is nevertheless a serious vagueness based upon a discrepancy between this abstract choice and the real choices confronted by this individual in his daily decision making. For example, in the abstract, I might rank listening to music over looking at paintings, although, in the concrete, because of particular circumstances, I always reverse this ranking. (My opportunities just happen to be limited to the few artists I appreciate and the few composers I dislike.) If we were to decipher an agent's values from concrete decision-making situations, we would then need a wide range to ensure a fair selection, as I said earlier. And if we are still in no position then to determine whether painting or music ranks higher, the reason may be that ranking at a sufficiently high level of abstraction is an ill-defined activity. It may make no sense to assign a higher priority to music except as an indication that one's most significant aesthetic experiences have been musical ones.

The demand for a wide range of choice situations prevents us from denigrating a value just because it happens in the actual world always to be cast against an alternative activity that affords sustained ecstasy. A more serious problem confronts the recasting of our criterion in more concrete terms. For one must consider the relations among one's values, including costs of fulfillment. If, in the abstract, I deem physical fitness a core value, it may well be that a commitment to its promotion is so demanding that I am prevented from realizing many other lesser values. I might find myself sacrificing the more important value of physical fitness to a lesser one in all actual choice situations and look to the world like a victim of self-deception, that is, a person whose behavior, which includes no physical exercise, is a more accurate indicator of value than his avowal. I might actually be prepared to begin an arduous regimen that is designed to produce a 100 pound weight loss, thereby establishing the value to me of physical fitness, but be unwilling to devote all my available energies to the truly Herculean task of dropping 250 pounds.

Thus, a fairer test of the value to me of physical fitness would obtain if we could exclude costs. The concept of cost is, however, obscure. For a cost is an outcome that has negative value, and that notion may be ill-defined in the context. Some consequences are, to be sure, of obviously negative value. Perhaps extreme muscular soreness is an example. But there are a whole range of activities I might have substituted for my series of workouts. Since we have replaced absolute value with relative value, even an alternative that I generally find pleasing might have negative value at least in the sense that it interferes with yet another I would prefer even more.

A simpler suggestion, then, is to restrict hypothetical choices to ones which ignore all nonintrinsic aspects of the options under consideration. We compare states of affairs without regard to the incidental positive and negative effects they may have, thereby obtaining a more precise evaluation of their actual value to the person. Thus, the only costs we consider are the intrinsic losses resulting from the rejection of the alternatives. We are not talking about wishing rather than choosing, for the question still concerns what the agent would choose. Thus, although it is indeed easy for a person who must lose a great deal of weight to "opt for" physical fitness, thereby revealing that it is a value to him, we can obtain a more precise measure by looking at the price he is prepared to pay. Although I may not ever be prepared to make the sacrifices needed to lose 250 pounds, the desirability of this state of affairs would be revealed in a choice to bring it about effortlessly that demanded the sacrifice of certain designated alternatives, each of which is also evaluated in terms of intrinsic value and/or disvalue. (We might propose a monetary test were that problem-free. The question, then, quite simply is: How much are you willing to pay for it?)

The capture of certain values would seem to elude a methodology narrowly focused upon choice situations. There are many experiences, encounters, and activities which have enormous meaning, but which one does not actively seek to promote. Some of the most meaningful episodes of anyone's life occur as the unintended consequences of a planned activity or even as totally fortuitous happenings. Indeed, the very significance that some of these moments have is bound up with their spontaneous character; the very same plot, as planned, would lose the very special excitement of the unpredictable and the delectable flavor of participating in a scene without a script, perhaps one not even written by nature. There is even an air of paradox in the effort to incorporate them through the act of choosing such situations. For the distinctive value of these situations resides in their *not* having been chosen. This paradox can be eliminated, however, if we permit reference to more general sorts of choices, for example, to the choice of a *life* (or an extended span) which incorporates spontaneity.

The evaluation conception of value

The Evaluation Conception of values sharply distinguishes mere motivation, no matter how idealized or broadly conceived, from evaluation, the assignment of worth to desired states of affairs. A hypothetical or actual second-order judgment regarding the worth of the strongest desire is essential to convert the desire into a value (for that person). Thus, even though I want trout now more than anything else, I must concede that my eating the trout is of little intrinsic worth. Values are not simply the most important aspects of a person's life; they are also elements deemed to have real worth or genuine value.

In insisting upon the importance of evaluation to freedom, Watson was emphasizing the crucial difference between motivation and evaluation, whether the desire is for a candied apple or the life of a monk. I can be moved to choose either without regard for considerations like merit, excellence, value, or ennoblement, considerations the umbrella term "worth" is designed to cover. He was, therefore, among other things, opting for what I am calling the Evaluation Conception of values.

Many philosophers, including Frankfurt, Taylor, Watson, Dworkin, Haworth, and Nerlich, have insisted that higher-order evaluation is central to any life worth living and some think it essential to personhood. And they are surely right in denigrating the life of one always caught up in her petty, local pursuits so that she never steps back to make basic decisions which may, if effective, produce a reorientation with possibly profound effects on her life. Since the Motivation Conception would be a nonstarter if it could not account for higher-order decisions on behalf of fundamental commitments and ways of life, we must be assured that its picture of these decisions is not a parody.

It is certainly true that an autonomous agent possesses the capacity for second-order critical reflection directed to any first-order desire, no matter how general. But generality per se is insignificant in this context: I can ponder the question of whether to succumb to my love of grilled trout by having it this evening or every evening. Choices about what kind of person to be are, however, not just general, but genuinely second-order. The desire to have grilled trout every night for the next month is more general than the desire to have grilled trout this evening, but it is directed to actions and is satisfied if the actions are performed regardless of motive. The desire to be a charitable person, on the other hand, is the desire to be *motivated* a certain way and is not fully satisfied by a mere set of acts, perhaps grudgingly performed. The desire to lose weight is a desire for results and is different, therefore, from the desire not to be a gluttonous person. Many people satisfy the first and not the second desire. They are thin, but they are unhappy with themselves because they think about food all the time.

As mature beings, we are supposed to choose the way to lead our lives. Evidently, these choices represent long-term commitments and are not focused upon a single action or even a narrow set of actions. We often find deeper significance in these extended projects which permit interaction with others and with the world and which engage a variety of interwoven actions, intentions, talents, and satisfactions, providing us with "*coherent* meaning" (Nerlich 1989: 170).

To be sure, most human beings use the language of worth and depth to describe the act of placing a value on those projects and modes of engagement which represent, for the person, his core commitments.[5] I shall argue nonetheless that the Evaluation Conception's construal of these acts of valuing is not the only way to understand them. The Motivation Conception, according to which values can be determined if we know the informed, dispassionate choices an agent would make in a wide variety of situations, allows us to take into account those motives directed to the sort of person the agent would like to be.

The assumption that these are contrary conceptions of value may be challenged by appropriating and revising a notion of Stephen White's, that of an unconditional desire (1991: 18). An unconditional desire is one we want to be realized whether or not we continue to desire its realization. I want to see an end to starvation in Somalia. But I realize that I might someday become callous and totally self-absorbed. Although I then would care no longer about the fate of the Somali people, I regard that fact as irrelevant to my current desire; I now want starvation to end then even if I come not to desire that outcome in the future. In valuing this outcome in a way which severs the valuing from desire-fulfillment, I would appear to be conferring not merely personal value on this state of affairs. Perhaps then the idea of regarding a state of affairs as possessing intrinsic or objective value can be analyzed in terms of the idea of an unconditional desire. In that case, since the concept of an unconditional desire makes no reference to objective value, the reductionist about values would be vindicated and we would have no need to introduce the Evaluation Conception. We might simply identify, as a subset of an agent's values, as determined by the Motivation Conception, the agent's unconditional desires. These desires would be the ones we have toward states of affairs we may also characterize as possessing objective or intrinsic worth or value.

This notion needs revision for the following reason. We can fail to desire states of affairs whose realization would be highly satisfying. A desire to engage in an activity that I regard as merely personally valuable, say hunting deer, would then be unconditional if I am convinced that I would find it enormously satisfying even during the time my desire to engage in it has waned. I shall then construe an unconditional desire for a state of affairs {S} as a desire to realize {S} even if one believes that the realization would not be personally satisfying.

The following example also raises difficulties for the original definition. Benjamin, a nineteenth-century African-American slave, was brought up to believe in the inferiority of his race. The inculcation of this and related beliefs was so successful that, as an adult, Benjamin saw nothing intrinsically worthwhile in the perpetuation of his race. Black people, as such, are of value only to serve their masters. The life of a Caucasian person, on the other hand, is valuable just because the person is Caucasian; life as such has no intrinsic value.

Benjamin, like everyone else, has a powerful impulse for survival. He wants to live. Yet he places no objective value on his life as such or on his life as an Afro-American. Thus, the value to him of his life is personal or individual. If Benjamin is now told that he will be given a pill tomorrow that will make him suicidal (although he will not otherwise change in a way that might provide a rational agent with objective grounds for suicide), it is unlikely that he will announce that he now wants to die tomorrow. He does not want to succumb to the desire to take his life. Thus, Benjamin has an unconditional desire to survive, although survival for him has no objective value.

On the revised version, however, Benjamin has an unconditional desire to survive only if this desire would survive the belief that the continuation of his life would not be personally satisfying.

If the desire does indeed persist, then the revised version fails to capture the notion of objective value as well. The only way to challenge the possibility of persistence is to contend that the tenacity of the desire shows that Benjamin believes that there will be something satisfying about his life. Yet there are many people who regard their lots as utterly miserable and who do not, largely out of fear, choose suicide. The desire for self-preservation may be one of a set of fundamental drives that are extraordinarily powerful, yet whose satisfaction is of a merely personal concern.[6] There is no a priori reason to believe that we have not been provided biologically with desires whose persistence is relatively invariant with respect to changes in other, normally relevant mental states, such as belief.

There are similar, powerful physical aversions that are the basis of desires that are quite irrational. Of the people who choose to be buried above ground in a mausoleum, many are motivated by the intolerable character of the thought of their bodies becoming putrefied through the action of the organic elements in the ground. If one feels, in response to the example of Benjamin, that even he has to believe that his life is worthwhile, it would be hard to make a case that people who choose this mode of burial regard above ground decomposition as of greater objective value than the more conventional kind. Yet their desire for this state of affairs is quite unconditional.

There is, therefore, reason to deny that "unconditional desire" and "value as conceived by the Evaluation Conception" are precisely extensionally equivalent. Moreover, an individual's unconditional desires are not necessarily more personally valuable than that agent's conditional desires. Bernard has a cat, Sneakers, of whom he has grown quite fond. Having discovered that he is allergic to cats, Bernard must ask his friend, Michael, to take care of Sneakers. Since Bernard wants Sneakers to thrive even if he grows to become indifferent to the fate of animals and derives no satisfaction from a knowledge of their well-being, his desire that Sneakers thrive is unconditional. Bernard also has a desire for a rich and varied sex life that is evidently conditional. Should the satisfaction of these desires be jointly impossible, Bernard may well choose to sacrifice Sneakers's well-being. This selfish decision is grounded on Bernard's preference for great personal satisfaction over an objective value he convinces himself is minor.

White's failure to distinguish satisfying (fulfilling) a desire and deriving satisfaction from the satisfaction (fulfillment) leads him to the erroneous conclusion that one will never be motivated to eliminate an unconditional desire in favor of a conditional one. For a conditional desire, he says, "there is nothing to choose between a future in which it is satisfied and one in which it no longer exists" (1991: 18). We saw that this is not so in the case of my desire for hunting deer. The ramifications of this error are profound for White bankrolls this idea into a result of great metaphysical significance. Unconditional desires form a conative core that "represents one's deepest commitments – those commitments that, to the extent that any set of commitments can, define who one is" (1991: 203) or "one's most fundamental values" (390). Like Wolf, White is drawn to the idea that an agent cannot freely choose a form of self-realization in which objective value is subordinated to personal liberation. Yet of the many women who choose abortion, surely some believe that they are sacrificing something of objective value. A woman who appreciates the sanctity of life and who has not considered abortion has an unconditional desire (in White's or my sense) that her fetus live. Yet if reflection leads her to conclude that the personal costs are too great, she may well opt for abortion even though she is choosing a set of conditional desires (in White's or my sense) over an unconditional one.

Granted an intimate connection between evaluation and unconditional desires, I shall, for the stated reasons, not interpret the former in terms of the latter.

Evaluation

In the evaluative process, there is an endless list of words we may use to condemn desires. shameful, ignoble, morally wrong, debased, trivial, unnatural, cheap, immature, unsophisticated.

Although the application of any of these suggests an internal conflict between motivation and evaluation, one way to diminish the impact of this apparent disunity is to deny that both components are internal to the self. Given the work of Frankfurt and others, we have become accustomed to locate the self and its stirrings on the reflective level, that is, *I* condemn (or condone) the goings on in that will (oh, all right, of mine). (See Frankfurt 1971, 1976.) But we must acknowledge the importance of including desires as mine even when their possession disturbs me (Berofsky 1980, 1983, 1987). I would regard as equally unacceptable the assumption that reservations about motives, arising through critical reflection, automatically renders those motives *valueless* to the person. First-order desires range from those which are trivial and peripheral to the self to ones which are resistant *both* to expulsion *and* to a reduction of their significance to the self by a variety of second-order misgivings. Knowledgeable desires which are the subject of condemnation by their owner often retain both their status as bona fide parts of the self as well as their value to the very individual who is advancing the personal indictment. If so, the Motivation Conception of values, according to which values just are the strongest knowledgeable desires (one would choose to realize in a wide variety of decision-making situations) is not as outrageous as some think.

Suppose I am addicted to gambling. I find enormous satisfaction in the dangers, the thrill of uncertainty, the prospect of large winnings. To suppose that my motivation is knowledgeable, we shall have to provide me with certain advantages such as wealth (for I would not otherwise knowingly risk the calamity of large losses) and the absence of close personal attachments (*only if* their condemnation of my pursuit affects me adversely and induces me to abandon this activity). Suppose also that the choices I have made to sustain this venture have been dispassionate in the required sense. Although quite passionate about gambling, I find that my commitment is a stable one: I do not regret these decisions during moments of cooler reflection. I view those who charge me with an incapacity for "sober" reflection as engaged in an effort to subvert my values and arbitrarily impose theirs. I will now argue that the value of gambling to me survives quite serious second-order reservations.

Moral values

There are at least three ways a personal conflict can be engendered. My addiction may come into conflict with my moral values, my ego ideal, or my personal morality. In each of these cases, the conflict is deeper and more unsettling to the extent that these items have been integrated at deep levels of the self. I hasten to explain.

My inclination to gamble is knowledgeable if I possess all relevant knowledge pertaining to possible outcomes including, therefore, the *personal* costs in the long run of my life style. Thus, even if my friends and family are dismayed at my life style, my aloofness nullifies the bearing of this fact; it staves off the emergence of guilt feelings that would normally be suffered by one who observes the disappointment of friends and relatives arising out of their concern with his life. Now I may come to believe that it is wrong to disappoint those who care about me so much and this belief may precede any revision in my attitude of aloofness. I see that I *should* not be so unconcerned, that I should care and I may or may not change in the direction I perceive I ought to. In this case my moral values dictate that I should not gamble because my doing so hurts so many others. Worse yet, the hurt is perceived to arise out of the caring attitude others have toward me; the object of their pain is the appalling state of *my* current life. The conflict will be more unsettling if this moral value is not just an article of intellectual assent, but evolves into a dominant conviction. Suppose that I come to dedicate myself to the promotion of communal values, including the value of family and the importance to a normal person of full participation in family life. I join organizations and spend a great deal of time campaigning for the return to family values. I am enormously frustrated when my efforts appear to be unsuccessful and delighted when I sense a glimmer of hope. My failure to overcome my addiction, so painful to the members of my family, will be even more disturbing then, especially if the onset of the urge still renders me indifferent to their pain. My emotional life lacks integration because I see that I should care, and it bothers me greatly that I do not care at those times when concern about the pain I am causing might actually induce me to reform. This is not an uncommon sort of conflict; often people must be told that charity (advice) begins at home. In spite of my moral convictions, I have to acknowledge the value gambling retains for me.

On the Motivation Conception of value, an agent's values are determined by the informed choices he would make under conditions meeting certain constraints such as dispassionateness, emotional stability, and freedom. When I suppose that I might continue to care deeply about gambling in spite of moral reservations about my life, I am, of course, supposing that this negative evaluation is also made under analogous conditions. The condemnation is significant just because it is advanced knowledgeably, freely, and dispassionately. The conflict can be real and deep. Just because the evaluation cannot be changed by the removal of a defective circumstance such as ignorance, blind passion, or enslavement to the interests of another, we must not, I am claiming, infer that I do not really confer value on gambling.

Ego ideals

We earlier conceded that mature persons occasionally reflect on their lives and consider adjustments depending on second-order attitudes about their primary motives. Thus, we can generate a conflict when the conception of myself as a gambler clashes with the picture of the person I would ideally like to be (where, again, we may suppose that this picture has been formed through a process that is free, dispassionate, emotionally stable, and informed). My ego ideal may, of course, include a conception of a moral agent, so that overlap with the first sort of conflict is possible. Then again, it may not. Also, ideals may be held shallowly or deeply. Although my failure to realize my ideal may be personally devastating, it is also true that I may adopt an uncritical and frivolous picture of the person I would like to be such that my failure to embody this picture is only temporarily and not deeply disturbing. Thus, the negative judgment of critical reflection may take place from the perspective of a personal ideal which is embedded in a shallow level of the self.[7] Just because a judgment is *higher-level* in virtue of its object, that is, a first-order desire, does not imply that the judgment is *deeper* than its object, the desire. The failure to satisfy the first-order level desire may have far more profound personal repercussions than the failure to satisfy the higher-order judgment directed against that desire. The failure to achieve what I deeply want (level 1) may contribute more to personal disintegration than the failure to honor reservations about that desire. The tendency for the locus of identification to remain on the primary level in spite of second-order misgivings is paradoxical only for those already committed to the hierarchical theory's account of self in terms of the higher-order act.

Personal morality

I think we need a third sort of conflict, between desire and personal morality, to capture certain judgments, for example, that my life as a gambler is wasted because I am not doing anything really important, that is, of "real" value. (I would not object to the incorporation of personal morality in the first category, moral values. That depends on whether morality is necessarily other-directed. For here, my worry is that I have wronged *myself*. A case for incorporating this in the first category is that the perspective from which judgment is made is impersonal. I am implying that others who live as I do are leading equally worthless lives.) In any event, this perspective is distinct from that of one who worries that he is not embodying his ego ideal. I may have to acknowledge that I am extraordinarily attracted to all facets of gambling (or race car driving), the thrill, the anxiety, the ancillary way of life, the people one meets, the sights, the sounds, and so on. It is not just that I *am* this way; it is the way I like to see myself and have others see me. I am pleased when others learn about my eccentric and picturesque way of life. I wish it had some redeeming features so that I could recommend it from a moral perspective. The problem is not that I am hurting others, for I may not be. And it is my ideal except that it falls short in failing to provide me with personal worth. (To those philosophers who find this last sentence incoherent, I would recommend that they direct their attention to real people, including ones who, although sane, cannot formulate the overriding "life plan" which gives their existence meaning and others who are pleased to make it through the day even if they cannot characterize the worth of their lives or that single "project" whose failure, according to this doctrine of the ivory tower, would require them to commit suicide.)

Thus, I can identify with a life style, one which incorporates little in the way of other-regarding sentiments, consider that I am fulfilling my personal ideal, yet deem my life basically worthless (beyond the minimal worth there is in my having fulfilled my goals and consequently not feeling frustrated). If I am right, the Evaluation Conception is committed to the paradoxical-sounding position that a person with ego ideals does not necessarily have values.

Is it really possible for an agent to embrace freely a form of life he is discerning enough to recognize as worthless? (Remember, too, that the judgment of worthlessness is not made out of misinformation, emotional instability, the passion of the moment, or the undue influence of another.) Of course, I did not actually select the life of gambling from a set of choices in an explicit deliberative act. I drifted into it for the reasons listed above: I feel most alive when I am gambling; it is thrilling; the people one meets are fascinating, if somewhat daffy; I love being thought of as a gambler, and so on. But in this respect, there is not that much difference between the gambler's life and most other more conventional lives. In spite of the call to mature people to "choose their lives," most of us find that circumstances over which we have little or no control play a major role in this project; that, although there are choice points along the way, there is also a lot of drift as well as a lot of luck, good and bad. By the time we are mature enough to make rational choices, we have accumulated habits, tastes, and responsibilities which narrow these choices drastically.

Moreover, my recognition of the worthlessness of this life indicates that I am not a psychopath. I have the concept of worth and the discrepancy between that sense of worth and the goals which fulfill my ego ideal may well be conflict-producing. Although my ideal – the gambling life – appears to be at right angles with morality, I at least have qualms about that myself. My moral stance does not differ from others; it is just that I have failed to incorporate it into the picture of the person I "really" want to be (and am). We must recall the current project: to establish that the Evaluation Conception's construal of the act of valuing one's *basic commitments* or *most important desires* is just one possible construal. To locate a person's deepest values is not necessarily to locate that which he deems worthwhile.

In choosing or at least continuing to endorse this career, I have adopted reasons which are de facto in conflict with worth. What I find thrilling and vital turns out unfortunately to conflict with my sense of worth. Why must these coincide?

Of course, in casting a negative moral judgment on my life, I am ipso facto advancing a reason to change. That is the basis of the conflict I face. But there are always reasons against any action or life style. Moreover, these can be reasons the person himself has to change. If, after secretly harboring yearnings for many years, I finally decide to become a monk, I may still have moral and nonmoral reasons against embracing my ideal. (Suppose I have to abandon persons financially dependent upon me.)

Or consider a scene from the movie *Patton*. George C. Scott portrays the flamboyant American general walking through a field of corpses of allied soldiers after a bloody engagement, saying "War; God, I love it!" Although Patton and no doubt many others thought that his life project was worthwhile, is it so difficult to imagine a deeply conflicted variant, in particular, one who finds himself with strong pacifist sentiments, whose firm moral conviction is that war is evil and ought never to be waged, and in whom such sentiments *coexist* with the deep love of war?

In alluding to the manner in which our psyche is shaped by powerful forces which realize much of their impact prior to the mature selection or endorsement of ideals, we must not lose sight of the way in which society provides the very options from which our ideals are molded. When, for example, a student enters the law, she enters a system or institution already possessed of an antecedent structure. Even when a rebel seeks to find his way by experimenting with a given structure, for example, entering an open marriage, his project is a reaction to and a variant upon this social structure.

Even if our imagination is limited by the options presented by the society we happen to enter – and it is not – individuals could only form their ideals from practices in which participation will not produce deep schisms between the individual and society *if* we assume that the society possesses a simplicity and cohesion lacking in almost every modern society.

In *actual* societies, we find sound and unsound "social forms,"[8] forms approved of by the majority and ones at variance with the prevailing moral point of view. A growing child has a variety of forms with which to identify: lawyers, doctors, laborers, sports figures, crack dealers, hit men for organized crime, arms smugglers, and Gestapo officials. Raz says that individuals define the contours of their own lives by drawing on the communal pool of values. These will, in well-ordered societies, contribute indiscriminately both to their self-interest and to other aspects of their well-being. They also define the field of moral values. There is but one source for morality and for personal well-being. (1986: 318–19)

Although the selection of a morally sound social form may be essential to one's well-being, the point I wish to stress is that, since every nonideal society contains *both* types of social forms, moral and immoral, why can't one choose from either? Or why can't one be conflicted as in my gambling example, where the ideal is taken from a morally unsound social form, but prevailing moral values, having also been inculcated, present me with a conflict between ego ideal and moral ideal?

Although it is clear that some of our desires express neither our ideals – we would not regard it as a genuine loss to be rid of certain desires along with their fulfillments – nor our moral values – there is, in the gambling example or in the example of the conflicted Patton, a clear conflict between desire and morality – there remains resistance to the distinction between ego ideal and moral ideal. Yet even if a desire is converted into an ideal only when the agent is proud of possessing or acting on it, it does not follow that the ideal is now a moral one. Pride is precisely what many young crooks have when they succeed at a life of crime. Taking their models from unsound social forms, they evince a sense of pride at their skills and their accomplishments. (A skilled safecracker can be very proud of his work.) Displays of pride can be extraordinarily irksome and ugly when observed by a law-abiding citizen. We seek out proper role models for the young because we worry that they will form their ideals from poor models.

If it is conceded that crooks and gamblers can see themselves as embodying ideals, it may be objected that these ideals must then at least embody a personal morality. But this objection mistakenly assumes that, even if a person can be *proud* of his ideals, he must then suppose they are *worthy*. One can, first of all, be proud of morally worthless behavior, say the ability to hold one's breath for three minutes under water. And if it is said that a person who is proud of this ability may not be proud of *himself* for organizing his life around this ability – suppose he wants to achieve a world record – I would agree. Moral notions creep in at that point. But I would insist that an agent, like the gambler or some petty crook, can have an ideal without being proud of himself for living in accordance with it. When a criminal obnoxiously displays pride at what he has done, and is asked if he is proud of *himself*, he may not say yes. He may never have confronted that question or, if he has, in a way, confronted it, he may be prepared to say that he is not proud of himself. But he may well have had personal ideals which he now finds are in conflict with poorly entrenched moral ideals.

Identification and the self

Earlier, in an effort to explain the continued significance of a desire on which we pass a negative judgment, I distinguished the depth of a desire from its level. A higher-level desire need not be as deep or significant to the person as a first-order desire against which it is directed. An even simpler explanation of certain cases in which a person both rejects a first-order desire, yet continues to identify with it can be provided. We tend to think of identification as an act in which we *both* praise *and* embrace a motive. Now, the case of the gambler is one in which we embrace the life as our own, but are not prepared to offer unadulterated praise. There are also people who lead inauthentic lives. They organize their world in order to satisfy certain desires which they would prefer not to have. They regard it as very important to please other people and do so even if they must sacrifice other desires of theirs they would much prefer to be acting from. The fear of personal confrontation is so great that projects whose realization would confer meaning on their lives are abandoned. Yet the depth and strength of this fear are so great and so central to their lives that they have to admit that it is very much a part of them.

The judgment that a life is inauthentic is really a value judgment, not a metaphysical one. If I have to acknowledge that I am a shallow person or a fearful person, I may judge my life as falling short of personal ideals. I have devoted my life to unworthy ends because the desires impelling me are ones whose realization has little significance. But how in good faith can I judge that those desires are not mine if I am honest? "Yes, that's me. Isn't it a shame!" Thus, "identification" is ambiguous between incorporation and endorsement. To think that incorporation is inevitably praise is to refuse to face the tragedy of a life the person knows is not worth living.

In construing identification as endorsement *and* as appropriation, Frankfurt (1976) conflates distinct notions. Consider Fred, whose ideal is Gandhi. He thinks it would be wonderful to be like him, even though he knows that he is not in any way similar to the Indian leader. Fred is a combative, meat and potatoes type, who takes no steps to form pacifist or vegetarian inclinations or to study Hinduism or to promote the self-reliance of oppressed people. Now we may rightly accuse Fred of disingenuousness, but every once in a while, Fred has a passing urge to refrain from initiating yet another brawl and finds in addition that he would actually prefer to be moved by this desire.[9] The feeling quickly passes, however. The point I want to stress is the importance of the connection of acts of endorsement to the rest of the psyche. One cannot honestly regard these acts as metaphysically serious unless the first-order desires which are their objects have an independent claim on the self! If that is so, the identification approach cannot be a sufficient account of appropriation to self.

In response to these concerns, an identification theorist might introduce the notion of unconscious identifications *or* endorsements. Thus,

Fred really identifies unconsciously with his omnivorous and bellicose nature. But there are good reasons that identification theorists do not take this tack. There is, first of all, a simplicity to the original version. We understand what a conscious act of endorsement is; whereas, even if we are sympathetic with the notion of unconscious *states*, we might be skeptical of the idea of our own mental *acts* that are inaccessible to us. Moreover, how do we distinguish the case in which bellicose Fred does and bellicose Fred does not perform this unconscious act of endorsement? For we surely want to permit both possibilities, just as we do on the conscious level. But if the unconscious act is posited just in virtue of the fact that Fred has a bellicose nature, its introduction becomes utterly gratuitous. Yet this unfortunate result obtains if the unconscious act is introduced in the original case on the grounds that the conscious act of identification with pacifism cannot be serious since Fred is obviously bellicose!

Frankfurt's (1992) more recent discussions of identification do incorporate a requirement concerning the link between identification and the psyche as a whole. Wholehearted identification demands that the person be satisfied in the sense that he possesses no tendency or inclination to alter his condition. Moreover, he has reached this state through an understanding and evaluation of his psychic condition. Even if it is possible that Fred consciously feels no dissatisfaction during this pacifist interlude, let us concede that, since contrary forces are undoubtedly at work even during this lull to restore him to a state of normalcy, that is, belligerency, he is actually *not* entirely satisfied. We do not have to count his real self as pacifist, therefore, for the identification was not wholehearted.

We must, however, still insist upon a distinction between appropriation and wholehearted identification just because the latter is conceived as an act of endorsement. We seriously underemphasize the significance of our first-order natures if we have no way to profess the reality of a self we cannot in good conscience condone.

There may well be an intellectualistic bias accounting for the identification of valuation with self. We expect the agent's own formulations to be the best source of information about himself. So, it is supposed, if he would condemn his own desires, that surely tells more than the mere possession of those desires. And Eleonore Stump (1988) argues that the agent must be identified with a first-order desire, even if the desire belongs to the person's darker nature, so long as the agent's reason, operating soundly *or* unsoundly, proclaims approval. But the self-determining status of the second-order will is not secured by the insistence that its deliverances be endorsed by the intellect. For the issue is not simply the arbitrariness of identifying the self with the intellect rather than the passions. We must not forget an elementary psychological observation that the intellect is often a tool of the passions and that reasoning on behalf of some desire may well be a rationalization designed to disguise an agent's true motivation, which lies hidden from consciousness, but whose dominance in the organization of the agent's personality is reflected in behavior, speech, and emotion. One cannot just take endorsements for granted without consideration of the overall psychological picture; a person's own judgment is but one datum whose status can become subordinate to others.

If powerful unconscious motives lead me to endorse an end as good, why should we think of the real me as defined by that process of reasoning which is a distorted expression of elements of my psyche far more central to my being? These elements, say, certain unconscious first-order desires, may dominate other facets of my existence and may produce profound disturbances if brought to consciousness or if efforts are made to eliminate them. When certain desires explain the dictates of reason and occupy a central place in the economy of a person's life, why choose the desires *endorsed* by reason rather than those which *explain* that endorsement, when they are in conflict?[10]

Like Alicia, might not our darker, nonrational impulses be superior candidates for our true selves than the possibly self-deceptive rationalizations of our second-order will? Might not the dedicated gambler honestly tender a negative evaluation on himself without identifying himself with that evaluation because the attractions of that sort of existence are just too powerful. Here, the second-order will is not guilty of self-deception; he knows very well that there is a lot to be said against his way of life.

Can powerful, unconscious motives lead me to identify wholeheartedly (in Frankfurt's sense) with some end or desire? Can I be ignorant of the forces which are closer to the core of my being and which account for my "satisfaction" with some desire that is in actuality peripheral or subordinate to that core? Perhaps not, for the structure of such cases would require the presence of forces that would be incompatible with complete satisfaction. If endorsement is a guise to prevent the pain of full disclosure, there are elements at work that can cause the endorsed desire to lose favor. If I profess total satisfaction with my job because I unconsciously fear confronting my boss, there must be elements in my psyche, the unpleasantness of aspects of the job I have repressed, which are straining to make their presence felt. Should they burst forth, I will admit that I dislike my job. Since "satisfaction is a state of the entire psychic system" (1992: 13), my original endorsement was not really wholehearted.

Wholehearted identification is, then, closer to appropriation just because it embeds a powerful requirement of psychic integration and thereby goes far beyond the idea of endorsement, no matter how enthusiastically proclaimed. Yet insofar as endorsement remains essential, the doctrine will be unable to accommodate the case of one who cannot endorse what is nevertheless a bona fide truth about himself.

Frankfurt's tendency to inflate the significance of the second-level appears as well in his characterization of importance or care. Whereas I have advanced an account of personal value that destresses the role of evaluation, Frankfurt sees the hand of reflective evaluation as essential in the determination of the objects of care. Now, if I could decide what it is that is important to me on the basis of reflection, this view would be understandable. But Frankfurt believes that we cannot resolve ambivalence through a decision that consummates our reflective activity. Wholehearted identification is not under volitional control; it arises, when it does, nondeliberately, "as an unmanaged consequence of the person's appreciation of his psychic condition" (1992: 14). Moreover, if this condition is essentially the absence of an interest in change, a total acceptance of things as they are, why do we need reflection to arrive at this state? I can be totally content without ever having thought much about it.

Clearly, Frankfurt is worried about wantons, individuals whose deliberations are exclusively calculative, never reflective. I certainly agree, as I have already said (and will elaborate upon in Chapter 9), that reflection in the sense intended here, that is, as incorporating a review of one's first-order motivational nature, is important and meritorious. But we can certainly require that persons be in general reflective without requiring that a person specifically engage in reflection about P as a prerequisite for his actually caring about P. More importantly, there is no simple relation between the consequence of reflection that Frankfurt spotlights, to wit, total psychic satisfaction, and the extent to which the person truly cares about P. The extent to which gambling is important in my life is not a simple function of the extent of my ambivalence. I care very much about gambling even though I have an interest in change. My acknowledgement of the worthlessness of my life and my sadness at the disappointment of my friends does not automatically undermine the love of this life I cannot help feeling.

I have stressed the valuational and metaphysical significance of a person's first-order will without regard to the accessibility of the person to his own will. Yet the tendency to locate the self in the aspect of the person most available to that person is pervasive in psychological theory. When psychologists theorize about the self, they usually talk about self-image, ego ideal, or self-conception. For example, a well-known anthology entitled *Psychological Perspectives on the Self* (Suls and Greenwald 1983) begins with a section on self-appraisal, which includes papers on self-definition, self-evaluation, and self-assessment. The second section is devoted to self-consciousness, and so on. One paper by W. B. Swann, "Self-Verification: Bringing Social Reality into Harmony With the Self," begins with the sentence, "One sure way to stir people up is to tell them that they are not what they think they are," and then proceeds: "The major purpose of this chapter is to examine the processes whereby people work to ensure the stability of their self-conceptions" (1983: 33). There is presumably then a subject matter constituted by the *actual* nature of the self that is being ignored by the psychologists!

Even Freud's thinking was dominated by this methodology. In his structural theory, presented in 1923 as a replacement for the earlier topographical model, the "Ich" is identified with the ego for that is the system which is associated with the sense of self (see Mausner, 1990). Behavior determined by the ego is experienced as "mine." As important as the id is – it is actually the source of the ego and provides it with all its energy – its unconscious status renders it ineligible to be counted a part of the self proper.[11] (There are, to be sure, other differences between the ego and the id, for example, only the ego qualifies as a system, an aggregate with its own activities, boundaries, and functions, and this consideration also plays a role in the differential treatment.)

Freud (1923) introduced the ego in "The Ego and the Id" as an hypothesized structure which explains aspects of behavior and experience. It is most ironic, therefore, that the thinker who, more than any other, taught us the extent to which our behavior and experience are controlled by unconscious factors, drew a line between self and nonself on the basis of an ideology his own profound contributions should have undermined! The insistence that the self is to be identified with the rational, epistemically accessible, conscious system makes sense when that system is also assumed to play the crucial role in explaining our behavior and our experience. But when that assumption is abandoned, it seems plausible to shift to the idea that the self incorporates whatever elements play a central role in the true explanatory theory of behavior and experience.

The new idea is not problem-free. For example, we criticized the identification approach for confusing endorsement with incorporation, insisting that the latter is the relevant notion. The suggestion is that the explanatory primacy approach will discard the hidden evaluative component of the identification view. A desire's causal role, for example, does not depend importantly on our approval or disapproval of its presence in our psyche. Yet evaluation must rear its head in terms of the delineation of the explananda, that is, the behavior and experience that are supposed to be explained by elements of the self. How, for example, are we to judge the explanatory importance of a component without judging the importance of that which is to be explained? If a person suffering from a twitch moves his toe far more frequently than he performs the act of deciding to marry, it does not follow that the explanation of his twitch reveals more about himself than the explanation of his decision. If the explanation of this result is in terms of the greater importance to the person of his decision, we have reintroduced valuational elements in the delineation of the self. For this and other reasons, the explanatory primacy approach will be rejected. We will not pursue this matter here for we will be forced to resume this discussion in Chapter 9 when we finally confront the issue of the connections between the concepts of self and autonomy.

The primacy of our first-order natures

There are passing whims a person has which he wholeheartedly repudiates. They conflict with his values and are unrelated to any other life purpose. They arise from some gratuitous source and express no deep meaning which would illumine other facets of the agent's personality. When the person abjures these whims, they may be relegated to limbo and ignored in an accounting of the structure of his psyche. The occasional urge to pull a chair away from a person about to sit on it, induced by a bizarre chemical imbalance in the brain and unconnected to any other facet of one's life, is a nuisance to be endured, not a feature to be incorporated, except in a footnote, in a psychological profile. Recall the demand for reasonable significance on a desire before we elevate it to the status of a value.

The significance of the act of rejection in such a case cannot be generalized into a model of the self. For, on the whole, our basic natures are given essentially by our primary motivations. Philosophers must not forget psychological commonplaces. Negative personal evaluations can be rationalizations on behalf of the protection of other first-order desires whose satisfaction is more important to the agent than the elimination of the rejected desire. And positive personal evaluations can express wishful thinking, the belief that a praiseworthy inclination is stronger and more important than it actually is.

We must remind ourselves that even an honest judgment can be a relatively shallow one, that although one can realize that it would be a good thing not to act on a desire, the significance of the desire can far surpass that of the reasoned judgment, and only the philosopher's traditional preference for the rational or the cognitive blurs philosophical vision and generates a misleading conception of the self.

Evaluation versus motivation conception of value

In spite of what has been said, a person can still reject an addictive urge as venal and destructive, even if he may have to concede it is *his* urge. Whether one holds an Evaluation or a Motivation Conception of values, *some* acts of rejection reflect the agent's values better than the object of the act. They may be honestly tendered and coherent with other aspects of the person's character. He really wants to be rid of this monkey on his back and is doing all he can to this end. The only positive value of the addiction is the temporary release of tension it affords, whereas its disvalue is great. Sometimes, *second*-order desires can issue from deep layers of the self. A person who is plagued by a desire he cannot banish from his psyche may deem action from that desire as having negative value just because he finds he will be unable to respect himself were he to succumb.

The Motivation Conception would explain the rejection of the addictive urge in terms of a set of hypothetical choices. The sympathetic reading accorded the Motivation Conception has been designed to correct for the Evaluation Conception's tendency to elevate second-order acts to a metaphysical and ethical status far beyond what many of them deserve.

But a full airing of this debate is unnecessary for present purposes for, if we were to suppose that an agent's values can be identified with the dominant or effective motive of a hypothetical choice situation, then the view that value is intrinsic to autonomy would be uncontested. I must concede that values are essential to autonomy if values are what the Motivation Conception says they are. For if a self without values is a self without any ranking of desires, we have a being no one would regard as autonomous. The person would have a vegetative-like status, such as we may approximate in certain extreme psychotic states, including perhaps an advanced case of anomie or extreme depression. Autonomy is a condition of agents, and agents are motivated to act in some way or another. We can, to be sure, describe a possible creature who ranks short-term and specific desires and never forms long-range projects or ego ideals. But I have already conceded that these agents lack essential conditions of autonomy. Out of polemical considerations, therefore, we take it that the insistence that autonomous agents be motivated by their values amounts to the belief that agents must be disposed to evaluate their desires or strongest preferences from the vantage point of worth. This interpretation is borne out by the texts. Taylor (1976) explicitly advances this point of view. And Haworth introduces values in a discussion of critical competence since an autonomous agent will evaluate his preferences in part in terms of their mesh with his values. Indeed, the essential link between autonomy and critical, independent evaluation of options provides the locus for values. They are in us, to be enunciated when the deliberative process requires it. We, therefore, treat the claim that autonomy requires values as the claim that an autonomous agent must be disposed to these higher-level acts of evaluation.

Incidentally, these thoughts may provide a further basis for the sense that there must be a more intimate connection between freedom and value than I have allowed. For as the preceding remarks make clear, I have never denied *either* that the powers that constitute freedom are ones possessed by beings who necessarily have values (in the sense of the Motivation Conception) *or* that the importance of these powers is their role in the furtherance of these values.

Granted that almost all autonomous agents engage in evaluation in the way demanded by the Evaluation Conception, can a case be made that evaluation is intrinsically important to the life of an autonomous agent *qua* autonomous agent? In this chapter, we have rejected efforts to answer this question affirmatively through the postulation of intimate links between selfhood and evaluation. We explore this question further in the next chapter. If the answer is no, then although the conclusion is strictly that an autonomous agent might be value-free, the more careful reading of this is that an autonomous agent might have values only in the sense given by the Motivation Conception. He ranks his preferences, but, qua autonomous, is in no way concerned to evaluate those preferences in terms of their worth.

6
Autonomy and rationality

We have focused until now on the connections between freedom and autonomy. With respect to dispositional autonomy, I have insisted that an autonomous agent in a certain sphere must be a free agent, that is, she must possess (and be disposed to use) the tools of critical competence needed for the exercise of freedom of decision in that sphere. She exhibits autonomy of choice in a particular decision-making situation only if she is unhindered from without in the exercise of these capacities. She is fully autonomous if, once the decision is made, she is proficient at its enactment. Proficiency is constituted by power or token ability, a combination of positive and negative freedom. An agent may possess virtually full autonomy within a certain sphere if all the deliberations in that sphere result in autonomous decisions to perform certain actions which the agent is proficient at executing and which are relatively easy to perform – actions that do not demand heroic effort or the thwarting of contrary powerful impulses, moods, or general tendencies. The scope of autonomy of such an agent may or may not be extensive, depending upon the character of the items within this sphere. The scope is narrow, for example, if there are few items and they are trivial ones. Insofar as all agents set out to achieve objectives and rank these objectives in importance, they may be said to have values. These values guide their decision-making in the form of motivations.

The question posed at the end of the last chapter is the extent to which autonomy requires the coordination of an agent's motivation with those higher-order judgments deemed to be judgments of value in accordance with the Evaluation Conception. Why should we believe that any of these high-level happenings is essential to the critical competence of an autonomous agent?

Self-control

We may worry that an agent who does not pass his impulses through a valuational filter lacks self-control. He is not his own ruler because he is a slave to his passions and impulses. Indeed, the function of critical reflection is to ensure control over one's life, and it is exactly in this domain that the psychopath appears to be deficient.[1]

Clearly, a person who can never control his appetites when he finds sufficient reason to do so lacks autonomy. But there are interesting permutations. Recall Alicia, who had difficulty controlling her *reason* when it opposed appetite. She felt victimized by her reason and identified with the loser in this struggle, her appetites. The identification account of the self would rightly count her as heteronomous; she is under the sway of an internal force, reason, with which she does not identify. Logocentrically-inclined philosophers just do not take seriously enough the possibility of an individual like Alicia, someone who appears to challenge the Aristotelian dictum that "reason more than anything else is man."

The psychopath is different from Alicia. He does not suffer even potential conflict for his reason does not pose a prima facie challenge to appetite. Moreover, he is capable of calculative rationality to a possibly very high degree, even if he apparently has few long-term interests to which he subordinates his current ones. Although psychopaths do have a scale of preferences and are capable of self-restraint (Haksar 1965), their general orientation toward immediate gratification and consequent ineptitude at the formation and sustaining of long-range projects does limit their autonomy in ways we delineated in Chapter 4. But it is unclear why his failure to consider whether his preferences cohere or conflict with his values (in the sense of the Evaluation Conception) should also count against his autonomy if he lacks values in the first place. A value-less agent evidently reflects, but only as much as he needs to. As a clever con artist, he is prudent enough to ensure the maximization of utility in the long run. Why is he any the less his own master because he lacks values?

Perhaps psychopaths are very unhappy. But there are many rational agents whose autonomy is not in doubt who are unhappy. Moreover, that an agent must have a personality sufficiently integrated so as to be able to exercise control over himself and his actions is also no insurance against unhappiness or eccentricity. Freedom and happiness are distinct goods: some slaves are happy, while others who fully recognize their absolute independence and total responsibility are engulfed with aloneness and respond, in Sartrean fashion, with a sense of dread.

The case for values, if there is one, must now be made by fleshing out the following argument. Autonomy is self-rule, rendered possible by critical self-regulation. We require then a self with its rational faculties. But a self totally denuded of value is disintegrated and consequently incapable of *self*-regulation, and rationality which is not informed by relevant values does not permit the right sort of self-control. In this chapter, we address the preliminaries to this question, a direct answer to which is begun in the next chapter.

Rationality and self

If one challenges the autonomy of the psychopath on the grounds that his (noncalculative) reason or capacity for higher-order evaluation is so stunted that he is better regarded as a child, as one without a fully developed self, we must again recall Alicia. For if an adult can identify her self with its nonrational components, as Alicia can, what is to prevent the psychopath from so doing?

How can anyone identify herself with her nonrational nature? Alicia is minimally rational; as such, she is able to engage in critical reflection, to evaluate arguments logically, to calculate strongest preference, to judge various possible means to her goals, to understand at least the basic laws of probability, to formulate long-range projects, and to recognize the difference between success and failure. She reaches a conclusion that demands that she suppress certain desires. The reasoning is not purely calculative in that it rests in part on moral premises which dictate the prohibition, independent of Alicia's other desires and concerns. She *accepts* the conclusion *as* a conclusion of reason, knowing that it would indeed be immoral to act on her desires. But she is frustrated because she regards this desire as a most intimate part of her self. So she has an internal conflict.

We saw in the previous chapter that, for independent reasons, an autonomous agent may well need to reject elements of the self so long as the rejection is mandated by *other* components of the self. The special problem in Alicia's case is that, if her conclusion that the wicked action is immoral *is* a conclusion of reason, then we cannot blithely apply the earlier principle to this case and announce that Alicia's reason is not a part of her! Alicia's reason, unlike a passing whim, is special. She must use it, even if she challenges its conclusions.

Conflict does not automatically require the expulsion of one element from the self in an effort to restore consistency (see Berofsky 1987: 160–87). Alicia *must* abide this conflict as an internal one. We are not making the absurd demand that an essential part of Alicia, her reason, be expelled from the self. The question then is: what is the difference between an ordinary state of conflict between two elements of the self and the state of conflict in which Alicia finds herself, in which she "identifies" with the nonrational element?

There is, obviously, the second-order judgment itself, a judgment of preference for the wicked desire over the mandate of reason proscribing its satisfaction or simply the judgment that the satisfaction of the desire would feel like genuine self-expression. Moreover, as I observed in Chapter 5, if we permit the reasoning on behalf of virtue to be faulty, we cannot conclude that the rationally sanctioned desire is more securely located in the self. For the act of reasoning can be an instance of self-deception in which the agent disguises to herself the real basis of her endorsement, to wit, her need to suppress the recognition that a *different* desire is the really dominant force in her personality. Thus, acts of identification, *supported or not by reason*, are not self-certifying!

And so it is with Alicia. Indeed, her feeling that she is more truly her appetitive self may well be delusive! It depends, as I said previously, on the role her appetites play in the overall economy of her psyche. This is shockingly vague, but is clear enough to ground the fallible character of acts of identification. Psychotherapy may come to reveal to her that she has been hesitant to acknowledge her purity of spirit because of a traumatic episode in which a powerful authority figure scoffed at her efforts to place her passions under rational control. Since this episode occurred at a time in life when Alicia was particularly sensitive, she responded to her fear of this person by identifying with her passions. In psychotherapy she comes to see that this segment of her life is relatively isolated from the mainstream so that as she begins to acknowledge consciously her feelings toward this person, she comes to recognize that her wicked desires are not nearly as attractive as they had been and that it is an easy matter to control them without the feeling that one is leading an inauthentic life.

As fanciful as this may sound, it highlights the fallible character of these acts of identification. A less fanciful – because genuine – example is that given by Frithjof Bergmann about himself. For many years, Bergmann (1977) tells us, he could not accept his status as a professor of philosophy. He went through the motions, but always felt he was living a lie. After many years, he came to realize that he had all along been doing what he most deeply wanted to do and that his failure to commit himself fully to his profession and his life was based on immature considerations having to do with image, the pressures of unrealized romantic dreams, and the like. This personal observation is particularly interesting because it shows that feelings of *estrangement* (nonidentification) are also not self-certifying.

Just as Alicia may be wrong about herself, she may – given a different story, of course – be *right* when she identifies with her passions. They may ultimately be very important to her even though she also condemns them. When she succumbs to reason, therefore, she is not expressing her deepest self. How is this possible?

On Wolf's conception of reason, according to which it enables us to discern the Right, if Alicia's rational faculty is not flawed, then she would indeed be behaving irrationally if she were to succumb to her passions. Many, of course, view reason as ill-equipped to discern intrinsic right from intrinsic wrong. On this alternative, since Alicia's moral promptings are not the voice of reason, a faculty intrinsic to her, she may, like the psychopath, regard these promptings as genuinely alien. The failed attempts to extract morality from reason (I will document some important ones in the next chapter) provide some support for this latter alternative.[2]

If ethical cognitivism fails, we would be able in addition to respond to the claim that autonomous agents must adhere to the canons of morality since their rejection of morality would imply ignorance in a sphere in which autonomous agents must be knowledgeable. If rejection of the fundamental principles of morality does not necessarily imply a defective cognitive mechanism, then autonomy does not imply morality via the demand that autonomous agents be knowledgeable. In the next chapter, we shall see how an autonomous agent may consistently reject as *irrele-*

vant or *nonbinding* moral data he is aware of. Like Alicia, although he knows that it is wrong to behave in certain ways, he yet has reasons to reject the claims of morality. Unlike Alicia, he then actually opts out of morality.

Rationality and autonomy

On the psychologically oriented approach taken in this book, the basic case for the inclusion of rationality as an essential ingredient in autonomy is easy to make out. As we view the development from childhood to maturity, we look primarily for the emergence of independence. Yet a person who is genuinely independent of others is nonetheless obliged to govern his life by some nomos, that is, some law or system, and we are forced at the beginning to take on those offered by our culture. If we adopt a nomos uncritically and retain it in the same way, we have failed to make it our own. Critical competence is, therefore, essential to self-governance. The autonomous individual, observes Benn,

rests neither on the unexamined shibboleths and conventions of a traditional culture nor on the fashionably outrageous heresies of a radical one when they lead him into palpable inconsistencies. The resources on which he will rely for this critical exploration must lie, necessarily, within the culture itself, supplemented, perhaps, by those elements of alien cultures with which he has become acquainted. But such elements, too, have to be assimilated into the network of his own cultural beliefs, to be located in and related to the overall framework of his intelligible world, before they can be accessible to him. Within this complex web – perhaps "tangle" would be more appropriate – he will try to create his own consistent pattern, appraising one aspect of it by critical canons derived from another. As an artist or a scientist must draw on the resources of an existing tradition to contribute creatively to its development, so an autarchical man must construe it for himself to become autonomous. (1988: 179–80)

Failure to submit the system to continuing scrutiny in this way invalidates the claim to *self*-governance, for the individual thereby remains indistinct from the group. Thus, in tribal society and in certain periods of great stability and routinization, autonomy, the emergence of individual self-government, is impossible. "Autonomy is an ideal available only within a plural tradition" (182). Even if an autonomous member of a religious order accepts the fundamental precepts and behavioral codes of that order, he does so on the basis of a critical review of its doctrines and practices, a review which is ongoing and which results in an individualization of those doctrines and practices in accordance with his assessment. Even if an individual looks like a totally assimilated member of the group (is *substantively* dependent), his autonomy (*procedural* independence) may be retained.[3] His critical powers have been at work and continue to be alert so that the absorption of practices and ideologies bears his individual stamp no matter how objectively indiscernible this may be. He is not a rubber stamp or an assembly line product identical to all the rest.

Ideal autonomy

Those who regard genuine or pure autonomy as inconsistent with the restrictive situation of human beings in nature and society are attracted to the model of radically independent self-creation. The truly autonomous agent would be able to select any goals, unencumbered by a psyche limited by its interaction with an environment bent on circumscription.[4]

Although ideal autonomy is an enormously appealing model to some, its nature is problematic. In order to describe it, we must, first of all, bracket the limitations imposed by our nature-cum-environment which restrict the power to secure all our objectives. Power or liberty *is* a feature of freedom, but not the one whose nature we are currently seeking to discover. We are here concerned with autonomy proper, not proficiency; we want to describe the features of an agent whose deliberations, including those concerning the choice of basic goals and values, are in no way limited by factors external to the self.

How would an ideally autonomous agent choose her goals? In the real world, it is naive to assume that an agent

has purposes, which spring perhaps from some wholly internal process of preference formation or from some inner process of deliberating, and confronts "out there," in the surrounding environment, his resources and constraints.... The family, school, or office is not simply an external environment which a person confronts. Rather, he belongs to it. This implies that it gives him his purpose: he has a place in the family as a parent, in the school as a student, in the office as a clerk, and having such a place involves having a purpose or way of life for which the resources are resources, and the constraints constraints. (Haworth 1986: 108–9)

The lover of radical self-creation views the autonomy that such a person may achieve even under optimal conditions as ersatz. That he makes the best of his dependence on his environment does not annul that dependence. In addition, the defender of ideal autonomy may well reject the notion of procedural independence used by advocates of the more pragmatic attitude as incoherent. Benn's autonomous agent is supposed to evaluate his culture's beliefs and practices from an *individual* perspective. From whence arises this perspective? Yes, concedes Benn, the critical resources themselves lie within the culture. But, he adds, the agent *assimilates* the resources in a distinctive way, thereby conferring his own special mark upon them.

From whence arises this capacity, asks the advocate of ideal autonomy. If the very way in which the individual processes and alters the materials provided by his culture is itself culturally determined, in what genuine sense is the person independent?

The rejoinder is very familiar. If creative activity cannot arise in response to materials extant in the culture and available as potential resources, it arises from no source and is in no clear sense creative. It would be better construed as pure caprice, the product of pure chance, without rhyme or reason. Benn says:

To be autonomous . . . is not to have a capacity for acting without reasons or for conjuring action commitments out of nowhere. And for reasons one must have a system of beliefs from which action commitments derive and into which new evidence can be assimilated, yielding new commitments. How could anyone come by these bits of basic equipment except by learning them in the first instance from parents, teachers, friends, and colleagues? Someone who had escaped such a socialization process . . . would be able to make nothing of himself, being hardly a person at all. (179)

Suppose that, in resistance to the familiar view, enunciated above, that the conception of a self, divorced from nature and society, is meaningless, we attempt to extract the conception of a being from the idea of pure autonomy. The goals of this ideally autonomous agent (IAA) are not determined by the contingencies of his situation, and are not restricted by possible limits on his actual ability to secure the goals he formulates. What might his goals then be?

A case has just been made that autonomy entails rationality. If this being must be perfectly rational, and reason dictates certain goals directly, he would have to have at least these. But is it clear that IAA must be rational? For the evidentiary value of rationality would be moot for such a being. If his goals are determined exclusively from "within," there is no need to be assured that he has sifted the intellectual and cultural offerings of his society through his rational filter. For these offerings have not been imposed upon him. Even if he lacks critical competence, we may still rest assured that, ex hypothesi, the values and goals he endorses have not been unself-consciously derived from *external* sources.

Independently of this consideration, however, rationality is of enormous instrumental value. Even if this agent does not need to peruse externally imposed values, mores, and practices to ensure that continued adherence to them will be satisfying or desirable in his eyes, he will be at a disadvantage in practical reasoning designed to secure whatever goals he happens to possess should he fail to be rational. If E is my goal, M is the only means to E, I assess the probability that M leads to E as 1, M does not interfere with any other goals of mine, and I know all of this, I will, as rational, choose M. If I were not rational, I would be more likely to frustrate myself since this bit of practical reasoning will not take place and there will not, therefore, be a high probability that M will be chosen.

Rational powers are general. A superstitious gambler may luck out in the short run; but he is more likely to run into trouble than one committed to a rational approach to life. One who fortuitously secures an objective by rejecting the scientific point of view in a particular domain may well reduce his chances of reaching the truth or advancing his goals in another domain. IAA knows, therefore, that a commitment to rationality is the best overall means to secure his objectives.

Would rationality be essential to IAA if we explicitly confer upon him perfect proficiency at the realization of his goals? If perfect proficiency is constituted by the existence of a routine or sequence of actions that is within the power of IAA for each decision he makes, rationality may be required to ensure a successful execution of the routine. (We might prefer to say that he cannot really be perfectly proficient unless he is rational.) Of course, we might posit omnipotence instead, understood as the imme- diate, automatic realization of any decision. (Perfect proficiency is inferior to omnipotence because a perfectly proficient agent cannot realize goal G without employing strategy S and cannot, therefore, achieve G-without- S.) Yet even for a truly omnipotent being, rationality will at least be required for decision making if we are to understand this process as at all akin to human decision making.

The only reason one might have for believing that IAA is not necessarily rational is that it does not befit such an agent to sacrifice his perfect freedom to the demands of rationality even on a purely instrumental construal of rationality.[5] But this concern can be allayed so long as IAA retains the option of being irrational. And if we ordinary rational mortals retain that option, why should it be foreclosed for an ideally autonomous agent?[6] It would surely be restrictive to deny him the power we all have and exercise even if he would rarely invoke this option.

Of course, we ordinary mortals retain this "power" because we are not perfectly rational. That is, we have the power to decide irrationally as a result of possible intellectual or emotional failings. The power we are permitting IAA, however, is rather the power of a fully competent agent to reject the promptings of his reason. "Reason" is ambiguous. As an objective notion, it stands for a body of norms pertaining to the manner one should draw inferences and make practical decisions. Given the fallibility of human beings, one totally committed to rationality may none- theless make an irrational decision. She may take herself as having a sufficient reason to do A when, objectively speaking, she has only a weak or no reason to do A. So a self-chosen irrational action can appear to have a point in the eyes of the (fallible) chooser. In fact, such an action can actually earn a point in this chooser's eyes, as happens in cases of weakness of will.

If we do not suppose that IAA would suffer weakness of will, are there any other circumstances under which a self-chosen irrational action can have a point for him? Would he *ever choose* to act irrationally? He cannot have a sufficient reason for doing so and he cannot be forced to do so. So how can an affirmative answer be defended? If he wants to act irrationally or he wants to prove that he can or he wants not to appear to have a stable and, therefore, constraining nature, he automatically *has* a reason to behave in the way he is contemplating, in which case the prospective action is not irrational. He is not irrational when he acts "contrary to reason" in order to show reverence for autonomy, for it is rational for one with this motivation to act in this way. But if a self-chosen irrational action is, as critics like Benn would say, random, pointless, and indistinguishable from an action without any origins, in what way is it really "self-chosen"? Imagine that an autonomous agent decides that it is important to display his power to reject reason occasionally and picks at random decision-making situations in which to select the "irrational" option. (It is irrational according to some appropriate standards accepted by him, although the information that he does not want to adhere to these standards in this case is omitted from the relevant data determining the rationally admissible and inadmissible options.) Even though he does not have a reason in each of these cases to select that case as the one in which he will act irrationally, his behavior does instantiate a policy he has a reason to adopt. In that respect, his decision is self-chosen, but is also, in a sense, rational.

IAA might be like Alicia once she overcomes her moral training and acts on behalf of her deepest feelings. Remember that Alicia believes correctly that her reasons to behave as she most wants to are overridden by her reasons to refrain since she realizes that the great harm she would inflict on others were she to act on her strongest desires is not offset by the satisfaction of those desires. If IAA were like that, he would be choosing and, moreover, choosing *against reason*.

We are not imagining that Alicia and IAA are acting for *no* reason whatsoever when they behave irrationally. It suffices for irrationality that one act contrary to the reason judged by the agent (and perhaps others) to be the best.

Thus, a self-chosen irrational action need not be pointless even for IAA. In special cases, the power to reject reason can be of great personal value. Perhaps then, the possession of this strange power actually enhances our autonomy. I might believe that freedom or autonomy, enhanced by the power to reject reason, is an even greater value than reason itself.

It is worth observing that perhaps only special people like Alicia or certain rebellious types place great stock in the power to reject reason. Most people are perfectly content with a less than perfect state of autonomy. Thus, mathematicians who are "constrained" to accept a rigorous proof do not feel cheated by their inability to reject a conclusion they recognize as logically required. Through submission to the principles of logic and mathematics, they may be deprived of a sort of freedom – a liberty of indifference – but most would conclude that it is of no value.

It would be fruitful to unfold further the logic of ideal autonomy if we could thereby gain insight into the autonomy of real human beings, bedeviled with a manifold of natural and circumstantial limitations. If certain substantive goals were implicit in the conception of ideal autonomy, we would be in a stronger position to make good use of this idea. But it is not clear that a self-chooser must choose Happiness, Truth, Beauty, and Goodness.

The limits of rationality

A weakened reason can advance certain goals. It enables religious fanatics to retain their faith and the resultant optimism and strength of purpose. It may help others to avoid awful truths and thereby retain the integration of their personality and the very possibility of a partially autonomous existence. But in each of these cases, the value of diminished rationality is relative to certain beliefs, desires, or personality traits (faith in God, fear and rejection of nihilism, a tendency to overlook depressing facts) which would not be chosen by an ideally autonomous agent.

In other words, I reject the possibility of a perfectly rational IAA, who becomes so despondent about the realization, achieved with the aid of complete rational competence, that the world will frustrate her desires for salvation or for the realization of all positive human values or for something of this sort, that she experiences personal disintegration so great as to undermine sufficient unity of her self required for continued autonomy. These desires would reflect weaknesses in character which would not be autonomously chosen.[7] They exist in conventional, but not in ideal human nature, perhaps because of the traumatic experience undergone by all children during the period when they lose a sense of their omnipotence. In any event, since this person is autonomous, whatever explains the onset of the desire as well as the onset of the despondence must be internal to the self. Even if "nothing" explains these phenomena, the self here is afraid, weak, and in need of a high level of support which is not forthcoming. Since this person is free of the biological, psychological, sociological, indeed all natural limitations which plague you and me, is there any way to explain why a self-determining creature would be like that? To be sure, one can always concoct some metaphysical account which would make a given set of personal features appropriate; but here we have to contend with a perfectly rational agent, one who is not easily bamboozled.

It is not easy to say what an agent totally divorced from nature and society would be like and what goals he would set himself. But how can a case be made that even *some* ideally autonomous agents would choose goals and desires which, when combined with exemplary rational powers, promote personal disintegration and the extinction of autonomy?

Of course, nonideal human creatures sometimes find their rationality a curse. Critical competence and intelligence make it difficult to accept the various pictures of the world dangled temptingly before us – pictures of a place congenial to some of our deepest longings. Thus, the manifestation of critical competence in a sensitive creature contains the potential for personal disintegration and the resultant loss of autonomy.

Accordingly, the adoption of autonomy as an ideal is itself a *real* choice a fully informed, rational agent must make. For, like other choices, there are costs associated with each option. Even if I am now autonomous, I might have the opportunity to relinquish this state to join a community or order which limits my autonomy in drastic ways. That human beings do this all the time is some evidence that there are important values associated with the heteronomous life. It supports the thesis, advanced in different ways by Eric Fromm (1941) and Jean-Paul Sartre (1956), that we dread the state of being free.

An interesting example of the values of the heteronomous life is provided by Jehovah's Witnesses. Bruno Bettelheim (1960) observed that, in concentration camps, Jehovah's Witnesses displayed extraordinary integrity, unselfishness, and an inner strength deriving from a firm commitment to internalized ideals. Their inner strength lay in part in the narrowness of their ideology, in the total inner conviction they refused to put to the test.

Jehovah's Witnesses lack autonomy because they lack rationality, a component of which is the willingness to defend principles by an appeal to relevant evidence and a readiness to revise and abandon these principles should the objective data warrant such actions. Under special circumstances, heteronomous individuals may be in a better position to preserve their identity than autonomous ones; the dangers of critical intelligence and knowledge have been mentioned previously. In subordinating their individuality to the group, they abandon self-determination for the comforts of group solidarity and subjective certainty, elements which stand them in good stead in times of crisis. If a Jehovah's Witness were forced to adopt the critical perspective of a truly autonomous agent and view therefrom his role in the universe and the meaning of his life, the resultant disintegration might well be serious. "The truth is terrible, says *The Iceman Cometh:* Let us gloss it over, although we always know it is there" (Raleigh 1968: 16). An increase in rationality is detrimental when the personality cannot tolerate it. But it is not the agent's autonomy that is adversely affected; the author of *Thirty Years a Watchtower Slave* is more autonomous after his liberation than before (see Young 1986: 70).[8]

Ideal, maximal, and realistic autonomy

Resuming the critique of the very notion of ideal autonomy, we may cite additional reasons for skepticism directed to this notion. For the concept is incompatible with the very idea of a human agent's choosing or forming a desire or goal and is, therefore, worthless for our purpose. When we attempt to impose the model of ideally autonomous choice on human creatures, we meet with incoherence. When God becomes man, He acquires the capacity for mortality. When a fully self-determining creature steps into the real world, even gingerly, she cannot help but take on the constraints and burdens of the finite creatures around her.

Suppose our ideally autonomous agent forms the desire to acquire and nurture friendships and suppose we bracket the familiar worries regarding the meaning of "self-determination" in a case in which the desire arises from no external circumstances as well as less familiar worries as to how a being totally set apart from the real world could even have acquired the concepts relevant to the formation of such a desire. Even if the desire is magically just there, it can only enter into deliberations, be acted upon, and modified by a *limited* being. For a friend is one with whom one enters certain relationships and in relation to whom one eschews certain modes of behavior. A friend is a person one does not mistreat in certain ways and to whom one has certain obligations. I cannot both want Willy to be my friend and also plan to steal his money and his ladyfriend.

Perhaps IAA is one who freely chooses to limit her actions by the adoption of certain desires and goals, but who retains complete autonomy through the power to abandon these goals at will. In entering into a friendship I do not really forsake the option of cruelty directed against the friend, for I do not forsake the option of abandoning the friendship. Thus, the limitations under which I operate are only logical and even God, according to most accounts, is bound by the laws of logic.

This reply is inadequate for IAA cannot really form friendships on these assumptions for these are relationships one cannot abandon so readily. One would not count a person as a friend if she could at the drop of a hat decide to become an enemy. One may call the limitation logical or conceptual, but the key conceptual connection is between becoming a friend to Walter at one time and finding it very painful to betray or act callously toward Walter at a later time. The extent to which a person retains the power to exercise with ease his capacity for betrayal is the extent to which he is unable to act on the desire to form friendships. If there are analogies with the paradoxes of divine omnipotence and, consequently, general lessons concerning ideal forms and perfection, so be it.

This conclusion survives the assumption that IAA is perfectly proficient in relation to the pursuit of her selected ends. For that IAA is able to achieve her goal of establishing a friendship with Walter does not annul her commitment to behave toward Walter in the immediate future in a friendly way. We may even suppose that IAA is omnipotent. For again, that IAA realizes this goal "with the wave of her hand" does not relieve her of the commitment to exercise the associated behavioral dispositions directed to the future. IAA's autonomy is as diminished as that of any other friend of Walter's.

IAA would then have to concede that the satisfaction of certain desires entails a certain loss of autonomy. The extreme example would be the desire to be a slave. The rub here is that all valuable human endeavors and institutions entail some loss of freedom and, hence, autonomy. Friendship is just one example; the relations of lover to loved, parent to child, employee to employer, civil servant to citizen are a few others. Thus, full participation in a meaningful life requires a significant abandonment of autonomy.

Perhaps autonomy is not what it is often cracked up to be. We shall consider that later. But if it is our goal, we may, for the sake of self-determination, have to eschew entanglements which some regard as essential to the good life. Perhaps, as a self-chooser, an ideally autonomous agent would not form desires which would restrict her capacities for continued self-choice. But this presupposes that a self-chooser wants to continue to be a self-chooser and it is unclear why this would have to be so, especially given the lonely character of this state. In any event, the problem is, as we shall see, more serious, especially for those perfectly proficient IAAs who are not truly omnipotent by dint of the need to execute a strategy for each selected goal.

The possession of any concept commits one to certain norms, if only the conventions of correct usage. To be sure, one can secretly understand a notion even if one publicly flouts these conventions. I can call anything I wish "water." So my autonomy is intact. But if I want a drink of water, I *must* direct my actions in one way rather than another. In general, the adoption of any goal, no matter how autonomously derived, constitutes a commitment and, as such, the positing of limits. For an imagined end constitutes a goal only when the agent is under a constraint, self-imposed to be sure, to take appropriate steps toward its realization when circumstances permit. One cannot both have a goal and also be entirely free to do whatever one has the capacity to do. The achievement of certain goals – to be a great violinist – exacts enormous demands and imposes severe limitations, at least on those IAAs who cannot *achieve* every goal just by *adopting* it. The critic may again point out that IAA can revise her goals any time she wishes. And the freedom to abandon a goal is compatible with the retention of that goal. But a person who each day reaffirms a commitment he can just as easily disavow is at least irresolute and, should he actually execute frequent changes, erratic and mercurial as well. He fails to take advantage of one of the most useful features of the practice of forming long-range goals, namely, the waiving of the exercise of reconsideration so as to permit the formation of firm dispositions required for the realization of the goal. The point we made earlier about friendship can then be generalized. Just as a friend must find it very hard to engage in certain actions, so an efficient goal seeker must find it hard to act contrary to the goal. If IAA has goals at all – and the concept of autonomy applies only to such creatures – she cannot have the level of perseverance displayed by ordinary creatures on behalf of their goals. This strikes me as a serious limitation on an ostensibly unlimited being.

If ideally autonomous agents are so different from us, it will be hard to understand how reflection on their nature can illumine the character of our imperfect autonomy. If, in response to these thoughts, we view ideal autonomy as incompatible with the possession of desires, a genuine exemplar would, of course, be terribly remote – even a devout Buddhist who wishes to be free from all desire is motivated by *that* desire, at least until he achieves realization. That in itself is not a decisive objection to the concept; perhaps the concept of the divine entails that divine beings must be transcendent and consequently flagrantly aloof. The special problem in the case of autonomy is that autonomous agents must choose, and it is not clear how a being who has no wants or motives can participate in this practice. When a Bodhisattva finally enters Nirvana, he does acquire one feature of an autonomous agent, to wit, independence from the influence of others. But the concept of an autonomous agent is the concept of one who *directs* his behavior independently and, again, the Arhat, he who has attained enlightenment, is not directing anything, certainly not his affairs, at least in any way that we can understand.

Although the notion of ideal autonomy may in the end be incoherent, it is worth observing that we do not think of self-imposed limitations as necessarily impairing human autonomy. Why, then, should we alter our thinking for IAA? Let us address this question by reflecting on the nature of one limited *only* by these conceptual restraints, an agent we call *maximally autonomous* (MAA). If MAA is constructed from scratch, we can provide her with a motivational structure only if we can find a criterion which would enable her to select and order a set of motives. Even a set of reasonable constraints on this motivational structure will not determine a unique set of desires. We can, for example, narrow the possibilities by assuming that MAA wants the scope of her autonomy to be as extensive as possible. In addition, since she is rational, she wants any set to be, in White's words, mutually supporting (1991: 201). Otherwise, she will face conflict and frustration resulting from an inability to satisfy some of her desires. We will surely still be left with an indefinitely large set of possible motivational structures.

If we have to order desires to determine priorities, we shall have to select MAA's deepest values and we cannot in this connection avail ourselves of the assumption we rejected in the previous chapter that those desires must be unconditional. Perhaps we may suppose that MAA wants to be happy. But the achievement of happiness depends on both the set of desires and the character of the world in which MAA is embedded, including aspects of MAA distinct from her motivational structure, for example, her cognitive makeup and her abilities. If MAA is supposed to be as close as possible to IAA, let us suppose a totally pliant world. She and her world will be as accommodating as possible once she chooses her motivational structure.

But even for MAA, there are many ways of being happy, even very happy. There will, therefore, still be many possible motivational structures. In itself, this may not pose a serious problem. If reason cannot narrow the range further, it does not forbid the random selection of one of these structures. Hence, MAA is free just to pick a set.

One cannot rule out the possibility that one of these sets provides a rather narrow scope of autonomy. A person who wants to be a good mother, lover, employee, citizen, and Jehovah's Witness may lead a very happy life, although she is making very few major decisions. (This observation is compatible with the proposition that the autonomous character of a decision in some way always enhances the happiness of the agent.) Although, unlike IAA, MAA is allowed the constraints implicit in her having goals, she ought to impose as the fundamental constraint on her motivational structure the selection of the set that preserves the widest possible scope of autonomy.

We must, however, recall that scope of autonomy is a normative notion. One extends this scope by adding decisions that have at least some significance. But MAA cannot then select a set of desires on this basis without a value system that will determine the significance that satisfying a particular desire has. But we cannot then determine MAA's value system simply on the basis of her desire to expand her scope of autonomy! There is no way to break into this circle.

Nor would we wish, in order to eliminate the normative component, to revert to a purely quantitative interpretation of scope of autonomy unless we want to count poor Chuzzlewit as a paradigmatic MAA (see Chapter 4).

The other alternative open to MAA is to choose only to promote her self-determination. In order to avoid this dilemma and to be as close to ideal autonomy as it is possible to be, she will not have truck with any other desires. Moreover, she will not have to be concerned about her happiness for the world and her nature will collaborate to ensure this outcome. (She will, like Nietzsche's Übermensch, revel in her isolation.)

It follows that MAA will face almost all her decisions with indifference. It is not even clear that she will be concerned about her own continued existence. She only becomes involved when someone or something threatens the number of options available to her. Power-mongering for its own sake is her sole preoccupation.

If this picture of a virtually denuded self is so remote as to be unhelpful when we try to understand the nature of our autonomy, we may then relativize the concept of a maximally autonomous agent to a motivational set. That individual who wants to be a good mother, lover, employee, citizen, and Jehovah's Witness may be maximally autonomous relative to this motivational set – the set would have to be ordered as well so that conflicts can be resolved by appeal to this person's priorities – just as the individual who simply wants to be a self-chooser may also be maximally autonomous relative to that motivational set. In each case, we must consider whether the individual is as autonomous as possible given the constraints imposed by the individual's motivational set.

Or we may turn directly to a more realistic model. We have been able to say little about the character of an ideally autonomous agent beyond the fact that she is a self-chooser with rational powers. If we place her in the real world, she will be under whatever conceptual restraints are implicit in her otherwise unrestricted selection of desires and goals. This model of a maximally autonomous agent is overly romantic in light of the fact that we have allowed this individual omnipotent control over nature so as to secure the conditions for the realization of her motivational set. If we are ever to understand the autonomy of real creatures, however, we must form our ideals out of materials taken from the real world. We would then have to accept our facticity and the numerous constraints implicit in our genetic and social embedding, no matter how ideal that might be. Our model of realistic autonomy is controlled by the conditions on autonomy we are in the process of specifying: freedom, knowledge, rationality, independence, integrity. If we wanted to make real people as autonomous as humanly possible, we would have to institute features like (a) a superior genetic endowment, (b) a loving, supportive family and friends, (c) an enriched, stimulating environment, (d) an excellent education, and (e) experiences which encourage independence, self-control, and critical reflection. Our goal will be to encourage the formation of dispositional autonomy by cultivating an appreciation of the autonomous life and the conditions of its pursuit and possibly the expansion of this disposition to ever wider domains to ensure that scope of autonomy is as extensive as possible. We must make this list of features more precise and we may have to add others. But the point I wish to stress is that by the time the child reaches the age at which she is becoming autonomous, she will happen to have many goals and ambitions that derive from the contingencies of her life and that were in no sense freely chosen. She may now evaluate those goals and that is what her autonomy basically consists of. She will also be burdened by physiological and psychological limitations on her freedom, for example, her memory, her information processing capacity, and her perceptual powers. For the best heredity and environment in the world fall far short of the ideal we can imagine a maximally autonomous agent to possess.

Having said this, we cannot but be impressed with advances in knowledge and technology which dramatically enhance our powers and hence our (realistic) autonomy. We are gaining control over natural realities hitherto regarded as immutable. The borders of these limitations are constantly moving. We are not as stuck with what we are as we used to be. Momentous issues concerning the value of these expansions of the scope of autonomy and the right of individuals to take advantage of these advances will be addressed in Chapter 10. Since we cannot yet start all over from scratch, we must talk about the matter of contingency and will do so after clarifying a notion which has played a key role in most conceptions of autonomy, procedural independence.

Procedural independence

For realistic autonomy, what can procedural independence be in light of our dependence on others for education, training, and information? Even if we concede a large role for heredity in the development of our critical powers, who can deny the essential role of our parents, teachers, and peers? And how can we reply to the worry raised about the appeal to individual perspectives and distinctive modes of assimilation in light of the leveling effect of determination, that is, the recognition that these are just as dependent on origin as are the most routinized bits of behavior?

One can, first of all, count as a component of procedural independence the adoption of any rule or principle used in deliberation, regardless of origin, so long as one fully understands the grounds of its acceptance and now uses the rule or principle because one has this understanding. Perhaps I would never have reached this point with respect to modus ponens were it not for the training I received in Mr. Simpson's class. But what went on in Mr. Simpson's class counts only as a cause *in fieri* (a producing cause), and a partial one at that, and plays no sustaining role in my deliberative life. What matters to my status as an autonomous agent is the current disposition of the items, my present ability to understand, use, and, if necessary reject or modify the rule or principle. We may have acquired the rule by rote, but so long as it is sustained in virtue of its rational ground and in such a way that, were there good reason to reconsider its acceptability, that earlier learning experience would not inhibit a rational reevaluation, our autonomy is not diminished.

If Mr. Simpson had also taught me to affirm the consequent by appealing to natural intellectual weaknesses to which the young are liable, and if I have never reconsidered the matter, then I *am* dependent on him because there are no grounds for accepting this rule which might have independently led me to embrace it. I was led to this distortion by him and would not have been so led were it not for that classroom experience. If I *have* reconsidered as an adult and continue to endorse this rule, then the fault may lie in my rationality, in which case my procedural independence is intact. Or it may rather be that the failure to see the truth depends on the persistence of an idea or mode of thinking created in that initial classroom experience. If Mr. Simpson steered my thinking processes along certain lines which currently inhibit the adult ability to get the matter right, then I am dependent upon him. If he simply led me astray in such a way that the normal development of my rational powers would include a rethinking and a realignment along the right lines, then my independence depends on my *actually* getting on track again.

We want to extend the idea of independence to evaluations invoking rules and principles which are not universally accepted as true or correct as well as to individual desires and preference rankings which do not even purport to have objectivity. A person who uses modus ponens because he sees that it is true has broken from his origins in the way autonomy demands. But a person who invokes in decision making the rule of maximin or his preference for the movies of Luis Buñuel over those of Oliver Stone cannot appeal to truth.

We can attempt to advance the same strategy that worked so well for the "objective" examples. It matters little that the agent came by his commitments uncritically; what matters is the way he sustains them. If he has thought through his preference rankings in an independent way and is prepared to offer reasons for them, it does not undermine his current autonomy to learn that those reasons played no role in the etiology of his preferences. If he is currently responding to reasons, even if those reasons do not have the ultimate grounding that modus ponens has, he has disengaged himself from his origins. He prefers Buñuel to Stone in part because he rejects the exploitative and simplistic components of Stone's films. But he is open-minded about this assessment and would revise his views if the other side could produce good reasons.

Of course, as soon as we heave a sigh of relief at the recognition that an *implanted* rule can be *sustained* rationally, we are reminded that the very manner in which we are disposed to conduct a rational reevaluation or perhaps the motivation to undertake this scrutinization might themselves have been implanted. And even if the principles and rules invoked in the deliberative process are not derived from the demon, perhaps he has cleverly arranged the agent's psychological dispositions so that the input into the deliberations will guarantee that its rational unraveling will be in accordance with his fiendish plan.[9]

A fully autonomous agent, no matter how rational, cannot review all his canons at once. It is a truism that, in any specific theoretical *or* practical context, some elements must be taken for granted so that other, more problematic components can be submitted for reconsideration. Moreover, the rational agent does not preclude the submission to review in another context of those principles or beliefs that were unchallenged in a prior context. We must, therefore, distinguish two distinct sorts of cases of inculcation. Suppose a demon with a pessimistic outlook on the world implants the maximin rule for decision making under uncertainty in Homer and Bart. Neither is aware of the origin of his propensity to invoke this rule, and neither has occasion ever to undertake a critical examination of this procedure. But Bart is guilty only of the familiar charge that elements of his life have in fact gone unexamined because he has never found himself in a situation in which a challenge seemed to be called for. He is not as self-conscious as he might be, but he is fully disposed to submit maximin for review should the matter be brought to his attention. More importantly, the review would be conducted as objectively as is possible in light of the limitations of the subject matter, that is, given that the issue is not as "objective" as modus ponens. Homer, on the other hand, has been rationally disabled by the pessimistic demon; if he were to think about this rule, he could not be as objective as a rational agent can be expected to be about such issues. His thinking would continue to be distorted in the same way my thinking about affirming the consequent is if I cannot cast off that faulty picture acquired as a student. Thus, the demon has "interfered" with Bart's autonomy in the absolutely minimal way necessitated by Bart's membership in the human species. The demon's action simply reflects the fact that Bart cannot possess ideal autonomy. We shall look further at the implications of contingency, but we simply note now that that is all we are dealing with – contingency. We are certain of some ways and not others. In addition, the personal element in this causation is irrelevant. For both Homer and Bart, the demon could just as readily have been a gene. Homer's loss of autonomy results from there having been *some* cause of his current inability to submit the rule of maximin to a thorough assessment. It is that inability which constitutes his heteronomy.

Thus, the interjection of the specter of the fiendish oppressor at each stage is unnecessarily pessimistic. For the defender of autonomy wins this game since he need only require *at any level* that the agent be prepared to submit that level to rational scrutiny, not that he be prepared to submit all levels at once. If all is theoretically open for grabs and if each review can be conducted as rationally as the context permits, then the apprehension concerning clouded origins is in that way disabled. Although no one can be perfectly autonomous, some can be more autonomous than others. And these limitations are a function of the human epistemic situation, *not* of the activity of some demon.

Thus, independence shades off into rationality. The demand for independence reflects the concern to discard the possibly rickety ladder that may have enabled us to reach the roof in favor of the tools we now need for the job at hand.

Independence is not always secured once reasons have transcended their origins. There is an important difference in interpersonal relationships between reasons that are *discovered* and reasons that are *created*. If action on a certain reason R does not undermine autonomy, no further threat to autonomy arises from the fact that a counselor had discovered R and brought it to one's attention for consideration. Matters are different when one person provides a reason for action for another through manipulation, terror, extortion, and the like. In these cases, the dominating party has provided a reason by bringing one into existence.

Heteronomy is not always the result of action from reasons created by another. I might choose to dine with you this evening because you have cooked a splendid meal. When do such cases pose a threat to autonomy?

It has frequently been maintained that the difference between persuasion and manipulation or between a threat and an offer must be explicated normatively. Certain interpersonal transactions violate norms constitutive of human decency. It is admissible to attempt to persuade someone that he ought to be more charitable by pointing to the benefits his money could provide. It is inadmissible to tell him that failure to respond will result in incarceration in a cell with poisonous snakes. Whether or not someone is behaving independently, therefore, may depend on whether or not someone else is adhering to certain standards.

It is important to see that these considerations do not undermine the current effort to formulate a value-free conception of autonomy. First of all, even if my autonomy depends on normative matters, such as whether or not I am being treated with respect or whether or not unfair advantage is being taken of me, *my* decisions and actions may be taken without regard for principles or values. Second, the manner in which an improper intervention into my affairs undermines my autonomy may itself be capable of nonnormative characterization. The latter requires elaboration.

The simplest case arises when one party destroys the freedom of another by rendering him powerless. If I have a pathological fear of snakes, your threat to throw me into that snake-filled cell renders me powerless to refrain from writing a check to your favorite charity. My autonomy is nullified by the diminution of my freedom, *not* by your having acted improperly. This should be clear when it is recognized that this fear can arise in the absence of an intentional origin. My autonomy is just as diminished should my action result from the sight of a snake which just happens to wander into the neighborhood. This conclusion is supported as well by the consideration that your unethical behavior need not adversely affect autonomy at all; I may refuse to succumb to your threat by fighting back, or I may stoically accept the penalty of incarceration with snakes just to avoid having to make a charitable contribution.

In many cases, a person's substandard behavior arises from the use of deception. In certain instances of manipulation, in subliminal advertising, in lying, one person uses another for his own ends and fails, thereby, to display the respect owed that person. Deception permeates extended relationships which may overall be deeply satisfying. In marriage, when each partner comes to obtain intimate knowledge of the manner of response to diverse stimuli of the loved one, it is extremely tempting to use this knowledge in a manipulative way. A husband may undertake a strategy involving displays of helpfulness, flattery, and generosity in the knowledge that his wife's response to the discovery of the little red sports car in the garage will thereby be muted. (Examples like these show that any complex and extended human activity which may in general *exemplify* autonomy will contain instances of heteronomy.)

Since successful deception entails the concealment of relevant information, the deceived party is deprived of knowledge, a component of freedom. In this way, we again have a ready explanation of the loss of autonomy arising from improper treatment that does not require reference to the impropriety. The wife's ignorance of the reason for her unusually compliant attitude toward the new addition to the family reduces her autonomy, regardless of the explanation of the ignorance.

Deception is not the only way in which one person can adversely affect another's autonomy by disconnecting the person from the springs of his behavior. A person may threaten to withdraw love in order to generate a desired response, without necessarily intending to conceal his motivation. The manipulated party may respond accordingly, but may offer specious explanations because she is unable to confront her actual motivation, the fear that she will be deprived of love. Here, too, although the man is behaving contemptibly, the woman's loss of autonomy is grounded in general in her emotional deficits and in particular in her lack of insight into herself.

Most instances of unethical treatment do not involve the rendering of the aggrieved party powerless to respond contrary to the wishes of the villain. If I find the prospect of incarceration with poisonous snakes only highly unpalatable, my freedom$_p$ to retain my money and accept the penalty is not thwarted, even though my freedom$_v$ is, perhaps, lost. In any event, I have already posited these distinctions in recognition of the limited relevance of normative matters. Dependency relations between two human beings are simply a prominent way in which to activate these conditions.

Although it is relatively uncontroversial that autonomy requires procedural independence, what are we to say of the person who autonomously abandons his independence? That is, he freely and rationally decides, in an act exhibiting procedural independence, to live the rest of his life according to the whims of his guru or his mother or the Führer. Having chosen his life in accordance with the strictest requirements for *self-choice*, Dworkin would count this individual autonomous (1988: 22–33). Since the person is substantively dependent on someone else, Dworkin concludes that substantive independence is inessential to autonomy.

Unless we introduce temporal qualifications here, confusion results. For a truly substantively dependent agent has in fact *also* abandoned procedural independence. Under normal circumstances, if I decide to throw in my lot with the Moonies, I may retain my right to reconsider. In that case, although I am following orders, I am not substantively dependent in the relevant sense. We often subordinate ourselves to persons and institutions of authority when we believe it is appropriate. We lose no autonomy, however, when we are prepared to submit these decisions to rational review and to action that is appropriate in light of the results of the review. We *do* lose our autonomy, however, if we surrender our right or power to conduct these reviews. But then we are abandoning our substantive independence in the relevant sense *only* when we abandon procedural independence.

The notions can only be pried apart if we count the *earlier* procedurally independent decision to surrender substantive independence as the only thing that matters. But I would prefer to say that, through the abandonment of procedural independence (I will not make decisions for myself) *and* substantive independence (my guru will), the agent has made an autonomous decision to become heteronomous. He was autonomous, but is so no longer.

I believe that the feeling that autonomy should be construed so that autonomous commitments of the sort just described do not make one heteronomous rests on a failure to appreciate fully differences among types of commitments.

Almost all people who display the virtues of loyalty, friendship, trust, or fidelity do *not* turn into mindless automata in relation to these spheres of their lives. In eschewing certain forms of behavior, most sensible people leave open the option of changing their minds under extreme circumstances, even if they are not prepared to specify the nature of these circumstances in advance. As Socrates observed, we don't return a weapon to a friend who has gone mad; we don't lend money to our child to underwrite his plan to blow up the World Trade Center; we don't remain faithful to a woman when we discover that she has been deceiving and manipulating us for years. In choosing to subordinate ourselves to other people, or for that matter, to institutions, practices, or projects, we do *not* necessarily abandon our autonomy. Indeed, the depth of the tie is enhanced by the reaffirmation of the bond implicit in the *autonomous* refusal to consider deceiving a loved one. A husband who binds himself in this way to his wife, yet who retains the right of reconsideration under *extreme* circumstances is surely a superior exemplar of the marriage ideal than a groom who autonomously chooses to undergo neurosurgery so that he will be rendered physically incapable of deceit "until death do us part." Also, I need not suppose that the husband who retains the capacity for deceit actually ever reviews his options. He thinks and acts just like the neurologically incapacitated husband, but would notice an occasion for defection if it were to arise.

The power of review retained by an autonomous agent is compatible with the bona fide limits imposed by autonomously chosen relationships. I still cannot plan to steal my friend Willy's ladyfriend even though I can wonder whether it would be wise to continue the relationship. For, given the nature of friendship, a person who has autonomously chosen to be Willy's friend cannot, qua rational, count the attractiveness of Willy's ladyfriend as a sufficient reason for disloyalty to Willy. Were I disposed to think this way, I would never have been a real friend.

Thus, an agent who is autonomous at a certain time is both procedurally and substantively independent, although he may be substantively dependent in the harmless, autonomy-preserving manner of a person who relies on an expert or a counselor or who joins a highly structured organization to see if it will work for him.

In defense of the view that autonomy is procedural, not substantive, independence, Dworkin (1988: 21–33) points out that the fundamental value assigned by so many to autonomy precludes the account of it as substantive independence. For, since there is great diversity in the selection of our ideals, any substantive conception will undoubtedly not be shared by all persons. Not everyone admires or emulates the rugged individualist. Many persons, therefore, who have freely and thoughtfully adopted ideals will have to be counted as heteronomous on the substantive conception. And if autonomy is a basis of respect or a ground for counting one a member of the moral community, we will have to exclude such individuals. We will not be under an obligation to value them as ends, to treat them with respect, and to grant them equality of treatment. Since Dworkin accepts the link between autonomy and morality, he urges a thin conception of autonomy, one "that has no particular content, that emphasizes self-definition in abstraction from the self that is so defined" (1988: 30).

First of all, it is arguable that autonomy is the basis of moral community. Others have been offered: sentience, the possession of interests, rationality. But even if Dworkin is essentially right, and the basis of universal respect has something to do with autonomy, perhaps the relevant feature is the *potentiality* for autonomy. Alternatively, as Dworkin himself says:

Our notion of who we are, of self-identity, of being *this* person is linked to our capacity to find and re-fine oneself. The exercise of the capacity is what makes a life *mine*. And, if I am to recognize others as persons, as independent centers of consciousness, as *them*, then there is a requirement that I give weight to the way they define and value the world in deciding how I should act. (32)

Since a *truly* substantively dependent person refuses to exercise the capacity to "re-fine" himself, he has presumably then absolved me of the responsibility to recognize him as a person and to respect his wishes. After all, they are not really *his* wishes.

Thus, a person cannot surrender his procedural independence and retain his autonomy, even if the act of surrender is fully autonomous.

Contingency

One of the virtues of the conception of autonomy as critical competence is the way it appears to circumvent the free will worry. The libertarian requires that desires be chosen by an individual in order for that individual to claim ownership of the desires. But who cares how I came to be critically competent? I may bemoan the fact that I happen to prefer vanilla ice cream because of experiences over which I had no control, but I cannot bemoan the fact that I am rational for analogous reasons. I may not think it right to take *credit* for this result. But the fact that I am not praiseworthy does not mean that this trait is not a necessary ingredient of my freedom. I can change certain psychological structures which have evolved without my mature participation along lines which will improve them. So the fortuitous character of the origin of my desires recedes in importance as my critical reflection, whose fortuitous origin is equally irrelevant, does its work. The freedom acquired by a slave from his master is not tainted by dint of its origin.

One problem with this argument is that, as we shall see, decision making often requires the adoption of principles that are not rationally certifiable. People who are equally rational will make different decisions in identical situations because they differ in the extent to which they can tolerate risk and the degree to which they tend to be optimistic or pessimistic. So contingency reappears; how cautious or optimistic one is depends on developmental matters which took place before one had control over one's life. And one cannot here say that one attitude is clearly better than the contrary one.

So pure contingency creates special problems. Those fundamental desires, preferences, goals, and values we just have and in terms of which we base all our other decisions comprise a domain which either cannot be submitted to rational appraisal or just happens for many people not to be regarded as open to such treatment. Hence, the strategy we extended from the narrow domain of the clearly objective to the wider domain of the rationally defensible won't work. Moreover, many of our most important links to the world belong here: occupation, religion, personal relationships, and life style.

And since most of us are not prepared to submit many of these important matters to critical scrutiny, we cannot establish procedural independence. Reason plays *some* role, to be sure. Many people *abandon* religions, occupations, and spouses for good reason. And we must continue to insist that the more autonomous an agent is, the more disposed he is to submit for periodic review his preferences, propensities, character traits, and components of personality. But the principal reason given for maintaining or adopting many values, relationships, or activities is a nonrational preference or inclination grounded in the contingency of one's development. There are many noble professions I might have chosen; I happen to like being a philosopher. Will is my friend because I just like being around people like him. I married Barbara in part because I am attracted to lively, energetic people. (My friend Norbert prefers phlegmatic types.) I am committed to the Jewish people and their ideals because I am a Jew. Sally is committed to the ideals of Catholicism because she grew up as a Catholic. Lenox is a nice place to live because I find the cultural resources stimulating. My friend Etan prefers a more rugged environment. I am a Knick fan because I grew up in New York City; John likes the Celtics.

It is true that these *non*rational determinants do not have to interfere with one's rationality (see Wolf 1990: 146). A religious commitment may blind one to the truth and may prevent one from seeing fairly, but many preferences are acknowledged as just that and do not hinder one's ability to appreciate human differences and treat people without prejudice. Nonetheless, if the issue is autonomy and, more specifically, procedural independence, it is undeniable that these elements create a prima facie problem. They are an essential component of any life and, therefore, of the life of a realistically autonomous person. Moreover, they are the source of much that gives that life meaning, in part because of the powerful human drive toward individuality. For, if reason is what we share, nonrational determinants are what distinguish us from one another.

The libertarian typically seeks refuge in an extracausal domain in which the self, when it is able, transcends these limits. Compatibilities seek accounts of self-determination which permit the agent to view these elements as self-chosen in spite of their origins. One well-known effort of this nature bids us to view these components as compatible with autonomy just in case the agent wholeheartedly identifies with them.

One cannot, however, evade the following truth. Imagine identical twins growing up in virtually identical ways in Boston. Selma and Thelma are Catholics and Celtic rooters; but one day, Selma mysteriously acquires the power to change her loyalty to her religion and to her basketball team. She may simply press a button and wake up the next day, a Congregationalist and a Trail Blazer fan. Since Thelma is stuck with her religion and her team, it is undeniable that Selma has acquired a power which confers greater freedom on her than that possessed by Thelma.

We suppose, of course, that the changes are genuine, that, were Selma to press the button, she would find herself *really* wanting the Trail Blazers to beat the Celtics and *really* not attracted to the mysteries of the Church, and so on.

It is worth noticing that the realization of this model of autonomy in the real world is paradoxical in ways I have already mentioned. Just as our ideally autonomous agent was seriously bound by the desires he autonomously formed, so may it be that a serious Catholic or Celtic fan is barred from displaying a power such as Selma's. For a commitment to Catholicism may, of course, be eroded, but it cannot be turned on and off, like a preference for dress style. In fact, it may be seriously argued that the very power, even left undisplayed, is impossible. One is not a real Celtic fan if one *can* be a Celtic fan every even numbered day and a Trail Blazer fan on the odd numbered days.

This objection applies more readily to more ordinary powers to change, that is, powers to change one's religious orientation by exploring the differences between the religions, talking with people whose views one respects and reflecting upon these conversations, and so on. For if a person is capable of shifting back and forth in this *active* way, the changes are a more serious indication of her underlying commitments and reveal herself to be a fickle person, one not really dedicated to Catholicism or the Celtics.

Psychologically, Selma might find the passive power, that is, the power to change by pressing a button, quite disturbing. It is important to human beings, as we have noted, that some commitments be very difficult to erase. And the deeper her commitment, the more undesirable these changes would appear to Selma. (Suppose that Selma has not taken these alternatives very seriously.) But the more central reason Selma should be disturbed is that, even if she has just flirted with such changes, she would certainly feel more autonomous if she undertook to *initiate* an exploration into the merits of such deep transformations. For, if Selma changes by pressing a button, she is totally passive. She has the power to bring it about that she ends up a Congregationalist. That is very different from the active power to convert. Ironically, therefore, the passive power *preserves* the intractable character of the religious bond. For it is logically conceivable that a person exercising this power take on the depth of commitment of a religious zealot. It is just that she takes on a new commitment daily. In any case, Selma is disturbed more about the loss of active control than she is about her fickleness. For, under the passive power, her fickleness, unlike that of one who comes to be convinced by a different television preacher each day, is only apparent.

The active power is indicative of greater autonomy if it is grounded in greater rational powers. An agent who is able to acknowledge the reasons to change his religion is more rational than one who cannot do so. Thus, the power which enhances autonomy is not the power to change as such, but more precisely the power to undertake a review which would result in change if reason required it. Even if one embraces Catholicism in a wholehearted way, then *if* it can be shown that the commitment to Catholicism is autonomous, the definitiveness of that commitment should not automatically make one a slave.

Let us not deny the obvious. If Selma is independently uncomfortable with her Catholicism, then the acquisition of this (passive) power is a boon to her autonomy. For she is now in a better position to express her self. She would be in an even stronger position if she could bring about these changes on her own, that is, through rational reappraisal. We can increase our autonomy through autonomous behavior or through drugs, psychotherapy, and the like. That Selma is frightened by the loss of control she undergoes in the aftermath of the button pressing does not imply that she does not end up with greater autonomy. The air of paradox arises from a failure to distinguish the heteronomy of the means from the autonomy of the end.

Suppose, on the other hand, that Selma is totally content with Catholicism and the Celtics. Even if Selma's freedom is enhanced by the addition of this power, the further conclusion that her autonomy is also enhanced follows only on the assumption that her devotion to these institutions is *not* wholehearted and irrevocable. The power to choose Congregationalism is important to her autonomy only if the exercise of this power is grounded in a point of view which potentially expresses her true self. But if she has not the slightest inkling to become a Congregationalist, how does the power to become one confer greater autonomy on her? The assumption must be that her current dedication is self-limiting. Her autonomy is increased by the addition of this power because she is now free to define herself from a wider range of genuinely feasible options.

In Chapter 2, I claimed that an agent retains her autonomy in a conflict situation if the effective desire originates in the self. Thus, even if Selma is mildly disposed to flirt with Congregationalism, she retains her autonomy once she reaffirms her Catholic convictions should the latter be heartfelt. Although I would not withdraw this claim – I cannot see that Selma is disadvantaged when her desire for Thai food remains unfulfilled by dint of her free decision to satisfy her stronger desire for sushi – I suppose that, from some sort of ideal perspective, Ted is a notch up on the autonomy ladder if he is identical to Fred except that Ted is able and Fred is not to satisfy a trivial desire each has. Our acknowledgment of the significance of real autonomy along with the fact that, except for ideal autonomy, autonomy is always a matter of degree should make us skeptical of the salience of these reflections. As I said in Chapter 2, an agent can possess virtually full autonomy even if intellect and will are not perfectly aligned, and he consequently experiences some conflict or temptation.

Selma's embrace of Catholicism is unlike her embrace of modus ponens. Even if she is a rational agent and regularly submits all her preferences, including religious ones, to a careful review, the results of this review rest in part on the contingency of her upbringing. To grow is to be confined. Moreover, assuming that her dedication to Catholicism is not irrationally grounded, then we cannot assimilate her situation to that of mine in the case of the adoption of an invalid argument form. My current infirmity, resulting from a peculiar incident in Mr. Simpson's class the effects of which I cannot shake, is an instance of heteronomy because of the limitation imposed by this episode on my rationality. My development has been limited not just in the way in which *any* process or mechanism is limited. Since the earlier stages of a process determine the later ones, the unfolding of any process brings with it the reduction of possibilities. This is true of the development of logical powers as well as the formation of religious attitudes and beliefs. The crucial difference is that my rationality and, therefore, my autonomy, has been impaired and Selma's has not.

The difference in the impact on autonomy is *not* based on the manner of human involvement in the etiology. Why should it matter whether Selma's attitude is the result of a supportive family, a manipulative priest, or a nonpersonal attraction to the pomp and circumstance of the religion? My thought processes can be distorted by my enemy or by my gout.

Consider again Laura, the woman whose childhood was highly confined and narrow.[10] In order to identify the specific contribution of her background, over and above any adverse effects on her rationality, to heteronomy, we supposed that Laura does submit her life to rational scrutiny. The problems are (1) that she remains ignorant of so much that would be relevant to the formation of attitudes, values, and aspirations, and (2) that the input into her practical deliberations is derived from such narrow sources. She can't imagine why anyone in her shoes would want to be other than a clerk in the general store in the village by the sea. Her evenings are spent watching a little TV and on weekends she always visits her sick mother, with whom she knits and gossips. She is not attracted to music, literature, deep personal relationships, travel, social causes, or education.

We can see her ignorance as a barrier to her autonomy. For suppose exposure to other ways of life reveals, promptly and dramatically, a latent desire to expand her horizons. We may then rightly see her previous existence as heteronomous in spite of the absence of discontent. For her decisions had been only partly reflecting her self. There was an unfulfilled side to her nature even she was ignorant of which she would have chosen to realize if only she had known better.

Suppose, on the other hand, that new inputs change nothing. Laura goes to the big city, meets new people, reads books, and so on, but continues to find her life in the village quite fine as is. She understands that the label of narrowness used by a woman who told her something about consciousness raising is a sort of charge against her, but she thinks her life is as full as it should be.

The difficulty this sort of example raises is that, whereas we can readily see how certain environments (or demons) are *freedom*-limiting because of the way they *currently* function to incapacitate the agent, we cannot see how Laura's environment is *autonomy*-limiting unless we can see her self as fuller than she does. We must suppose that her development has distorted or suppressed natural impulses. And we must address this question with Berlin's fears ever before us; we must, that is, not impose on Laura a self that expresses *our* views of what she really should be. We must take care not to impose our models of flourishing unless we abandon a central enterprise of this book, to wit, to define autonomy in a value-free way.

We must reserve final judgment on Laura until I disclose a crucial dimension of autonomy in Chapter 8 which will be the basis of an ultimate verdict concerning her autonomy. The verdict itself will be delivered in Chapter 9 once I make a limited concession to the role of origins. We will at that point distinguish the view of autonomy taken in this book from those which demand a more serious role for personal history or etiology.

Principles of rationality

We have made claims about rationality and its connection to autonomy without advancing a view about the actual principles a rational agent should invoke in reasoning and decision making. Indeed, to do so would be to write a different book. Clearly, many of the issues confronting decision theory have little or no bearing on the conditions of autonomy or freedom. And, in a general way we have justified the connection of the two ideas by defending the need of an autonomous agent to establish her independence by evaluating beliefs and values in a critically competent fashion. Moreover, agents like us, possessed of desires, including the higher-order desire to secure a preponderance of our first-order desires, will be frustrated and ineffective on the whole if we fail to adhere to the standard rules of inference. Even if one occasionally, even frequently, flouts the principles of rationality, extensive violations are tantamount to self-disintegration.

Much energy has been expended on strengthening the instrumental conception of rationality. Although it is reasonable to require of a rational agent that the beliefs and desires which render his action rational actually play a role in determining or sustaining that action,[11] many would like in addition to find a way to prove that Hume was wrong when he judged reason utterly impotent at passing judgment on the rationality of our ultimate ends. We do, after all, abandon ultimate ends and look back on earlier goals as shallow, immature, or silly. If we refuse to challenge the intrinsic worthiness of some selected end, that is, as Dewey said, the way it is in *that* context at *that* stage of life or growth. Tomorrow it may be otherwise. No end is immune to challenge at some time or another.

But the question remains: if we come upon an agent with abhorrent, foolish, or outrageous desires, is there a rational procedure which can convince him to abandon those desires other than by showing him that they are based on false or improbable beliefs or that their pursuit would interfere with other goals of his?

Current accounts of rationality do not hold a great deal of promise in this regard. According to many, a rational assessment must be done in a dispassionate, informed, and vivid manner (Darwall 1983: 94–100; Brandt 1990). The rational outcome is a matter then of empirical discovery. Desires which survive this process of appraisal cannot be judged irrational, no matter how bizarre they seem to be. If vivid, informed reflection on a fact fails to cause a psychological change, there is no independent criterion of relevance which would permit us to say that the facts which are the objects of reflection are *semantically* relevant to a change even though they are in this case not *causally* relevant to one.

Advocates of this sort of account do not suppose that human nature is sufficiently uniform so that we may expect to eliminate all instances of the bizarre and the abhorrent by this procedure. Perhaps then we need additional conditions. We may anyway for independent reasons since, as Alan Gibbard (1983) observes, this approach suffers from the false assumption that "we are reliable transformers of vivid realizations into rational desires" (206). If an honest civil servant who refuses all bribes would succumb to temptation should he vividly reflect on the pleasures made available by dishonesty, the causal account counterintuitively judges the dishonest act the rational one. There are people who are better off *not* thinking too vividly about suicide.

I shall later argue that behavior that strikes us as contrary to reason is often a failure of a condition called "objectivity."[12] Since objectivity is a component of autonomy, we can often establish a judgment of heteronomy in a way that bypasses the question of the agent's rationality. This result is desirable for theories of rationality provide limited payoffs in this domain.

For example, in recognition of the deficiencies of the causal approach to rationality, Robert Audi (1985) proposes a condition of well-groundedness, an epistemic analogue of justified belief. Whereas Richard Brandt, unlike the instrumentalists, demanded at least that ultimate desires meet the test of information saturation and cognitive psychotherapy,

Audi wants to add the demand that intrinsic desires and valuations originate in relevant experiences such as the experience of the characteristics which make an object or activity valuable.

Audi rightly notes that the objective grounding of desires does not guarantee the exclusion of the bizarre, for whatever one finds pleasure in thereby contains a characteristic valuable to that person. Thus, in spite of the demand that rational desires be grounded in the world, the ultimacy of individual authority is preserved. Although our discussion of contingency suggests agreement with Audi on this score, his condition does not rule out those aberrant cases that happen also to be ones of heteronomy. For, on Audi's view, the desires of a neurotic which lead him to self-destructive behavior are well-grounded. It is satisfying to please your father, assuage guilt feelings, or relieve the tension caused by the unresolved conflicts of childhood. Now, it may well be that Audi is able to judge the neurotic irrational in virtue of *other* conditions of rationality, perhaps the requirement that one seek to maximize total satisfaction (or something of this sort), and may, therefore, agree that well-groundedness of desire does not in itself imply autonomy. In any case, I shall later argue that this neurotic may be deficient in objectivity, a component of autonomy not included under current accounts of rationality.

Autonomous irrationality

Some philosophers do not understand why autonomy has anything to do with rationality (see Crocker 1980: 36–43). I have identified bona fide reasons to link these notions. But I do not see that an autonomous agent need be *as* rational as most criteria of rationality demand. There are constraints on autonomous agents that rational agents are exempt from and vice-versa.

For example, if I am an adventurous sort, I may seek a novel and unfamiliar experience, ignorant of the likelihood of its satisfying me. If I know it is not dangerous, I am perhaps not irrational; in the light of my ignorance, however, I am not rational either. I do not think that autonomous agents must be *so* rational that they compromise their autonomy when they choose ungrounded actions, such as this one, which are neither rational nor irrational. If I choose autonomously to lead an adventurous life or if I just happen to be that way and am pleased about it, there is no reason to deny the autonomy of an instantiation of this policy.

Certain instances of tenacity are actually cases of autonomous *irrationality*. Many great achievements have been effected by irrational persons who ignored the odds against success. It was quite unreasonable for Pasteur, partially paralyzed as the result of a brain stroke, to jeopardize his health further by his tireless efforts to discover a vaccine for rabies. Yet it would be a mistake to deny autonomy to Pasteur on this basis even had he failed.

Ironically, Pasteur may have maximized expected utility and thereby passed this familiar test of rationality. For this test does not judge the rationality of (1) those preferences for gambles which permit us to construct interval scales from his preference ordering or (2) his assignments of probability to outcomes. Thus, Pasteur maximizes expected utility relative to the assignments of "irrationally" low values to all the alternatives to the creation of a vaccine for rabies and the assignment of an "irrationally" high estimate of the probability of success. There are various ways an agent can be irrational. He can invoke principles beyond expected utility theory, such as those of prospect theory, which lead to clear violations of rationality (Kahneman and Tversky 1990: 154–5); or he can, like Pasteur, adhere to expected utility theory, but grossly misrepresent or ignore objective probabilities (Allais 1990: 115).

Nonetheless, the charge of heteronomy applied to a particular decision of a tenacious person has a false ring, especially when he succeeds, because the reasons autonomous agents should be rational are inherently general. If, for example, adherence to rational principles is the preferred policy because it is more likely than any other to lead to success and is the best way to avoid clearly unacceptable outcomes, for example, becoming a "money pump," then one can identify a violation of rationality independent of outcome. That is, one can be irrational and luckily successful. But if that success pertains to a goal, adopted by an emotionally healthy individual, which has been independently crafted and has served to unify the personality and mobilize all its resources, the failure of rationality may not offset the autonomy of this particular choice and action. Since rationality, with its general thrust, is more important to dispositional than to occurrent autonomy, occasional breaches which are not indicative of a general breakdown of rationality and which preserve other elements of autonomy are permitted.[13]

Autonomy and omniscience

If it is a priori odd that an autonomous agent is permitted a certain amount of irrationality, it is even odder to suppose that enhanced freedom can *reduce* one's autonomy. Yet freedom includes knowledge, and there is an argument that too much knowledge is a dangerous thing, at least in terms of its effects on autonomy.

The argument in one form or another has been frequently made. (See Ginet 1962; Shackle 1958; Schick 1979; Levi 1986: 53–67; and Levi 1994.) If I know enough about myself and the world, I will be able to predict how I will choose in a decision-making situation I know I shall confront in the future. For example, if I know, or even just believe, that I will be faced with a set of options O_1, O_2, ... , O_n determinate enough to permit application of a decision-making policy with a unique outcome in each case, and if I possess all relevant information needed to apply the policy, then, if I am "deductively thorough" (Schick 1979: 240), I will believe the deductive consequences of my beliefs, in this case, say, that I will choose

O_1. And if, to use Schick's language again, I am "belief retentive," I will retain this belief until the moment of choice. But the presence of this belief precludes my choosing among the options. "Since A *believes* that he will do x, he cannot ask himself whether he will" (Schick 1979: 241). So I cannot predict a *choice*.

If the prediction rests upon premises which include particular information about the predictor's beliefs, preferences, and policies, then we are forced to accept the somewhat paradoxical conclusion that choice is incompatible with self-omniscience. I accepted that conclusion in response to Ginet's version of the conundrum (Berofsky 1964) and Schick agrees.

Levi's (1986: 61–4) discussion of the problem is governed by his concern to retain principles of rationality as norms for self-criticism. Since norms are useful only if they lack vacuity, we must ensure against self-omniscience for, as we have seen, that precludes genuine choice. On Levi's scheme, an agent who can deduce how he will choose reduces the set of feasible options – those to which the principles of choice are supposed to be applied – to the admissible options, that is, those which are permitted by his principles of choice, and thereby renders the principles useless. The agent must, therefore, abandon some assumption needed to derive the conclusion as to her choice and, since Levi's purposes require the retention of principles of rationality, he suggests that the agent abandon the assumption that she will act rationally at the moment of choice. Although the derivation can be blocked just as readily by abandoning assumptions about her applicable beliefs and values or assumptions about which options are feasible, the abandonment of the assumption that she will pursue the rational policy when the time of decision arrives permits the retention of information crucial to decision making.

Full self-knowledge of the information required to determine admissibility is a regulative ideal for deliberation before the moment of choice.... Much activity in deliberation involves calculation so as to identify the assumptions to which the deliberating agent is tacitly or implicitly committed (Levi 1986: 63–4).

These reflections warrant the inclusion of information about beliefs and values which permit a deliberating agent to determine admissibility. And since decision making is the reduction of the feasible options to the admissible ones, we ought also to know what the feasible options are. But we do not require for successful deliberation the assumption that the agent will at the moment of choice select an option determined to be admissible.

The model of deliberation we are being offered, then, is an ideal one. For not only do people in fact fall short of full self-knowledge; they also do not always use rational principles of decision making (on any reasonable conception of rationality). But the impossibility of first-person prediction of choice is a phenomenon which applies just as much to agents who are irrational. A person who happens to be irrational or who explicitly disavows principles of rationality and does not, therefore, care to use them in self-criticism is just as unable to predict his choice as one who is rational. For the puzzle arises in virtue of the agent's adoption of *any* decision-making procedure which permits a unique outcome based upon the relevant information at his disposal, for example, his beliefs, preferences, and values. The problem is created, as Schick (1979: 230 40) notes, by the ability of the agent to predict his own decision, whether he does so by the invocation of rational *or* irrational principles of decision making.

It is, therefore, misleading to represent this problem as one that pertains particularly to *rational* choice. An irrational agent's principles of choice are also vacuous under the assumption of self-omniscience, although he may know that he will not act rationally. Yet Levi can generalize his solution if he describes the assumption he would abandon more generally, to wit, as the assumption that the agent will not choose from the admissible options.[14] For an irrational agent's admissible options are simply the ones which are permitted by his principles of choice, no matter how irrational they may be. And he needs his principles to make decisions as much as we rational folk do.[15]

Irrationality aside, it must be noted that deliberation is still possible if we imagine that some element of self-knowledge other than the knowledge that one will choose an admissible option be abandoned. After all, almost every real decision-making situation occurs in the absence of some relevant information about one's own beliefs or values. Such decisions are often wise, even if they are not perfectly rational. Levi's central point, then, is that *effective* deliberation is hampered by this sort of ignorance, but not by ignorance concerning how one will choose. So a perfectly effective deliberator, whether his principles are rational or not, will lack some self-knowledge, but not knowledge that is relevant to deliberation.

The application of Levi's solution to autonomous agents, as we have characterized them, dissolves this conundrum for this group. I have insisted that autonomous agents are basically rational and possessed of knowledge bearing on their decisions. They may, thus, possess the principles, beliefs, and values which will inhibit effective decision making should they also know or believe that they will act on their choices when the moment of decision arrives. But since autonomous agents need not be omniscient, we do not have to suppose that they know they will choose rationally. They do not need this belief to deliberate rationally or effectively and they do not need this belief to *be* rational, for there is a difference between being rational and knowing that one is rational. So "perfect" freedom per se is not incompatible with effective deliberation or perfect autonomy of choice for perfect freedom demands all *relevant* knowledge, not omniscience. We may thus resume our reflections without fear of paradox.

7
Rationality, values, and integrity

We turn finally to the role of values in rational decision making.

It is well known that theorists disagree on the principles a rational agent must invoke when making decisions under uncertainty. One might try to assimilate such situations to ones of decision making under risk and recommend the maximization of expected utility, or one might invoke minimax, maximax, Hurwicz's variant of the latter, or the strategy of minimizing maximum regret. It is commonly supposed that reason per se does not dictate this decision, in which case rational agents are obliged to adopt principles grounded extrarationally. If some such principles are associated with values, then rational agents, all of whom must confront decision making under uncertainty at one time or another, must have values, although these values cannot be derived from the assumption of rationality.

Now the term "value" is used so widely that even these general methodological principles may be said to reflect values. The maximin rule expresses the value of conservatism or caution, the maximax rule that of optimism. If the term "value" is to be stretched this far, it is indeed impossible for any but the most seriously disturbed psychotics to proceed through life without values. The thesis we would then be examining would be reduced to triviality. It behooves us then to retain the conception of value advanced by the Evaluation Conception. One may adopt a rule for decision making under uncertainty which expresses an inclination toward risk taking without deeming the life of a gambler intrinsically worthwhile.

Although I reject this facile manner of importing values into rational decision making, there are more serious arguments for the necessity of values on the part of rational decision makers. For example, we must consider the case that value-free deliberators are so impoverished that we can barely recognize them as models for the deliberative process of normal humans. We, thus, distinguish these appeals from the distinct set of arguments which attempt to extract values from the concept of rationality itself.

From the point of view of formal decision theory, a rational agent is neither precluded from undertaking a rational evaluation of preferences nor required to submit his preferences for the sorts of scrutiny demanded by the Evaluation Conception. Nonetheless, since the theory requires preferences to be transitive, and people's preferences often seem to be intransitive, then it must be supposed that people are being irrational when they make intransitive choices. Hence, to get preferences in a usable form, they must be submitted to rational criticism (see Darwall 1983: 67–73).

We may then suppose that either the preferences of our rational and autonomous agent are transitive and satisfy any other formal requirements of decision theory or that occasional minor adjustments do not require personal evaluations of the sort demanded by the Evaluation Conception. We want now to see if a person meeting these and all other reasonable requirements on rationality can be value-free in accordance with this conception.

Although we earlier conceded to rational, autonomous agents the freedom to flout rationality on occasion, since the thrust of the following discussion is negative, it can only enhance my case to suppose that an autonomous agent must *always* be rational. For we wish to reject the inferences some draw from this, in particular, inferences concerning the extent to which such agents are required (by reason) to adopt certain values, including morality itself.

The rationality of altruism: D. Gauthier and S. Darwall

Many philosophers have attempted to improve on Kant's celebrated efforts to derive morality from rationality. Some of these efforts are guided by the thought that the most powerful sort of derivation would be one whose starting point assumes an absolutely uncontroversial conception of reason. Thus, we are asked to picture an individual agent who initially acknowledges as a reason for action only an expected personal benefit. Unless one wishes, in the manner of Kant, to isolate practical reason in the noumenal realm, no one can object to instrumental reason as at least *part* of a unified rational faculty. Disputes arise when it is just taken for granted that rationality occasionally dictates action whose expected outcomes benefit others at the expense of the agent. A derivation of morality from rationality which eschews such question-begging assumptions would then be formidable, and we turn then to efforts of this nature. (I cannot hope to canvas all interesting proposals for a rationally grounded morality. There have, of course, been a variety of such efforts, e.g., those of Kurt Baier [1958], Thomas Nagel [1970], and Alan Gewirth (1978); the difficulties in their formulations have been cited by others.)

The structure of Gauthier's (1986) impressive argument is highly complex, and I can only offer a conscientious effort at a simplified reconstruction of that portion of it which is relevant to the point I wish to make.

Gauthier sees morality arising out of agreements voluntarily entered into by rational agents who find that the unfettered pursuit of self-interest by all is counterproductive. If the world were a perfectly competitive market, one in which Adam Smith's invisible hand ensures an optimal outcome for all market transactions, then each person's pursuit of individual gain would result in outcomes for each which can only be bettered at the expense of someone else. Morality is required precisely because the world is not like this.

The prevalence of situations with the structure of the Prisoner's Dilemma (PD) also reveals the limits of a world of individual maximizers. To fix our ideas, let us recall the payoffs in the Prisoner's Dilemma case. Suppose that Dave and his friend, after having been arrested for a crime, are each told the following: If you confess and your partner refuses to, you will receive only 1 year in prison, while your partner will get 10. If neither confesses, each will be convicted on a lesser charge and spend 2 years in prison. If both confess, the sentence will be 5 years. Here are the options, with Dave's on the left.

		Friend	
		confess	**do not confess**
Dave	**confess**	(a) 5, 5	(c) 1, 10
	do not confess	(b) 10, 1	(d) 2, 2

The rational strategy for a participant in a Prisoner's Dilemma who seeks to maximize his expected utility results in a nonoptimal outcome. Each would select (a), reasoning that he would be better off regardless of the other's decision. Had the participants cooperated with one another, they would have achieved an alternative outcome which is better for *every* one, namely, (d). Cooperation, or the adoption of joint strategies, permits benefits unavailable to the loner.

Thus, rational agents are induced to the bargaining table to consider the formulation of agreements that would improve upon the current state of nature, that is, agreements that would result in cooperative arrangements which at least ensure optimality. In order to beg no questions, we must suppose that the bargainers' rationality is constituted by pure self-interest, that each participant prior to the creation of a contract is concerned only to maximize her expected utility. Hence, if we succeed in showing that a rational agent can emerge a cooperator, she must have undergone a fundamental change at the bargaining table; for there, her behavior is purely utility maximizing.

How can it be rational for a purely self-interested agent to become a cooperator? First of all, an agent must expect from cooperation a utility at least equal to what she would expect from noncooperative interaction. Thus, it is to her interest not to drive others from the table or to be excluded from the table herself. These considerations will limit the demands she can make for her share of the surplus benefits cooperation is expected to secure. Since concessions must then be made, we demand that they be made by the person with a lesser relative concession. Gauthier then advances a principle, minimax relative concession, which limits outcomes to those in which the maximum relative concession is as small as possible. Rational bargainers adhere to this principle in forming a joint strategy which affords each person expected utilities governed by the principle. Moreover, it is rational for one who has agreed to this principle to conduct his affairs in accordance with it, that is, to forego individual utility maximization for the optimal outcome determined by the principle of minimax relative concession.

Gauthier supposes, and his critics generally agree (see, for example, Campbell, 1988) that the more serious problem he confronts is the rationality of compliance. Even if we can get a rational agent to agree to constraint by exhibiting the benefits of cooperation, how can we keep one who began as an individual utility maximizer in line once he finds himself in a situation in which he can revert to form and resume free riding and exploitation? If he can gain a benefit from breaking his agreement, what is to prevent him rationally from doing so?

Of course, we can imagine or create social arrangements which, through sanctions such as punishment, the withdrawal of benefits acquired through violation of the agreement, or the exclusion of the person from subsequent participation in the venture which has secured to him the special fruits of cooperation, severely limit the discrepancy between the behavior of a "straightforward maximizer" and that of a "constrained maximizer," that is, one who constrains his pursuit of individual utility by adhering to the joint strategy to which he has agreed.

Although the constrained maximizer, motivated by the increased benefits of cooperation over universal noncooperation, exercises constraint only if he expects others to do likewise, situations requiring genuine self-sacrifice will sometimes be required. Thus, he, rather than the straightforward maximizer who happens to act morally, but is actually motivated by self-interest, is the prototype for the moral agent. The straightforward maximizer returns money which does not belong to him because he would otherwise be penalized or because he would lose the benefits accrued from the trust others place in him. The constrained maximizer returns money because he has agreed to participate in a practice he expected would benefit him and is now disposed to act on the strategy dictated by the agreement, assuming he expects others to comply as well, even if he could retain the money and suffer no adverse indirect consequences from doing so. From this strain, the fully moral agent will emerge.

Is constrained maximization (CM) rational? Gauthier concedes that it is pointless to defend the rationality of CM on the assumption of transparency, that is, universal knowledge of the disposition of each person. For transparent straightforward maximizers will suffer from the responses of the community to their imminent defections and associated deceptions. Hence, the overall benefits of CM outweigh the occasional sacrifices which must be endured in order to prevent social ostracism and worse.

CM becomes the prudent policy for a straightforward maximizer bedeviled with a penchant for self-disclosure. Gauthier realizes that this sort of victory for his case would be pyrrhic. For those who, from Plato on, have sought a rational reply to the case for the pursuit of pure self-interest, have conceded that the real issue is posed by the perfectly deceptive individual utility maximizer.

Yet Gauthier attempts to salvage this sort of strategy by upholding the rationality of CM on the more realistic assumption of translucency, a condition between transparency and opaqueness, that is, complete ignorance of the dispositions of others. There follows a complicated and conditional defense of CM, resting on facts such as: (1) the more constrained maximizers there are, the greater the risk of noncooperation and exploitation any one of them can assume; (2) constrained maximizers must be disposed to exclude straightforward maximizers from the benefits of cooperation; and (3) constrained maximizers must cultivate the ability to detect insincere straightforward maximizers.

The obvious response to this line is: "Yes, but what if the special conditions for successful straightforward maximization obtain?" We have not really moved significantly from the transparency case. We have simply learned that it is harder than we thought to be a truly successful devotee of SM. At this point, Gauthier shifts to his real argument.

The example that is supposed to create this difficulty is that of one who has rationally contracted to cooperate, but constantly seeks occasions to violate the agreement. Now in a rational resolution of the bargaining problem, the agent, having reached a joint strategy in accordance with the principle of minimax relative concession, is thereby constrained in his pursuit of individual utility. He thus forms a disposition to CM. Yet his subsequent attitude in the example under consideration reveals that he has not actually formed the disposition to CM at all.

Only the person truly disposed to honesty and justice may expect fully to realize their benefits, for only such a person may rationally be admitted to those mutually beneficial arrangements ... that rest on honesty and justice, on voluntary compliance. But such a person is not able, given her disposition, to take advantage of the "exceptions"; she rightly judges such conduct irrational. (1986: 182)

A choice is rational if and only if it expresses a rational *disposition* to choose. CM is rational because one who is so disposed will reap the benefits of inclusion in a cooperative strategy. Hence, an action which expresses this disposition is rational even if it does not maximize expected utility. We may then charge the person ever on the alert for opportunities for defection with irrationality; he lacks the rational disposition and, therefore, does not make rational choices.

Gauthier's critics have challenged the assumption that the primary loci of rationality are dispositions to choose rather than individual choices. I shall not adopt this strategy for I believe that it was never rational for the person participating in the bargaining process to become disposed to CM in the first place.

To see this, let us retrace our steps. Rational agents dismayed by the outcomes of individual strategies of straightforward maximization are led to see that cooperation can yield improved outcomes, that optimization can be achieved under conditions of universal cooperation.

One of these individuals is Devious Dave, a brilliant and scheming individual maximizer who is trained in the art of deception and practices it whenever it is to his advantage to do so. Since the members of Dave's community are unaware of his uncurable propensity to exploitation, they ingenuously invite him to the bargaining table.

Although Dave sees the advantages cooperation furnishes him, he realizes that the bargaining situation itself provides an opportunity to achieve an outcome for him that is even better than the one formulated in accordance with the principle of minimax relative concession. He realizes that the concerns which have led his neighbors to consider the adoption of joint strategies to improve their lot provide a unique opportunity to reap more than his fair share of the fruits of cooperation. He, therefore, takes his place at the table, prepared to behave just like the others. He will act as if he is making concessions in the hope that others will in fact do so. He will acknowledge the force that arguments demanding concession have even to pure individual maximizers, but will privately retain the policy of straightforward maximization. In the evening, after a full day of haggling, while the other participants relax, Devious Dave secretly takes courses in advanced methods of deception.

Actually, Dave would benefit from the respites taken by the others even more than they do, for the psychological demands on him are great. The others, who, we shall suppose, are sincere, proceed singlemindedly. For example, they do not make excessive demands for fear of inducing a breakdown in negotiations. Dave does the same thing, except that his public affirmations are always superseded by private thoughts, in this case the thought "I will do everything I can to get more than my fair share, but will say otherwise to induce others to retain the cooperative spirit I will someday be able to exploit."

This is not to say that Dave is not committed to a solution to the bargaining problem which secures optimality. Look again at the PD situation. Outcomes (b), (c), and (d) are all optimal. For in each of these cases, it is impossible to improve one's lot without adverse effect on the other. Outcome (d) can be achieved by a cooperative endeavor and is to be preferred by all to the outcome which is arrived at in the state of nature, (a). But for Dave, (c) would be even better than (d); so that is the goal he sets himself. He is delighted that Friend is prepared to cooperate so as to permit the exploitation hitherto unavailable.

Dave may not be able to pull it off. After all, it will be difficult for Friend to be kept in the dark as he languishes in prison for 10 years. So it may be that, in this case, Devious Dave becomes Prudent Dave, does not confess, reaps the benefit of the renewed trust of his community, and proceeds to seek out better opportunities for exploitation by defection from joint strategies to which adherents to the bargain have committed themselves. And if they are difficult or impossible to come by, that will prove again a thesis far duller than the one Gauthier had set out to prove, to wit, that social arrangements may be devisable under which a pure utility maximizer, acting strictly from prudence, will behave just like a morally good person.

It may be objected that the reasoning that is available to Dave is available to every other person at the bargaining table. Moreover, since each starts out, like Dave, as a straightforward maximizer, she is likely to be tempted to reach the same practical conclusion as Dave. If so, then the bargaining will break down even though there will be the appearance of an agreement. There are different scenarios depending on the extent to which people are duped by others. That is, some or many may actually believe that others are genuinely committed to the agreement and are, therefore, ripe for exploitation. In any event, the possibility of improving upon the prior state of things is excluded.

This consideration only strengthens the case against Gauthier for it shows just how hard it is to convert a straightforward maximizer to CM on a conception of reason as maximization of expected utility. Thus, the view of Hobbes's Foole, as presented for refutation by Gauthier, is actually vindicated:

The benefits that could be realized through cooperative arrangements that do not afford each person at least his non-compliance utility remain forever beyond the reach of rational human beings – forever denied us because our very rationality would lead us to violate the agreements necessary to realize these benefits. Such agreements will not be made. (1986: 165)

It is curious that Gauthier reports the Foole's view here as the impossibility of *making* agreements, whereas in the next sentence, he formulates it as the rejection of the position that "it is rational to comply with an agreement if it is rational to make it" (165). We have pressed the case for the former interpretation, arguing that the problem is not really compliance, but agreement.

So, Devious Dave, the sensible knave, "seeing the advantages to be gained from . . . the advantageous breaches in honesty and compliance" (182) never does form or acquire the disposition to CM and may not rationally "be admitted to those mutually beneficial arrangements . . . that rest on honesty and justice, on voluntary compliance" (182). It certainly is irrational to admit him if you *know* he is a knave. But the relevant thought is that Gauthier has not shown that it is irrational for Dave to seek admission if he is reasonably sure that he will not reveal his true colors.

Although a straightforward maximizer like Devious Dave retains this general disposition after the formulation of a contract, its specific instantiations are now more complex. His actions are now based on strategies whose implementation requires him to calculate the actions those he believes are complying with the agreement will take. He must be familiar with the terms of the agreement, of course, as well as the manner in which the agreement applies to a particular case. In addition, he must calculate the probability that someone will, under the circumstances that prevail, comply with the agreement.

Thus, straightforward maximizers may have to form quite complex lower-level dispositions or strategies as we indicated above. In the end, the emotional and intellectual demands may prove too great for Devious Dave and he may convert to CM. That may be Gauthier's message: It is just too hard to be a successful straightforward maximizer.

The parallels between Gauthier and Stephen Darwall (1983) are instructive. Darwall's elaboration of the case against an exclusively self-centered theory of practical reason is complex and subtle and I wish only to draw attention to a difficulty relevant to the issue before us. In a Kantian vein, Darwall proposes that a norm is bona fide only if a rational agent *can* choose from an impartial perspective that all agents act on it. He characterizes a perspective as impartial in terms of a veil of ignorance somewhat thicker than Rawls's. S is an arbitrary rational agent ignorant of any preferences not intrinsic to and psychological facts not implicit in rationality. Under these circumstances, it would clearly be irrational for S to choose that each person act on the unconstrained principle of individual utility for, in the event that S would find herself in a world like ours, the possibility of maximizing individual utility is generally poorer than it would be were people to constrain their pursuit of self-interest by requirements of morally right conduct in situations involving potential cooperation or conflict with other agents. It would then be preferable for S to adopt a conditional principle dictating the subordination of self-centered activity to morality when agents interact in ways affecting each other's interests and projects. Pure practical reason, therefore, directs agents to give priority to moral requirements over ones of self-interest.

Darwall observes that the rationality of a choice in the real world, the only place where it matters, depends on a variety of relevant facts, including the actual behavior of people and the prevailing conventions. Behavior would reasonably vary depending on whether one lands in a den of thieves or a monastery.

Of course, these contingencies can all be accommodated by conditional principles formed behind the veil. But Darwall fails to draw this suggestion out. Since a preference is more rational, other things being equal, the more informed it is, would not a perfectly rational agent attempt to formulate far more specific principles than the two very general ones stated by Darwall? We know that the following so-called conjunctive principle is superior to the solitary principle of maximizing individual utility:

If there are not other agents with whom cooperation or conflict is possible, then maximize informed individual utility.

If there are other agents with whom cooperation or conflict is possible, then constrain pursuit of informed individual utility by requirements of morally right conduct (for example, by the requirement of nonmalificence). (1983: 232)

But why should we not add the following disjunct to the second part?

... unless one can maximize individual utility because (a) the other agents are sufficiently weaker or (b) the other agents are less intelligent or less capable in relevant respects or (c) a decisive advantage over the other agents can be achieved by an act of deception or by the use of some element in the situation, whether or not such use violates a principle of morally right conduct.

Now Darwall might claim that this modification (call it the principle of prudence) is worse than the conjunctive principle on the obvious grounds that a society in which everyone acted on it would contain so much mistrust, resentment, and fear that the interests of most would be served quite poorly. But Darwall cannot invoke this rebuttal because the relevant question is not: What would the world be like if everyone adopted this principle? It is certainly true that the world would be a better place if everyone adopted the conjunctive principle rather than the principle of prudence (and an even better one if everyone practiced saintliness). But the issue before us is: What should I do given the way the world *is*, including facts about actual moral behavior? Darwall himself says that we are not obliged to be moral in a den of thieves.

Thus, I need not worry that everyone will be as immoral as I contemplate myself being. The universal component of concern to Darwall is retained insofar as the principle of prudence is recommended to *any* rational agent who finds himself in a world like ours, that is, one populated with people varying a great deal in moral and nonmoral traits.

To see the force of this, consider what principle applies to an agent who finds himself in a community of wealthy and simple saints. What would constrain him from robbing his neighbors blind? *Any* rational agent would be better off were he to take advantage of this situation. Thus, this course of action is rationally preferable to those who find no intrinsic value in sainthood.

Even if the principle of prudence is unacceptable, it seems reasonable to suppose that the standards one should adopt on Darwall's grounds are not very high. It is certainly foolish to be "too good" and is probably wise to be morally lax when one can get away with it, for example, by cheating on one's income tax, stealing office supplies, jaywalking, lying for convenience, refusing to give to charity, taking more than one's fair share, and may well be advised to be very cruel in special circumstances. For in the end, reason, for Darwall, can but dictate prudence in one way or another. Thank goodness we do in fact have the sorts of intersubjective values we do, that we genuinely care about other people and certain traits, activities, and institutions. There is no reason to impugn the rationality – and, therefore, the autonomy – of a person who behaves altruistically because he loves, appreciates, and finds joy in the happiness of others.

One who finds no value in the things most of us hold dear, therefore, will find no argument in Darwall which can convince him rationally to change.

The person who adopts the principle of prudence is, therefore, like Devious Dave. Darwall shows the superiority of the conjunctive principle over the principle of maximization just as Gauthier shows the superiority of the principle of minimax relative concession to the unfettered pursuit of self-interest. But where each offers a dichotomy, there is really a trichotomy. A rational agent will prefer the principle of prudence to the conjunctive principle because it permits one to bypass the rules of morality when an opportunity arises and it is in one's interest to do so. A rational agent will prefer the appearance of agreement to a contract to genuine agreement for the same reasons. Of course, the trichotomy is only apparent, since the new response to the demand for cooperation is just a version of the old response, straightforward maximization.

The amoralist

It may be easier to establish the irrationality of an amoralist by abandoning Darwall's version of internalism, to wit, that p's being a reason for S to do A is constituted by S's preferring A, other things being equal, upon rational consideration of p. For we might then be in a position to insist that the amoralist has a reason to behave better even if he prefers not to do so.

Internalism is attractive because it demystifies the concept of a reason by providing a naturalistic account of it in terms of the way we are in fact motivated. Also, by regarding a reason as a fact that motivates when rightly considered, we automatically explain why reasons move us to act. But the very permissiveness of internalism has been deemed an argument against it. Does Wilbur have a reason to remove Lois's toenails just because he is moved to do so by dispassionate reflection on the act and the way it enhances the goal of human toenaillessness? For those not convinced by these cases, Michael Stocker (1979) argues against internalism by appeal to the converse situation, that is, cases of people who acknowledge certain values, but are not moved to promote them. The veteran social worker, weary of the struggle to improve people's lot, is now apathetic and feels useless. He knows it is good to do the sort of work he has been doing, but just no longer cares to continue the battle himself. It would be difficult to challenge the rational character of his consideration, for it may well be dispassionate, informed, and as vivid as possible relative to his current psychological state.

To be sure, this social worker once was motivated and Darwall may try to capitalize on that by a reformulation of internalism. Or he may demand more before he confers the honorific label "rational" upon his considerations. In any event, the rejection of internalism is not enough. For example, on G. E. Moore's externalism, the failure to acknowledge or to be moved to promote the good is not a failure of rationality. It is rather a defect of a separate moral faculty. Since a perfectly rational agent might have a defective moral faculty, rationality does not guarantee morality. The version of intuitionism one needs here is rather that of Richard Price's (1948), for on his interpretation, it is the understanding rather than a separate moral faculty which apprehends rightness.

Although it is difficult to defend a doctrine like Price's, the same issues can be raised from a slightly different perspective. Suppose that ethical objectivism is true. Since ethical facts would then be as objective as any others, an amoralist would be counted *cognitively* deficient. For if it is a fact that unprovoked cruelty is immoral, the failure to acknowledge that is a failure to accept a truth. And since knowledge is a component of positive freedom, the absence of relevant knowledge diminishes one's autonomy. Thus, amoralists must be, to some extent, heteronomous. If a decision to behave cruelly is made in the absence of the *information* that unprovoked cruelty is wrong, the amoralist is not as critically competent as he might ideally be.

One cannot always blame reason for a failure to acknowledge ethical facts. If we are dealing with a psychopath, then the problem is not his rationality, but rather the impoverished state of his moral emotions. He does not accept moral principles because he lacks the relevant moral emotions. If he is incapable of feeling compassion or if he cannot empathize with one who is suffering, then an improvement in his rational powers will be useless. He is defective on the evaluative level because he is defective on the primary level. In a recent experiment with convicted rapists, it was observed that the only effective way to change their attitudes toward their behavior was through extended efforts at expanding their capacities for empathy toward their victims. They were repeatedly confronted, via personal meetings and videotapes, with their victims' reports and responses, both verbal and emotional, until the cumulative weight of these encounters produced a breach in their personal defenses and they began to feel the pain they had caused.

When a cognitive deficiency rests on deficits of an emotional nature, the individual's heteronomy may be grounded, not on his amorality, but rather on the implications of his amorality to projects and ambitions of great importance to him. If people ostracize and shun him, he will be unable satisfactorily to pursue many goals, some of which are important to him. His autonomy of choice and his proficiency may accordingly be seriously impaired.

If these considerations do not suffice to explain the amoralist's heteronomy, we shall discover in Chapter 9 that the explanation may lie in a developmental deficit. It may be reasonable to believe that a normal development will provide a normal person with the experiences which enable him to appreciate the pull of morality. Without surrendering the possibility of rejecting the dictates of morality by one fully adept at appreciating their hold on human beings, we may certainly sympathize with a person whose upbringing or native endowment has rendered her deficient in this sphere. We can see this as relevant to autonomy because the self has been stunted in its development in such a way as to limit the options available to the agent. I am not confusing autonomy with flourishing for I am not resting my case on the failure of an adult to choose to express a mode of response that is in his repertoire of possible responses. He is not freely stifling certain natural tendencies and fundamental forms of human expression. Rather, they have been stifled for him in ways we will later elaborate for spheres other than the moral. An amoralist has lost something he never had the chance to appreciate and that would have been an integral part of his adult mode of interaction with the world and other persons. (If the problem is constitutional, if the amoralist is born that way, then indeed he may be as autonomous as he is ever capable of becoming.)

This amoralist is heteronomous not because he fails to engage in evaluations, but rather because of emotional impoverishment sufficiently serious to interfere with his status as a free, full-fledged adult. Although moral values play no role in his life *and* he is heteronomous, the explanation of the latter is provided, not by the Evaluation Conception's interpretation of the former, but rather by a profound deficit in his emotional makeup. Even assuming ethical objectivism and, therefore, ignorance on his part, this case does not support the necessity of values to autonomy. The more interesting case, therefore, is that of the person who possesses an adequate range of moral emotions, but refuses to introduce values into his deliberations in accordance with the Evaluation Conception.

If this latter individual is at the opposite end of the spectrum from the psychopath, the jaded social worker falls somewhere in between. A person may have had a sufficiently normal character development so as to recognize different forms of immorality. Yet his moral beliefs are compartmentalized in such a way that they play no role in deliberation; there is a chasm between the intellect and the will. Consider a thief who succumbs to the urge to steal without any sense of conflict, but who later honestly reports that he believes that what he did was wrong. Although his moral reflections lack practical import, they are advanced by one who feels their force. Like the jaded social worker, the moral emotions either were there and have lost their force or they accompany the moral judgments in the form of remorse, guilt, frustration, and/or a poor self-image. This individual is similar to one suffering from weakness of will except that the schism in his personality is more profound. The moral emotions of a merely weak person are pervasive in the ways we would expect. They arise in deliberation as well as retrospective evaluation even if they are too weak to be effective in the former. The heteronomy of the thief is more serious for he must deem deeply unsatisfactory a life of impulsive or spontaneous immoral behavior followed by moral condemnation which, as sincere, would itself be accompanied by remorse and other negative emotions.

Nor is an impaired reason necessarily the explanation in a case, not of amorality, but rather the adoption of an immoral code of behavior. (One who believes that morality derives from rationality will have to charge both amoralists and immoralists with irrationality.) A person who is capable of experiencing moral emotions may suppress those emotions on behalf of a distorted moral world view which demands the eradication or subjugation of certain racial groups. Although the explanation of immoral behavior of this sort is highly controversial and may vary from case to case, it is implausible to believe that all such persons just need rational rejuvenation. My eyes are not defective if I fail to see the suffering of another human being because I avert my gaze or unconsciously repress a normal level of attentiveness to my environment. Not all failures to see the world for what it is implicate the visual or the rational faculty. If reason is, as Wolf says, the faculty that guides us to the True and the Good, "reason" is really a name for a group of diverse faculties.

Since we are interested in the possibility of value-free autonomy, amoralists should be the focus of our interest, and is it not in any case true that, on the assumption of ethical objectivism, all persons who reject the correct moral principles are heteronomous?

The more difficult case, as I said, is presented by the amoralist who acknowledges the force of moral principles, but insists that they are irrelevant to one like him. His failure to be moved by moral truths is akin to the failure to be moved by visual features of the world on the part of one who has voluntarily chosen blindness. If a blind person can be autonomous – and Dr. Roy did in a sense choose his blindness – why can't an amoralist be autonomous? We must recall that autonomy is not flourishing: if a blind man's failure to flourish in the visual domain is not an automatic bar to his autonomy, why would his failure to flourish morally count against his autonomy?

There is a difference, to be sure. Since moral behavior is everyone's concern, we do not permit people readily to opt out of morality. It is permissible to become temporarily blind; it is *not* permissible for a normal person who feels the force of moral principles to choose a temporary suspension from the moral game. Special circumstances, such as extreme duress or temporary insanity, might permit the suspension of the normal sanctions against immoral behavior, but a person can casually rest his eyes, not his honesty. The difference between one sphere and the other is captured in the principle that a person who has both abilities is automatically bound by the moral features, not by the visual features, of the world.

One must at least try to flourish morally if one can. Morality is inherently universal.

Yet this difference is itself grounded in the moral perspective. Hence, only when one acknowledges the force of morality will one see morality as categorically binding. Consider then an even more extreme case, one not involving retrospective guilt or the acknowledgment of some sort of conflict, to wit, that of the person who rejects morality for theoretical or philosophical reasons and manages to square this stance with his first-order will. A person committed to a Nietzschean transvaluation of values may concede that an act is contrary to morality (not just contrary to some moral code or other), yet believe that the institution of morality is not ultimately binding upon him.[1] He may, as Nietzsche did, advance an explanation of the institution which reveals its flawed character and the ground of its violability. Many philosophers not sympathetic with this stance have nonetheless granted the meaningfulness of the practical question "Why should I be moral?" and have, therefore, conceded the underpinning of this point of view. It is not incoherent to say: "Yes, it is immoral to steal, but I will have nothing to do with morality." If he actually succeeds psychologically at unshackling himself from the bonds of morality, is there any basis for the judgment that he lacks autonomy? If his reasoning is just a rationalization to secure the advantages of immorality, we may find that he is lacking in critical competence. But if this is not so, we have a case of knowledge which is judged by the agent as irrelevant to practice. If this cannot be overturned, he cannot be judged heteronomous. To be sure, there are arguments within morality which might permit us ways of condemning this person. But this fact does not render the conception of such a person incoherent. If this Übermensch is just plain wrong, if, that is, morality applies to him as objectively as gravity, then his dismissal of values is a case of *relevant* ignorance and we shall have to conclude that he is heteronomous.

Suppose he grounds his case on the assumption that moral principles bind only the weak and he is strong. If he is deluded about his strength, then he would clearly lack autonomy for the straightforward reason of ignorance. But otherwise, a defender of ethical objectivism is constrained to show that an otherwise knowledgeable, competent, rational, free adult, possessed of the physical and psychological ability to violate moral principles along with a willingness to do so is nevertheless bound by them in a sense analogous to that in which he is *physically* bound by principles he is physically unable to violate. The defender must find a fact about this Übermensch which, like Kant's rationality, renders his self-proclaimed liberation from moral rules null and void. That is a tall order, especially in light of the difficulties attendant upon efforts to achieve this outcome by extracting it from rational self-interest.

According to one version of the internalist point of view, the Übermensch is incoherent. For in "denouncing" an action as wrong, he must *have* a sufficient motive to refrain from performing it. But even if the denunciation of an action as wrong is *in part* constituted by a motive to refrain, that motive need not be sufficient. The akratic, motivated to do *A* because he sees that he has a sufficient reason to do so, may nonetheless fail to do *A*. Since, in the akratic, a reason deemed sufficient does not evolve into a sufficient motivation, the possibility of the Übermensch, even assuming internalism, is guaranteed. Indeed, the failure of this argument was implicit in the earlier suggestion that our amoralist has to unshackle himself from the bonds of morality. The autonomous amoralist is not the emotionally scarred psychopath. The former understands the case for morality and counts the moral emotions as a part of his normal repertoire. He wants rather to pry apart his natural, first-order moral dispositions, for example, compassion, from those second-order judgments of worth he would be rid of. If he is compassionate, he has no objection to acting from that emotion. But he is impatient with second-order reflections designed to modify action in accordance with views of moral worth, even if he acknowledges their pull.

It may be misleading to press the analogy between Nietzsche's Übermensch and the autonomous individual. Nietzsche was so concerned to emphasize the supremacy of the will of the Übermensch as a counterweight to the traditional demands of a morality imposed from without that he felt it necessary to place him in a state of splendid isolation. (Nietzsche says: "They will live alone, and probably know the torments of all the loneliest forms of loneliness" [1964: 383].) In creating values from within, "he is his own judge from whom is no appeal" (1964: 367) and is consequently barred from the conventional delights of shared enterprises and relationships in which reciprocity and mutual respect are the order of the day. Obsessed with his own authority, he manages to avoid entanglements which demand his subordination.

Must we then suppose that an autonomous individual had better choose the high (moral) road anyway just to avoid the chilling aloneness of Nietzsche's great man? I shall answer in the negative and have already begun this answer first of all by limiting autonomy to agents who are automatically bound by their status as choosing and desiring beings. If I am right that this limitation is required by the incoherence of the notion of an ideally autonomous agent, then I cannot be accused of begging any questions in this context. If we are talking about realistic autonomy – and our earlier discussion of grander ideals forced a choice between those that are incoherent and those that are merely outrageous – we would then acknowledge the embeddedness of this individual in a tradition that sets the parameters for his preferences, selection of goals, and modes of thought and perception. We are thereby simply acknowledging the place of contingency in the life of any agent, autonomous or otherwise. So far, however, no case has emerged for the necessity of morality in the life of this person should he have the vision to contemplate its abandonment.

But surely some of this person's goals are very likely to involve relationship and community. Without morality, any commitments on this agent's part can only then be hypothetical. It is ludicrous to suppose, however, that he will, therefore, not find satisfaction, perhaps deep, in these enterprises just because he is prepared to submit his commitments to a periodic review governed by personal rather than moral criteria.

It is important to see once again that I am not denying the limits of autonomy. Although a truly autonomous agent cannot experience the delights and personal advantages of total submission to the community, it does not follow that he must stand totally apart from society once he adopts an amoral stance. The picture of a being who withdraws not only from the practice of moral evaluation, but also from the associated emotions and motivations of his moral community is indeed an unnerving one. It is not, however, intrinsic to the concept of an autonomous amoralist for the moral values that guide others may find their counterpart in him in personal motives such as compassion, charity, and love. That an autonomous agent, disinclined to invoke moral evaluation, can be guided and find satisfaction in these ways will be argued later in this chapter. I will also claim that he is not seriously disadvantaged by the absence of a propensity for moral evaluation and, in fact, sustains possible advantages.[2]

The burden of one who would charge the amoralist with irrationality is rendered even greater by the rejection of the analogy between factual and ethical knowledge. Both Rawls and Habermas would like to find a rational grounding of principles of justice; but neither is prepared to accept an ontological grounding of these principles akin to that of natural laws. The world does not have a moral structure in the way it has a physical structure. Rawls says:

What justifies a conception of justice is not its being true to an order antecedent to and given to us, but its congruence with our deeper understanding of ourselves and our aspirations. . . . Moral objectivity is to be understood in terms of a suitably constructed social point of view that all can accept. Apart from the procedure of constructing the principles of justice, there are no moral facts. (1980: 519)

For Habermas, moral claims appeal to a different type of validity than is appealed to by assertoric claims because "the orders of society, which we either conform to or deviate from, are not constituted *independently of validity*, as are the orders of nature, toward which we can assume an objectivating attitude" (1991: 60). The amoralist cannot, therefore, be mistaken in the straightforward way the advocates of the geocentric hypothesis are; he does not simply suffer from an informational deficit.

It is absolutely crucial to bear the difference between autonomy and morality in mind. We shall later in this chapter see that an autonomous agent who fails to be guided by moral principles cannot go it alone on the basis of a first-order motivational structure rich in a variety of moral-like emotions *if* we seek to replicate in him the complex structure of conventional morality. Moral reasoning is absolutely essential to the *moral* life. Intuitions and feelings pertaining to justice, for example, are hopelessly inept guides to one who wishes to embody this virtue in her life. One has to have a cogent theory of justice, one whose principles have met the tests of consistency, scope, compatibility with other plausible principles, and coherence with central intuitions which themselves have been submitted to scrutiny to ensure against distortions arising from a variety of possible sources. An autonomous agent who eschews values, interpreted along the lines of the Evaluation Conception, cannot be a moral exemplar.

Discourse ethics

One who does not pass judgment on the worth of his own inclinations is not likely to appreciate the communal practice of moral criticism and dialogue whose goals are the elucidation of shared value commitments and the promotion of agents with moral sensitivity and a readiness to engage in moral evaluation whenever it is called for. We may try to disarm this objection in a variety of ways, but the claim that one who withdraws from moral discourse surrenders the right to continue the practice of argumentation, *moral or otherwise*, would surely suffice to convert the picture of an autonomous agent we are trying to draw into a caricature of a human being.

Jürgen Habermas has advanced such a charge and carefully defends it against circularity on the grounds that no moral premises are invoked to reach this conclusion. The practice of argumentation, Habermas contends, embodies presuppositions which all participants must adopt (on pain of abandoning the practice). The content of these presuppositions entails a principle which functions as a rule of argumentation (U) which permits moral judgments to be justified only if "all affected can *freely* accept the consequences and the side effects that the *general* observance of a controversial norm can be expected to have for the satisfaction of *each individual*" (1991: 93). One cannot, therefore, rationally engage in argument without being bound by this rule.

The appeal to rationality as the ground of morality places Habermas in the same Kantian tradition as Gauthier, but the differences with Gauthier are stark. For Habermas rejects the project of deriving morality from features of strategic action. An agent seated at the bargaining table is engaged in strategic action insofar as he is concerned to reach a solution that will further as much as possible his individual interests. When Habermas talks about argumentation, however, he has in mind a form of "communicative action" in which each participant is guided solely by the force of argument. Although an agent engaged in strategic action may serendipitously find that he can rationally validate his position, he is not exclusively concerned to motivate others and to be motivated by the quality of arguments. Argumentation in the "ideal speech situation," by contrast, demands as well that each potentially affected person be permitted to participate, free of coercion, committed to truthfulness. Moreover, each party must be prepared to reverse her interpretive perspective in full and sympathetic response to the expression by others of their points of view, self-understandings, and interest structures.

The most controversial feature of the ideal speech situation is the need to reach a unanimous conclusion. Since argumentation arises when a consensus is disrupted, the goal of this activity is the restoration of consensus. This can only occur when each party freely embraces an outcome each recognizes to be in the common interest. Adherence to the democratic process is insufficient in this regard for the universal commitment to majority rule is compatible with continued minority dissent. In argumentation designed to reach a consensus, on the other hand, each member must be convinced that the agreement is equally good for each participant and is, therefore, committed to the principle that the general adoption of a norm is justified only if *all* affected agree (U).

The term "argumentation" is thus used by Habermas in such a specialized way that, even if an agent who opts out of morality is precluded from this activity, it would appear that he is not seriously disadvantaged. In fact, given that *no* real-life discourse realizes the conditions of an ideal speech situation – each participant must be fully committed to and perfectly competent at realizing all the procedures – in what way is a refusal to "argue" any disadvantage? If argumentation is, by definition, the search for valid norms, why may I not ask to draw a bye? In response, Habermas insists that this attitude of withdrawal is tantamount to taking "refuge in suicide or serious mental illness" (1991: 100). He believes that argumentation is a species of communicative action oriented toward reaching an understanding and that this mode of activity is at the core of our sociocultural natures. We might just as well propose that we stop breathing. "Because the idea of coming to a rationally motivated mutual understanding is to be found in the very structure of language, it is no mere demand of practical reason but is built into the reproduction of social life" (1987: 96).

Even if we agree that the procedures which define this form of discourse – universal participation, equality of respect, truthfulness, reciprocal sharing of perspectives – are, in some way, socially hard-wired, even a perfect exemplification which is *designed* to produce consensus on a moral norm can backfire. Habermas concedes, for example, that we may discover that certain issues will simply not yield to consensus.

But it might transpire that descriptions of the problem of abortion are always inextricably interwoven with individual self-descriptions of persons and groups, and thus with their identities and life projects. Where an internal connection of this sort exists, the question must be formulated differently, specifically in ethical terms. ... The (moral) question would be how the integrity and the coexistence of ways of life and worldviews that generate different ethical conceptions of abortion can be secured under conditions of equal rights. (1993: 59–60)

The discovery that a question is an ethical one is an acknowledgement that it is embedded in culturally specific conceptions of identity and ways of life that do not admit of consensual regulation. Morality, in contrast, is essentially concerned with the identification of just principles by which to govern social interactions.

A second explanation for the failure to reach consensus on the part of agents fully committed to the procedures of the ideal speech situation is simply the absence of generalizable interests. (Moral principles can play some role here, just as they can in the abortion dispute, to secure the integrity of each point of view, by ensuring a fair compromise.)

Third, there are the limits imposed by time and circumstance, quite serious ones in light of the need to produce assent in all affected parties.

Even assuming Habermas's view that socialization is impossible without a commitment to communicative action in general and argumentation designed to reach a consensus in particular, an individual can at best be generally disposed to adopt the procedures which make consensus possible, even if, through no fault of his own, he never in fact succeeds. In light of this, I want to interpret the nature of this individual's alleged commitment to (U).

On one reading, the view is trivial. If I am disposed to adopt principles in argumentation which commit me to (U), I am evidently committed to (U). The declaration that one is bound by (U) becomes uninteresting as soon as one learns that one is only bound in those contexts whose structure requires (U). Whatever interest remains is captured by the thought, conceded previously, that, as social creatures, we are disposed to resolve disputes by positing such structures and imposing the requisite demands upon ourselves.

Habermas has grander designs. He would derive the commitment to (U) from presuppositions governing any argumentation, moral or otherwise, designed to produce the truth or to redeem claims to validity. And the case is indeed strong that such a search ought to embody open-ended and free participation, equality of respect, truthfulness, and absence of coercion. We now imagine a participant entering the arena of *moral* argumentation. Habermas says: "It follows from the aforementioned rules of discourse that a contested norm cannot meet with the consent of the participants in a practical discourse unless (U) holds" (1991: 93). The inference Habermas immediately draws, to wit, that his project has now succeeded, presupposes that the procedural requirements embodying universal respect entail, in the case of moral argumentation, the further demand for universal consent. But if, after a full and honest dialogue in which I have listened as openly and sympathetically as I can to the arguments and expressions of interest and concern of all others, consensus has not been reached, I cannot understand why I am constrained to reject a principle that satisfies *almost* everyone. Habermas insists on real dialogue with real people – the more, the better – rather than a meeting of select philosopher-kings who have, to boot, successfully completed a grueling regimen of sensitivity training and 20 years of psychoanalysis.

Habermas is well aware of the gap between the real and the ideal. But even if we attempt to close this gap by supposing that all participants are motivated only by the search for truth, one of these who will be adversely affected by a proposed norm may refuse for that reason to accept the norm even though he knows that no other norm would be nearly as acceptable from a utilitarian (or deontological) point of view. A commitment to the truth is no obstacle to selfishness (or perversity). A rich person may not want to pay more taxes even though he fully acknowledges the feelings of the poor participants that they would be hurt more by other systems of taxation. Having reached an impasse, must the members acquiesce to the rich participant and reject as invalid the system of taxation he opposes? What in the nature of argumentation or morality grounds this demand?

We saw above that there are a variety of reasons for a failure to reach consensus that oust the discourse from the domain of the moral and, consequently, render it beyond the reach of the above refutation. Habermas must, of course, render the domain of the moral sufficiently precise so as to remove the suspicion of question begging. He would charge the rich participant with a failure to engage in moral argumentation on the grounds of his failure to engage in imaginative role reversal in the required spirit, that is, from the standpoint of impartiality. The moral point of view concerns justice and that does not enter into his motivation. Looking at the matter from the point of view of his own interests, he has failed to transcend the confines of purely strategic action.

We then derive (U) via the constraint on the moral point of view that a participating agent be engaged in communicative, not strategic action, for communicative action is action designed to secure a *common* interest. Thus, each interested party maintains a veto.

Habermas believes that the determination of interests is not a private affair. An individual's expression of her interests is embedded in a language and an interpretive scheme open to critical input from and possible revision by others. This may help to explain why Sue can sometimes be convinced that she is in a better position to know Lou's interests than Lou himself. Of course, Lou's fallibility raises doubts about the acceptability of universal veto, even assuming common interests. Perhaps the respect owed Lou by Sue along with the open-ended, complete, and honest exchange we expect in this discourse combine to legitimate Habermas's position over paternalism, with its greater inherent dangers.

In the increasing pluralism of modern life, it is becoming more and more difficult to share interpretations and, hence, to find genuinely common interests. Habermas is forced, therefore, to accept Thomas McCarthy's reconstruction of his doctrine according to which "normative disagreements turn on value disagreements" (1991: 185). Instead of acquiescing to the criticism that he has failed to produce an independent identification of the domain of the moral, Habermas sees the difficulty posed by the increasing differentiation of forms of life as necessitating the greater abstractness of "the rules and principles that protect the integrity and egalitarian coexistence of subjects who are becoming increasingly unfamiliar with one another in their difference and otherness" (1993: 90–1). Whether or not there are any generalizable interests is an empirical question. Habermas thus believes that it is in principle possible for the domain of the moral to be absorbed by that of the ethical, although he believes that that condition does not in fact obtain.

There are two important implications of Habermas's point of view for our position. Normally, we think of morality as potentially pitted against the individual interests of an agent. We wonder then how an autonomous agent can be induced to bind himself to a system which is likely to threaten his personal concerns. We began by concentrating on rationality: What reason can this agent have to adopt moral principles? On Habermas's conception of morality, however, this tension is dissipated; morality is not contrasted with individual interest; it rather concerns the promotion of those individual interests that happen also to be shared by all others. Insofar as an autonomous agent can be rationally motivated to promote his own interests, there is no barrier in principle to his adherence to moral norms or the process of their validation in discourse. Habermas's narrow conception of the moral annuls its sting for an autonomous agent who, as possessed of rationality and self-insight, need not be threatened by moral argumentation.

The second implication concerns the response to the narrowness of the moral domain. Many critics are disturbed about the remoteness of the circumstances that are essential to genuine moral discourse, grounded on the many varieties of human frailty that can obstruct its realization, the virtual impossibility of securing universal participation, and the uncertainty of consensus for one of a variety of reasons having nothing to do with failings of the participants, for example, the incommensurability of the participants' world views and language. They conclude that this ideal is just too remote from the circumstances of actual "moral" discourse to be of much use.

Habermas objects to McCarthy's response to this worry according to which the framework should be modified by admitting other modes of validating moral rules, such as the legally institutionalized processes of opinion formation in a democratic society. Habermas argues that these processes do not confer validity on legal coercion except insofar as they are ultimately grounded on the principles of discourse ethics.

But the framework necessarily remains limited in a formal way to methods of legitimation of norms governing social arrangements through discursive practices. Although Habermas pays homage to Strawson's account of the phenomenology of the moral and the need "to maintain our focus on the web of moral feelings that is embedded in the communicative practice of everyday life" (1991: 50), he is interested primarily in emotional responses because he sees them as pointing to suprapersonal standards for judging norms. Since Habermas views moral judgments as the core of moral theory, Seyla Benhabib calls him an "ethical rationalist," one who "neglects that the moral self is not a moral geometer but an embodied, finite, suffering, and emotive being" and is, therefore, "blind to the variety and richness as well as significance of emotional and moral development" (1990: 356). This sort of critique, which charges ethical rationalism with promoting a distorted view of the moral texture of human relationships by subordinating the interest in moral development to its role in the creation of rational agents, often takes a feminist turn. The doctrine is alleged to promote the ideal of the disengaged decision maker, thoroughly rational and free of the distorting influences of emotional dependency. In Chapter 10, we will look more closely at the charge that doctrines like ethical rationalism promote a male-painted picture of the autonomous agent as an aggressive CEO or Paul Bunyan-type.

In his defense, Habermas might cite the nonintellectualistic elements of the ideal speech situation, in particular, the demand that each party enter empathetically into the mind-set of the other in order to grasp her personal perspective. This act is not just designed to gain access to the other's beliefs, but is ideally supposed to result in role reversal, so that one assumes as much as is humanly possible the feelings, attitudes, and perceptions of the other. In entering into the emotional and affective thicket of another's life, one is better prepared to satisfy the demands of the moral conversation for impartiality. Rationality rests on the nonrational condition of having "walked in another's shoes."

If we look more closely at the nonrational components of the moral life, we may easily find a host of affective states, attitudes, and character traits which are entitled to a role comparable to that of judgment. Pace Kant, a person moved by compassion rather than respect for a moral principle dictating compassionate action deserves our moral admiration even if (1) he is not intellectually equipped to formulate a maxim that guides his action which can meet appropriate validity tests and (2) he is likely to act unwisely, even immorally on occasion, because his feelings get the better of him. I want to show, in the remainder of this chapter, some of the advantages of a life guided essentially by first-order volitional states and the disadvantages of a life excessively controlled by second-order evaluations. The excessive preoccupation with judgment on the part of moral theories like that of Habermas has indeed made it difficult for some to see the bona fide moral character of a person who possesses values only in the sense of the Motivation Conception.

Value-free autonomy and deprivation

One strategy available to the critic of value-free autonomy involves the possible deprivation and impoverishment of one who makes such a radical adjustment to his will and to his emotions. Would not the failure to evaluate his preferences reduce significantly the possibility of a variety of self-regarding attitudes we take as central? If we do not esteem any qualities we find in ourselves, we cannot feel self-esteem; if we do not believe we are worthy of respect, we cannot feel self-respect; if we do not view our lives as worthwhile, we cannot in one sense think of our lives as having meaning.

These conceptual observations, resting on the connection between judgments of value and attitudes, a connection noted by Hume and emphasized in several twentieth-century moral theories, must be tempered by relevant psychological considerations. A person whose self-esteem rests upon the discovery of qualities in himself which are objectively estimable may be a highly insecure person. He may seek and not find qualities which determine successful performance or achievement. Even if he is successful, the propensity to undertake frequent evaluations of one's esteem is a sign that he *lacks* the very trait he purports to find. Psychotherapists who treat patients with low self-esteem achieve success, they report, when their patients gradually replace inferiority feelings "not by an equally self-conscious pride or self-appreciation but by a diminished interest in the matter. They simply become less concerned with measuring themselves and more interested in activity and life" (Shapiro 1981: 60).

Obviously occasional expressions of pride in one's accomplishments are normal; but genuine self-esteem is not constituted by dispositions to make such judgments because it does not rest upon comparisons of performance with standards.

It is inaccurate, therefore, to construe self-esteem as esteem of certain qualities which one happens to possess, but which are admirable wherever found. In support of this for the case of self-respect, Shapiro argues that "if effective, competent activity is a direct and principal source of self-respect, the reason is not obvious why, to put the matter simply, self-respect should not be largely the possession of the brightest, the most competent, the most successful" (1981: 61).

The point applies as well to the closely related trait of self-esteem. Since it is not grounded in psychological makeup, similar sets of psychological traits are not necessarily correlated with similar levels of self-esteem. (Obviously, certain emotions, like pride, *are* intimately related to specific objects, qualities, or achievements.)

The conceptual chasm between self-esteem and the possession of estimable qualities has launched a cottage industry in the United States. In every sphere and stage of life, we are bombarded by the peddlers of self-esteem. It may take the form of "an explosion of awards, gold stars and happy-face stickers for the most routine accomplishments of childhood" (*Newsweek*, February 17, 1992), pleas from the pulpit ("People who do not love themselves can't believe in God": the Reverend Robert Schuller), or even a California State task force which concluded that "lack of self-esteem is central to most personal and social ills plaguing our state and nation" (*Newsweek*, February 17, 1992). All these expressions of this movement agree that low self-esteem should be taken on directly; there is little need to be bothered by "irrelevant" matters, such as the criminal, sinful, ignorant, unskilled, unproductive, or self-destructive behavior of the subset of all those afflicted with this disease. As disturbing as this attitude is, it does rest on the conceptual truth that ungrounded self-esteem is still self-esteem.

Shapiro draws an analogy between self-esteem and health. Health is a normal condition not requiring explanation and reflected in an absence of specific disease-related symptoms. It is a generalized sense of well-being and vitality. Analogously, persons with self-esteem do not necessarily direct this attitude toward specific first-order characteristics. Rather, they initiate their projects without excessive self-consciousness, with a sense of independence incorporating a tendency to trust their own judgments and to see their actions as bearing a sense of their own personal authority. Basically, self-esteem is the sense of one's autonomy. If I believe myself to be in control of my environment, to have a wide range of options I can exercise, to be independent, to be regulating my activity in accordance with my rationally grounded preferences, I will have self-esteem. An autonomous person may come to doubt that he is exercising his auton-omy wisely or properly. But this reverberates on his self-esteem only if he finds himself paralyzed or incapable of change. And then the problem is that he no longer *is* in control; he is not regulating his activity as he would wish. He senses a loss of power or will. He has lost the capacity to make his distinctive mark on the world and take responsibility for it.

Thus, an autonomous agent, not disposed to higher-order evaluation, need not be as impoverished as one might suppose. Built into his auton-omy is a sense of self-worth, self-esteem, and purposiveness. And the fact that these attitudes are not grounded in specific traits or ways of life suggests not only the milder thesis that no specific values are intrinsic to full freedom, but the more radical doctrine that autonomy requires no values at all. What is wrong with the picture of the Übermensch, powerful, competent, expressing his vitality unencumbered by any second-order reservations, especially from the sphere of conventional morality, about his impulses? Reveling in his autonomy, he projects a sense of self-worth and self-confidence.

The clinical literature is replete with confirmations of this view. Over and over again, the contrast with defensiveness, self-destructiveness, and depression is autonomy, independence, mastery of the environment, en-joyment of the vital, overcoming of the morbid, the capacity to express feelings, the lack of undue concern about pleasing others. Many with a poor self-image, for example, solve whatever problems caused this and other debilitating states like depression and detachment of affect when they are able to activate themselves, when they can respond indepen-dently on the basis of an insight into their own affective states. Again, the improved self-image arises not as a disposition to second-order judgments, but rather as a conceptual by-product of genuinely autonomous behavior.

Having said this, we must amend the conclusion to allow for a distinction between the metaphysical and the merely psychological dimensions. A person with self-esteem may be deluded. His self-esteem may be grounded in the sense that he is autonomous, when in fact he is not. A heteronomous person may project this confident and vital image when, as lacking in insight and full of conceit, he fails to realize how impotent he really is, how dependent on others his decisions are, or how irrational his decision-making activity is. He may also be attempting to conceal a deep sense of shame which would emerge in consciousness if he were to engage more seriously in open and honest reflection.

In psychoanalytic literature, there are accounts of this false sense of autonomy as arising in borderline and narcissistic personality disorders where a "false self" emerges to defend the "real self," which is impaired, against painful affect. This false self can appear to be quite autonomous.

The patient feels grand. . . . and this feeling is reinforced by his perception of the world and the world's reinforcing feedback. . . .

The illusory quality of this defensive self is revealed by its content, its motives, and the denial or devaluation of reality required. The content revolves around grandiosity and omnipotence, while the motivation is to seek narcissistic supplies. . . . Joined to this is the extraordinary denial of the reality of any stimuli that frustrate these projections.

The patient's sensitivity to narcissistic wounds makes him extremely perceptive of and sensitive to other people's narcissistic needs and he uses this perception to coerce or manipulate them, through gratifying their narcissistic needs, into reinforcing his grandiose self projection. The very real cleverness, charm or charisma possessed by some narcissistic personality disorders can make an extremely convincing illusion of relatedness. (Masterson 1985: 42–4)

This behavior is guided by a very narrow goal, defense and protection of the self. Ultimately, however, situations will arise which reveal to the person that his real self is unstable, ineffective, felt to be unworthy. For example, he may enter a relationship in which his inability to form a genuine emotional commitment becomes evident. Even if there had been the appearance for a long time of autonomous functioning, the narcissistic personality eventually becomes debilitated and perhaps dysfunctional. Successful treatment permits the emergence of a distinct system felt by the patient to embody his genuine feelings and needs, ones he has had all along and whose expression, not grounded in a neurotic need, is genuinely satisfying. Whatever the underlying cause of this phenomenon, for example, abandonment depression, the criterion of successful resolution is the reassertion of the real self, its spontaneity and capacity for commitment and creativity.

It would thus be a mistake to define autonomy as a purely psychological trait. Autonomy is a condition whose presence is not just grasped by its possessor in an act of introspection. Conversely, can't an autonomous agent be ignorant of this condition? Can't I *under*estimate my rationality, personal integration, or independence? A powerful person can suffer from self-doubt without being so debilitated that her power is actually stifled.

However one distinguishes the apparent autonomy of the false self from the genuine autonomy of the real self, the point is that the emphasis is not on self-evaluation, but rather healthy engagement. Although, from the psychotherapist's point of view, the goal is the restoration of spontaneity, the capacity for commitment and vital engagement, unencumbered by self-doubt and excessive personal evaluation, the objective dimension of autonomy is also crucial. For, if this goal is achieved at the expense of reality distortion, if, as the psychoanalyst would put it, the real self remains suppressed, the subject has not achieved a level of personal integration which ensures continued satisfactory functioning. He is very likely to encounter frustration and distress by dint of his failure to understand the world and his relation to it, by dint, in other words, of his lack of objectivity, a notion we will study more carefully in Chapter 8.

In the context of the current polemic, the key point is that, since a person impoverished by the lack of self-esteem is often inclined to evaluate himself (negatively), it does not follow that all who lack such inclinations are autonomous; some, for example, may be suffering from narcissistic personality disorders and will only appear upbeat and invulnerable. Conversely, one can underestimate one's autonomy. But even if therapy requires the patient consciously to judge himself so that he will come to be aware of his bona fide abilities, the confidence he may acquire will not then be constituted by continued self-evaluations, as helpful as these may be to sustain or prop up a flagging ego. For autonomous persons at least *can* have self-esteem in virtue of their manner of engagement in the world, not in terms of second-order evaluations.

The formation of values

The normal development of a human being incorporates conditions leading to the formation of an ego ideal. Although this observation is not controversial, theorists will evidently differ on details. According to Heinz Kohut (1971, 1977), the integration of functions into what he calls a cohesive self depends in part on two types of narcissistic transference, one of which, the idealizing transference, occurs when the idealization of the parental figure is transformed into an internalized system of values. "The parents' apparent greatness infuses the child's feeble sense of self with power, value and cohesion" (Wolf 1977: 214). The cohesive self initially includes a nuclear idealized self-object, that is, the admired qualities of the parent, experienced by the child as a part of his own self. This component of the self in normal maturation becomes the ego ideal which, as part of the person's value system, undergoes major and minor modifi-

cation through life. If the parent or caretaker is empathetic and supportive, he will facilitate the development of this cohesive self which includes
both a mature self-love as well as a capacity for empathy.

Our account has not denied the importance of ego ideals (or a value
system) to autonomy (Chapter 5). But we do not require that a person's
ideals or values be construed as *worthy* end-states. Their value to the
person might be constituted simply by his wanting to realize them in
light of all relevant information, perhaps because they have indeed been
internalized through the transference process described by Kohut. The
issue we want now to consider is whether there are elements of Kohut's
account which might be appealed to by one who believes that a self
without a sense of worth must be a fragmented self. It would appear that,
on Kohut's account, an amoralist cannot have a cohesive self for something must have disrupted the evolution of the nuclear idealized self-
object into an essential ingredient of that total configuration he calls a
cohesive self. Moreover, the person will experience himself as fragmented
and will lack a sense of well-being. Thus, for Kohut, there is ultimately a
direct relation between ego ideals and self-integrity.

Having incorporated the importance of ego ideals into the repertoire of
an autonomous agent who lacks values (on the Evaluation Conception),
we also can show that a value-less agent, one not driven, among other
things, by moral principles, need not suffer from as impoverished a set of
motivations as a critic might suppose. Although a pure egoist, one driven
by an interest in maximizing personal utility, is not disposed to make
personal evaluations, he may nonetheless want those things his community regards as intrinsically valuable. Indeed, who today is sympathetic
with the Kantian model of a moral agent, driven by principles rather than
inclinations? If one can find a person who enjoys the pursuit of noble
goals, whose predominant motives are compassion and love, few would
take the Kantian stance and view this person as devoid of moral worth.
We not only prefer such persons; we also realize that they are more
reliable partners insofar as they do not need to intervene on behalf of
duty when the occasion requires it. For if the intervention takes place
against a motivational system pulling in the opposite direction, we face
the possibility of moral weakness.

But is a virtuous amoralist a psychological possibility? Even Mother
Teresa must have struggled against selfish impulses so as to coordinate
her principles and her inclinations, thereby permitting the atrophying of
those principles from the point of view of motivational efficacy. Many
saints report lives of constant struggle with their base impulses.[3]

We may bolster the idea of a virtuous amoralist by the following theoretical speculation. Let us suppose, as Kohut believes, that self-integrity
requires the phase in which the nuclear idealized self-object appears. For
as the young child grows, he discovers, to his increasing dismay, that his
grandeur is a fantasy, having been grounded in a false omnipotence. The

disappointment would be psychologically crushing were he unable to replace his grandeur with that of the parent. But then the objective qualities must be absorbed by the child's self and the result is, as we saw earlier, the nucleus of the self's value system.

If something like this must go on in order to have a cohesive self, then since autonomy requires a cohesive self, this story is a condition of autonomy. Now if we postulate as an example of autonomy the amoralist, perhaps even the virtuous amoralist, we must specify a plausible psychological story whereby the second-order life of our growing child, that is, his personal evaluations embodying his morality and sense of worth, is absorbed by the primary level of motivation. Then, and only then, will the amoralist be moved strictly by a preference for, say, altruistic behavior rather than some principle of altruism used to evaluate his motivational structure.

Psychological theory has often addressed a prior question, namely, how in the world does a person ever get moved by personal evaluations? We cannot consider how motivationally effective personal evaluations might be replaced unless we have some idea as to how they got there in the first place. This becomes a problem in the context of a theoretical approach which takes explanation of behavior by (first-order) desires and beliefs as paradigmatic for personal evaluations are not desires (whose objects happen to be other desires). On the conception of value we are currently required to suppose (the Evaluation Conception), the conflict between value and desire is not to be reduced to a clash of desires. As Watson and Taylor would have it, it rather represents a battle between fundamentally distinct components of the person. (The issue cannot even be raised on the competing Motivation Conception of value.) Thus, if we have a theory as to how desire moves us to act, we may not be able to extend this theory to principles or values. This is W. P. Alston's (1977) conclusion, one which provides support for the libertarian line of C. A. Campbell (1940, 1951) that in no plausible way can one extend current theories of motivation to the experience of effort of will (Campbell) or self-intervention (Alston). The argument is that, on behaviorist and behaviorist-inspired accounts, the motivational force of a desire which is not innate derives via conditioning and more sophisticated techniques of generalization from desires which are innate only because the acquired desire takes on an effective anticipation similar to that attached to the innate desire. (There are alternative accounts, but none plausibly explains how principles per se can motivate.) Yet in cases of temptation, we sometimes have the sense that we can form tendencies in opposition to the strongest desire. Alston observes, as Campbell did before him, that psychologists can attempt to defuse this circumstance by pointing out the many ways in which the weaker desire on behalf of principle just becomes the stronger when it is supplemented by various considerations, for example, the desire for a good reputation in the community. The puzzle remains, however, for we are invariably left with bona fide cases when this just does not happen, and we nonetheless intervene successfully on behalf of the weaker desire.

Perhaps, as Philippa Foot (1972), Thomas Nagel (1970), and John McDowell (1978) have contended, the culprit is the belief-desire model itself, in particular, the assumption that all intentional action requires an antecedent desire. If we reject this assumption in favor of the possibility that the acceptance of a principle can directly motivate, it will be less puzzling that a principle motivates in the face of a strong desire in opposition to it. For if we can be moved to act by seeing that a course of action is right, the strength of the motivation might suffice to overcome a strong, contrary desire.

One of the powerful reasons for believing that desires are empirically necessary for intentional action is that the position appears to explain why two persons in the same cognitive states act differently. Why would Wilbur, but not William, offer aid to the homeless person they both see, unless Wilbur has a stronger desire to help? And the fact that we often act in the absence of a discernible urge or impulse is inconclusive since desires are not identical with, although they can evidently be manifested in, conscious mental episodes. If desires are internal states which explain various sorts of dispositions, for example, to act certain ways, to say certain things, and to have certain conscious states, they may well be independent of and prior to an intentional action they explain, in spite of the absence of a felt urge. And I agree with Martha Klein (1990: 144), in response to McDowell, that the *cognitive* fact that only Wilbur sees the plight of the homeless person as a reason for acting explains the difference in response only on the assumption that Wilbur has and William lacks an appropriate underlying *affective* disposition. Also, since desires or affective dispositions can differ in strength, we have a natural way of explaining why a person sometimes rises to duty and sometimes succumbs to temptation. To be sure, cognitive states can differ in epistemic "strength"; there are degrees of belief. But they are irrelevant in explaining why a person who is *certain* that he ought not to do *A* sometimes does *A* anyway. So we still do not understand how a motivation to do the right thing can be strong unless the strength is really a feature of a desire, in which case we are not really allowing that a principle as such can overcome a powerful desire to act contrary to the principle. In some way, a principle must get associated with an appropriate underlying affective state.[4]

To establish this link, Alston looks for help outside behaviorist literature and finds it in psychoanalysis. There is general agreement among psychoanalytic theorists concerning the existence of the phenomenon of identification. If we suppose that the satisfaction the child takes in the presence of the parent is generalized to the parent's traits, we have explained the identification with the behavior and attitudes of the parent. The traits are introjected and imitated in spite of the possibility that there is *no* affective anticipation in relation to the action expressing such a trait, including those acquired by association, for example, the anticipation of guilt or anxiety which would accrue from the performance of a "forbidden" act. Thus, even when the anticipated *total* satisfaction of the unprincipled alternative is greater, the child acts from principles adopted through the process of identification with the parent's traits. Since the child's motivation is not grounded in the anticipation of positive affect in the *objects* of the parent's attitudes and behavior, a comparison of positive and negative affect arising from the performance of the principled alternative with those arising from the performance of the unprincipled alternative will overlook a motivationally relevant consideration which might make the difference.

Although the psychanalytic account, therefore, apparently permits an explanation where stimulus-response theories have failed, we may challenge its efficacy by questioning the ability of the theory to explain the transition from the child's satisfaction at the appearance of the parent to identification with the parent's traits. If the psychoanalytic account is based on simple associationist principles, we have a loophole through which the S-R theorists can enter. That is, if the child simply associates the presence of the parent with the presence of someone with certain traits, transferring the pleasure accompanying the former to pleasure now linked with the latter, we still seem to have resorted to principles of stimulus-response psychology, namely, the conditioned response. Moreover, we may also want to know why the child takes the further step, to wit, introjection and imitation. For the pleasure the child receives or anticipates may explain why she *seeks* the parent or one who possesses the parent's traits, but not why she herself *takes on* those characteristics.

(We may, in fact, push the difficulty back even further. Why should the child take pleasure in the presence of the parents? Assuming the child's cognitive development is not sufficiently advanced so as to permit a judgment that the parent satisfies the child's needs, we must suppose the operation of associationist principles. The child is pleased at the appearance of that in whose presence needs are satisfied. On this score, Kohut's doctrine is not better because it demands rather sophisticated judgments of the child. In fact, this raises the whole issue of the way psychoanalytic theory can operate when it appears to attribute extraordinarily sophisticated judgments to infants.)

In other respects, however, Kohut's version of the doctrine of identification is particularly compelling. Kohut's idea is that the child's self would disintegrate unless she *adopts* the traits of one who is so powerful. Recall that the discovery by the child that her omnipotence is a delusion is a personal threat so powerful that the very preservation of the self demands an immediate substitute. Only by incorporating the qualities of the omnipotent parent can the child be restored to her early grandeur. Kohut's doctrine, thus, explains *both* why identification occurs *and* why the child specifically identifies with the parent's traits.

Although we may understand why the child takes on the parent's traits without expecting rewards from the resultant behavior, the restoration of a sense of power constituting an adequate reward in and of itself, typically the child will be rewarded for imitative behavior and will reward herself so that the positive tone of these responses will be generalized to the objects of the attitudes themselves.[5]

Although there are theories other than psychoanalysis which offer explanations of principled behavior, let us suppose that the phenomenon of identification is indeed central. So the child starts out with principles taken over from parents. As the child grows, these principles should be submitted to criticism since the child's needs, perceptions, knowledge, and experience change. After all, there is no necessary connection between the principles and values a child happens to acquire and the principles and values which would be most appropriate relative to *other* facets of the child's personality and abilities in relation to the world of which he is a part. Even if the internalization of the parent's standards is successful and their imbedding pervasive, there is no guarantee that the fit will be permanently satisfactory. That is an all too familiar fact of life. Eventually this process reaches an equilibrium and a relatively stable system of values emerges.

Now, although identification may explain how one can acquire principles which motivate us to act without expectation of standard rewards, we must note that the objects of these principles not only may, but in all likelihood will, acquire affect through association with parental, and then, self-approval. The child's need and admiration of his parents are the initial reasons he imitates their displays of prejudice. But then he may well acquire a genuine aversion for the targeted group. We see then a way in which action by principle acquired through parental identification can reenter the primary level of motivation. Not only do our principles change, but the reinforcement acquired by principles which persist may well be transmitted by association to the content of those principles. The person who was taught to be punctual and initially acted from this principle may learn to enjoy the positive reaction of those she does not keep waiting; the person who was taught to be honest may enjoy the admiration of those who praise her honesty.

Thus, even if Kohut is right, and autonomy requires at least ego ideals, if not a set of moral values, the sense in which they must be present does not require the second level on which personal evaluations are made. They may be present as simple preferences, entering into the calculation of one whose decisions are always efforts to maximize utility.

Evaluations, virtues, and altruism

I do not deny that a person who lacks values is impoverished. So, if I am right in thinking that autonomy does not per se implicate values, we shall have to view certain lives as enriched in virtue of elements independent of autonomy and this conclusion must have a bearing on the overall judgment concerning the value of autonomy I render in Chapter 10. On the other hand, whatever autonomy is, an account that permits autonomous agents to fall short of full personhood is to countenance an intolerable level of impoverishment.

An autonomous agent who lacks values on the Evaluation Conception's interpretation is barred from grounding his preferences on the basis of considerations of worth. To use an illustration of Taylor's (1977), a person might be moved to diet out of a sense that overindulgence is undignified and that self-control and autonomy are essential components of a model he wishes to emulate. Alternatively, he may attempt to explain his inclination in quantitative terms by viewing the amount of satisfaction derived from a successful diet as greater than the pleasures of gluttony. For he can anticipate health, longevity, a sense of well-being, and a capacity to participate in many pleasurable activities unavailable to the obese.

We thus appeal to the model which permits us to understand how a person not disposed to make personal evaluations may nonetheless have preferences which embody ego ideals because of the manner by which they have arisen through the identification process described above. Thus, I may simply prefer self-discipline to overindulgence without viewing the matter in terms of the number of utiles or the amount of satisfaction (unless such descriptions are treated as recastings of the fact of my preference).

Even if we ignore the effort to capture the notion of *self*-worth by the idea of a robust, confident engagement rather than a propensity for second-order judgments of worthiness, we must concede that certain evaluations are *necessarily* second-level and cannot, therefore, enter into the life of even a virtuous amoralist. For example, a judgment that one's central life activity is ultimately worthless is available only to a person who reflects. (An amoralist who shows signs of depression as he engages in his work may experience vigorous and wholehearted rededication when he changes jobs. He now eagerly looks forward to his work and has no thoughts or feelings which can be interpreted as a sense of emptiness, meaninglessness, or worthlessness. Nonetheless, to distinguish the undiluted enjoyment from a judgment of worth, we need that second-order evaluation.)

In general, the virtuous amoralist can have first-order dispositions without being disposed to further dispositions to judge those first-order ones. So he can feel compassion for others without approving it or deeming himself a good fellow for being that way. And he is surely capable of emotions we associate with love, including a sense of dedication and commitment to the loved one. For that is constituted by a set of preferences in which the loved one's interests take precedence over others, including perhaps the lover himself.

On the Motivation Conception, values are determined by choices that are then reflected in behavior and emotion. But are there not second-

order evaluations implicit in many emotions and character traits? Taylor
(1977) claims, for example, that a first-order analysis of the virtue of
courage must fail. Although a courageous person need not judge that he
is virtuous, he must make judgments of worth, in particular, that the
sacrifice he is prepared to make is on behalf of a *noble* cause. And this
judgment is bound up with others which collectively characterize the
quality of life the person wishes his inclinations to express and sustain.
Without these evaluations, acts of courage would appear foolhardy, masochistic, or irrational. Without a sense of the quality of life one would
choose, one is not much of a person.

It is, first of all, simply untrue that courage imports these second-order
evaluations. For a man who knowingly places himself in great danger in
order to protect his son acts courageously. He is not foolhardy, masochistic, or irrational because he fails to acknowledge that his cause is noble.
His son may be a lout; his father loves him nonetheless and, given that,
we see the point of the father's action and deem it courageous. The son's
welfare is of great value to the father even if we treat the concept of value
as the Motivation Theory demands. Accounts of courage that presuppose
the Evaluation Theory treat this virtue as more than plain courage.[6]

With respect to virtues other than courage, I suggested previously that
it is easy to understand how an amoralist can acquire them on the primary
level of motivation through the identification process, even though a strict
Kantian may regard these traits as ersatz in the absence of a motivation
by respect for the moral law.

It is possible without a moral dimension to sustain other-regarding
feelings, to look upon another person's well-being as a constituent of
one's own venture. But can the depth or motivational efficacy of these
feelings be sustained on a Motivation Conception of value in light of the
latter's proscription of an attitude of respect for the other? Such an
attitude incorporates a second-order evaluation for if the other person is
perceived as an object of respect, he is someone who is *entitled* to these
other-regarding feelings.[7] Without the acknowledgement of respect, it
may be argued, the amoralist can treat another at best the way a pet
owner treats her pets or a possessive mother treats her child. She may
take pleasure in the happiness of her charges, but can never fully appreciate the importance to the objects of her affection of their own projects.

The other-regarding amoralist, the objection continues, cannot really
be as other-regarding as one whose feelings of love or compassion are
inclusive of those moral emotions, basically respect, which implicate
evaluations. (Mature) love is not, as I earlier described it, a prioritization
of interests unless an interest in the loved one's autonomy is grounded in
an evaluation, to wit, that the other is deserving of respect. Amoralists
cannot really experience love.

But an interest in another's autonomy need not be grounded in respect.
Animals promote the independence of their offspring better than humans.
It is interesting to watch a cat permit her newborn what a human on-

looker might regard as a very high level of independence before she intervenes to protect the kitten. At a certain stage, the baby must fend entirely for herself, free of any worry about continued maternal meddling.

Although we regard a mutual concern for independence as a component of mature romantic love in human beings, the extent to which we fall short of the ideal is profound. Relationships which are less prone to include possessiveness and jealousy may well display one person's interest in the independence of another. This happens – not always, to be sure – between teacher and student or between therapist and patient. It is not uncommon for a teacher, free of possessive feelings for his students, to delight in the development of a student's capacity to work independently. It is compatible with this feeling for the teacher to take delight in his own contribution to the student's intellectual growth. Thus, the promotion of the student's well-being becomes a constituent of the teacher's own enterprise.

The teacher may well believe that his student *is* entitled to respect. Yet it is not clear that this belief must play an essential role in the teacher's actions. One can take great pleasure in observing another's intellectual maturation and want to promote it without invoking moral notions to sustain these interests.

The acid test takes place when the student's development demands that the teacher sacrifice his own interests for the sake of the student's independence. A genuine concern for the student's autonomy will permit some intrusions of this nature. For the critic must believe that only a moral commitment is strong enough to underwrite the teacher's continued support.

It is, first of all, worth noting that a person with this moral commitment may not be able to sustain support for his student. In spite of his acknowledgement of the student as a moral agent, the conflict between his own interests and those of this student may, as it often does, result in the teacher's opting for his own concerns. To be sure, in some cases, the teacher may be able to appeal to a moral principle in defense of his actions. The student wants the teacher to abandon all his other students so that he can devote himself exclusively to him. The teacher rightly protests. But if the student needs money to further his studies and the teacher is consequently asked to forego the purchase of a pool table he has longed to own, the teacher's acknowledgment of the rights of his student will *neither* automatically result in *nor* morally require the abandonment of his personal goal.

Moreover, it is perfectly clear that self-sacrifice is very common in those defective relationships which fall short of ideal love. Overprotective parents and jealous lovers often renounce their own needs for the sake of the loved one. To be sure, they have a special problem when it comes to the promotion of the other's independence. But it may well be that a tinge of possessiveness is a more reliable basis in certain cases, for example, for the sort of self-sacrifice demanded by the student. A genuine relish for the student's advancement, partly motivated by egoistic considerations, may well promote greater self-sacrifice than moral commitments.

We must place the matter in context. It is a tautology that a person with moral commitments is prone to behave more morally than persons without them. We will later explore additional ramifications of the model of an autonomous agent without values. The point I am currently trying to stress is that a person need not be hampered inordinately by a failure to engage in second-order evaluations, including moral evaluations. He may experience love, for example. He may certainly experience that romantic feeling which many persons who happen also to be victimized by feelings of possessiveness experience. He may also experience a genuine delight in the other's development, even if, like the "moral" agent, he reverts in the end to selfish motivation.

Or consider friendship. Is it so clear that a person is more likely to be moved to act out of a genuine concern for the well-being of her friend because she believes her friend is entitled to this treatment or because she is grateful for the association, wants to do what she can to sustain it, relishes the reciprocity inherent in the relationship, and takes pleasure in the happiness of her friend? The case for a radical separation between those who can love and those who cannot, based on the capacity for moral reflection, remains to be made.

It should go without saying by now that I am not supposing that the amoralist is driven solely by the anticipation of pleasure in his appreciation of ostensibly noble pursuits such as friendship, love, the raising of consciousness about the environment, and painting. For no premise prevents me from adopting the stance of Bishop Butler on that old chestnut: Although I would not give money to environmental causes unless it pleases me to do so, my motive is the improvement of the environment, not the pleasure. A value-free agent, in the special sense we are assigning this term, can find value and meaning in her world. We must simply understand value as the Motivation Conception understands it.

But will a value-free agent really be acting out of concern for the other? If compassion rather than principle moves me, am I not admitting that I do not now *really* care about the sufferings of Rwandans? For if compassion is a first-order state, is it not conditional in the sense of White?[8] How then can my concern be directed to the world when I do not care what happens when I die? Even if my feeling of compassion is phenomenologically indistinguishable from the motivation of a Kantian, does it even deserve the label "compassion" if I do not care what happens to the Rwandans tomorrow because I know that a pill I am about to take will bring it about tomorrow that I will not care or that I will not be disposed to have a warm feeling at the sight of food deliveries reaching the Rwandan people? Would not analogous thoughts apply to love and friendship? Is my concern for my friend's recovery genuine if it is a concern that my friend recover so long as the concern persists?

The issue before us is vague. Since I have conceded that my morality is flawed, the critic must show that this concession forces a quite radical breach between me and the rest of humanity. In response, I can point out that, so long as I remain compassionate in my own way, my behavior, feelings, and avowals will be virtually indistinguishable from the rest of my fellow creatures. The conditional nature of my concern will only make itself felt practically in special situations, such as those in which I have an opportunity to promote a certain end at a time when I may no longer desire that end. It would be irrational for me, for example, to take out an insurance policy or to specify a beneficiary. Why should I plan to dissipate my wealth among causes I now appreciate when the benefits will accrue to these groups and individuals at a time I no longer can appreciate the outcome?

Notice, by the way, that it would not be necessarily irrational for me to distribute my wealth *now* among these causes, even if so doing affects my welfare adversely. For nothing in the nature of this amoralist requires that he take greater satisfaction in those interests which provide him with personal benefits rather than those which are directed to the benefit of others. That I am not concerned to promote interests whenever I lose my interest does not imply that altruistic interests are necessarily weaker than selfish ones.

The argument I am resisting is as follows. If feelings like compassion and relations like friendship must embody unconditional desires, and if unconditional desires embody implicit judgments of objective worth, then only a person with values as the Evaluation Conception conceives them can sustain these fundamental components of humanity.

In response to the first premise, I have tried to narrow the gap between full-blooded and "second-rate" compassion. Although the second premise has already been refuted – I earlier cited examples of individuals with unconditional desires whose objects are not deemed objectively valuable by those individuals[9] – it does seem difficult to deny that an unconditional desire for the alleviation of Rwandans' suffering must be grounded in or presuppose a belief in the objective value of this outcome. If the alleviation of suffering is just personally valuable, why would my care extend to a time at which I believe that this result will be of no personal value?

I do believe, however, that it is unnecessary to invoke a notion like objective value to explain the unconditional character of this sort of desire in the case of many people. Vivid and extensive reflection on the suffering of individuals can produce a set of intense emotions and a powerful disposition to engage in imaginative projections of these emotions. These imaginative extensions are not under the control of reason. They are very much like the imaginative extensions of those persons who choose to be buried above ground because they are repelled by the thought of their own disintegration at the hands of underground creatures. In each case, revulsion at a prospect is so strong that the individual is thereby induced to promote a state of affairs the attainment of which will arrive too late to provide him with personal satisfaction.

This sort of thing happens in the case of love, for example, love of one's children, and may, like the other examples of powerful emotions such as self-preservation and certain primitive fears, have a genetic basis and an evolutionary explanation. These feelings, like Hume's sympathy, are natural, powerful, and operate independently of our rational faculties.

I have not denied that most people would use the language of objective worth in certain of these cases (children, Rwandans). My point is that, since the language of objective worth cannot be invoked in others of these cases (bodily decay) which are similar in crucial respects to the first group, an alternative explanation of the element of unconditionality may be more plausible for at least some individuals, including autonomous amoralists.

How, then, does a value-free agent differ from an animal? For both can loosely be said to rank desires. Human rankings are more complex for they are infused with language, information, emotions directed to sophisticated intentional objects, and high-level processing. But how do we get from there to meaning? There is, first of all, critical reflection, including second-order reflection leading to the formation and transformation of ego ideals, and secondly, the importance of long-range projects. There is also far more individual variation within the human species than in the rest of the animal kingdom. Yet meaning seems to be remote from all these elements.

If we turn to the unique content of human desires, we might wonder how the satisfaction of playing the cello, reserved for our species, is converted into the meaningfulness of this experience. (The satisfaction derived from the use of cosmetics is also unique to our species.) A value-free agent finds meaning *only* in the sense that, in virtue of the distinctive satisfaction he receives from this activity, he has a strong overall preference to pursue it. He stops short, as most of us do not, of making those further evaluations that the activity is especially worthwhile. He can revel in the experience and savor its special character, as my cat cannot, but has no use for evaluations beyond the calculative ones he must make at moments of choice. He can judge that sounds are beautiful, and that the sound of a cello is distinctively beautiful – rich, sonorous, piercing, sublime – perhaps because the beauty is there, waiting to be discerned by a trained human listener.

I affirm again that the amoralist *is* somewhat impoverished, but not nearly as many suppose. He will not feel a sense of injustice and he will neither feel nor miss feelings of indignation and resentment. He can feel gratitude (and others can be grateful to him) for the feeling does not require the belief that he is entitled to the favor bestowed on him, and he can feel trust. To feel confident in another in virtue of one's belief in the other's reliability, one need not adopt a moral stance. I certainly do not have to suppose that the other is driven by moral concerns.

Those who are prone to draw a sharp line between the two types must be reminded that action out of moral principle is not necessarily action issuing from strong or unambiguous motivation. The agent may in fact have to struggle with temptation in a battle won frequently by temptation. And when morality is the victor, the agent may harbor resentment and dwell bitterly on the sacrifice he has made. In certain situations, it would be more rational to trust the one driven by nonmoral motivations.

In addition, the concern to produce principled adults can backfire, as we will see in the next section.

Rigid personality

We turn to our growing child to consider various scenarios of development. Our natural tendency to idealize the agent disposed to second-order evaluation explains the tendency to overlook certain dangers resident in this personality type, certainly in the extreme form of the rigid personality.

Rigid persons (Shapiro 1981) act deliberately, purposefully, with a self-awareness that does not permit spontaneity or the relaxation of willful self-direction. They often delude themselves into thinking that they really want what their principles dictate and are then concerned about the loss of self-control arising from their inability to act on these false beliefs. They are thus estranged from their feelings and motivations.

The volitional behavior of the rigid individual, in other words, is not guided by conscious aims and purposes that arise, as they normally do, out of objective attention to the world, out of a continuous judgment and a "trying on" in imagination of the possibilities of action. The rigid person's behavior is guided by fixed and already established purposes and is merely technically informed by data selected according to relevancy to those purposes. . . . The relationship of the rigid person to such authoritative rules and images substitutes for and makes unnecessary an objective relationship with the external world. (1981: 75–6)

In the development of normal autonomy, the inequality between adult and child is replaced by a sense of personal authority, whereas "the rigid individual's self-respect remains invested in the achievements of his will, in what he has 'made of himself' " (77).

Values take on the status of duties or rules by the rigid character and are conceived as superior to her own inclinations.

When the compulsive person, for example, reminds himself that he should do something because it is the right thing, the nice thing, or the generous thing, he is prompted not by kindness, generosity, or concern for justice but by a sense of rules and duty obliging him to do something kind, generous, or nice. (80)

The rigid character is not only preoccupied with rules and principles; he also has a great deal of difficulty making decisions which cannot be referred to the judgments of this inner authority.

The rigid individual refers to these authoritative rules, as well as to actual models and images of authoritative figures at exactly the point where the next person's attention and interest are directed to the external world. This is evident, for example, whenever an obsessive-compulsive person attempts to decide between x and y by referring to some rule, principle, or authoritative purpose or to what he imagines some respected figure would do – instead of simply looking at x and y. (76)

The psychologist Shapiro will receive a sympathetic hearing from the philosopher Bernard Williams (1985). For the latter notes that reference to the world is precisely what we need in the case of those fundamental moral concepts he designates as thick, for example, treachery, promising, courage. They are moral notions whose applicability is determined by the way the world is in fact, so that people tend to agree on their application.

Autonomy and morality

It is not as if the path of the amoralist fails itself to be strewn with dangers. Let us first remind ourselves that our amoralist is motivated in part by first-order feelings such as compassion and love, which distinguish him from the psychopath. Now if our point of view were moral, which it is not, we would have a great deal to be concerned about. For it is naive to believe that a moral agent can get by just with the proper motivational set. A healthy infusion of judgment along with discriminations grounded in a careful evaluation of principles and their application to cases are an antidote to various ills which can beset even natural saints. Consider the flower child, an easy prey for sects with nefarious purposes; or the political radical, so moved by compassion for the disadvantaged that he is swayed to support policies which ultimately work against that group. But it should not be necessary to preach the benefits of intelligence to an audience of philosophers.

Thus, Shapiro would have us attend to but part of the story. We cannot always just look at x and y and act on the basis of that alone. We do not wish to replace the excesses of the rigid character with a dangerous mindlessness. Oftimes the most important thing morally to do is to get someone really to take a good, hard look at aspects of the world he is seeking to subordinate to some principle acceptable to his moral consciousness. But to decide, for example, whether or not an act or institution is fair, we may have to do a lot more than that. Looking carefully is an important part of the story. Evaluating the act or institution in terms of principles whose acceptability may themselves be challenged because of their inconsistency with other principles we are committed to is another part of that story.

The foregoing critique has been undertaken, as I said, from the moral point of view. But this is not the relevant point of view. I have never claimed that autonomy leads to morality. We have, to be sure, contrasted a virtuous amoralist with a psychopath to emphasize the fact that autonomy does not preclude other-regarding motives and related feelings. But there is no doubt that a virtuous amoralist lacks an essential ingredient of a perfectly moral agent. Never evaluating his motives, he can only use his rationality in a calculative way. Thus, even if he is able to maximize utility, he will fall short of our moral ideal.

A simple illustration, again involving fairness, will suffice. A virtuous amoralist loves his two children, but loves his daughter a little more than his son. He decides, therefore, to leave a greater portion of his estate to his daughter. Assuming that his daughter is not in greater need and that his preference is not grounded in any relevant difference, this act is unfair. But how can we convince the father? He may insist that the discrepancy be kept secret from his children so he will not have to contemplate the disappointment of his son. There is nothing clearly irrational about his act, and it does embody his feelings of love toward his children. But as an amoralist, he does not evaluate his motives from a moral perspective, for example, from a consideration like fairness. He is not as moral as a principled person might be, but it does not follow that he is not fully autonomous.

If, from the perspective of morality, one moved by love of family or tribe or nation needs to reflect diligently upon her circumstances in light of moral principles which have been submitted to the tests of reason and experience, this conclusion applies even more conspicuously to one whose other-directed actions are *limited* to those who enter into these special relations. Thus, we have the familiar examples of the criminal who treats family members with love and respect, but has no compunctions about harming others for the sake of himself or his family, or the tribal member who sees himself bound only by intratribal obligations. Most moral systems – all legitimate ones, some would say – whether or not they acknowledge a special moral place for obligations arising out of particular relations like family and religion, insist on the need for constraints upon action arising from the interests of persons outside self or family or religion. Without these constraints, the result is ethnic, religious, national, or racial strife. If morality cannot be derived from autonomy, it does not follow that its significance is thereby undermined. Indeed, we may choose morality *over* autonomy – the supremacy of autonomy as a value cannot just be assumed.

Although we have yet to find anything seriously amiss about the Überfrau from the point of view of her autonomy, I may be charged with trivializing my own doctrine by conceding the necessity of values for autonomy and shifting the claim to a weaker one concerning the *way* in which values can be embedded in the personality. This charge can be answered.

1. Certain evaluations must be second-level and cannot, therefore, enter the life of a virtuous amoralist. For example, as I said previously, a judgment that one's central life activity is ultimately worthless is available only to a person who reflects.

This is *not* to say that one who does not make personal evaluations lacks *self*-worth or *self*-esteem. In fact, self-esteem is best thought of as an awareness of one's autonomy, as we earlier saw.

2. We must recall the earlier discussion of value in which the adoption of the Evaluative Conception was seen to be required to give substance to the issue of value-free autonomy. If values are to be identified with the strongest knowledgeable choice, à la the Motivation Conception, only extreme psychotics or those in a vegetative-like state lack values.

3. Thus, it would be preferable to say, as I suggested earlier, that in those unusual cases in which the ego ideals are totally reabsorbed by the primary level, the agent, even if he is driven by compassion and love, is *not* acting from value, that is, personal evaluations. We may, in other words, concede the psychological correctness of Kohut's views on the conditions of self-cohesion without denying the significance of the distinction between the amoralist and the value-driven person, even if they are behaviorally similar.

4. These arguments presuppose that a cohesive self does not specifically require a level of personal evaluation. Indeed this level can degenerate into the rigid character, one whose autonomy is threatened by his own principles. We saw as well that a perfectly moral agent will make personal evaluations. But since autonomy does not require perfect morality, we cannot conclude that it requires personal evaluations.

Normal persons who act immorally may appear to be similar superficially to autonomous agents who are genuinely value-free. An agent is not value-free just because she acts immorally or strangely or from ignorance, compulsion, or great stress, or because of a bout of weakness of will. Nor, of course, are we concerned with those who stray from the path of righteousness for any of the reasons available to the average person: selfishness, a propensity to divert one's attention from human suffering, the refusal to acknowledge one's weaknesses, fears, and dispositions to cruelty, the need to protect a vulnerable ego, and so on. For all these persons may *have* values they fail to act on for one or another reason.

Having repeatedly stressed the possibility of autonomy without morality, I might be interpreted as denying the capatibility of autonomy *with* morality. Although I have highlighted types of examples, for example, the rigid personality, in which the moral temperament does indeed preclude autonomy, I have never denied that moral agents as such can be autonomous. In light of examples like the rigid personality, it is not a simple matter to lay out the contours of the moral life for one committed to autonomy. It goes without saying that such an individual has adopted a moral code independently in the sense specified in Chapter 6. Thus, it may have originated from and be substantively identical with the moral outlook of his group, but it is sustained by this individual for "the" reasons that can be advanced on its behalf.

In fact, the account of objectivity defended in this work is quite congenial to the possibility of autonomous morality. The reason is linked to the situating of objectivity, a notion that will be described more fully in the next chapter, at the core of my conception of autonomy. The argument begins with a reminder that the earlier rejection of ideal autonomy prepares the ground for autonomous subordination (objectivity), that is, open, informed, and flexible response to the materials, structure, and constraints of those disciplines, institutions, and enterprises interaction with which constitutes our life and provides it with meaning. If a painter remains autonomous even when his artistic vision imposes what he might describe as severe constraints on his activity, why may not a moral person be permitted to feel analogous constraints? Indeed, the analogy may be pressed to defend against the objection that the moral life is distinctively incompatible with autonomy on the grounds that a moral agent (who is not a saint) is sometimes required to act against his own interests. For clashes with self-interest are the staple of many forms of life, not just the moral one. In adopting certain constraints on his behavior, the moral agent thereby opens himself to the possibility of conflict. But that is true of any complex life. The inability to satisfy two conflicting desires does not automatically make one heteronomous, except in a trivial way.[10] And although it is true that moral conflicts, unlike many others, often demand the sacrifice of significant personal interests, it is also true that many nonmoral commitments – to become a prima ballerina or thrive as a painter, for example – make equally formidable claims upon us.

I shall not ponder further the constraints that must be imposed on a moral agent who refuses to abandon personal autonomy. I see no insuperable barriers to the definition of this type. Of course, wherever we find a set of fundamental commitments, moral or otherwise, barriers to the fulfillment of said commitments can nullify the very freedoms whose absence also annuls this particular individual's personal autonomy. Although certain conflicts are easy to abide, unremitting frustration and the associated loss of a significant amount of autonomy may well be the consequence of imposing great demands on life.

8
The liberation theory of autonomy: Objectivity

The picture of the autonomous agent that has evolved so far incorporates the following elements: (1) Freedom: an autonomous agent possesses a variety of intellectual and physical skills and capacities which confer upon him the further capacity to assess his options competently. His autonomy is enhanced by a strong rational will. (2) Values: an autonomous agent has and acts on values, but it is not necessary that these values be understood as the Evaluative Theory demands. That is, he is not necessarily disposed to evaluate his desires and options from a moral point of view or from the point view of the worth of his motivations. (3) Rationality: an autonomous agent is basically rational. He possesses rational powers and is generally disposed to use these powers in decision making, even though he may retain and occasionally act on the power to flout rational principles. (4) Independence: the procedures and principles of decision making adopted by an autonomous agent are held by that agent on the grounds of their reliability in the process of decision making. Regardless of origin, they are subject to evaluation in terms of criteria that are as objective as possible. Although an autonomous agent may enter relationships which entail (self-imposed) limitations, he does not thereby abandon either his ultimate capacity for or his right to rational review. (5) Contingency: given the unintelligibility of the model of ideal autonomy, the fact of contingency must be conceded. Since all autonomous agents are limited by their development, I have proposed criteria to determine the ways in which one agent can be more autonomous than another. (6) Emotional and characterological viability: an autonomous agent who happens not to possess values in the sense of the Evaluation Conception is nonetheless capable of a wide range of attitudes, emotions, and character traits, even though he is not capable of moral emotions and attitudes. He is capable of love, friendship, courage, gratitude, and trust, for example. He possesses self-respect and self-esteem in terms of dispositions to act rather than dispositions to judge, including the disposition to engage the world robustly, confidently, vitally, and independently.

Must we not finally introduce the notion of self-determination as the very essence of autonomy? I believe, however, that the problems philosophers have confronted in explicating autonomy derive from their failure to see that autonomy is *not* internal generation. In spite of the etymology of the term, we must look not to the internal connection, not to the origin in self, but rather to the way the agent enters his world. That has in fact been the thrust of the discussion so far. Philosophers have freely introduced into their accounts of the nature of freedom the reasons that freedom is valuable to us. Consequently, we are often told that autonomy (or freedom) and value are intertwined. I believe that a more significant connection relates autonomy not to values, but rather to the manner in which the agent is immersed in her surroundings.

I have expressed the common feeling that we would not have greater freedom of a worthwhile sort if we retained the power to reject a proposition whose truth is staring us in the face. Although my endorsement of this view was slightly qualified in Chapter 6, I want now to affirm that we should feel similarly unafraid by the correlative need to subordinate ourselves to the other arenas in which we act and find our satisfactions. For it is in this way that autonomy is achieved.

Autonomy and objectivity

As a child begins to assert himself, his natural intellectual and physical development permits a deeper and more pervasive relation to the external world. He can do a lot more and he can represent the world in sophisticated ways to himself so that his goals are now becoming diversified, and he is also able to defer the gratification of some of them. At the same time, he identifies with the traits, values, and principles of his parents. If these are successfully incorporated, the conflict will not be great. But the conflict must be there to some extent for he inevitably plays off these incorporated elements with those arising from his own relation to the world. Indeed, his self-esteem is grounded in a growing awareness of his own ability to formulate and carry out his goals whether or not they are the introjected ones; this is his awareness of his own autonomy.

Successful identification is clearly not sufficient for autonomy. The identification process submits itself to a continuing struggle through childhood and adolescence as the growing person asserts his own authority and tests the adequacy of inculcated values and principles against the world as he comes to understand and appreciate it.

Given that the process is successful, the result is an autonomous adult. Psychologists have no qualms describing it in this way despite the ultimate "origin" of the psyche in the identification process. If the introjected values and aims of the authority figures survive the maturation process pretty well intact, so be it. The demands of the friends of ideal autonomy for greater independence than this are unreasonable, as I demonstrated in Chapter 6.

As we know, this process must fulfill certain conditions if autonomy is the outcome. The requirement of rationality, for example, explains why a dogmatic person, one who retains a doctrine even when it conflicts with the preponderance of evidence, is heteronomous. Whether his dogmatism is mere tenacity – persistence in the pursuit of a goal even when (the person knows that) it is very unlikely to be attained – or a genuine failure of *competence*, he is likely to get into trouble. But even if he is a frequent failure, he may be one of those people who do not respond badly to adversity. If a goal is very important to a person, he may wish to pursue it even if other objectives are thereby frustrated, and even if he is not very efficient or competent.

This resistance to frustration helps to explain some of the commendable features of Jehovah's Witnesses and similar groups. When the dogmatism of certain religious people or members of cults pertains to matters taken to be absolutely central to the core of the person, a shield against the frustration of other goals resulting from this irrational, unscientific, and narrow posture is thereby activated. For since all one's important goals are subordinated to the core ideology, protection against the failure of the subordinate goals is virtually guaranteed. If submission to my master requires the suppression of my desires to participate in the life of my family, then I may well try to suppress or to reconceive those desires in such a way as to permit me to pursue my religious quest without internal conflict. We are, therefore, impressed by members of Jehovah's Witnesses, who are locked into a narrow, all-encompassing ideology, who suppress whatever individuality they once possessed, and who then convert this total dedication and assurance in times of deep stress into equanimity and fortitude.

In addition to failures of independence and critical competence, Jehovah's Witnesses share an important trait with rigid persons. They both respond to the world by the invocation of principles rather than by an objective and open examination of relevant features of that world. They both look to the world for confirmation of principles which are never really put to the test; the world for them is a place to apply, not test, their convictions. This propensity is, of course, invaluable for the protection against failure of the core ideology. In other words, they lack what Shapiro calls "objectivity."

The conception of an agent's response to the world as being governed by features of that world has played a role in both epistemology and value theory. Nozick (1981: 167–288) claimed that a person with knowledge is essentially one whose beliefs "track" the true, that is, one who adjusts his beliefs in light of the actual state of the world; and in the sphere of value, we similarly seek to be sensitive to the values in the world, adjusting our reactions accordingly. So knowledgeable and good persons direct their inner lives (beliefs, desires, feelings) by the objective state of the world. The value of free will lies in this ability to align ourselves with value. Striking a similar chord, Wolf (1990: 67–93) defines freedom (as a condition of moral responsibility) in terms of the ability to be governed by the right. But, interestingly, neither Nozick nor Wolf think of *autonomy* in this way at all. Both interpret autonomy as what I have called ideal autonomy, and Wolf concludes, as many have, that the idea is incoherent. Nozick attempts to unravel the implications of this radical idea and the result borders on the incomprehensible or is at least of negligible value to an understanding of the autonomy of real people. If objectivity is the key to knowledge and morality, might it not also be a crucial component of nonideal autonomy?

The nature of objectivity

Since *all* action incorporates objective and subjective components, we must look more closely at the distinction between the autonomous agent's purposes arising from the world and the rigid person's arising from (partially) introjected parental principles. If a young musician is growing up to be an autonomous person, is it not also true that his purposes do not just derive from the "world" as he daily confronts it? His parents encouraged and nurtured his musical growth. He himself was reassured by the recognition of his own (internal) talent. His musical activity is also in part the reflection of principles of technique and performance he has learned and consistently applies.

Objectivity, as I would characterize it, is in part an epistemic condition, distinguished by the degree to which the acquisition of information, particularly in perception, is independent of subjective principles or nonuniversal physiological defects. That is involved in seeing things "as they really are" (or at least as a normal, competent, impartial spectator would), seeing facets of things whether or not they would conflict with principles, and not being limited by flaws of a physiological character. In this regard, objectivity is reminiscent of procedural independence; it matters not how the perceptual powers of an agent came about; it is rather their current reliability which confers objectivity upon them.

The proviso that permits objectivity to be satisfied should a spectator see things as a normal, competent, impartial spectator would is designed to deal with matters like optical illusions. Not only is it determined that we see color emanating from the purely black rings of Benham's Disk when the disk spins. It is also true that the knowledge that there is no light source other than black or white does not change this universal, involuntary response. We might well call this a failure of objectivity. But in the context, there is little point in doing so for we wish to isolate responses to the world which the individual distorts not just in virtue of his membership in the human species. If we had been more sympathetic with the viability of the concept of ideal autonomy, we might well regard the response to Benham's Disk as a breakdown of objectivity and, therefore, an instance of heteronomy. (This is not to say that our rejection of ideal autonomy prohibits us from viewing a defective *behavioral* response to Benham's Disk as an instance of heteronomy. A person who *believes* and *bets in accordance with the belief* that the rings are really green suffers from the same sort of unfreedom and consequent reduction of autonomy as any other ignorant person.) Insofar as we found it necessary to shift to notions like maximal and real autonomy, each conceived in terms of degrees and limited to creatures who have contingent purposes and natures, the identification of universal limitations is interesting, but not to the point. It might be entertaining to ponder the greater autonomy of a creature who can "see" nonvisible light; but it is even more interesting to see if we can formulate a conception of autonomy for human creatures.

There is point, therefore, in identifying *non*universal limitations occasioned by purely physiological conditions. The color blind person suffers from a condition which, like ignorance, can affect his freedom and autonomy. He does not see things as a normal person would and is in danger, therefore, of behaving inappropriately. Evidently, this defect can be and often is minimized, but the fact that it is physiologically induced does not render it less harmless in terms of its potential effect on our freedom and autonomy. A similar conclusion obtains in the case of temporary infirmities such as intoxication and severe stress. This provision again highlights the point that autonomy is a matter of degree; one with good hearing has more freedom and potential autonomy than one with poor hearing.

It would be simplistic to suggest that our responses to the world can be dichotomized, depending on whether they are grounded in fact or in fancy. Our interpretations of the world are not just right or wrong, but rather fall on a continuum which includes intermediate positions such as "exaggerated," "shallow," "biased," "fragmentary," "contextually inappropriate," and "distorted." We will, however, dichotomize the problem at another point by drawing a somewhat arbitrary line between the agent's description of the world and her behavioral response to that description. With respect to the latter, a rigid or otherwise inappropriate response to the agent's description is a breakdown of objectivity. Before we turn to the nexus of problems surrounding these ideas of appropriateness and flexibility, I want first to say a few words about the issues which pertain to the other term, the agent's description.

Evidently, the notion of objectivity presupposes the possibility of neutral, objectively grounded descriptions of the world. This is not the occasion for a defense of scientific realism. I would only wish to point out that there is obviously a connection between the realism-relativism controversy and controversies about the nature of mental illness and the nature of autonomy on psychologically based characterizations of the latter, such as mine. Relativism encourages radical conceptions of mental illness as either nonexistent (see Thomas Szasz 1970) or as a set of appropriate responses to the person's own "world" (see R. D. Laing 1969).

So I shall assume a canonical, objectively accurate or at least well-grounded description of the world. We observe first that this description can incorporate all bona fide perspectives, physical, chemical, biological, historical, anthropological, sociological, and so on. So one is not wrong to describe that chair as a Queen Anne, made of walnut in 1730, weighing 10 pounds, used for sitting, a family heirloom, easily stained, coveted by Aunt Louise, and so on. Second, an incomplete description is clearly not necessarily an inaccurate one, and the latter is what matters.

But there are still a variety of ways of deviating from these descriptions without being plain wrong. It would be convenient to deal with the continuum (between pure fact and pure fancy) by an appeal to the hypothetical normal, perfectly competent, and impartial ("ideal") observer. But, even ignoring purely evaluative responses ("beautiful," "disgusting"), we have no reason to expect uniform responses with respect to adjectives like "cluttered" or "noisy." That is, even "ideal observers" can vary, depending on circumstance or culture. Differential responses to a variety of matters do not impugn the partiality, competence, or normality of the observer. Accordingly, we ought not judge Jack, the farmer, *or* Jill, the city dweller, as deficient in objectivity because they form different judgments of noisiness. It would be advisable, therefore, to adopt a conservative account according to which discrepant responses of ideal observers nullifies conclusions of nonobjectivity based on that category of response.

This proposal presupposes that one can isolate features of the "ideal observer" that bear on his role as determiner of the objective. And we do indeed have tests of various sorts of competence. We should note as well that normality is not to be understood so as to preclude trained expertise. A normal oenologist possesses a highly developed olfactory faculty, and a normal pilot can see better than most people.

Impartiality is the most difficult characteristic to describe. It is necessary but not sufficient to insist that an impartial spectator be disinterested, that is, either not have a stake in the matter or not know what his stake is. For a distorted response can arise even in a disinterested spectator. A misogynist judge has no stake in the outcome of a trial of a woman he is conducting. Yet the guilty verdict he delivers displays his partiality; he knowingly or unknowingly bases his verdict on his antipathy toward women rather than on the evidence.

It may not suffice to require that there be a preponderance of opinion against the judge's verdict on the part of otherwise normal, competent individuals, for discrimination based on gender may be endemic to the society. If we are to condemn an entire group's objectivity, we shall have to do so by appeal to the distortions created by a defective environment. And we once again find ourselves assuming a perspective from which this judgment may be rendered. These judgments are sometimes very difficult, and we must often wait upon the cumulative impact of an extended debate, much as we must cull the transcript of a lengthy trial. A charge of partiality or irrationality may rest on subtle matters that are difficult even for rational, scientific observers to identify. Only the give and take of the informed, competent, and conscientious members of the society can produce a reliable result. The complexity of this process is augmented by the ill-defined nature of the very class which is supposed to be issuing this expert judgment. For membership in the class of ideal observers rests on judgments made by that class itself.

Given that we do not require of an objective response that it be offered from a particular perspective or that it be complete, and given that we do require unanimity among "ideal observers" before we proffer a judgment of nonobjectivity, I can abide the inconclusiveness that attends many of these judgments. And the ill-defined character of the class of ideal observers along with the effects of that imprecision are elements we have to live with anyway. For the judgment of a scientific community that one of its members is a crackpot usually gets sorted out over time through the interaction between the ongoing dialogue within the (imperfectly defined) community and the theoretical and experimental results that come to light.[1]

A second component of objectivity is flexibility, the disposition to change one's behavior, views, and responses in light of new and relevant information. A person may have an excellent grasp of the world as it is, but be too set in his ways to change. He sees that the situation calls for a novel response, including perhaps a fundamental change of goals, but cannot muster the resources to make one. As much as our autonomous musician responds to internal signals, he is also objective in these ways. He is prepared to estimate his talent accurately; he will not seek confirmation of his deepest wishes about himself where more impartial observers see only wishful thinking. He is ready to rethink the principles of performance if his musical growth is blocked by a possibly rigid adherence to a teacher's dogmas. And he listens carefully, ever ready to hear afresh, and to be nourished by new sources of musical inspiration. Although he may, of course, be engaged in self-evaluation, he does not brood upon the quality of his performance and his potential as a professional. And, as much as he was initially propelled and inspired by his parents, he is now internally motivated. He contrasts dramatically with the rigid individual, Shapiro's paradigm heteronomous person. The features of this person are: inflexibility, a disposition to constant self-evaluation, a failure of internalization, reflected in the feeling that values are external constraints, willfulness, nonspontaneity, and the absence of a propensity to engage in a fair test of principles of action, which are constantly invoked as a source of comfort and a bulwark against self-confrontation.

Other things being equal, an objective person is more likely to be informed than one who is not. The cognitive dimension of autonomy, an openness to the world as it appears to be to one who is not disposed to distort his perceptions so as to render them compatible with, and confirmation of, antecedently held principles and beliefs, is more likely to give rise to knowledge than its contradictory attitude. There are, of course, other conditions determining the extent to which a person is informed. One must actually have made relevant observations, and one must have the capacity to interpret them accordingly. Since we must have sufficient information to be able competently to evaluate our choices, autonomy requires a certain amount of relevant knowledge; however, we must not confuse objectivity as an attitude essential to autonomy with knowledge, a component of positive freedom.

The failure of objectivity in debilitating neuroses and personality disorders is documented in the work of psychologists from a variety of traditions. Although the psychoanalytic tradition, in which, in a broad sense, Shapiro works, has been challenged by cognitive therapy, proponents of the latter school of thought are equally insistent on characterizing neurotics as those who respond inappropriately to the world. A. T. Beck writes,

Despite the similarities, the person with acute anxiety reaction differs significantly from the person exposed to a realistic threat. The danger the patient perceives is nonexistent or blown out of proportion. He is not only preoccupied with the idea of danger, but he consistently misinterprets innocuous stimuli as indicative of danger. (1976: 81)

In fact, cognitive therapy's core idea, that emotional disorders are cognitive failures, that is, misinterpretations of the world, based perhaps on defects in the learning experience, places the failure of objectivity at the core of mental illness. "Our inner workings can shut out or twist around the signals from the outside so that we may be completely out of phase with what is going on around us. A profound or chronic discrepancy may culminate in psychological disorders" (Beck 1976: 25).

Inappropriateness is a difficult notion and we have yet to explain it satisfactorily. Beck notes that neurotics can be *over*sensitive to stimuli. A husband can listen too carefully to the remarks of his wife in order to find a basis for a hostile response. The inappropriateness of his response has to do with the distortion of stimuli on behalf of a mode of relating that is determined by his internal, unresolved conflicts rather than an objective appraisal of his relationship.

Before we attempt to clarify these vague remarks, it will be helpful to relate the epistemic dimension of objectivity to the matter of rationality. Beck's comment about acute anxiety reaction and the common response to phobias suggest that these conditions are in part cases of irrationality. Since snakes and mice are not as dangerous as the phobic reaction to them would suggest, we may be disposed to conclude that phobic patients either grossly misinterpret the likelihood of danger or employ an irrational principle of decision making. But a more plausible interpretation would refuse to construe their behavior as an instance of decision making at all. The withdrawal behavior is more typically an automatic response to an inner emotional state, itself elicited by the sight of the relevant object. A person afflicted with a phobia may well *concede* the objective unlikelihood of danger, but still be victimized by the emotional reaction induced by the presence of the feared object.

Thus, the irrationality of the fear response must be explained in another way or we must at least understand the sense in which the response is "inappropriate." There are dangers in invoking the debilitating character of phobias in this context. For example, a person with the fear of snakes who happens to spend his entire adult life on the east side of Manhattan is likely to get by quite well with his "affliction," whereas a man with agoraphobia who has just been hired to lead a caravan across the Sahara Desert is in deep trouble. The resident of Manhattan may be just as irrational as the caravan leader, although there is cause for concern and a reason to seek treatment only in the latter case.

If one views the behavior as a choice, one is entitled to introduce as relevant in the utility assignments the reduction of the fear or terror that an avoidance reaction would certainly produce. What this shows, in fact, is that the behavior is *not* irrational – the avoidance of the unpleasant is a clear case of rationality; if anything is irrational, then, it must be the emotion of fear and not the response of flight to that emotion. And that result applies both to the full-fledged phobic response as well as the response to an exaggerated fear (in which the person retains the power to choose). Thus, the theory of rational *choice* cannot teach us anything useful in this context.

Since responses to the world are objective only if one retains the capacity for flexible response, we are supposing that objective behavioral (as opposed to perceptual) responses must be voluntary. This is not, of course, to say that the response must actually be preceded by choice or deliberation, but only that it is open to intelligent control. Habitual and spontaneous actions can be voluntary in this sense, but phobic behavior is not. In looking to psychology, then, to help us to determine the ways in which the range of objective response is narrowed, we might think that we are learning how our repertoire of involuntary responses expands.

But the issue of the voluntary character of neurotic response is itself highly controversial for both psychological and philosophical reasons. With respect to the former, even within the broadly psychoanalytic tradition, views range from the traditional Freudian doctrine which construes action as impulse- rather than choice-driven to Shapiro's view, according to which all neurotic action (and virtually all normal action), is voluntary. Although I think it evident that the classical doctrine fails, I also agree with Mausner (1990) that Shapiro's doctrine goes too far in the opposite direction. When neurotic symptoms arise in response to unmanageable conflict, the result is panic, a state which precludes the possibility of mediation by volitional processes. The person is in no position to evaluate the potential means for alleviating tension and is, therefore, in worse shape than the robbery victim who can *choose* the option of minimizing danger by succumbing to the robber's demands.

Yet the agent with neurotic symptoms does alleviate his panic through the adoption of these symptoms in the same way the phobic reduces his fear response. The rationality of behavior in these cases is more than the use of innate adaptive mechanisms such as those accounting for perspiration in hot weather. For one thing, the responses are individual, not species-wide; moreover, they are symbolically mediated, thereby permitting us to see the goal of the behavior as determined by intentions of the agent. Consciously, of course, there is no choice, but that is true of voluntary actions like habits. So the involuntary character of these actions must be grounded on the hypothetical fact that the agent would be unable to process relevant information which suggests the irrationality of the panic reaction. And, of course, neurotics do stubbornly resist such information, for example, when it points to the way in which their actions have an adverse impact on other goals of theirs. In any event, the philosophical issues bearing on the nature of the voluntary are live, and I will develop my thoughts on the connection of psychology to the idea of objectivity without further consideration of them.

A breakdown of objectivity: The phobic response

It would be presumptuous to characterize objectivity in a way which commits us to a psychoanalytic approach to mental illness. The idea of an adult open to the world as it is and responding to it in an appropriate manner ought to admit of an explication which does not preclude alternative accounts of the manner in which emotional factors can interfere with objectivity. In order to see how we might best provide a neutral account of objectivity, it will be helpful to contrast the principal psychological accounts of a type of affliction, phobia, concentrating on those elements that bear on the matter of objectivity.

A typical psychoanalytic account of phobia is provided by N. Cameron (1963) in his description of the famous case of "Little Hans."

This boy of five years refused to go out into the street because he was afraid of horses, actually feared being bitten by them. In the course of therapy it turned out that the horses symbolized the hated and feared aspect of his father. The phobic solution was about as follows. . . . The love for his father was retained, while the hatred for him was displaced on the horses. This had the added advantage that the horse could easily be avoided, whereas his father could not. . . . the boy expected primitive retaliation from his father for the primitive hostility he himself felt. This expectation likewise was displaced. It became the regressive oral fear that horses would bite him. (294–5)

We have then a conscious intentional state explained by an unconscious intentional state whose object (father, retaliation by father) is symbolized by the object of the former (horses, being bitten by horses). Now *given* the conscious fear, the avoidance behavior is fully understandable without the aid of psychoanalytic theory. The theory, then, enables us to explain the conscious fear itself in terms of the unconscious fear and its symbolic connection to the conscious fear.

It is often said that psychoanalytic explanations provide the agent's reason for an action which appears to lack one. This psychoanalytic explanation tells us that Hans avoids horses because he does not wish to be castrated by his father. But notice first that we do not need to know why Hans avoids horses once we know that he is afraid of them. So psychoanalytic theory has to remove the puzzlement over the fear itself, and it does that by the symbolic connection together with the belief about retaliation. But even if this removes some of our puzzlement, it leaves unanswered a question about the irrationality of this belief. Why should Hans hold such an erroneous belief?

Evidently, the psychoanalytic account of the Oedipal conflict must be brought to bear on this question. Even if that account adequately explains *young* Hans's castration fears, his current fear of horses can only be explained by reference to that childhood fear if we suppose that the conflict, including his belief about his father, was repressed as a child and, therefore, never submitted to subsequent rational scrutiny. Otherwise, we would expect he might learn that his father is not such a bad chap. Thus, the ossified belief festered in his unconscious, affecting him in ways he could not control. His freedom was impaired by the influence of a false and ill-grounded belief. Its effect is more pernicious than a conscious analogue, for the latter has at least a chance of being found out once critical reflection commences.

As we have said often, any response to the world implicates both the world and the respondent. In order to justify the conclusion that Hans's behavior displays a failure of objectivity, we must find a basis for concentration on the respondent rather than the world. Psychoanalytic theory tells us that Hans is not "really" responding to the horse, but is rather responding to his own childhood fears which have become displaced on the horse. The horse is a peg on which to rest his Oedipal fixation. He avoids horses ultimately because of unconscious intentional states (fears, beliefs) which were formed in childhood, rendered inaccessible to consciousness because of their painful content, and which are now activated by triggering experiences like the presence of horses. If Hans's behavior were genuinely objective, then the actual features of horses that are causally relevant to his behavior would not just be those which render them a candidate for symbolic representation of the father.

The profound impact of childhood on adult behavior postulated by psychoanalysis enables it to characterize failures of objectivity without having to invoke the debilitating character of phobias and other neurotic disorders. According to psychoanalytic theory, childhood experiences become causes *in esse* or *sustaining* causes of adult behaviors. For this reason, the theory threatens human freedom more than do other theories, even those which are *completely deterministic*. The desires, beliefs, and fears formed when the person was uncritical *persist* to do their dirty work. And since they operate on the unconscious level, the agent's critical capacity, as we noted previously, is impotent to affect these states. They are like genetic factors, contingencies which cannot be altered (unless the person enters treatment) and which can function to diminish our autonomy.

Although we called Hans's belief about his father both false and ill-grounded, it might be neither. And if we identify as the relevant belief of the adult Hans "My father is *now* a danger," we might even imagine *that* belief to be epistemically impeccable. Now, if poor Hans's father, with evil intent, has been brandishing a kitchen knife before his hapless son since the poor boy's Oedipal phase began, we would certainly expect dire psychological consequences. But the standard psychoanalytic account supposes that the belief arises independently of the normal, reliable channels. Hans conjures up this belief out of his own desires and feelings of guilt, whether or not the belief is true or justified. And it is that process which explains the onset of the phobia. So the belief is epistemically tainted in terms of the unreliability of the actual process leading to its formation. For the sake of brevity, we shall simply call such beliefs unreliable. They can produce the same unfortunate effects when they are screened off from the critical review process even if they happen to be true and justifiable.

Freudian theory has spawned an enormous number of variations. We can, therefore, find psychoanalytic accounts which preserve those features permitting ubiquitous judgments of nonobjectivity, while rejecting other key elements of the Freudian point of view. The elements accounting for a breakdown of objectivity are essentially the persistence and causal relevance of unconscious intentional states, unreliably formed and resistant to revision through normal review processes.

The cognitive therapist agrees with the psychoanalyst that the "real" object of fear is not necessarily the manifest one, the object the patient reports is inducing his avoidance reaction. But, unlike the psychoanalyst, the cognitive therapist believes that the deeper fear is accessible to the patient and can be elicited through discussion and reflection. Extraction of the "ideational core" (Beck 1976: 168) of the phobia does not require the mediation of an elaborate theory to provide us with symbolic interpretations. Patients with agoraphobia may reveal after questioning that they fear being stricken with an illness under circumstances in which medical help is difficult to obtain or that they will lose personal control and do something very embarrassing out in the open.

In addition to agreement about the need for some sort of distinction between manifest and latent content, the cognitive therapist also concedes that, in the case of "fixation phobias," the "conceptual maturation with respect to this fear was arrested at an early stage of development" (Beck 1976: 180). A normal childhood fear, of animals, the dark, or doctors, is removed from the domain which is submitted to learning through experience, maturation, and reflection.

Beck has little to say about the reason this happens. He does note that parents may reinforce these fears, especially if they experience the same fears. Truth aside, psychoanalytic theory at least offers an explanation for the burial of the fear in a corner of the mind inaccessible to the reflections of the individual.

The reference to reinforcement is reminiscent of the explanation of phobias provided by the school of behavior therapy. For, although the latter eschews reference to cognitive elements, relying instead on traditional behaviorist notions of learning as classical or operant conditioning, Beck's explanation of the *persistence* of the fear and, therefore, the evolution into adulthood of the phobia does not itself invoke any distinctively cognitive elements. If the only explanation of the retention of the fear is the reinforcement of the parent, why might we not construe that in terms of the standard conditioning paradigm? To be sure, Beck is not committed to the behaviorist's (e.g., Wolpe's 1969) views about the *onset* of fears in terms of "accidental conditioning." Indeed, he rejects the view that phobias arise from the displacement of the fear directed to a genuinely frightening object onto a stimulus which happens to be presented along with that object. The presumed virtue of this position, to wit, its ability to explain bizarre fears in terms of the fact that anything might be in the vicinity of a frightening object, is only apparent once we see, after some probing, that phobias are not as bizarre as they initially seem. The real fear is a common one linked *nonaccidentally* to the ostensible fear. A woman is afraid of eating solid food because she once almost choked to death on a piece of meat.

With respect to the issue of objectivity in the case of cognitive therapy, we have noted a similarity to the psychoanalytic account insofar as the phobic adult is plagued with the fears and beliefs he has both retained and failed to submit to critical review. The inability to eradicate unreliable beliefs – evidently more disabling than simple ignorance – is an epistemic limitation on his freedom, as well. The cognitive therapist may well regard phobias as sufficiently difficult to alleviate on one's own, so that his views on the limitations on freedom of the afflicted individual turn out to be practically the same as those of the psychoanalyst. Yet psychoanalysis does view such afflictions as more intractable than the cognitive therapist believes they are, for, according to psychoanalysis, the beliefs and desires which explain the condition are highly resistant to reemergence in consciousness.

If we remind ourselves that a phobic reaction is not a decision, we may wonder what the relevance of the unavailability of relevant information is. Although it is clear enough why a decision maker needs reliable information, a phobic does not use information to decide to engage in avoidance behavior. Nonetheless, the phobic response, as an emotion, can be assessed in terms of its rationality, where an irrational emotion is one that is based on misinformation. One can be angry or saddened that P when not-P is the case. In learning the truth, therefore, one hopes that appropriate emotional adjustments are made. And the fact that adjustments are not always made does not diminish the significance of information. Any decision depends on a multitude of factors. That I continue to smoke in the full knowledge that it is bad for my health does not imply that my freedom is not diminished by ignorance concerning the consequences of smoking to my health. So why would it not be equally important for a person afflicted with arachnaphobia to know that spiders are not dangerous, even if he remains afflicted?[]

On psychoanalytic assumptions, we may similarly suppose that Hans can come to learn, through a purely intellectual process, that he fears castration. If, for example this is explained to him by someone whose views he respects, perhaps his therapist, the information will play no role in his cure. According to psychoanalytic theory, successful therapy requires that he come to *recognize* this fact.

So whether or not the relevant information and access to states like desires and fears are available to the person, they are not available in a *usable form*. For the psychoanalyst, they are buried in the unconscious, thereby providing protection from painful emotions; for the cognitive therapist, the misconceptions on which the phobic reaction is based are not as inaccessible. The therapist must avail himself of a variety of cognitive techniques, for example, identifying misconceptions, pointing to experiences which show the patient to be in error, isolating illicit inferences, and teaching a patient how to learn from his experiences. Beck concedes that simple "intellectual acquiescence" to the truth is insufficient and that attitudinal and emotional factors can facilitate the transition to genuine acceptance and the initiation of emotional transformation. The patient who fears solid food may acknowledge that incidences of choking are very rare. Yet she may need to go through a process of unlearning in which the "automatic thought" linking solid food and choking confronts the facts in a supportive setting which encourages heightened awareness and objective self-examination.

So both positions agree that the patient must "recognize" the truth. For the cognitive therapist, the agoraphobic has a pretty good idea of the immediate reason for his behavior. He thinks he will make a fool of himself when he is exposed. But it is not that easy to relieve him of this conviction. Since he misinterprets the world, he lacks freedom, and since this propensity has become fairly entrenched, his objectivity is implicated – he responds inappropriately because he has a hard time seeing things as they really are. The problem is more severe, according to the psychoanalyst, because the patient lacks self-knowledge in key respects – little Hans does not know that he fears his father – and his capacity to recognize the truth in a therapeutically useful way depends on the emergence of repressed states in consciousness.

According to both, the one who suffers is stifled by the past because cognitively deficient mental states, acquired long ago and rigidified through immunity from the normal processes of rational review, occasioned by maturation and fresh experience, continue to be causally active. Highly minimal features of the stimuli are causally relevant to behavior: Hans responds in an automatic manner to signs of horses; the phobic responds similarly to the thought of solid food as such. The richness of experience is dissipated by a filter which permits only information bearing on the fear or desire ("it is a horse") automatically activated by the object to pass through, undergo symbolic transformation, at least according to psychoanalysis ("it is my father") and activate first the unreliable belief ("my father will castrate me") and then the behavior (avoidance).

It must be noted that these features which interfere with objectivity are not themselves sufficient for mental illness. There may be deeply ingrained, perhaps even innate, beliefs which operate during one's life, but are never submitted for review. The belief in an external world might be one of these. And Kantian epistemology is a rich source of examples, of course. The most obvious difference between these and the ones which enter into mental and emotional disorders is that these are not evidently unreliable. Yet this difference may not be crucial. The discovery that Berkeley's case against the rationality of the belief in an external world succeeds would not automatically make me mentally ill. A less frivolous example would be provided by one whose religious upbringing leads her to see a divine hand in all that happens. This belief is typically not put to the test; it is imparted to experience by the believer and plays a crucial role in attitude and behavior. Many would see it as ill-grounded, false, and unreliably formed; however, even if that is correct, the adherence to this outlook on the world cannot be counted automatically as a sign of mental illness.

Since this is not a treatise on mental illness, I shall not advance a view as to the difference between a phobic and a religious person, assuming both to be nonobjective and irrational. Is the former an instance of mental illness because his behavior is harmful to himself, very unpleasant, or not conducive to satisfactory functioning? Or is there an alternative account?

We alluded above to the behaviorist account of phobias in terms of accidental conditioning. Watson managed to induce a fear of rats in Little Albert by presenting a loud noise together with a rat. After several repetitions, Albert's natural fear of loud noises was extended to rats and, it was claimed, to other furry objects by the principle of generalization. It has become clear, however, that the behaviorist picture must be incomplete because it is not possible to condition people to be afraid of just any stimulus associated with a genuinely frightening one. One cannot induce a fear of wooden ducks, opera glasses, and curtains, for example (see Claridge 1985: 68). There is experimental evidence that many fears are innate and that the development of childhood fears takes a very definite chronological course (see Gray 1971). It may well be, then,

that the human nervous system is in some way "hard wired" to react to certain very specific stimuli, like snakes, which signal threat and which, as a result of evolution, have been left residually represented in Man and are more likely to be triggered into action in some people than in others. (Claridge 1985: 69–70)

We turn then to what I shall call the biological theory of phobias (and mental illness, in general).

The latter portion of this quotation alludes to individual differences in order to explain why phobias are distributed unevenly, given their alleged origin in a common feature of the human nervous system. Hans Eysenck (1967), basing his work on a fundamental principle of Pavlovian theory, argued that personality traits, extreme forms of which represent different types of mental illness, are themselves grounded in individual differences in the brain's excitability (which itself is modified by built-in inhibitory feedback loops). Thus, properties of the nervous system account for dimensions of temperament, such as anxiety, impulsivity, and aggressiveness, as well as the extreme forms of these which make people more susceptible to varieties of mental illness.

These ideas come together to indicate that certain aspects of phobic reactions may not actually be learned at all. They may simply arise in the first place because some very anxiety-prone people are more likely to show strong emotional responses to stimuli which in a real, perhaps evolutionary, sense *are* fear-producing, the behavior that they lead to being later elaborated through learning. (Claridge 1985: 68)

Physiology is relevant even in the explanation of the *persistence* of the fear, according to Gordon Claridge. Anxious individuals, for example, adapt extremely slowly to arousing stimuli. Anticipating fear, they avoid the source and thereby permit the level of anxiety to remain high over extended periods of time. Yet Claridge concedes, as his remark about the relevance of learning indicates, that physiology is insufficient to explain the manner by which phobias are elaborated. First of all, the behaviorists are right to emphasize the reinforcing properties of adult behaviors, for example, displays of the fear which then are imitated by the child. Secondly, the cognitive psychologists are right to emphasize the reinforcing properties of higher mental activities such as imagination – dwelling on the feared object exacerbates the anxiety, for example.

Cognitive elements play a more significant role in other disorders, for example, obsessive-compulsive neurosis. Some cognitive psychologists find a characteristic cognitive *style* in the obsessional personality, in particular, a narrowly focused attentional style, which leads to a rigidity in conceptualization. The biological perspective bids us to seek out the physiological foundation of such differences. Claridge observes in this connection that there is an established link between the mechanisms associated with the general arousal of the brain and the processes which control the breadth and narrowness of attention (1985: 75). In addition, the psychological style of obsessionals might be linked to the way the functions of the two cerebral hemispheres are organized. It goes without saying that the detailed way the psychology of the individual is mapped on to the concomitant neurophysiology has yet to be discovered.

Enough detail has been presented to identify the similarities and differences between the biological perspective on objectivity and the two psychological approaches discussed previously. For the former, the onset of the fear is determined by a combination of a genetically based trait transmitted through the processes of evolution, a temperamental propensity grounded in features of the central nervous system, and perhaps some environmental contingencies. The breakdown of objectivity derives from the causal significance of the person's contribution to the response in relation to the object's. The perception of the object sets in motion an inflexible, automatic response. The fear response cannot be adjusted based on information about the actual danger of the object. Although the response may be rooted in one that played a useful role for our biological ancestors, it is no longer grounded in an understanding of the world as it now is. Whereas the psychological positions emphasize the causal role of rigid, (relatively) inaccessible mental states, the biological outlook attributes the essential causal powers to the central nervous system.

The differences diminish if we choose a moderate version of the biological approach, such as Claridge's. For since learning enters the picture to sustain the phobia, learning can also work to eradicate the phobia. The moderate biological approach does not necessarily suppose, therefore, that phobias are more difficult to eradicate than the psychoanalysts believe. We cannot control the propensity to fear snakes, but the fear response, unlike the knee jerk, may be eliminable.

Society, through its treatment and corrective agencies, *does* bring about change in the sick, unhappy or deviant person. . . . But in none of these cases, if we are honest, is there a pretension that the remedies are anything other than palliative, or that the underlying temperamental dispositions are essentially altered. (Claridge 1985: 188)

Although the disposition is unalterable, we must remember that

temperament does not provide a blueprint for behavior as such, only for *styles* of behavior, similar temperaments finding expression in different ways. The evidence for this is all around us: the hysteric and the actress, the obsessive and the librarian, the schizoid and the Oxford don are often seen to come from, respectively, the same temperamental bags. (Claridge 1985: 189)

With respect to the issue of *autonomy*, the position of the biological approach has already been addressed in the discussion of contingency in Chapter 6. There are limitations which can adversely affect our autonomy through the interest we have in change. In the case of mental illness, therefore, the limitations would almost inevitably affect our autonomy – most people would prefer to be rid of these conditions. We distinguished the extrinsic origin of the trait from the capacity to change just as Claridge distinguishes the origin of the phobic reaction or the temperamental disposition which enhances the tendency for such a reaction from both the power to change the reaction, which we have, and the power to change our temperaments, which we do not. Since, according to Claridge, we lack the freedom to change our fundamental disposition, our (maximal) autonomy would be diminished were we to desire this change. Yet we may have a great deal of realistic autonomy as well as the freedom to change our phobic behavior.

But the current issue is the narrower one of objectivity. All responses to the world depend in part on our physiological and psychological condition. The three theories we have canvassed posit additional conditions which limit our response. The term "limit" is used instead of "determine" because the condition is an internal one, preventing the respondent from adjusting his response in light of relevant information emanating from the object. According to psychoanalytic theory, information about fathers and horses does not alter the inaccessible belief which accounts for the phobic reaction and the avoidance behavior. According to the cognitive theory, information about the likelihood of choking does not alter the automatic thought that links solid food and choking. According to the biological perspective, information about the dangers of mice does not alter the genetically determined fear response.

Although we have canvassed several psychological perspectives on the origin of phobias, there are, of course, other theories. Also, complexities emerge when we examine the ways in which each theory extends its ideas to mental disabilities other than phobias. Thus, the above discussion is severely limited in at least these two ways. Yet we have been able to identify, in major theories selected across a broad spectrum, the common view that barriers to objectivity are created by inner states, unreliably formed early in life in response to a common childhood situation and persisting in a way which removes them from experiential review and the influence of newly acquired information. Although these states are causally active, they induce insensitivity to individual differences among the objects on which they are directed and they inhibit flexible response. Let us call such states "backward-directed." Insofar as each theory's version of this general idea is applied to other instances of mental illness, we need not worry that backward-directed psychological states are peculiar to phobias.

The emphasis of the biological approach on temperament has been echoed in some psychoanalytic literature by the effort to bring to the focus the significance of character styles in the understanding of mental illness. Shapiro has been critical of psychoanalysis for its preoccupation with instinctual drives, stimuli, and tensions as factors determining development, mode of adaptive and defensive functioning, and neurotic style to the exclusion of an innately determined configuration of psychological equipment which imposes form and organization on experience and helps to determine, along with environmental input and biological drives, a style of psychological functioning. The style, which incorporates both a cognitive and an affective element, helps to explain the individual's "choice of neurosis" or character pathology. In contrast to the rigid character we have already described is the more "fluid" type, such as the impulsive, of which the psychopath is a variant, and the hysteric.

In Chapter 4, I talked briefly about the impulsive style and observed there what can now be described as a failure of objectivity on the part of an impulsive person. For, again, a person who is dominated by whim and a failure to form long-term attachments is likely to have a narrow and distorted understanding of the objects of his interests, observing only what is relevant to the satisfaction of the moment. I mention this to ward off the objection that the picture of the autonomous agent that is being offered here is that of one who lives from moment to moment, ever alive to the transient satisfaction and ever ready to abandon long-range commitments should they interfere with the pleasures of the here and now.

A capacity for spontaneity is highly valuable, but it is not necessarily accompanied by the cognitive and affective deficits of the impulsive. The impulsive, through his failure to be able *in general* to plan and to sustain a level of attention essential to intelligent deliberation, is paradigmatically heteronomous – he lacks critical competence or rationality. As difficult as it is to decide when deliberation is "complete," a seriously abbreviated decision-making process is likely to display inadequate compilation of data, including data known to, but not accessed by, the person, or insufficient processing, which itself can take a variety of forms. The inadequacy of the process can be characterized in the most fundamental way: the impulsive, through his cognitive style, is likely to hurt himself or frustrate his desires.

The analogous attenuation of his affective processes is exhibited in the experience of motivation, in particular, in the absence of both a sense of deliberateness and a tendency to convert a whim into action only after a controlled evolution. Instead, the whim is abruptly executed, without ever having been transformed into an intention, no less a reasonable one. Understandably, the impulsive is unlikely to enter into deep or meaningful relationships.

It is more difficult to identify a defect of autonomy in the affective sphere for it is always possible for the impulsive to claim autonomy relative to his own peculiar makeup, to insist that his distinctive affective style is perfectly suited to one who is simply not interested in sustained or deep relationships. The problem was identified in the previous chapter where we acknowledged that the heteronomy of psychopaths, a type of impulsive whose amorality creates serious social problems, is grounded in part in a developmental deficit which stunted the development of affect or emotion in ways we promised to describe. We shall discharge that obligation in the next chapter.

Earlier, we identified a barrier to objectivity acknowledged in different forms by competing psychological schools of thought, to wit, backward-directed psychological states. There can evidently be barriers of an intellectual sort, for example, limitations of intelligence, memory, and perceptual powers. And we have just seen that there are barriers to objectivity of a third sort, to wit, character styles. Thus, in acknowledging the distorting role of subjective *principles* in our initial description of objectivity, we failed to countenance as well the distorting role of subjective *cognitive styles*. The impulsive fails to be open to the world as it is not because of a principle, but rather because she addresses subject matter in a way which encourages ignorance of all but the most narrow band of data.

Although psychoanalytic cures are difficult to come by, there are presumably examples such as Little Hans. But we can do virtually nothing about basic temperamental disposition or character style. Although Claridge is not overly skeptical about behavioral modification in light of the variations available to a person falling under a general disposition, Shapiro reminds us that there are basic cognitive and affective styles which can directly impair objectivity and, therefore, the capacity for adult autonomy. Although every innate characteristic is potentially autonomy-limiting simply because it is impossible to change, some innate characteristics are *essentially* autonomy-limiting because they interfere directly with the defining features of autonomy. We know that this is true of characteristics related to critical competence such as low intelligence; we now realize that there are more subtle forms of limitation.

A hypothetical example will help to fix our ideas on the relevance of objectivity.

Jean becomes a painter and deems this activity his life's work. It provides him with his deepest satisfaction and he cannot conceive abandoning it. He has become a painter because his third-grade teacher, Ms. Webster, encouraged his initial efforts in this direction, and he began his early artistic education in order to please her. Thus, the desire to please Ms. Webster is *explanatorily* prior to the desire to be a painter. But, as Jean's interest and training develop, the initial motivation drops out of the picture and the character and contours of his adult activity are determined instead by contemporary features of this activity. What Jean *specifically* does is not determined by his relationship to Ms. Webster. The subjects he paints, his style, his related activities, are unrelated to this origin. The childhood experience is a cause *in fieri* (producing cause), not a cause *in esse* (sustaining cause), of his painting. His early infatuation with Ms. Webster does not sustain the activity or its character.

His brother, George, on the other hand, also infatuated with Ms. Webster and also led to pursue the life of a painter for this reason, continues as an adult to use the canvas as a way of working through these early childhood attachments. All his subjects are similar to or symbolic of Ms. Webster, his preferred colors are those of her clothes, and his style is the one she approved of. The significance of the early experience, thus, persists beyond its purely initiatory role. George's growth as an artist is impeded because he is unable to draw on the resources of his world in a way which might permit the utilization of his talents for the creation of novel artistic responses. George's psychotherapist, but not Jean's, tells him that his painting is a way of fulfilling his continued desire to please his teacher. He describes George's activity in the language of reasons: He is trying to please Ms. Webster; the reason he paints that dress blue is that Ms. Webster wore a blue dress, and the like.

George may deny this and he may, like Jean, regard his immersion in this world as defining his essence. But regardless of George's assessment of the personal importance of painting, his therapist may find indirect sources of confirmation of the hypothesis regarding the *reasons* George paints in George's behavior and feelings, including behavior and feelings (and dreams perhaps) not manifestly linked to his painting. Thus, the effects of the childhood experiences, never submitted to rational reflection prior to therapy, permeate a variety of facets of his adult existence, and, for that reason, retain their significance.

As Jean becomes immersed in his life, and as we seek to understand his work, we must turn to the features of his adult experiences and relationships, for these will be the relevant causal ones. Thus, Jean will not change his life if he works through this early relationship and discards all vestiges of romantic feeling for the teacher. George, on the other hand, may be profoundly affected by a significant change in the traces left by this relationship. For the importance to George of his art is subordinate to the importance of his feelings and desires pertaining to Ms. Webster. There is a fragility to George's career. As immersed as he may be in his painting, as important as it *appears* to him to be, it is not clear that his interest can survive a "successful" psychotherapy. For in his professional life, he has not really been responding to the situations as they present themselves. Jean chooses blue because it looks to him as if that fits, given the surrounding colors and the subject; George chooses blue because that is Ms. Webster's favorite color. What happens then when neither cares about pleasing Ms. Webster?

It will be true for each person that the importance of his life as a painter "depends on" these early experiences. But the difference in the nature of the dependence is crucial. For George, the meaning of the childhood experience continues to permeate his professional life, requiring us to allude to it in an effort to understand why he does what he does. Not so for Jean.

Jean's identification with his artistic world is bona fide; George's is not, or at least not entirely. Jean's choice of a career is autonomous; George's is not.

George's problem is similar to that of the rigid person. He is still acting out his childhood fantasies and needs. He has not transcended the stage to adulthood. He is responding to voices from within rather than conditions from without. The key here is objectivity as we earlier characterized it – the ability to see the world, including one's own psychological states, for what it is and to respond to it appropriately.

(Jean and George represent two extremes. The real world, always murkier than our categories, undoubtedly contains persons who fall on a spectrum between these two cases.)

Appropriateness of response

In zeroing in on objectivity as a key component of autonomy, we characterized it in part in terms of the propensity to respond to the world as it is (or as it would appear to an impartial adult with intact faculties). But people respond differently to the same stimuli even if they are mentally and physically healthy. Is objectivity compatible with *any* set of responses? If not, how do we define "appropriate" response? We would expect far too much of our theory, for example, if we supposed that all eccentric responses can be accounted for in terms of their being governed by a backward-looking state.

Is it similarly a problem for the objective account that it imposes no constraints on the *source* of our motivations? If, under the influence of incompatibilist arguments which challenge the freedom of persons whose desires arise in the normal way, that is, through the external sources of heredity and environment, we require of an autonomous agent that his desires not be determined or limited by the real world, then they might be utterly mad, that is, actually impossible or, if possible, utterly silly. Ferne, an autonomous agent, might spend her life trying to promote the merits of tattoos of crushed grapes.

What I wish to emphasize here is that autonomy as such imposes very little in the way of constraints. Yes, an autonomous person must be independent, rational enough, and possessed of relevant freedoms and personal integrity. I would now add objectivity to this list, but the addition does not permit us automatically to judge eccentric persons as heteronomous.

We ought not underestimate the possibility that Ferne is irrational. It may well be, for example, that this idiosyncratic venture is linked to one or several goals shared by her community. There might then be a handle for a critical exchange. For example, if this project is grounded in the thought that these tattoos are beautiful, we may have a focal point for an aesthetic dialogue. And the outcome of such an encounter may well be the rational revision of the mission. A similar outcome may result from a variety of scenarios in which Ferne undergoes reeducation or socialization in response to her dismay at the isolation she suffers. But if she is *not* diverted from her path, if she remains an eccentric, even an extreme eccentric, we cannot automatically count this development against her autonomy.

A certain sort of neurotic personality poses another difficulty for this account of objectivity. If the core idea of objectivity is the immersion of the agent in a situation he appreciates accurately and responds to appropriately, how are we to assess Gideon, a highly sensitive, fearful individual, who, in an effort to be liked by others, nervously attempts to

anticipate their needs and reactions so that he can do whatever he believes will ingratiate themselves in his eyes? Gideon is *overly* immersed in
the present because of his desperate need to be loved combined with the
fear that he is unlovable. And he may in fact achieve a certain amount of
success. People like this, if they do not transmit their own nervousness,
make excellent hosts because they are alert to their guests' needs and
comforts. If they do not produce love, they at least produce appreciation.

But there is a failure of "accurate appreciation," the cognitive component of objectivity. While Gideon may be highly sensitive to others' needs
and reactions, and while he may in fact not be "lovable," he often errs
about the way to rectify this inadequacy. He receives admiration, when
he really wants love. Secondly, Gideon is inflexible. He does not accept
the fact that he does not have to go to these extremes, that the people
who do care about him would prefer that he relax and consider his own
needs as well. His responses are inappropriate in the most fundamental
sense – they are designed to achieve an objective that they will not
achieve because they are grounded in false beliefs.

We may, of course, supplement these failures of objectivity with ones
based upon the underlying reasons for Gideon's behavior. It may be that
he is seeking, not the love of his friends and acquaintances, but instead
the love of a parent who abandoned him. Like George, he is responding
not to his current environment, but rather an earlier phase of his life. He
is the victim of a backward-looking state.

There are other forms of excessive sensitivity or flexibility which pose
merely prima facie problems for this account. A competent performer
who is paralyzed by stage fright – as distinct from one who rationally
responds to a frightening situation – is over-responding because she, not
her environment, prevents herself from doing what she is capable of
doing and what she wants to do. Since her response prevents her from
achieving a fundamental goal, its inappropriateness is based simply on its
irrationality. We can then on this score judge her as heteronomous. Or we
can count her failure as one of proficiency for she is unable to act
successfully on her decision to perform up to capacity.

Another example of intemperate fine tuning is the phenomenon Jon
Elster calls "adaptive preference formation" (1989: 170). Some individuals,
in order to ensure against frustration, adjust their preference rankings on
the basis of their beliefs about the feasibility of the options. They achieve
contentment by coming to want what they learn is available to them. And
if they do not necessarily misperceive the situation in order to bring the
change about, they are not guilty of a failure of epistemic objectivity. (The
fox in the French fable, for example, is guilty of this sort of failure for he
comes not to want the grapes because "they are too green.")

The manner in which this mode of preference formation undermines a
person's autonomy is subtle for it does not incorporate frustration or
goal obstruction, as in the case of stage fright or an overly ingratiating
personality. The point of this practice of adjusting one's preference rank-

ings to the state of the world is, of course, precisely to avoid these unsatisfactory results.

In spite of the assumption that epistemic failures are not necessarily involved, it may yet seem promising to invoke a failure of objectivity. The person is not responding to the "world" in that he is not responding to intrinsic features of the potential object of desire. That is, his strength of preference is not determined by an appraisal of the object's potential for satisfaction. The cause of the object's rank is extrinsic – the likelihood of attainment.

This strategy fails for we often permit extrinsic considerations to play such a role. We may choose to modify our preference rankings as a result of input from religious or moral sources. If I renounce an option I know will be highly pleasurable because I view the associated action as wicked or because I believe that I would be disobeying the will of God, I am not necessarily heteronomous in so doing. If so, what is wrong about adjusting my preferences on the basis of a different sort of extrinsic factor? From the point of view of autonomy, the answer is "nothing." But the key consideration is that the mode must be self-consciously chosen. If the agent autonomously selects this manner of preference formation, he may be faulted for excessive submissiveness or pliability, but those are different failings. In the bona fide case of heteronomy, the person is unaware or dimly aware that his preferences are being driven in this manner, and is, therefore, reminiscent of the person whose character style or temperament is exerting a powerful influence on his behavior in ways he would repudiate if he gave himself the opportunity to do so. In the discussion of contingency in Chapter 6, I conceded the limitations on autonomy of many of our modes of response, but I also insisted, therefore, on the importance of a disposition to review periodically the ways in which we relate to the world. That is, of course, crucial to autonomy.

In order to accommodate the ultimate reference to the individual, we must construe appropriateness as a causal notion and relativize it to an individual. An appropriate response is any response of A's to a situation not governed by a backward-looking state which would be chosen by A, conceived as otherwise autonomous, that is, as possessing personal integrity, adequate rationality, freedom, independence, and the features of objectivity that have been independently identified. Notice that we do not say that only autonomous agents can respond appropriately, but rather that an appropriate response is one that would, in a sense, be endorsed by that agent on the assumption that he is conceived under conditions of occurrent autonomy. One modification must, however, be made. Appropriateness varies depending on the agent's information. A person may respond in a way that appears inappropriate due to ignorance. Although this failing adversely affects his freedom and, therefore, his autonomy, it seems more natural to say that it is nonetheless appropriate under *his* epistemic circumstances. Since we demand objectivity and rationality, we know that the hypothetical choice would be made by one who is open to the world as it is and who processes data in accordance with rational principles. I also insist that the hypothetical response arise out of reflection which is dispassionate, careful, intensive, and stable (in the sense that responses are uniform over time when similar conditions obtain).

Imagine a person who naturally responds to those close to her by concern, caring, and a desire to nurture and serve. She rarely thinks of herself in her quest to please others and to discharge what she assumes is her responsibility to the people around her. She has interests, but they are sacrificed for the other person because mutual satisfaction is impossible. Are her responses appropriate? Can this person be autonomous? Should this person be autonomous? The questions are of great significance because some have alleged that this description fits the natural condition of the female sex or, at least, many of its members. If so, then perhaps autonomy is an unnatural or inapplicable standard for half the human population. Since that would be a devastating result for the many proponents of this ideal, we shall return to this issue when we consider the value of autonomy in Chapter 10.

The distinctions invoked here have nothing to do with determination versus indetermination. The autonomy of Jean, George, or Ferne is not based upon the determined or undetermined character of the choice or the persistence of their respective goals. If determinism is true, not only does George remain heteronomous; Jean remains autonomous. For the relevant causal factors are still different. Jean is responding to features of his current environment in relation to his current psychological state, and that fact is not undermined *either* by the discovery of universal laws underwriting these causal connections *or* by the discovery of the causal antecedents of these interactions.

Those who believe that any viable conception of autonomy demands an indeterministic world for its realization will no doubt regard the preceding comments as facile and cavalier. I think that the fear of determination is grounded in the fear that subsumption under law is tantamount to subjection to necessity and the latter is incompatible with freedom or autonomy. So the urge to be free of necessity is the basis of the fear of determinism. In *Freedom from Necessity* (1987), I attempted to show that these fears are groundless and, not wanting to restate that case here, I am going simply to rely upon it.

Autonomy and mental health

Are we assuming that autonomy and neurosis are incompatible? We might defend this connection by reference to the supposition that a neurotic would wish to be rid of this affliction under complete information, including information of an autobiographical nature; so he is not the way he ideally would like to be. But this will not do for there are people who would concede that their personality is conditioned by a neurotic upbringing, yet who would not wish to change. So this sort of etiological inquiry is irrelevant.

To be sure, one can describe conditions under which the neurotic would wish to change. But if those conditions are radical, if they involve surgery, the introduction of powerful methods of suggestion, deep psychoanalysis, and the like, the person who forms the desire to change may not be the same person in the relevant sense of "same person." The test of autonomy becomes meaningless if any changes of condition are permitted for, no matter how content with himself a person is, one can always introduce modifications so that the person ends up unhappy.

Thus, even if, in light of the dependence of autonomy on rationality, we demand that this review be conducted rationally, we shall not find that the rational decision is inevitably the eradication of neurotic traits. This finding is upheld even if we demand the normal sorts of strictures, for example, that the agent possess complete relevant information, that she be able to process it rationally, free of the influence of a strong, temporary mood or passion, and that the person reflect vividly on all relevant considerations.

For example, the judgment that mentally ill people cannot be autonomous often arises from the thought that mental illness involves internal psychic conflict and self-regulation is impossible if a self acts out of conflict. In Chapter 6 I challenged the assumption that it is essential to the autonomy of a self in conflict that it *expel* elements to eliminate the conflict. Furthermore, only some conflicts, such as those of the rigid person, are serious and antithetical to autonomy. It is not a serious diminution of my freedom to have to choose between the Ferrari and the Lamborghini.

There is a sort of conflict which must be involved in mental illness for all illness involves self-harm and, barring the anomaly of the masochist or the suicidal person, all persons have a desire to be well. In fact, this conflict is necessary if we are to believe the familiar dictum that no one would be in a state of self-harm unless there is some advantage and an advantage will be evidently painful to eliminate.

But again, even with conflict, the neurosis may be so satisfying, the pain of removal so great, and the dysfunctional condition so minor that the agent chooses to retain his neurosis, even after a rational review. He is deciding carefully and dispassionately, under complete information (about etiology and the consequences of alternative courses of action), incorporating in the deliberation information about his fears and the role played by certain behaviors which promote his sense of security and relief from anxiety. He may see that it would be better to be different, but may not wish to pay the exorbitant price. Yes, he is in the grips of a neurosis which influences his decision by exaggerating the significance of certain feelings at the expense of others. But although his vision is influenced by his fears, it is not necessarily distorted. We cannot assume that this choice is not an autonomous one. The influence of his condition may operate rationally in the sense that he would recommend the retention of the neurosis to anyone similarly situated even if he were to reflect on the matter not as one under the grip of this neurotic condition. There was a time when the choice to remain neurotic inevitably would have been looked on as just another sign of madness. Those times are thankfully behind us. One can choose rationally to be sick even on the assumption that the desire to be well is natural and universal.

But just because it is rational to remain neurotic, it does not follow that such a neurotic is autonomous. We must, first of all, recall the difference between occurrent and dispositional autonomy. A person generally disposed to heteronomy may be capable of occasional episodes of autonomy, just as a slave may be capable of autonomously choosing to remain a slave. So, if neurosis entails a general disposition to heteronomy, it does not follow that a neurotic is incapable of making an autonomous decision to remain neurotic. When we inquire about the autonomous status of a person suffering from neurosis or mental illness of a more serious nature, we want information of a more general nature about the impact of the affliction on her life – her choices, her actions, her values.

In an earlier work on autonomy, I dealt with the issue mental illness raises by insisting on a distinction between autonomy and moral responsibility. I argued that, if a self is sick, that does not automatically tell against its autonomy (see Wolf 1987). If autonomy is self-rule and a self is sick, then some autonomous agents are sick. We simply treat some – not necessarily all – as morally blameless. George is autonomous, but not necessarily responsible for his behavior.

In that work, I was guided by the requirement that autonomous choices and actions originate in the self. I would modify this earlier conclusion about the connection between autonomy and origination for I now believe the origin requirement to be mistaken. I think it is grounded in a false metaphysics or model of the mind. I observed earlier that the origin of the term "autonomy" provides the rationale for the inclusion of independence and competence – an autonomous state *rules itself*. It is interesting that political autonomy does not go on from there to invoke an origin requirement. If the sovereign is a king, whether or not he has *personal* autonomy, the country has *political* autonomy if he effectively rules it without undue interference from outside political forces. Thus, Russia under its last czar, Nicholas II, was an autonomous nation, although its sovereign, under the domination of the notorious Rasputin, was notably lacking in personal autonomy.

In the sphere of personal autonomy, we, of course, demand independence from another *person*. But, in addition to the further requirements of rationality and personal integrity, requirements grounded on the analogous demand for minimally effective rule, we feel obliged to postulate internal origins for the motives of an autonomous agent, construing internality as stronger than mere *personal* independence. We are not autonomous if we act out of desires instilled in us by a hypnotist, demonic neurosurgeon, or skillful manipulator. But that is perceived to be insufficient – the unwilling addict cannot appeal to personal causes such as these to explain his condition. So if he is heteronomous, we have to find more subtle means to eject his addictive urges from the self. That is, of course, the role of devices like identification.

A final judgment on the connection between autonomy and mental health must wait upon a resolution of other matters, including the status of the origin requirement.

9
The liberation theory of autonomy: The place of self

As we have just seen, the case of the addict or compulsive initiates a quest for an internal difference between the genuine autonomy of the normal person and the heteronomy of the addict. But there are features of an addict's life having nothing to do with the origin of his addiction which can explain his heteronomy. First of all, an unwilling addict lacks proficiency, the capacity to control his environment in accordance with his desires. However he came to this state, the loss of proficiency is grounded in his current condition, independently of origin. He is a cripple even if he freely chose to become one. More likely, the evolution to addiction was not initiated by a free choice. A fully informed, rational adult would not choose to become an addict, especially since one item of information at his disposal is that he would come seriously to regret the decision later. But here again the heteronomy of the original decision has to do with contemporaneous features of the decision, namely, ignorance or irrationality.

But we cannot just ignore the etiological component. People become addicts out of hopelessness, the need to become oblivious to their desperate condition, the desire to be free of physical and emotional pain, and the anticipation of intensely satisfying experiences. And they are often not responsible for the conditions which led them to addiction. The point again is that these elements are relevant not because they ultimately derive from sources external to the self, which is true of *everything* that influences our behavior. The relevance has rather to do with the influence they bear upon the rationality or independence of the decision-making process. If they blind the agent to relevant consequences, if they make it impossible for him to deliberate coherently or independently, then the agent fails to be autonomous for he fails to be rational, fully informed, or free of the undue influence of another.

We must not forget that autonomy is a matter of degree. A prospective addict may be aware of many, but not all relevant consequences of his decision. He may be able to contemplate the consequences of some, but not all of his actions with a certain amount of clarity. He is being egged on by a drug pusher who is highly experienced in the art of manipulation. He is able to desist, but it is very hard to do so.

So if he is autonomous, he is certainly not nearly as autonomous as a well-educated, well-informed yuppie making the same decision out of boredom and the desire to experiment. Again, we are "victims of our

210

environment"; certain environments are more conducive than others to the creation of autonomous adults. *But, even for realistic autonomy, the autonomy that emerges is a feature of the agent grounded in his current relation to himself and his world.*

We have talked about the importance of the decision-making process and the possibility of its being (relatively) autonomous in spite of the defective character of the origin of the components entering into the process. We may also count as defective the impoverishment which results from an early environment which has greatly narrowed a person's mode of thinking, range of experience, or vision. So when he attempts rationally to deliberate, he is bound to view fewer options as feasible. This contraction demands expansion; he must open himself to new options and be prepared to respond to them. In other words, he needs objectivity. If that makes him autonomous, it is not in virtue of his having found the right way to express his self. Meaningful engagement may be designated "self-expression," but we are just redescribing the feature of objectivity in a misleading metaphysical way. The *person* has a history and, like the process of painting, that history is causally responsible for his current state. Nonetheless, that process can have an independence and authenticity depending on the character of current interactions. The painter's goals are his even if he constantly redefines them, basing these redefinitions on provisional results. And the autonomy of the process is grounded on the openness and ability of the artist to respond to all relevant inputs.

The rejection of the origin requirement

Through contemporary limitations on freedom, therefore, we acknowledge the limits created by physical infirmities, influences of an exploitative nature, and deficiencies of an economic or social character. We *are* to a very large extent the "victims" of our heredity and environment. There are biological givens, innate dispositions and personality propensities, impoverished environments, and all the other afflictions and limitations bemoaned by hard determinists. But these are limitations not because they are determined, but rather because they are potential obstacles to the deliberating agent, some of which are impossible to remove. Yes, we would have greater autonomy if, like Selma (see Chapter 6), we could, by the snap of our fingers, enhance our positive freedom by increasing our intelligence, removing innate infirmities, and eliminating emotional barriers to full participation in a wide range of satisfying relationships and activities. But that we cannot do this indicates that we have maximal or ideal autonomy in mind, in which case we should recognize that our universal inadequacy in this respect does not nullify real differences of freedom and autonomy between one person and another in a deterministic world.

We identify differences in autonomy in terms of differences in rationality, independence, objectivity, or personal integrity. We do not automatically suppose that these criteria will eliminate immoral or strange people. And among the strange people who remain, some will be flourishing far less than others. For they will either have freely chosen to suppress certain modes of expression, or they find they just have no interest in developing them.

There are significant differences among limitations. Some incapacities are pervasive, affecting our proficiency, as well as our freedom of decision, in a variety of tasks in areas we judge important. In most cases, this is what is wrong with blindness, poverty, severe emotional deprivation, and inferior educational opportunities. It is better to be limited by an inability to appreciate urban life or hard rock music than by an inability to see or by an inability to afford a decent education.

In this nonhistorical spirit, I would also affirm the irrelevance to autonomy of acquiescence to the process which led to the formation of one's current will. One may reasonably have objections to that process without having any qualms about results. And if one does have qualms, the relevant matter is the current capacity to change.[1]

As I said in Chapter 6 in the discussions of independence and contingency, and have just reiterated, the current autonomy of an agent has essentially to do with the current relation of that agent to the world. Another dimension of this outlook is reflected in the conviction that autonomy can evolve into heteronomy and vice-versa. An autonomous agent may choose to become a slave, and a (heteronomous) Jehovah's Witness may be reeducated so as to emerge as an autonomous adult. (We may find the former conceptually puzzling because of a confusion between autonomy and responsibility. That we may *blame* a slave for having freely chosen this condition no more annuls his [current] slavery than the fact that I am morally reprehensible for having intentionally ensured that I will be unable to keep a promise makes it the case that I *can* [now] keep the promise. We hold people derivatively responsible for failings they are impotent to change now just because they once were in a position to suppress the emergence of these failings.)

Challenges to each sort of counterexample to an historical conception of autonomy may be grounded on the key role of rationality. How, for example, can an autonomous agent choose slavery given that such a person must be rational? This question is indeed impossible to answer once it is assumed that nothing is of value unless it is coupled with autonomy. In rejecting this extreme position (see the arguments in Chapter 10), I am free to present examples of rational selections of a heteronomous life. Although we admire people who valiantly combat efforts to force or lure them into a life of slavery, it is evidently easy to imagine circumstances in which the prospects of a protracted struggle are so unbearable and perilous and the appeal of a fun-filled life under a benign dictator so beguiling that a rational person chooses to succumb. If this example is unsatisfactory, consider a decision to enter a community whose cohesiveness is great enough to demand the abandonment of a considerable degree of autonomy. The possible rationality of such a decision is grounded on the incompatibility of autonomy with those values of community or relationship associated with commitments to the other or to the group so fundamental that they clash with the rationality requirement of autonomy. An autonomous agent is free to commit herself to another person or group so long as she retains the ultimate authority to withdraw from the commitment when the going gets sufficiently rough. She is, therefore, barred from feeling the depth of community sentiment and the sense of belonging unique to those groups in which self-expression *is* the expression of the community. I have argued, for example, in Chapter 6, that the defects of such groups do not nullify the values of membership arising from the intimacy of shared commitments, ideals, and emotions. So it is not a priori true that an autonomous agent would choose rationally to continue to be autonomous regardless of circumstances. It is unlikely that the preference for a tight-knit community over an autonomous one is demonstratively irrational in all conceivable circumstances.

In looking at the converse counterexample – the transition from heteronomy to autonomy – it is striking to observe that all autonomous agents begin their lives as heteronomous. Why should we then think that current autonomy demands an etiology that itself displays the signs of the state which *emerges* from the process?

Evidently, I do not mean to deny that the process of becoming autonomous is a gradual one; a heteronomous person does not wake up one morning to the pleasant discovery that, overnight, he has become autonomous. And should the agent have participated actively in the process by displays of nascent rationality and periodic acts of reflective approval, we might count him "more" autonomous in a cumulative sense. If Wilfred has been charitable his whole adult life, whereas Wilbur has only recently overcome his selfish impulses to reach the same level of commitment, we may regard Wilfred as the more charitable man even if they are currently indistinguishable. Clearly, unless those who cite the importance of the engagement of elements of autonomy in the development of full autonomy are thinking of current, not cumulative, autonomy, their thesis is as trivial as the thesis that Wilfred is more charitable than Wilbur.

Although I will soon argue for the importance to autonomy of reflective endorsement, I am not convinced of the importance of actual or hypothetical endorsement of the *process* by which one arrived at one's current state. Suppose we wish to deprogram a cult member or convert a Jehovah's Witness to an autonomous life style. Why should our success be logically contingent on the cooperation of our charges? Although it is easier when a child does not fight the progression to independence, some children must be dragged kicking and screaming into adulthood. We may well imagine that the Jehovah's Witness displays resistance. He may balk at my heavy-handed efforts just because he knows his own limitations and is well aware of the values that he is being induced to forego for the sake of a value – autonomy – that frightens him. So I am again relying on the position that a rational assessment of these life styles, made under conditions whose specific character might be quite crucial, will not inevitably lead to an endorsement of autonomy. The individual may in fact regret the change once it has taken place. He misses the comforts, congeniality, and security of his former life. If he now sees the universe more clearly, he sees it, notwithstanding, as an unfriendly place. He has been uprooted and he feels very much alone. Although he is autonomous and is capable of unfettered rational reflection, free of self-deception, on the process which led to that outcome, he fails to endorse it.[2]

There is an important exception to the principle of the irrelevance of history to which we now turn.

Laura revisited

Looking again at Laura, who, we must recall, is not rationally deficient, is there any reason to suppose she fails the test of objectivity? Her liberated neighbor, Wanda, is immersed in music, responding to it with great intensity and love. Can't we say that Wanda's responses are more objective than Laura's on the grounds that they, not Laura's, are appropriate? The sounds of Beethoven's Violin Concerto speak to Wanda in just the way they once spoke to Joachim and Brahms and more recently to Heifetz and Goldberg, that is, as a near perfect creation in which compositional construction and spirituality merge in a sublime fusion. Laura, out of politeness, spends time listening to Beethoven and even takes some courses at the community college, but finds all of this boring and would prefer to return to her jigsaw puzzles. There are no circumstances under which she can come to appreciate this form of music.

Can we charge Laura with a failure of objectivity? We would have to justify this move without obliterating the distinction between autonomy and flourishing. We do not want to characterize Laura's actual self in terms of *our* ideals.

Laura may indeed be suffering from a failure of objectivity for, in all likelihood, her incapacities in this area are at least cognitive or perceptual. Many people who fail to appreciate certain forms of music acknowledged as great suffer from cognitive and/or perceptual deficits. Those who do not appreciate this music often cannot, or at least find it very difficult to, discern what is there to discern. Fundamentally, one must be able to recognize the form of a piece, that is, the exposition, the development, and the recapitulation in sonata form. It is hard to find a person sensitive to all the nuances of variation in pulse, harmony, texture, voicing, and so on, in a Beethoven sonata who then announces that he does not like Beethoven (or classical music). It goes without saying that this point is easily generalized to other dimensions of culture.

So we are likely to be left with far fewer eccentrics once we demand genuine objectivity. But if we suppose the unusual, that Laura continues to be satisfied with her shallow existence in spite of her cognitive *adequacy*, is there any further way of narrowing the gap between autonomy and flourishing?

It is not far-fetched to suppose that the environmental forces bearing on Laura's musical development led to the breakdown of objectivity. Spontaneous responses which would have cultivated her natural instincts were suppressed. The reinforcement was not there; any gropings in that direction were met with derision. Of course, the usual consequence of this failure is the erosion of cognitive powers. Laura has the *capacity* to develop the *ability* to perceive the form and harmonic scheme of a Beethoven sonata; given this ability, she is then possessed of the *capacity* to develop the *ability* to recognize the phrase, the musical equivalent of a sentence. A poor musical education results in the loss of these capacities and a consequent failure of objectivity through a failure of flexible response. Responses are not adjusted in accordance with perceived changes in subject matter. But Laura, as we now imagine her, *was* taught and *did* acquire the tools of appreciation; yet she remains cold to all forms of classical music.

The finding of nonobjectivity may nonetheless be warranted on the assumption that Laura's early experiences left her incapable of responding appreciatively to classical music. Suppose she was a musical prodigy and, like Nicolo Paganini or Michael Rabin, forced during her childhood to spend hours each day at practice, without food or water. Although the effects of these cruel regimens are often horrific – Rabin committed suicide – they are not usually the inability to appreciate the art form being mastered. We shall suppose that, in Laura's case, even though she can understand music as well as the most discriminating listener, that is precisely the effect. And in order to ensure that she is not simply blocked, we must imagine that she never really loved music, that her motivation as a child had been exclusively extrinsic. It is not as if deep psychoanalysis might enable her to reclaim a lost love.

We can readily suppose that, even though Laura's cognitive powers were not blocked, her *capacity* for developing the ability to sustain affect in this sphere *was* blocked. Even if she never loved music, she would have at least developed this ability under normal conditions of growth. If we look at her as an adult, we see a narrow self, incapable *even under hypothetical circumstances* of appreciating the finer things of life.

Now if, from this perspective, we complain that she does not flourish, we are making a value judgment. From her point of view, there is nothing deficient about her life. And she appears to be autonomous, for she has chosen her path rationally and independently. With respect to the former, she periodically reviews her life, using her vast critical resources. With respect to the latter, we cannot treat her as dependent on her cruel father in the way I am dependent for my logical failings on the bumbling Mr. Simpson, for we cannot assimilate her deficiencies in this sphere to those of one poorly trained in logic. Again, without an objective way of converting contingent narrowness into heteronomy, we are guilty of bias.

If, on the other hand, we pass judgment on one who never had the chance to choose fairly, whose self was quashed in its growth, we are not merely denying that she is flourishing and bemoaning her failure to live to the fullest. We are rather denying autonomy. For, although we may, as adults, autonomously choose to stifle the expression of certain natural tendencies and reject fundamental forms of human expression, we do so as fully developed selves, with basic commitments and ideals in terms of which this choice makes sense. Since Laura was never given this opportunity, her *ability* to flourish and, consequently, her autonomy, was thwarted. In this special case, an appeal to history must be introduced to distinguish what might have been (Laura's appreciation of classical music) from what never could be (Laura's running a three-minute mile).

We may even see this deficit as pertaining to positive freedom, the set of intellectual, emotional, practical, and social tools we need to exercise critical competence in the diverse adult world. The ability to appreciate is as much an ability as the ability to discern. Laura is at a disadvantage in certain decision-making situations if she cannot empathize with people who love music. When an Amish parent, motivated by a deeply held ideology, interferes with his child's natural musical talents, he is interfering with his autonomous development. In general, of course, children are heteronomous. But, as I observed earlier (Chapter 5), in a democratic society, we try to develop autonomy as early as possible by cultivating a child's gropings toward critical competence. We suppose that all persons are innately equipped with rational powers and hope to improve these through the educational process. Educators are supposed also to seek out other talents and nurture those as well. To fail to do so is to interfere with the autonomy of the adult by suppressing forces *actually* present in the child.

I emphasize the actual presence of these impulses to justify the description as autonomy-interference. For the effect on the child is analogous to the effect of long-term suppression of desire on the autonomy of an agent whose freedom of decision eventually erodes and, with it, his autonomy.

A similar diagnosis may be applicable to the psychopath if she began life with the same emotional potentialities as normal persons. If this condition is environmentally induced, we have the same basis to deny autonomy – the individual did not choose to suppress the development of compassion and empathy even if, as an adult, she identifies with her basic psychological makeup, and even if she does so after informed, vivid, and dispassionate reflection. Failing to find fault with her currently impoverished state, she is nonetheless heteronomous because her development was seriously impaired in a way similar to that of Laura's.

I again want to minimize the importance of the human element. A child never exposed to music, a feral child, for example, is just as disadvantaged as Laura. He may, in fact, be less so, but only if the influences on him did not quash forever the ability to respond sympathetically to music. The effect is important, not the cause.

Are we then in a backhanded way endorsing a modified version of *romantic self-expression*, the demand that we at least be taught to appreciate all, even if we reject some of this heritage when we know better? So the teacher will have to nurture the antisocial tendencies of his charges, since they seem naturally to display these as readily as the artistic ones. He will cultivate and refine the instincts toward property destruction, uncleanliness, and aggressive and unsympathetic behavior toward others. Are we not unfairly placing our children at a disadvantage by denying them the right to develop aspects of their natures so as to be in a better informed position as adults when they decide whether and how to pursue these tendencies?

It is a truism that education is supposed also to civilize its charges, even if this requires suppression. Some of this is justified by the resultant creation of a disciplined person, one who is in a superior position to exercise and display her talents and thereby to choose from a wider range of options and to make more rational choices. Discipline generally enhances freedom even if it is sometimes heavy-handed and sometimes a convenient excuse to suppress desires which do not in fact enhance the future freedom of its recipient.

One would have to be Pollyanna, however, to believe that all the restrictions intelligent adults allow schools to impose are justified on the basis of their beneficial effects on freedom. If we do not want our primary schools to permit sexually precocious boys or girls with dirty fingernails to express themselves, at least part of the reason is that they will adjust better in the society in which they are growing up, independent of any judgment about the merits of that society. If it is true, as some have said, that the standards of cleanliness in middle-class American society are irrationally high, we still want our kids to adjust to our society, even if that society is irrational.

In defending another truism, that schools express the values of the community, I am conceding that they also interfere to some extent with the autonomy of children. It is far less important to encourage the love of clean fingernails than the love of fine music even if, in some circles, one will get further with clean fingernails. So I am not recommending that Summerhill[3] be the model of all schools because I do not believe that all values should be subordinated to that of autonomy.

Although we are then not endorsing a modified version of romantic self-expression since we are not advocating the development of all potentialities, we are nonetheless upholding a modified metaphysical egalitarianism, the idea that there is no metaphysical basis to deny a locus in the self for potentialities that are universal and natural.

To return to Laura. We are now in a position to say that Wanda has more autonomy than Laura for, even though Laura's adult self is not more limited than Wanda's – it is, to be sure, narrower than Wanda's – its development was. And this judgment reflects, not the value of music, but the fact that Laura's childhood capacities were suppressed.

We note as well that this result does not depend on the distinction between normal and abnormal development. Given Laura's childhood potential, she might have been trained so that she would be disposed now to listen to music. True, she lost the capacity because of an abnormal upbringing, but we need not bring that in. This loss is different from that of the power to babble, for the inclination to resume babbling would be abnormal since it would interfere with the ability to speak and, consequently, the ability to act rationally, whereas musical activity does not interfere with the other essential components of the autonomous life.

Again, though, if Laura is less autonomous because she cannot appreciate music, why am I not less autonomous for having (thankfully) outgrown the petty jealousies and insensitivity to others typical of children? The answer is obviously to be found in the evident irrationality such behavior would be evidence of *now*, that is, in light of my fuller understanding and mature desires. And I *am* less autonomous for having lost the capacity for physical spontaneity and a variety of fresh perspectives on the world, elements of my childhood – so I am told – which would not conflict with rationality, and so on.

Thus, Laura has lost something that would have been a part of her and would not have adversely affected her rationality, independence, or personal integrity. She lacks objectivity, in an extended sense of the term. She is not as open to the world as *she* might be.

Aren't these also traits of Dr. Roy, the blind teacher of religion who chose to retain his blindness primarily because he feared the effects of sight on his religious quest? Yes, but we must remember that Dr. Roy's autonomy is contingent on the fact that his decision was not based on ignorance. His suppression of self-realization fails to be autonomous if it is not informed, if, for example, he would have come to believe that the ability to see is worth the increased difficulty of his religious quest. If Dr. Roy is autonomous, his infirmity does not interfere with a rational and informed life choice, whereas Laura's infirmity does. She does not know what she is missing.

Of course, it is conceivable that Laura was not quashed, that she could never come to appreciate classical music even if she could come to understand it. She might be like the student of a foreign culture; she must study carefully the forms of music and be able to perceive and describe them with care and specificity. But in this sort of case, learning, even absorption, does not necessarily bring appreciation with it. But if Laura's problem is constitutional, then she may be as autonomous as possible. In the end, we must allow the possibility of a real difference between autonomy and flourishing. There are limits imposed by genetics. But if we do not believe that our autonomy is adversely affected by our failure to appreciate the aesthetic nuances of nonvisible light, then our worry about

Laura is not a worry about her realistic autonomy. We are concerned about her in the way I would be concerned about my autonomy in a world of people most of whom *do* appreciate the aesthetic nuances of nonvisible light. Given the self she might have been, however, she may be as autonomous as possible.

Identification revisited

If we take the origin requirement seriously, we evidently need a principled way to distinguish motivation that originates in the self from motivation whose origin is extrinsic. The principal difficulty with the identification criterion in this connection, cited in Chapter 5, is that the act of embrace might be a disguise to conceal the significance of a hidden trait which is preeminent in the agent's psychological makeup or that a trait may not be embraced for reasons which do not undermine its centrality to the person. A person may be swayed by a powerful, unconscious motive to endorse one of his motives as good or to identify with that motive when in truth this unconscious desire, whose unveiling would produce profound disturbances in his psyche, dominates various facets of his life.

The act of identification, understood as appropriation, is, in other words, fallible. When I say "That's really me!" I might be wrong. These acts are not self-certifying.

In fact, as noted in Chapter 6, a personal observation by Bergmann (1977) shows that feelings of *estrangement* are also not self-certifying. During the early years of his career, Bergmann tells us, he felt alienated from his position as a professor of philosophy. He carried out his duties with the sense that it was all a sham. He eventually came to realize that he had all along been fulfilling his deepest desires and that his failure to embrace unconditionally his profession and his life was based on immature considerations which led him to retain romantic dreams which he had, without knowing it, outgrown.

But if a person can lead an inauthentic life, yet feel that it is authentic, or, like Bergmann, lead an authentic life and feel that it is inauthentic, it does not follow that the agent's reports of estrangement or identification are to be ignored. Perhaps they are to be trusted when made under ideal conditions. After all, Bergmann did correct himself in another act of recognition, one grounded in greater insight and experience. Might it then be that acts of identification are self-certifying when they are based on reliable and complete information? What is wrong with invoking for the act of identification the sort of demands we just made for appropriateness, that is, rationality, stability, dispassionateness, and careful and attentive reflection. We then explicitly add relevant information since, unlike appropriateness, *trustworthy* identification depends on self-knowledge. Call this *rational identification.*

Even with these additions, however, what is to prevent me from identifying with a passing whim, too weak to issue in action, to be more sensitive to my mate? I might honestly say that this desire feels like the "real me" even though, since we are supposing complete information, I know very well that I almost always act insensitively and that I feel this way because I like to present a more acceptable image to the world. If there is neither a requirement that a desire actually be explanatorily central in one's life, nor that one respond in a "genuinely appropriate" way to such information, there is no way of showing that my act of identification is not genuine. A vivid, stable, mood-independent reflection does not change my proneness to identify with this desire, to "feel" that it is close to the core of my being. The legitimate complaint that the act is illicit is based on the plausible assumption that explanatory centrality is essential to the self (at its "core"). When I am forced to confess that the desire does not really express me, I am conceding that it plays little role in my actual behavior.

We must not forget that the notion of identification we are working with is incorporation, not endorsement. Unless we suppose that we are always what we would like to be – a foolish assumption – we have to concede that a person may have to acknowledge as his own a desire he would prefer to be rid of or disclaim a desire he actually has, no matter how intimate the desire presents itself as. Once we see the difference between ouster from self and condemnation by self, we might be obliged to expel a praiseworthy desire like the desire to be sensitive to my mate. Our ideals can be idle; if I feel that I would like to be Gandhi, but do nothing about it, if I occasionally have pacifist impulses which I endorse, but do not act on, then I am in fact *not* Gandhi-like. A doctrine which fails to acknowledge a potential gap between the actual self and the ego ideal is incapable of comprehending the tragedy of a life judged a failure by the one who lived it.

Having emphasized, as a corrective to much current literature, the intransigent character of adult, first-order natures along with the possibly ephemeral, fragile, or deluded character of second-order evaluations, I now contend in addition that the demand that second-order evaluations leading to acts of identification be rational will not suffice to save the identification view of self.

Theories of self versus theories of autonomy

I have rejected the effort to predicate ownership of an act of identification in part on the grounds that an unconscious desire which explains the act of identification and which plays a far more prominent role in the organization of the life of the agent has a greater claim to this status. But then, if the self, like that of George's (Chapter 8), is neurotic or more seriously disturbed, a choice emanating from its governing impulse should be a case of self-rule, that is, autonomy. In fact, it will be difficult to locate a case of heteronomy, for we shall have to find someone who is *not* acting or choosing from motives that are the dominant ones in his personality.

There is something seriously amiss. For example, the thrust of the argument is that George is autonomous. His deepest desire is to ingratiate himself in Ms. Webster's eyes and that is motivating his actions. (To be sure, he is abysmally lacking in proficiency.) Our earlier discussion, on the other hand, concluded that George's failure to satisfy the objectivity condition renders him heteronomous!

We have reached this point in the following way. The identification approach defines autonomy roughly as action motivated by desires the agent identifies with. It is an account of autonomy because autonomy is self-regulation, and the desires which are truly ours are the ones we identify with. I have rejected the identification account of the *self* and replaced it provisionally with an account in terms of explanatory centrality. The desires which are most truly ours are the ones which play a central role in the mechanisms accounting for our behavior and our mental life. But if we then go on to characterize autonomy in terms of self-regulation, we shall be unable to find anyone deficient in this regard. For we all act from desires which explain our actions! If we must concede that the desire for crack is central to a crack addict, what makes this poor person heteronomous?

The solution to this dilemma is a surprising one. It requires the separation of the conditions of selfhood from the conditions of autonomy. It is certainly clear that we must permit an autonomous rejection of self on the explanatory centrality account. For otherwise, crack addicts must be counted autonomous!

In a preliminary way, we note first that, in spite of the claims made about our first-order natures, it is still true that a second-order desire *might* be more powerful and central than a particular first-order desire. *Sometimes*, a person's rejection of his first-order effective desire is accounted for in terms of features of the agent's personality which are deeper than the effective desire. We observed earlier that an immature impulse can retain its strength while having become quite peripheral in the life of the person dogged by it. Strength per se is but one component of centrality. Behavioral dispositions that used to be important can become bad habits, annoying traits whose dislodging would be entirely welcome and is being actively promoted.

Second, addiction exemplifies most perspicuously the difference between decision and action, so that an autonomous decision to change may well fail to be effected. Concentrating, as we are wont to do, on action rather than choice, we forget that agents lacking in proficiency may exercise autonomous choice.

Suppose, however, that a case cannot be made that the urge to seek crack is not central to the life of the addict on the basis of her second-order rejection of her addiction. Her second-order desire is bona fide, but just too weak to counteract the addiction. She is conflicted, to be sure, but not all conflicts, interlevel or otherwise, reveal heteronomy. Why should we count an individual's rejection of her addiction as necessarily more central to herself, even if no self-delusion is involved? We have argued that there is no good reason always to locate the self on the higher level in all cases of conflict and we may well lack sufficient reason in this case to find the self above the first level. On the explanatory centrality conception of self, therefore, why should we conclude that this agent lacks autonomy?

We might appeal to Raz's idea that an autonomous agent cannot be exclusively absorbed by one overriding concern. I think, however, that it is more important to ask whether she chose to live such a life. If she did indeed choose this life, can we conclude that she lacks autonomy now just because she has regrets?

The dilemma is this. We can only say that the urge to seek crack is not a genuine part of the addict on an endorsement model of the self and that model is, as we have argued, too Pollyanna-like. If, then, we insist on an explanatory centrality model, we shall have to view addicts who attempt unsuccessfully to quit, but in whom the urge is a deeper part of the self than the urge to desist, as autonomous.

In this difficult case of the addict whose interlevel conflict does not warrant a judgment of expulsion for the effective, first-order desire, we do not suppose as a consequence that her repudiation is frivolous. Although we are assuming that the second-order desire lacks a greater hold on the self – for otherwise the explanatory centrality model can provide the judgment of heteronomy – we still want to distinguish her conflict from that of the admirer of Gandhi. As a belligerent person, Fred does not necessarily lack autonomy in virtue of a romantic and tenuous flirtation with pacifism. Our addict's unwillingness is at least serious; otherwise, we have a person who entertains regrets about her life, just like anyone, autonomous or not, whose life is not ideal.

Perhaps then the heteronomy of the addict is based on a *rational repudiation* of the addictive urge. For a judgment which is rational, informed, dispassionate, stable, and vivid must be a serious one. Earlier, we rejected the rational identification model of the *self* for even a rational identification can be deluded. I might rationally identify with a rationalization; in spite of my rational powers, information, and detached, yet heedful frame of mind, I find the thought of myself as that which I *know* I am not as intimate or cozy. (Once we reject the endorsement interpretation of identification, we are left with a purely psychological reading of this act of "appropriation.") Lacking a viable account of "emotionally appropriate response," we have no way of ruling out disturbed and faulty acts of rational identification.

Here, we are concerned with autonomy, not self. We are *conceding* that rational repudiation does not entail expulsion from self. Thus, we repeat the question: Is the rational repudiation of the addictive urge the basis of the addict's heteronomy?

Should an addict be in a position to execute a rational repudiation, the answer is "yes." She lacks autonomy if, temporarily free of certain disabling effects of her condition, she is able to render a rational, informed, stable, and dispassionate condemnation of her lifestyle, one that confers negative value on her addiction *understood in accordance with the Motivation Conception of value.* (Of course, she may in addition confer negative value via a judgment that her life lacks genuine worth.)

Acts of rational identification or repudiation are usually hypothetical, for we are hardly ever under the ideal conditions required for such an act. Addicts, of course, are even further removed from these conditions. In many of these cases, the very absence of certain conditions suffices for heteronomy. Agents who are irrational or misinformed are cases in point. Or suppose that reflection about this choice occurs under the domination of external forces bent on subjugating the reviewer by indirectly controlling the very manner through which the review is pursued. Suppose, in other words, that the agent is not procedurally independent during the decision-making process. We would surely not trust the resultant judgment.

We must remember as well that we cannot count a rational identification as sufficient for autonomy unless the agent's natural potentialities have been permitted to develop. Thus, an addict who "knows" that there are other life styles that provide satisfaction without the debilitating effects of addiction may nonetheless fail to be in a position to make an autonomous judgment to choose an alternative life just because her upbringing has quashed her ability to appreciate and to be attracted to such an alternative.

An addict who fulfills the basic requirements of rationality, knowledge, freedom, objectivity, independence, and integrity, but who fails to endorse or reject in an explicit act her addictive way of life, may be said to have autonomously chosen this life style if she would endorse it were she to reflect dispassionately, yet vividly and attentively, on the matter. We need not add further conditions on the hypothetical choice since her autonomy provides all that is needed. For example, if she satisfies objectivity, she is liberated from the onerous burden imposed by the unmanageable craving, a burden under which most addicts actually make their decisions.

The agent lacks autonomy if she would not choose to be an addict were she, as she now is, to make general life choices under optimally cognitive conditions of the sort demanded for rational identification. ("As she now is" means "As close to her actual current self as she can be once we assume that she is changed just enough to meet the conditions required to exercise this choice." We choose the word "choice" rather than "preference" to emphasize the genuineness of the commitment. Repudiation in the absence of an unequivocal intention to act is insufficient.)

The upshot of this is that we are demanding that this hypothetical choice be made autonomously. If this agent would autonomously reject her addiction, she is heteronomous. And that is what is meant by the earlier, cryptic remark that the self can be autonomously rejected. She is not denying that she is an addict; nor is she saying that her true self is reflected in the second-order act of rejection. The metaphysics is second-ary. The truth embodied in the identification approach can only be cashed by rejecting the sense of the term "autonomy" provided by its etymology. Although an autonomous decision must not be "externally generated," it need not flow from the deepest level of the self. We pay homage to our natures as choosing and valuing human beings by construing an autonomous decision as one which expresses values (not necessarily understood in accordance with the Evaluation Conception), adopted rationally and honestly and seriously held, even when those values do not have a strong hold on the person. This is the germ of truth in the idea that autonomy is the domination or control of the lower self by the higher or true self.

Our general account of autonomy incorporates a demand for objectivity. That demand is warranted in this case as well if only to rule out those emotionally unsound decisions which arise as a response to the emotional springs of the agent's psychological condition and which result in a failure to govern reflections by the features of the components which enter into the objects of reflection. An individual considering a decision to become an addict should be influenced by the character of the life she would lead. Since we have conceded the logical possibility that such a decision is autonomous, we must concede as well that the condition of objectivity may be satisfied. If she is confident that she will not entertain serious regrets about this choice later on in life, if she has no strong desires that conflict with the addictive life, if she is fully aware of the consequences of her decision, if she is emotionally sound in the relevant way, if her natural potentialities have been adequately nurtured, if her reflections about the matter are rational and procedurally independent, if she will retain sufficient personal integrity, if she is prepared to review her decision in the light of changing circumstances to the extent that her addiction permits this, then her decision is autonomous. It is, of course, difficult to believe that this possibility is other than merely logical.

This account of autonomy in terms of an actual or hypothetical rational choice is not undermined by a difficulty which plagues the analogous account of self. We saw earlier that even a rational identification with a particular desire can be misguided. We will be frustrated by the absence of a theory of semantic relevance when we wish to charge a person with self-deception, given that he finds himself, after informed and dispassionate reflection, identifying with a desire we know is peripheral and fleeting. But we need not be similarly frustrated by the commitment to judge as autonomous the adoption of a bizarre decision made under similarly ideal conditions. These conditions – rationality, relevant knowledge, procedural independence, objectivity – are quite stringent, but they are not intended to smuggle semantic relevance back into the picture. They are designed instead to permit the ultimate authority of the individual.

Accordingly, I adopt the view that persons who are mentally ill can be autonomous so long as they meet the specified conditions: rationality, freedom, objectivity, independence, and integrity. These conditions are, of course, not distinct from mental health. But it is not my task to consider *the extent if any* to which there can be autonomous persons who are not mentally healthy. Our task is difficult enough without adding to it the project of defining mental illness.

Thus, the most sensible way to address the dilemma posed by the unwilling addict is implicit in the earlier rejection of the origin requirement. The metaphysical or psychological inquiry designed to discover the nature of a person is distinct from the inquiry as to the autonomous or heteronomous nature of his choices and actions. As we undermine the metaphysical nature of the quest for an account of autonomy, we provide a further rationale for replacing the demand for proper origination with the requirement of objectivity. And we undermine as well the significance of the concept of the self as a concept distinct from whatever idea of the "whole," embodied person is allowed to develop out of a scientific psychology.

In defense of objectivity

And now we see the fundamental reason that objectivity is a key component of autonomy. For, to put it in a slogan, *autonomy is not the freedom to express our origins; it is the freedom from those origins.* This is precisely the quality we find in Jean, not George (Chapter 8). Jean may be very grateful that he was placed in Ms. Webster's class. That fortuitous circumstance determined his life, a life permeated with meaning and joy. But he has transcended his origins in a way George has failed to do. George is still dealing with Ms. Webster; Jean is dealing with materials, subjects, current relationships.

Objectivity is the transcendence of and liberation from origin. It is the ability to respond to the world and to the current condition of the agent. As such, it implies the core sense of the term "autonomy," independence, a sense which was never intended to include all the elements we interact with daily. We need to be independent of the factors which led us to our current state rather than those which give our current life its meaning. Objectivity is denied to George and Gideon and to the unfortunate addict. The reasons may be different. George's reasons for acting as he does are bound up with desires directed at features of his childhood. Whether or not this is also true of the addict, the more visible repercussion of his early environment is the negative impact on his rationality and certain components of freedom such as knowledge.

It should go without saying that an agent can autonomously choose to retain elements of her past in light of reasons which of necessity pertain to her current state, including her understanding of and engagement with the world. To be freed from one's past is in part to be able to *select* to preserve parts or all of that past. An autonomous person may well be a rabid conservative – but he opts freely for the perpetuation of tradition and is prepared to reconsider that choice should circumstances change.

Had we succeeded in constructing an intelligible picture of an ideally autonomous agent, we might be in a position to confront the ideal currently being promoted with a superior model. We would not have to submit to the depiction of an autonomous agent as one beholden to the world. Since the ideally autonomous agent answers to no one and to no thing, he is not under the control of anything external to himself and is accordingly the sole proper subject of the designation "autonomous."

But the elaboration of the concept of ideal autonomy collapsed under its own weight and turned out to be either unintelligible or useless as a model for human beings. Yes, autonomous agents are beholden to the world. For life is action in that world, including even the act of committing suicide. A baseball player operates under the standing commitment to run to first, not third, base after he hits the ball. For he has concluded on the basis of informed, rational, and nonneurotic deliberations that participation in this activity is valuable to him and that decision is occasionally revisited and freely reconfirmed. He is not less autonomous by dint of his refusal to deliberate each moment whether or not to abide by the rules of the game.

I am suggesting that we are freed from the impossible task of delineating the inner from the outer. We are not physical structures, say balls, with a clear inside and outside. (Even if we were, the inner-outer dichotomy would be problematic because it does not pertain to the spatial location of objects, but rather to traits or events. Is the movement of a ball inside or outside the ball?)

It is good to be free of this burden. For the task is impossible. As bodies, we may be able to make some sensible judgments about what is a part of and what is not a part of our bodies. As philosophers, however, we are capable of endless disputes about the connection of our bodies to our selves; so that a clear delineation of the body is of little help in delineating the self. Before elaborating further on this important theme, I want first to ensure a proper understanding of the role of second-order evaluations in the life of an autonomous agent.

Second-order evaluations

My concern to deflate the status of higher-order evaluation has operated in the context of an enterprise of correction directed against the exaggerated claims made on its behalf by intellectuals who are inclined to elevate to the first metaphysical rank those aspects of their nature with which they tend most to identify, to wit, reflection. Although I have zealously pursued the task of restoring flesh and blood to our souls and have warned against the dangers inherent in the (overly) reflective life, I have at the same time permitted the existence of contexts in which second-order evaluation achieves ascendancy. There are people who are centrally engaged in personal redirection a good portion of their lives and who can make a convincing case that their values are not embodied in their effective wills. The importance of elements of autonomy such as critical competence and objectivity are as crucial here as they would be in any conative context. Whether my desire is first- or second-order, my autonomy and proficiency are enhanced to the extent that I make and execute my decision rationally, freely, independently, and so on. To the extent that I am displeased with the direction of my life, the propensity for second-order *reflective* evaluation (as opposed to isolated acts of condemnation) might well goad me into action which will restore contentment or add significance to my life. And since the capacity for objectivity, grounded in an ability to respond to the world rather than the fetters of our personal heritage, is universally imperfect, we can all benefit from at least a restricted inclination toward reevaluation.

If we do not call attention to this inclination by including it in a list of autonomy-enhancing features, the reason is the same as the reason we do not underscore the fact that autonomous agents have desires and purposes and deliberate in order to reach decisions that will enable them to achieve their purposes and satisfy their desires. Whether one holds an Evaluation or Motivation Conception of value, people are permitted (and expected) to adopt attitudes toward their first-order wills and are accordingly supposed as a matter of course to engage in practical reasoning at both the first and the second level. These are givens, fundamental facts about the sorts of entities for which we seek a definition of autonomy. And since that definition will distinguish the *manner* of making these decisions, it will not automatically rule out as nonautonomous an entire *level* of decision-making.

Thus, an intelligent response to frustration or the failure to attain happiness may well be a reexamination of one's motivational structure rather than a shift of strategy in an effort to achieve the greatest amount of overall satisfaction of one's desires as given. The former may (but also may not) lead to an enhancement of autonomy. For example, a person's objectivity might be improved through the attenuation of crippling fears or the reinforcement of certain desires, results attainable through informed and rational choices leading to appropriate action directed to fundamental internal changes. Moreover, the importance of opting for personal reflection is not diminished by a refusal to construe reevaluation in the terms of the Evaluation Conception. If I happen not to judge my desires as lacking worth, I may yet, as frustrated, miserable, bored, or unfulfilled, have excellent reason to consider pervasive personal changes.[4]

If the sense persists that the significance of higher-order reflection has still not been captured, the reason may be that our appreciation of this trait is based in part on matters distinct from its connection to autonomy. For example, Frankfurt is surely right, as I said in Chapter 5, that even people who never experience serious alienation from their wills are expected to submit their lives to occasional review. This expectation is, of course, grounded in part on the obvious fact that second-order reflection is useful; we expect that conclusions are likely to be sounder the more carefully one submits them to rational scrutiny. Although we have high-lighted the benefits of spontaneity in one's personal life, no one can sensibly deny the dangers of impulsiveness. Yet one can imagine some extraordinarily lucky person who is blessed with all the innate gifts and environmental requirements necessary for a rich and satisfying existence. Although he cannot perhaps be faulted for not ever being impelled to review his life, we see him nonetheless as lacking in depth. Since we imagine that these higher-order powers of personal reflection are more difficult to replicate outside our species, we tend to think of them as conferring a distinctive worth on us, even if, like Hamlet, we often abuse them. Thus, we find that the utility maximizer, no matter how sophisti-cated her desires may be, lacks a crucial component of the fully worth-while life.

Whatever the reason for this preference, it need not be linked to auton-omy. I have argued and will, in the next chapter, pursue the case that there are values distinct from autonomy – morality and community, for example – and the capacity for higher-order reflection may be one of these.

The significance of second-order reflection may be grounded on the alleged unintelligibility of denying its existence in creatures with a first-order will. Since, in general, we cannot have mental states without know-ing or at least believing that we have them, we cannot be utterly ignorant of our desires, some of which lead to effective action. And given that (1) we can find any fact about the world attractive or repellent and (2) we are naturally deeply interested in facts that bear upon our own welfare and interests, the fact that we must know what our wills are more or less up to implies that it is at least perfectly natural, if not implicit in our natures, to possess a second-order will.

Although the legitimacy and importance of second-order evaluations have been established, the primacy of our first-order will remains undis-turbed. For, from the point of view of autonomy, the role of second-order evaluation is the restructuring of the will. However essential this activity is, it remains subordinate to the first-order will. So long as there is harmony, there is no inclination to identify with the higher levels of the will. We must also recall the failures of those who argue that life on the first level must be bereft of complex emotional and motivational states.[5]

Personal integrity

The surprising conclusion we have just reached is that sense can be assigned to my idea of autonomy only if we distinguish it from the idea of self-origination. If we invoke the slogan of liberation from self, instead, we will better understand the force of doctrines like those of identifica-tion. The unwilling addict is heteronomous, not because his actions are not under the control of forces originating in his self – he is after all an addict – but rather because his behavior does not reflect the choices he would make under ideal conditions. His current bondage is constituted by his inability to realize values which are not yet adequately represented in the makeup of his actual personality. His objectivity is impaired for he cannot respond to the world as his practical reason dictates.

Before I embark on a defense of the view that the notion of self-determination cannot be given a viable metaphysical interpretation in this context, it will be useful to say something about the requirement of personal integrity. For whatever account of the self appears ultimately to be plausible, we do have a vague idea that an individual must have some internal coherence or unity before we can even broach the subject of his autonomy. It is difficult to understand what the autonomy of Smith can consist of if Smith is a multiple personality, dramatically and uncontrollably shifting from one persona to the next throughout his life.

Of course, if $Smith_1$ is the name of one of Smith's personalities, it may well be that $Smith_1$ has sufficient integrity to count as autonomous. In light of his unusual circumstances, $Smith_1$ may not have the capacity to formulate long-term goals; however, if we can count $Smith_1$ as a person in his own right and if we can bracket the empirical data that are likely to suggest failures of relevant knowledge or objectivity, it is not clear that he is utterly unqualified occasionally to perform an autonomous act or choice.

Split-brain persons raise difficult issues as well. At one extreme is the view that such persons are really two people locked inside a single body. (In fact, some conclude that normal people are essentially the same as split-brain persons and are, therefore, really two persons as well, each person being associated with one hemisphere.) At the other extreme is the position that split-brain persons are simply unusual, but unitary, persons.

The case of self-deception raises problems too for it has been argued that this phenomenon requires us to construe the mind as compartmentalized in a way which surely raises doubts about its "unity" (Davidson 1982). If self-deception is assimilated to two-person deception, we need a deceiver and a deceived within the confines of a "single" mind. Yet most theorists either deny that we are forced to adopt the model of two-person deception (see Johnston 1988) or deny that the adoption of such a model constitutes a serious fragmentation of the self (see White 1991: 163–224). The latter point of view is based in part on the fact that the division of the mind into component subsystems, so-called homunculi, in which each system is relatively isolated from the others and possessed of its own intentional states and a capacity to process information intelligently, is an independent requirement of most current theories in cognitive psychology. If self-deception raises special problems for the unity of the self, then, it must demand an even greater splintering of the self than that which is assumed by psychologists as a matter of course.

Although self-deception is uniquely perplexing, I do not believe that we need worry that an individual who succumbs to it cannot be an autonomous agent. After all, he can certainly be autonomous in those spheres in which his deceptions play no role. And in the case of those decisions in which he is under the influence of a belief he has convinced himself is true, while at the same time knowing that it is not, we may argue for heteronomy on grounds that have been independently postulated. For example, the belief that guides his decision cannot be an instance of (relevant) knowledge, even if it happens to be true. (Suppose his deceiving self holds a belief it fails to recognize as false and unwittingly deceives himself into believing a truth.) Nor is this mechanism of belief acquisition a very reliable one, in which case we have grounds to deny the individual's objectivity.

Thus, our theory contains features which permit some decisions regarding autonomy to be made when the unity of the self is breached. Some instances of disintegration, for example, would involve violations of the rationality requirement. Also, although I have argued that an amoral person is not necessarily disintegrated or radically bereft of fundamental humanity, it does not follow that psychopaths are autonomous. They may suffer from a developmental deficit which has resulted in serious impoverishment. (Impoverishment is, of course, different from disintegration, but I have tried to defend this conception of autonomy from the criticism that it permits as autonomous persons who are so impoverished that they fail to exhibit personal unity, that is, a rich enough complex of emotion, attitude, and judgment, sufficient to be counted a member of the community of persons.) And I have talked about an important component of mental illness which is incompatible with autonomy, to wit, a breakdown of objectivity.

There are so many difficult cases, however, that only an extended discussion of personal integrity, not to be undertaken here, can do justice to the topic. Although I will not, therefore, provide even a first stab at a respectable account of the concept, I would observe that autonomy is not to be identified with motivational integration, an ideal that is fully realized by an individual when each of her desires is a component of a tight-knit system of desires, organized around a life plan or overarching value that confers significance on and determines a ranking for the individual desires. For, although a profoundly disintegrated personality cannot exemplify autonomy, why should the degree to which one is autonomous be a function of the extent to which one exhibits motivational integration? There are people with multiple passions. Although some of them confront deep conflicts when they must choose among their passions, some do not. Of the latter, some may be unable to integrate their lives into a single theme in which each passion takes its proper place. Why should that absence of perfect unity undermine their autonomy?

In an era in which the demands on the individual are so numerous and conflicting, the many possibilities for satisfaction and enrichment dangled before us so tempting, and the bombardment of stimuli so unrelenting, the preceding remarks may be seen as a component of an irresponsible conspiracy to bolster the continued fragmentation of the self. As Kenneth Gergen (1991) says, "this virtual cacophony of potentials" not only makes committed identity "an increasingly arduous achievement"; it also undermines the meaningfulness of the individual elements. "As social saturation adds incrementally to the population of self, each impulse toward well-formed identity is cast into increasing doubt; each is found absurd, shallow, limited, or flawed by the onlooking audience of the interior" (73). Should we not insist on a centered self, one with roots deep enough to avert the forces of disintegration? Is a pastiche personality a viable one or do we not instead all need moorings which permit us to endure as stable and coherent beings?

These questions admit of no straightforward answers. David Miller (1974), for example, describes the "new person" as experiencing "equally real, but mutually exclusive aspects of the self. . . . The person experiences himself as many selves, each of which is felt to have . . . a life of its own, coming and going without regard to the centered will of a single ego" (193). Yet, "surprisingly, the experience is not sensed as pathology" (78). And Louis Zurcher (1977) is not disturbed by the transition to a mutable, rather than stable, self for he sees there the virtues I have posited for the autonomous self, for example, tolerance, openness, and flexibility.

Since I am actually sympathetic with the worries of those who view with alarm the forces threatening the personal integration of so many individuals, I would regard the interpretation of my words as a celebration of these developments a misunderstanding of the doctrine.

Let me first recall the remarks of Chapter 8 that were designed to distinguish the impulsive from the genuinely liberated individual. The requirement of objectivity ensures against total subjugation to the stimulus of the moment. The autonomous individual has the cognitive and affective equipment needed to assess the big picture. He has the physical, intellectual, and emotional skills and the disposition to reflect rationally concerning the options available to him, especially when his life is not proceeding along satisfactory lines. If one is free from limitations to engage the world in a satisfying way, one is not also required to submit to every prima facie demand, to savor every new stimulus, and always to eschew withdrawal or disengagement. I have indeed just made a case for the importance of reflective evaluation (understood in the terms of my doctrine) as a means to retain control over one's life.

In fact, one worry which I attempted to dispel in Chapter 7 concerns the possibility that the autonomous person would be, like Nietzsche's Übermensch, too *dis*engaged. I have said repeatedly that the autonomous individual cannot savor the delight of total submission to the group, but he is certainly capable of emotions that would sustain satisfying engagement.

I would, therefore, leave to each autonomous individual the decision regarding the importance in his or her life of a motivational core or a strict hierarchy of values. If some people demand a center, others may indeed find the patchwork life utterly liberating.

A similar result obtains when we think of integration temporally. If someone, someday, for want of something better to do, writes my life story, he will, of course, find all those threads and continuities we expect to find in the life of any single person. But again, I take it that integration is more than the absence of disintegration. And it is not clear that the narrative of each autonomous life must have a more significant unity. Of course, we can always represent ex post facto almost any life as unified, but the story is oftimes more properly construed as a feat of the literary imagination rather than a piece of honest history.[6] At this stage in my story, time has been as cruel to me as it has to others – most doors are closed, even locked. But I still see several, dramatically different ways of completing the story. No matter which I choose – assuming that I choose at all – I am sure that my biographer will be able to represent the final stages as my destiny, imminent in the life I have led until now. But these interpretive acts, as Sartre saw, do not capture the lived life, the life alive with at least some open possibilities. Of course, I might be wrong about myself. But so long as we see this as an *issue*, as something more than the juxtaposition of incommensurable acts of interpretation, we allow that my biographer, as good as he is at his work, is not an historian and, therefore, that the demand for motivational integration as a serious requirement on autonomy is ill-conceived.

Having declined to offer a positive account of personal unity, I should at least say that an autonomous agent must possess psychological continuity sufficient to countenance and sustain long-range plans and to deliberate rationally concerning them. It is not as clear that physical continuity must be preserved for it is not self-evident that bodily continuity is a necessary condition of the persistence of a project. If I know that I am going to change bodies, I can take that contingency into account. Of course, certain bodily transfers are detrimental to certain projects. If, just before a performance, Placido Domingo acquires the body and vocal chords of Henry Kissinger, his plans might be seriously thwarted. But people always confront frustration and barriers to the realization of their goals.[7]

The self

The question of the nature of the self can be a type or a token question. The type question concerns the kind of entity a self is: biological, psychological, social, moral, rational, pure, or perhaps some sort of combination. The more relevant question in the context of self-determination is the token one. If selves are the sorts of entities that can possess motives, drives, or desires, we want to know which of these have their origins in the self and which do not. What makes a desire a state of a particular self? When I challenged the identification conception on the grounds that rejected desires can be an important part of the self, I was *assuming* that desires are states of selves, and *challenging* the position that a particular desire fails to belong to a particular self just because the person (?) fails to identify with it.

Although I explicitly rejected the identification account of the self, I hinted that the explanatory centrality account also fails. I observed in Chapter 5 that the latter, like the identification account, is not free of evaluative notions since we must first distinguish important from unimportant behavior before we are warranted in calling explanatory elements "central." Thus, the purported contrast between the tough-minded account in terms of explanatory primacy versus the tender-minded alternative of identification turns out to be fuzzy. Not only must advocates of the explanatory primacy model explain what importance is, but they must do so in terms of a personal judgment not all that different from an act of identification. But the coup de grâce was more recently administered through the recognition that the sources of paradigmatic forms of *heteronomous* behavior – addiction and internal compulsion – must have their origins in explanatorily central components.

I noted in Chapter 5 that even the father of the unconscious resisted the explanatory centrality conception of the self when he identified the *Ich* with the ego, the rational and epistemically accessible system. We can all trace the roots of Freud's identification of self with conscious accessibility to Descartes. These roots are deep and are reflected in both common and philosophical accounts of self. White says that "selves . . . are persons as they are represented to themselves from the first-person point of view" (1991: 1).

If expulsion from self through conscious rejection of a desire which might in some sense be "important" to the person is indeed illicit, it is also true that the conscious level of the self has a primacy, even if its character is difficult to articulate.

We begin our self-articulation on the level of conscious reflection; that may well be a tautology. We discover that the conscious level does not provide all the resources for a fully adequate explanation of our conscious life and our behavior. So we turn to psychological structures, for example, the unconscious, or neurological structures, patterns of discharge, more or less remote from that level. It may well turn out, as the Churchlands argue, that the explanatory theory requires us to reconceptualize and finally abandon the starting point. When we contemplate radical reductions of the significance of the conscious domain, we cannot but suppose as well that the self has withered away. If the eliminative materialists are right and the ultimate theory of human behavior is one which eschews intentionality and replaces the concepts of folk and cognitive psychology with those of neurophysiology, then the self has surely been just a chimera – we are a complex organism, nothing more. But that result only reinforces the inextricable link between self and consciousness.

Yet, of the many deficiencies of the Cartesian view, several pertain uniquely to the context of our concern, namely, the elaboration of a conception of self that can serve to illuminate the idea of self-regulation or self-determination. We are barred from adopting a Cartesian account of self for we would not count an action that flows from an obsessive thought as autonomous just because the agent was aware of the thought. Nor do we view as paradigmatically autonomous a person who mistakenly cites a conscious desire as motivation when, in truth, he is ignorant of the true nature of his action and would decisively choose to act otherwise were he fully informed and not emotionally impaired. If a slave may be aware as a free agent of the forces driving behavior, Cartesian-driven accounts of the self are useless for our purposes.

We must then either turn to other conceptions of self which can better illuminate the distinction between autonomy and heteronomy or perhaps abandon the concept of self altogether. One danger in the adoption of the latter strategy is that, since it is a truism that there are many concepts of self, we might criticize one account and fail thereby to notice another, perfectly good one. Both Hume and Daniel Dennett (1989) reject the self, but they are rejecting very different things. Hume rejects an experienceable subject of all those mental states I call "mine," whereas Dennett rejects a single command center (in favor of a modularity approach to mind).

Nevertheless, as we peruse the variety of projects that may appropriately be regarded as elucidations of the concept of self, it is noteworthy how so many are ill-equipped to serve our purposes. Since Hume denies the self, his ideas are unhelpful. The Cartesian idea of a single subject of "my" experienced states will not do, as we have seen. Similarly ill-equipped would be the conception of the self as the bearer of personal identity over time. For whatever one's view on this matter, I can recall or anticipate and, therefore, render mine those mental states obtaining during episodes of slavery or addiction as well as I can recall or anticipate those mental states accompanying exemplary displays of my autonomy. Although we acknowledge the necessity of psychological continuity in some form, no further basis for a distinction between autonomy and heteronomy emerges from these elements.

Ditto for the self as the focal point of sensory orientation. Ever-changing optical and kinesthetic information provided by the environment in relation to our bodies together with our own responses to the actions we perform cohere to produce a unified referent of a significant number of instances of "I." But this self is as present to a prisoner as to his jailor.

The result is the same if we explore the implications of interactive accounts of the self. By this sort of account, I have in mind those that emphasize the component of contrast, especially in the etiology of the idea of self. We form a sense of ourself in relation to the other, where the latter comprises both the natural and the personal world. When the inanimate objects in our experience resist our will, we lose our sense of omnipotence and, in confronting the other, we acquire a sense of ourself.

And in those interactions with the significant human others of our infancy, we become aware of ourself as a person among persons, as one who shares emotions and engages in a reciprocity of expressive gestures. Again, however, the establishment of natural or social boundaries to the self is a feat for a slave or a freeman; one can be set off from the natural or social world as its victim or its master. We need another conception of self to anchor the latter distinctions.

Moreover, it matters little whether these differing concepts can be unified in some way. Whether we have different selves or one self with a variety of facets, we still face this deficit. Even a collective concept will not generate the required dimension that will permit us to draw the right line between one set of motivations and another.

Some philosophers view the self in moral terms. Charles Taylor (1989), for example, characterizes morality in such a way as to render it a sine qua non of selfhood. To have a morality, for Taylor, is to regard certain things as supremely important, valuable, or worthy in a sense in which contrasting items fall short in a qualitative way. And to have an identity is to be possessed of a framework in which judgments of this nature constitute a background against which all the discriminations necessary for a specific identity as a self are formed.

A notion of autonomy formed from this perspective would indeed possess the feature missing from most of the other accounts. It would afford a way of distinguishing self-directed from other-directed motivations; the former would reflect my evaluations.

If we replace a Kantian metaphysics of morality with moral frameworks à la Taylor, it seems to me that we inevitably invite the possibility of a conflict *internal to the self* between moral ideal (or ego ideal) and psychological reality. For the framework which constitutes my identity cannot be identified simpliciter with the self unless we make a sham of moral struggle, frustration, and guilt. The moral framework which defines my identity is at best my personal *ideal* and, as such, potentially unrealized by my weak self.

To be sure, the frameworks point of view is not narrowly restricted to the blatant sort of Kantian conflict between duty and temptation. Nonetheless, Taylor insists that the qualitative distinctions that define a framework are not psychological distinctions. To regard Bach as more profound than Liszt is not to want to listen to Bach more; to elevate courage to a core virtue is not to have a strong desire to be courageous. There is, therefore, no way to avoid a potential conflict between the ideal and the actual which renders this approach unusable. Even conceding to Taylor the Evaluation Conception of value, the structure of my motivations may well conflict with the structure of my values.

Efforts to ground a fusion of the actual and the ideal based on an inherent telos are seriously problematic. If my ideals or values are constitutive of my self as fulfillments of potentiality, then we evidently need a theory which will demarcate bona fide instances of self-realization from the fulfillment of unnatural potentialities. The biological model will not do for biology does not determine, even if it sets limits, on our goals or ends. And if we propose our sociological constitution instead, we confront a dilemma. If I am incompletely acculturated, then I may be in rebellion against the values of my group (even if the terms of the discussion have, to be sure, been set in the acculturation process). Why, in this case, should my values not be the ones I reflectively proclaim just because they differ from those of the group? If, on the other hand, I am perfectly acculturated, then the union of actual and ideal is achieved at the expense of the very state we set out to find. As we have noted, the most perfect exemplification of the merger of self and society takes place in tribal cultures, in which the capacity for autonomy has not yet been formed. If the perfect union of the individual with his group is the essence of self-determination, then self-determination cannot be the nature of autonomy. Autonomy demands that one's immersion in the group be at most partial, that one retains the capacity for withdrawal occasioned by reflective redirection of the course of one's life. One may try to "go between the horns" of this dilemma by noting that this redirection must be partial, that nobody can reform his values and purposes from scratch. But this fact is too weak in the context; that my ideals are formed in interaction with my environment does not entail the impossibility of a serious breach and, therefore, the need to look at the individual, not the group, to determine the individual's values.

If, having failed to locate a serviceable conception of self, we are inclined to scuttle the whole idea of metaphysical self-determination, we will be in a position to take seriously not only skeptical views of the self, but the more radical idea that there are no *states* of the self. It is one thing to abandon the idea of a unitary subject, or a single command center, or an individual continuant underlying psychological change. It is another to deny the existence of discoverable facts about the self.

The explanatory centrality theory is a version of *psychological realism;* there are truths about my self awaiting discovery, even if the mode of discovery is not conscious introspection. These truths are independent of interpretive acts, both mine and others. I am a certain way whether I see myself this way or am so treated by others. *Psychological constructivism,* as I will call it, on the other hand, goes beyond the familiar idea that the self is formed through interaction with others; it contends that the self is constituted through this interaction. To learn about ourself is simply to enter into an interpretive scheme, one that is not right or wrong. So-called self-knowledge is, therefore, socially relative. In learning a language, modes of interaction, and schemes of interpretation, we are not acquiring tools for the construction of theories about an independent domain of inner facts. We have rather all along been constructing that domain.

I mention this debate simply to make the point that the rejection of the concept of the self in an account of autonomy frees us up to pursue these issues without the worry that our views on autonomy are going to be profoundly affected. I would indeed recommend this option. We ought to abandon the *token* dispute, that is, the disagreement over the criterion of participation in the self, once it is conceded that a state belongs to the person in a wide sense.[8] I am, as a consequence, obliged to provide sense for the various remarks about inclusion and exclusion from self that have dotted this book. It will suffice to explain the most contentious of these, in particular, those claims about conflict "within" the self.

On a wide construal, every experienced conflict is within the self and that is the construal I would take. I have said that an autonomous agent can abide conflict that does not paralyze or disable the self so long as the effective desire resides within the self. That sort of remark cannot stand as is, and it is most fortunate that I can construct a plausible recasting in terms of the nonmetaphysical account of autonomy presented in this chapter. The criterion of autonomous choice that was explicitly designed to separate out autonomy from selfhood tells us that a conflicted person can achieve autonomy by deciding and acting on that desire she rationally identifies with, assuming that all other conditions of autonomy are met.

This liberal attitude toward self-inclusion permits us to bemoan Laura's failure to develop within her self a love of classical music. For this capacity for appreciation would indeed have been a part of Laura had it been allowed to blossom even if, as an adult, she would have autonomously refused to nourish it.

Liberalism also sustains the neutral attitude on the cultural issue of fragmentation I advocated earlier. If I am skeptical of the sanguine or even exuberant attitude toward what Robert Jay Lifton (1987) calls the protean life style, the flow through time, without coherence or permanence, of ever-changing impulses and images, my reasons are psychological or moral, not metaphysical. If the satisfactions of the autonomous life, as I have presented them, are essentially those of unfettered engagement, it is not necessarily a sign of emotional immaturity, at least for some people, to impose rules and boundaries to ensure that one remains in charge of one's life.

The way to tell where one stands on these matters is not through the discovery that one is actually realizing one's self for, as I have said, that is not a matter for discovery. Milan Kundera (1974) describes a pitiable girl who thinks otherwise in his story "The Hitchhiking Game." After participating in a bit of game playing with her lover, the girl takes on her coquettish role so well and so fully that

on the bed there were soon two bodies in perfect harmony, two sensual bodies alien to each other. This was exactly what the girl had most dreaded all her life and had scrupulously avoided till now: love-making without emotion or love. She knew that she had crossed the forbidden boundary, but she proceeded across it without objection and as a full participant; only somewhere, far off in a corner of her consciousness, did she feel horror at the thought that she had never known such pleasure, never so much pleasure as at this moment – beyond that boundary. (1974: 65)

His girlfriend's complete absorption in the role of the lascivious miss frightened and irritated the boy to the point of rejection. He refused to respond to her sobs and her efforts at return. She says: "I am me, I am me."

The young man was silent, he didn't move, and he was aware of the sad emptiness of the girl's assertion, in which the unknown was defined by the same unknown.

And the girl soon passed from sobbing to loud crying and went on endlessly repeating this pitiful tautology: "I am me, I am me, I am me." (88)

The failure to express her personal crisis in satisfactory metaphysical terms ought not to detract from the tragic character of her hysterical quest to distinguish authenticity from role-playing and the shattering nature of the erosion of her identity. As philosophically illuminating as I would like to think my reflections on autonomy and self are, I must remind myself, with sadness, of Wittgenstein's observation that philosophy leaves everything as it is.

Having found no basis for a metaphysical embellishment on the requirements of freedom, strength of rational will, knowledge, rationality, independence, objectivity, and personal integrity, I conclude my presentation of this theory of autonomy.

10

The value of autonomy

Most people believe they have a right to be autonomous, at least in many domains. The value of autonomy may then be construed as the value of conferring or possessing this right – the right to be a certain way and the right not to be interfered with as one cultivates this state – and that depends on the precise nature and scope of this right. The right will not be of much value to a person who finds that he only has a right to exercise autonomy over matters of little moment to him. I do not propose to address the scope of this right for such a discussion would have to rest on a general theory of rights I am not in a position to offer.

Instead, I wish rather to seek to know the value of that state, autonomy, to which one may or may not have a limited or unlimited right. Here, again, the question may be divided. For one may wish to know the value of making a decision autonomously rather than heteronomously, regardless of the specific content of the decision. Or one may want to know the value of incorporating a particular domain into the scope of one's autonomy.

The latter issue is the one most commonly in mind when the value of autonomy is discussed. Those who see autonomy as a value usually wish to extend its scope indefinitely. The more autonomy, the better. Devotees of certain forms of mysticism and certain religious practices found in the East are perhaps the only advocates of the other extreme – total personal surrender. Less extreme critics of the lovers of autonomy worry about the unbridled extension of this condition: Is it an unmixed blessing to look upon every sphere of human concern as a potential candidate for a takeover? Do we really want to be able to choose our religion, our sex, our intelligence, our talents, our genes, our body parts, our bodies? Can there not be a surfeit of autonomy? A more restrained attitude may be a viable option once we reflect on the parochial character of this ideal. Advocacy of autonomy as a foundational value is both geographically local and historically recent. It may be wise to take a broader perspective before we jump on the bandwagon.

Here again a division of questions is helpful. If we look at the matter individually, it is undeniable that, with respect to many, perhaps all, of these items, the answer would be affirmative for *some* individuals. For the possession of any trait can be an enormous burden for some individuals. The freedom to choose his sex would be a boon to a potential transsexual. Indeed, it is unclear what would be wrong in expanding

239

options given that everyone retains the freedom *not* to exercise this right. If I am content with my sex, I would not be burdened by the introduction of a right I have no interest in exercising.

If we look at the issue socially, on the other hand, the specter of a general extension raises deep and difficult questions about relations between the individual and society. If we are not burdened with the constraints imposed by the natural order and our historic development, we might find that *everybody* chooses individually to be a brilliant and handsome male, a Buddhist, a violist, and to live in Paris. Before long, of course, this order of nature would have to be subordinated to an order of society and we would all lose our perfect autonomy.

Even if we bracket the issue of the social chaos that would result, we have to wonder how individuals would make decisions when they lack the perspectives we commonly assume in normal decision-making situations. If there are no or few givens, if the background against which reflection makes sense is withdrawn, one would not know how to begin. If I need a new suit, I normally choose between Barney's and Moe Ginsburg. But if I can change my sex, perhaps I should contemplate shopping at that new boutique down the street. There is also that nudist colony I could join. I don't really want to be a nudist, but a quick trip to my therapist will cure that. Can there be too many options?

People often complain about the enormous burdens of decisions hitherto left to authority figures or nature that social changes or advances in knowledge and technology thrust upon them. Not only are there new burdens; there are also new opportunities to be blamed for bad decisions. Of course, we may imagine ourselves acquiring the power to change our psychology so that we are more amenable to the assumption of greater responsibility. Until that day comes, however, this psychological cost has to be taken into account.

The psychological and moral burdens of enhanced choice are but a proper subset of transaction costs. Gerald Dworkin (1988: 65–7) lists others, such as the costs of acquiring information, including the time and effort involved.

Yet, it is better that individuals assume many of the burdens they have been forced to assume. It may be quite distressing to decide on a course of treatment when that decision is a life and death one. But it is better that the (informed) individual take this responsibility rather than the physician, as used to be the case. Given that the decision is not necessarily more rational or wise, we may wonder why that is so. The answer flows from an answer we will later give to the question posed previously: What is the value of making a decision autonomously rather than heteronomously, regardless of the specific content of the decision?

For Kant, autonomy is the supreme practical virtue, for it merges with rationality, independence, and morality. Although many others have been critical of the Kantian scheme, my efforts have been directed against Kant's insistence that an autonomous agent act from (moral) principle rather than inclination. In rejecting the link to morality in particular, I have undercut efforts to justify autonomy in terms of the automatic promotion of moral values. Although an autonomous agent can lack moral values, it is worth observing that autonomy is a clear value in an agent otherwise committed to a moral life. One obvious reason for this is that we have *not* severed the link between autonomy and rationality and, whether or not it is invoked on behalf of moral ends, rationality is a powerful tool to achieve one's objectives. A rational agent is more prone to judge dispassionately and impartially and would, therefore, advance the moral cause if he were pledged to adhere to moral principles. In addition, since an autonomous agent is disposed to think for himself and is not prone to be swayed by the crowd, he is not tempted to subvert individual rights or to ignore morally relevant discriminations whose subtlety would otherwise result in their dissipation in a mob setting.

Those who place a supreme value on morality will show little enthusiasm for an autonomous agent who is unmoved by moral principles, even if she happens to act roughly in accordance with morality. The absence of moral feelings which implicate second-order evaluations, like a sense of injustice and a feeling of resentment, will be viewed as prominent deficiencies, as is the inability to participate in the communal practice of moral discussion and criticism. Even when an amoralist is driven by feelings of love, he is likely to direct these feelings toward individuals with whom he has a special relationship and is unlikely, therefore, to be able to subordinate these feelings to the demands of principles which require the moral agent at times to sacrifice the particular for the universal, the lover, relative, or tribesman for humanity at large.

My position that autonomy does not guarantee morality is different from a position to which we now turn, namely, that moral reservations may be directed to autonomy *itself*.

C. Gilligan's views

Minority groups often place autonomy at the core of their demands, and the women's movement is no exception. Yet Carol Gilligan (1982) has charged that autonomy is a male ideal, one whose advancement tends to further the subjugation of women or, at least, their confusion about themselves, their roles, and their natural feelings. Specifically, women find their identity, not in individual and independent achievement, but rather in the way they connect to others, in the responsibility they feel to bestow care, support, and protection.

Women naturally rebel against conceptions of autonomy like Erik Erikson's, whose description of the developmental path marks all experience intervening between childhood and adulthood as steps toward autonomy and independence, because on this account, "separation becomes the model and the measure of growth" (Gilligan 1982: 98). Female fantasies and thoughts on development have been little explored, but to the extent that they are known, they differ from men's. "Illuminating life as a web rather than a succession of relationships, women portray autonomy rather than attachment as the illusory and dangerous quest. In this way, women's development points toward a different history of human attachment, stressing continuity and change in configuration, rather than replacement and separation" (Gilligan 1982: 48).

Indeed, as Gilligan stresses, in women, identity and intimacy are fused. Even highly successful and achieving women, when asked to describe themselves, depict "their identity *in* the connection of future mother, present wife, adopted child, or past lover. Similarly the standard of moral judgment that informs their assessment of self is a standard of relationship, an ethic of nurturance, responsibility, and care" (1982: 159).

Had women rather than men controlled the formation of our ethic, affiliation might have attained a value equal to or surpassing individual attainment. And "if one begins with the premise that 'all morality consists in respect for rules' (Piaget 1965) or 'virtue is one and its name is justice' (Kohlberg 1984), then women are likely to appear problematic within moral theory" (Gilligan 1987: 26).

If autonomy is portrayed as a goal to be reached, it is also a means, to wit, independent choice. Women have difficulty with both. In the case of the latter,

while society may affirm publicly the woman's right to choose for herself, the exercise of such choice brings her privately into conflict with the conventions of femininity, particularly the moral equation of goodness with self-sacrifice. Although independent assertion in judgment and action is considered to be the hallmark of adulthood, it is rather in their care and concern for others that women have both judged themselves and been judged. (Gilligan 1982: 70)

Is the account of autonomy developed in this work subject to these criticisms? In one respect, the answer is clearly "no." I have never offered as the paradigm of autonomy the self-made, driven executive, who places his career ahead of family and personal attachments. Choices are autonomous not in virtue of content, but rather in terms of methodology. In emphasizing the primacy of contingency and the real limits of a critique of goals and desires based on the requirements of rationality, procedural independence, integrity, and objectivity, I have surely permitted a life of attachments, caring, and compassion as much as one driven by a need for individual achievement. If basic natures differ drastically, whether or not these differences are gender-based, they will be reflected in different life choices many of which can pass the tests of autonomy.

The lives must, to be sure, be autonomously chosen, that is, the product of a rational process, informed and objective, conducted carefully and independently. There is a real conflict between autonomy and female psychology if the very prospect of individual choice is, as Gilligan suggests, disturbing. A woman may autonomously choose a life of self-sacrifice and nurturing, but she is not autonomous if she just finds herself this way, no matter how content she may be.

As Benn observed, autonomy is not an ideal for a totally cohesive society. An Amish man may lead a life enriched by the values of communal caring, security, and tribal cohesiveness, punctuated by public displays of cooperation, compassion, and a common spiritual bond. He, like a woman who is fully, but not self-consciously, content with her role of male support, lacks autonomy.

Thus, autonomy is preserved if a woman self-consciously endorses the nurturing and supportive life to which she finds herself naturally drawn, so long as the decision meets the conditions of an autonomous decision laid down in the previous chapter. An independent agent can not only accept advice from others, but can also decide to get married or to nurture her son. The decision to form an attachment satisfies the condition of independence so long as the reasons leading the person to make this decision have been submitted to as much objective and rational scrutiny as the nature of the decision permits.

Although a nurturing and caring woman need not be utterly servile (see Friedman 1985: 145), there is a prima facie paradox in the specter of an autonomous life whose agenda and pulse are set by another person. According to Gilligan, the sorts of attachments a woman is prone to form are those in which her instinct for nurturing and caring will place her in positions of self-sacrifice. That is, she will be likely to subordinate her own needs to those of others. Is the traditional mother, waiting on her son's every need, tending to his ills, paying for his misdeeds, bolstering his flagging ego, adjusting her every response to his independent actions and her estimate of his state of mind, and ignoring her personal dreams so as better to fulfill her chosen mission, a possibly autonomous being? If not, it appears that we should reconsider the argument of Chapter 8. For the portrait now being painted of this woman accords with the sketch of objectivity, an essential ingredient in the autonomous life, presented there. We there depicted an objective person as one whose reactions and behavioral responses are tuned to the subject matter in which she is immersed. Unfortunately for this theory, this depiction is satisfied by the current example, which appears to exhibit the very antithesis of autonomy.

We must first reiterate the importance to autonomy of the emergence into self-consciousness of a fully informed recognition of the state of things. But if this way of life then persists, how does it differ essentially from the life of an angel of mercy, such as Mother Teresa? I have insisted that an agent can retain her autonomy in conflict so long as the decision on behalf of one of the conflicting elements does not originate externally. And surely the concern for others is quite internal to the woman.

I think a healthy skepticism about the case of the compleat mother will persist and that it is based on the belief that a typical instance is one in which the line between freedom and slavery, unlike the case of an angel of mercy, has been crossed. Once a woman loses the capacity to reassert her self concerns, she has lost her autonomy, whether or not her current state has evolved from an original, autonomous decision. That, indeed, has approximated the plight of many women. Their own ingrained habits combined with the expectations of others collectively form a powerful barrier to change. If, 30 or 40 years ago, a loving wife and mother flirted with the thought of self-assertion, she would not only have had to confront the reactions of her family and her society, but also the strength of her own habits and tendencies to self-sacrifice as well as a host of feelings, such as guilt, worries about ostracism and detachment from various sources of sustenance, and even the fear of a loss of identity. In my terms, the combined weight of these factors entails a lack of the freedom necessary for a display of autonomy. I note, in addition, that, on the account of freedom defended here, this woman lacks it even if she never *in fact* was tempted by the possibility of self-assertion or rebellion.

But the women's movement has changed women's moral thinking along lines which confirm Gilligan's view that the constraints imposed by female psychology are not entirely unmalleable. "The issue of inclusion first raised by the feminists in the public domain reverberate through the psychology of women as they begin to notice their own exclusion of themselves" (1982: 149). Judgment becomes complex "as selfishness and self-sacrifice become matters of interpretation and responsibilities live in tension with rights" (149). Thus, Gilligan does not find an irreconcilable tension between women's psychology and the demands of autonomous choice. She suggests indeed that a self-conscious awareness of the complicity of women in their own subjugation is desirable. If men have used a woman's natural bent for nurturing and self-sacrifice for their own selfish purposes, an awareness of this fact can at least initiate the sort of reconsideration which acknowledges a woman's personal needs as a part of the total picture.

This conclusion does not undermine the special thrust of Gilligan's view, that a woman's starting point cannot be ignored and that it ought to serve as a basis for a reconsideration of the assumptions about morality and value that have been driven by a male-dominated society. A woman can assert her rights to satisfy her own needs without adopting the total package – individual achievement, separation, morality as justice (so that the bloody battle is at least a fair one) rather than caring and responsibility for others. A more fundamental challenge to her position is provided by recent studies of responses to personal dilemmas, which indicate that gender differences are not statistically significant. (See Walker 1984; Walker, DeVries, and Trevethan 1987.) Gilligan has challenged the 1984 result, contending that, in one important study, "although care focus was by no means characteristic of all women, it was almost exclusively a female phenomenon" (1987: 25). Others have charged that Gilligan's psychological insights can be accommodated within the confines of traditional ethical theory. (See Sher 1987.)

In the critique of ideal autonomy, presented in Chapter 6, I concluded that one reason for thinking that this idea is incoherent is that the adoption of any goals is automatically limiting. If agents are inherently motivated, they are inherently limited by those motives. To want A is to be committed to seek means provided by the world for procuring A, to forego conflicting desires, to participate in the restrictions the possession of A demands, and so on. As we noted there, the most important goals we humans have seem generally to be bound to the most severe restrictions: love and friendship, to name two.

Accordingly, I then proposed relativizing the concept of maximal autonomy to an agent's actual desires. An agent who wants to be a father, friend, citizen, Jehovah's Witness, pool hustler, and U.S. Marine can have as much maximal autonomy as an agent whose sole desire is the desire to remain autonomous, although the former will evidently be severely limited by his freely chosen commitments.

This notion of maximal autonomy, therefore, underwrites the plausibility of the view that a woman who chooses the life of nurturing might well be autonomous. But these conclusions do not provide *further* support for the view that autonomy is valuable. Whatever value there is in the *choice* of the nurturing life over its nonself-conscious adoption is to be found in the value of self-conscious rationality and that is independent of the particular issues raised by these cases. If we believe that the nurturing, self-sacrificing life can be a valuable one, we will reject autonomy as an essential component of all ideals *if* it is incompatible with this sort of life. But I deny this incompatibility and am accordingly left with two possibilities. (1) Autonomy is not essential to all ideals for there is value in the life of a heteronomous nurturer, even if there is greater value in the life of an autonomous one. The greater value, which I will adumbrate shortly, is constituted by the usual features of self-awareness, control, and a critical competence whose value transcends any particular use of it. (2) Autonomy is essential to all ideals and there is, therefore, no real value in the life of a heteronomous nurturer. Autonomous nurturing is possible and the only valuable sort of nurturing.

Before we reflect on these two possibilities, I want to raise a question about the status of a heteronomous nurturer. If such a life is devoid of value, then one cannot think that such a person is a moral agent. Although I believe that autonomy does not imply morality, I have yet to pass judgment on the converse relation. Kant would concede that a caring and compassionate person might do good things, but if she does them out of an attachment to those things rather than principles derived from her rational nature, she lacks any moral worth. The issue then is the status of a nurturing person whose life was not chosen, who found herself drawn into such a life by her own natural impulses combined with external pressures she never had the opportunity to reflect adequately on in a context in which she was in a position to accept or reject the options placed before her. Rather, she responded unself-consciously to the prevailing pressures against the development of her own talents and abilities and in favor of the subordination of her personal interests to her interests in caring for her family and perhaps others to whom she extends her charity.

Only a discussion of the nature of morality more extended than I can here proffer will provide a satisfactory resolution of this woman's moral status. But when we consider that she finds great satisfaction in caring for others, that she is moved by compassion and love, it seems clear, as I have argued before, that only a dubious commitment to the Kantian insistence on action from principle prevents us from ascribing moral worth to this person. Perhaps it would be morally better for her to have chosen her life, but it does not follow that she is *devoid* of moral worth.

The autonomism of L. Haworth

I reject the extreme position, dubbed "autonomism" by Haworth (1986: 7), that autonomy is essential to all other fundamental values, that it is, in fact, "*the* fundamental value" (184).

In Chapter 2, I noted that negative freedom is inconsequential if it is offered to one without the skills to take advantage of it, without positive freedom in other words. And even the combination of negative and positive freedom is valuable only if the agent actually exercises critical competence and independence in his deliberations concerning the way to use his total freedom. If he is a tool of another or chooses blindly or impulsively, neglecting the opportunity provided by the combination of a wide range of options together with the ability to act intelligently on them, he has annulled the value this total freedom would have in a genuinely autonomous agent.

Although, autonomy is essential to the value of other ideals, it is not essential to all values. In particular, I believe that pleasures which are not chosen by an autonomous agent (or by an autonomous agent who happens in the case of this choice to be acting heteronomously) may well be valuable. If that were not so, why would a rational agent, forced to choose from completely heteronomous lives, choose a life filled with diverse and intense pleasures over one racked with perpetual pain? It may well be that the decision about value must rest with the agent; so that the preference for the life of pleasure over pain must be *endorsed* by the person. But the value of the pleasurable life does not depend on the *origin* of the pleasure (even if autonomously determined pleasures are more valuable than others).[1]

Autonomy and individuality

Many have waxed quite eloquently on the value of autonomy as a feature of decision making as such and there is little point in rehashing the case. For the critics of autonomy are generally either those who have construed it along more substantive lines than I or those who object to the exaggerated claims made on its behalf, for example, claims that it is the supreme value, that it is presupposed in all other values, or that the extension of its scope is always desirable.

The values of procedural independence, rationality, integrity, and self-control are evident. We can actually bolster the case for autonomy by referring to the elements I have insisted should be added to the more familiar ones. I have argued that an autonomous agent must be objective, that is, responsive to the world as it really is and prepared to adjust her reactions in light of relevant changes. She is engaged in whatever commitments she has freely, rationally, and independently entered into and is liberated from the voices and pressures of her earlier years which are prone to impair the flow of activity in a way which inhibits the mature satisfaction of pursuing and fulfilling these commitments. She must as a corollary possess whatever degree of emotional stability (along with its consequent advantages) is implicit in objectivity. Her upbringing has included the nurturing of all those basic capacities which will not interfere with her autonomous development so that she is in a position as an adult to choose those she wishes to cultivate. She is, as she enters adulthood, fully equipped to make an intelligent choice about how to lead her life, a choice that will be *her* choice as to the way her life can be given meaning. If she possesses proficiency as well as autonomy of choice, she is in a position to secure her self-proclaimed objectives. She, thus, controls the implementation of her values as well as their formation.

This account both highlights elements of value not identified in other conceptions and endorses more familiar sources of value. For example, although I have expressed serious doubts about a metaphysical reading of self-expression, the individual thrust pervades my account of autonomy as much as it does others.

This emphasis on individuality is central to many justifications of autonomy.

What makes an individual the particular person he is is his life-plan, his projects. In pursuing autonomy, one shapes one's life, one constructs its meaning. (Dworkin 1988: 31)

Autonomy is a capacity that is (partly) constitutive of what it is to be an agent. ... Our notion of who we are, of self-identity, of being *this* person is linked to our capacity to find and re-fine ourself. (Dworkin 1988: 32)

By losing autonomy ... we wouldn't be a self. In any serious sense, we wouldn't be a person, or individual. (Haworth 1986: 185)

The value to one of barely being alive largely derives from the value one places on being autonomous, individual ... One simply wants to *be* as an individual, to continue to stand out. This interest in existing as an individual is probably more fundamental than any other interest we have. (Haworth 1986: 187)

Being autonomous consists in having a measure of critical competence. Such competence establishes one as an effective agent and as such brings the ability to make a mark on the world that is distinctively one's own. (Haworth 1986: 188)

There is a weak and a strong interpretation of these claims. It is undeniable that many persons place great value on an independent selection of goals, a reflective endorsement of basic decisions, and the right to decide how to lead one's own life. For whatever reason, independence and individuality rank very high on most people's preference scales.

The stronger claim is that autonomy expresses the very essence of the individual person qua agent. Autonomy is not just a supreme value of the person, but rather the very condition of personhood. To be an agent is to be autonomous.

In one sense, the strong claim is trivial. If we recall that autonomy is a matter of degree, we will realize that all persons are autonomous to some extent. For no one is literally totally dependent or utterly irrational or completely lacking in personal integrity, at least with respect to certain domains. To imagine a creature totally devoid of these traits is indeed to imagine a nonperson. Thus, to recommend autonomy is tantamount to recommending one's continued existence as a person and an actor in the world.

If the strong claim is to be interesting, therefore, it must express the position that enhanced autonomy is so important to our nature that all values are to be subordinated to the value of expanding whatever autonomy we have. If the weak claim is basically the endorsement of independence, a claim I find hard to take issue with, the strong claim must be that all values must give way to the furtherance of the goal of increased individual autonomy.

I have already drawn the drastic implications of this outlook when it is advanced as social policy. I wish now to look again at this issue from the perspective of the individual.

There are examples of lives which conflict with the recommendation of the strong claim, for example, those which are led by members of tight-knit communities such as Jehovah's Witnesses and the Amish. We may expect, for example, that defenders of the strong claim would demand that the state require Amish children to receive as much public education as possible (in the hopes that these children would receive the tools to lead an independent life as well as the impetus to defect from the flawed life they have been leading).

In tribal society, the individual is indistinct from the group, and self-governance is not then possible. Yet we saw earlier, in the example of Jehovah's Witnesses, not only that values shared by lovers of autonomy – personal strength, dignity, equanimity in the face of profound crisis – can be found in such communities, but that their presence is in part a function of the very absence of individual autonomy!

We must recall that, since autonomy is a matter of degree, a Jehovah's Witness has *some* autonomy. We concede the claim that a member of this group ought not to surrender even this small amount if he needs to do so in order to retain those other values resident in his group. Now a strong version of the strong claim is that, unless a community reaches a threshold of autonomy for its members, a threshold the Jehovah's Witnesses do not meet, the community is utterly devoid of value. In light of the values perspicuously displayed by this group, the strong version is clearly unacceptable. So the strong claim must be read so as to entail the view that the presence of other values in a complex which falls below a minimally acceptable level of autonomy never outweighs one in which that threshold level is reached.

The claim is unclear. It does not, for example, imply that one ought rationally to choose membership in any group that surpasses the threshold over membership in any group that does not. For extrinsic considerations may dictate otherwise. A group of autonomous agents may be on the verge of extinction or be the target of another powerful group's wrath. So if the thesis is to be cashed out in terms of the rationality of such a choice, we would have to hold constant all extrinsic factors.

We can attempt further clarification, but I prefer to bypass these preliminaries and concede that the view can receive a reasonably clear formulation in order to address the claim head on.

There are values provided by a cohesive community that are unavailable outside that community. The mutual support, the confidence, the sense of belonging to something greater than oneself, the comfort provided by an ideology one does not question, the readiness to confront the perils of life, and the ability to help others in distress as a consequence of a reduced self-concern are goods one may scoff at in light of the genuine deficiencies of many tight-knit communities, for example, insularity, dogmatism, ignorance, and hostility to outsiders. And it is not irrelevant to cite the potential tyranny of the mob, so frequently actualized by groups whose members are unaccustomed to think for themselves. But it is not clear to me how it is to be shown that such a society is inferior to *every* group of autonomous agents, since the advantages of these latter groups are purchased at the cost of these communal values. One cannot ignore the tendency of autonomous individuals to place personal gratification over public goods and to extract the heart from relational and communal undertakings through the adoption of a self-serving stance that conflicts with that of deep commitment.[2] It is a wonderful thing to live one's own life, but there is surely *something* to be said for living *our* life.

My case has been overstated. There can be communal values, for example, cooperation and a shared ideology, in a community of autonomous individuals, but it is also true that the depth of community sentiment and the extent to which persons experience a sense of belonging are unique to those more intimate assemblages in which the demand for individual expression has not yet been spawned.

Notes

1. Introduction

1. In their writings on autonomy, Stanley Benn (1988) and Lawrence Haworth (1986) make some references to portions of the psychological literature.
2. Haworth (1986) develops a theory of autonomy along these general lines.
3. Hegel (1969: 133ff; 1971: 182–302; 1977: ch. 6, section C) was one of the earliest important critics of Kant's moral theory. Of the many contemporary critiques, see David Ross (1954).
4. The term is Haworth's (1986: 7).

2. Freedom and autonomy

1. See, for example, the discussion by Timothy Renick (1990) of Nozick (1974) as well as the critique of negative liberty by Charles Taylor (1979).
2. It may well be that efforts to characterize negative freedom break down just because they bypass accounts of the self. For example, an agent can be limited by incapacity or by restraint. But only the latter, as "external," diminishes negative freedom. But Lawrence Crocker (1980: 11–15) has convincingly shown that there is no principled way of drawing this distinction and has consequently impugned the very idea of two types of freedom. So in the end, we may not be able to evade the self in these discussions either.
3. As noted by Renick (1990: 332).
4. See also Joseph Raz (1986: 375–6).
5. I will very soon explain the difference between autonomy and proficiency.
6. He may well have had forebodings which are borne out by cases of the sort described by Oliver Sacks (1993). In the particular case of Virgil, the restoration of all the physical requirements for sight both failed even over time to permit anything close to normal visual perception and brought in its wake physical and psychological harm so devastating as to necessitate a return to blindness. At the conclusion of this odyssey, "Virgil is allowed to not see, allowed to escape from the glaring, confusing world of sight and space, and to return to his own being, the touch world that has been his home for almost fifty years" (73).
7. The point is made by Shapiro (1981), Haworth (1986), and Benson (1987b), among others.
8. For a defense of the view that the notion of freedom is invariant over action and choice, see Berofsky (1992).
9. For example, Haworth (1986, 2, 14, 16–18, 42–6).
10. Even if there are cases in which the will is moved by nothing – I act intentionally for no reason whatsoever – they are not cases of action resulting from an autonomous decision.

I do not regard the thesis that all intentional action is motivated as conceptually necessary. See Berofsky (1970).

3. Freedom of action

1. Throughout this discussion, the term "power" does not mean "influence" or "social power." Senator Boren has more power (in the latter sense) than I do since he can bring about the defeat of President Clinton's deficit reduction package and I cannot and that conclusion is not overturned by the fact that I can wiggle my ears and he cannot.

2. The more familiar route to the demise of the hypothetical analysis was taken by Roderick Chisholm (1964), who observed that, since there are things we cannot even try to do, we must add the proviso that the agent *can try* to act. Keith Lehrer (1968) buttressed Chisholm's critique by noting that a person's very failure to try (choose) may render her incapable of acting, in which case she cannot act although she would if she tried. Bruce Aune (1970) objected to Lehrer's proof on the grounds that Lehrer failed to show that the manner in which one is incapacitated by a failure to choose is a relevant manner. For example, if I am unable to raise my arm because there is a 200 kilogram weight on it that *I can easily remove*, I am incapacitated in an irrelevant sense. I really can raise my arm and could be blamed for failing to do so. But Aune's example fails to refute Lehrer for it is possible that a failure to try (choose) renders one incapable of acting *in the relevant sense*. If I am so incapacitated, I may well be able to remove the incapacity by trying, but be unable to try. Since Aune cannot just assume that I can try, then the incapacity induced by the failure to try is in this case too a relevant incapacity and Lehrer has made his point.

3. The sentence actually says "legally free" rather than "free"; but I think that must be a mistake.

4. See Crocker (1980: 15–22).

5. For a discussion of compartmentalization and related matters, see Jon Elster's introduction to Elster (1986) as well as other papers in that volume.

6. "Calling someone free ... amounts to a claim about the reasonableness of making certain practical *demands* on that person. ... if my argument succeeds, it ... may suggest a way of recasting the problem of freedom and determinism." (Greenspan 1987: 64).

7. Recognizing that coercion per se does not absolve an agent from responsibility, Harry Frankfurt (1973) seeks conditions beyond the submission to a threat that would absolve an agent by obliterating choice.

> If the victim's desire or motive to avoid the penalty ... is ... so powerful that he *cannot* prevent it from leading him to submit to the threat, then he really has no alternative other than to submit (italics mine). (77)

Notice the modal notion in the analysis. A person is absolved from moral responsibility when coerced only if he cannot but act on the desire motivating him. This is, of course, part of what the incompatibilist is saying, though he adds that a deterministic account of the action implies this inability. Once again, the fundamental status of token ability emerges to foil those who would displace metaphysics by value theory. I believe that, to the pile of traditional, unsuccessful attempts to reduce these modalities by the various hypothetical analyses of ability, we must add, as equally unsuccessful, attempts to reduce these modalities to normative ideas.

8. There are stronger constraints on free action according to some hierarchical theorists. For example, besides doing what she wants to do and wanting to be moved by that desire, some require that she also value her action, whereas others demand that she must have the desire upon which she acted *because* she wanted to have that desire. But these fine points will be ignored at this stage.

9. Since the hierarchical theory does not explicitly posit the Stoic identification of freedom with tranquility, it is then in a position to regard frail creatures like us who successfully overcome some weakness as thereby ennobled. We have displayed freedom and deserve moral praise by having chosen to make our mark on the world and then having struggled against our own natures to secure that mark. The hierarchical theory can count this person free in spite of the internal conflict because the victorious first-order desire coincides either with the second-order desire or, if there is conflict on the second-level, with the stronger second-order desire.

Nor is the absence of conflict sufficient for freedom. Consider young children, lobotomized persons, the inhabitants of Brave New World, and those responding to post-hypnotic suggestion. Contentment is one thing and freedom another. (See David Shatz 1985.)

We are ennobled by the possession of freedom even when we abuse it. The wise or proper use of freedom merits tribute distinct from the commendation of freedom itself. Hence, the credit to which a person is entitled by dint of a successful struggle against temptation accrues in part to the character of the goal he has selected. (A follower of Himmler who successfully overcomes his feelings of compassion for the victims of Nazism is due no credit.) There are actually a variety of facets of the person which may be appraised. There is his persistence (on behalf of a noble goal) and perhaps the freedom of will, that is, his having freely selected the noble goal.

4. **Agent freedom**

1. See, for example, the discussions in Paul Benson (1987b) and Wolf (1990).
2. There are other conditions of autonomy which will be identified in later chapters.
3. Ideas similar to these can be found in Benn 1976, 1988; Young 1980, 1986; Haworth 1986; Watson 1987a.
4. The reader must again be reminded that there are other relevant conditions of autonomy to be identified later. For example, Guzzlewit must have had an upbringing which permitted him to develop all his basic capacities.
5. The position to be taken here is opposed to that of Benson (1987b), who holds the view that freedom "demands that one hold the values one ought to hold" (472).
6. See Watson (1975).
7. For a defense of this position, see Zimmerman (1989: 128-39).
8. Robert Kane brought to my attention the need in this context to distinguish compulsion from weakness of will. My reflections on these matters have also benefited from conversations with Bashshar Haydar.
9. To his credit, in my judgment, Haworth (1986: 157) exempts moral values, allowing that an autonomous agent might be immoral or amoral.

5. **Values and the self**

1. The neurotic may be free$_p$, but not free$_v$. Although she can barely summon the strength to choose to enter a relationship, the emotional cost is so great that it is unfair to make this demand. We may decide that, in this context, freedom$_v$ is the relevant sort of freedom.

2. Among those who reject this identification is Raz, who denies what he calls the transparency of value, the view roughly that a value-conferring feature of a state of affairs makes it good for someone for whom, consequently, the state of affairs is preferred to its absence (1986: 269).

3. Discrepancies between behavior and avowal do not automatically preclude talk of desire (or value). The coherence of behavior and avowal is the norm because it is an essential ingredient in *paradigmatic* instances of the concept.

   We have not yet introduced the assumption that preference is rational. Evidently this will incorporate constraints, especially if preference relations are to permit a definition of utility as a measure of strength of preference, and one of these may indeed be a coherence of behavioral and attitudinal expression.

4. As Nerlich (1989: 88) observes, one may wish for a million dollars and yet want *not* to be doing any of the things which might enable one to procure it. Although a point about the difference between wishing and wanting, it could be extended to the difference between wanting and choosing.

5. Many philosophers insist that creatures who place value on things must express their values in these ways. Nerlich (1989), for example, conflates the choice of the person we would like to be with the definition of a sense of personal worth, a conflation which automatically precludes the possibility of a Motivation Conception of Value. Taylor's (1977) insistence that valuing individuals engage in strong evaluation and Hill's (1991: 185–6) contention that a desire becomes a reason for a rational agent only when the agent can respect himself for choosing to act on that desire are other illustrations.

6. Many people, of course, regard the life of a (any) human being as intrinsically and objectively desirable. But since others, like Benjamin, do not, we cannot identify the states we unconditionally desire with the states we regard as objectively valuable.

   As a good father, Benjamin wants his son to grow to adulthood even if he believes he will no longer derive any satisfaction from the relationship or even the bare knowledge that his son is still alive. Yet here, too, it does not follow that Benjamin regards the continued existence of his son as of more than merely personal value.

7. This matter of depth may help to explain Watson's (1987a) observation that we sometimes fail to identify with our own valuations. In criticism of his earlier account, he correctly notes that a value judgment concerning one's desire, reflectively arrived at, may still clash not just with the desire—that is ordinary interlevel conflict and potential weakness of will—but also with the locus of identification. That is, the person still identifies with the desire. Part of the air of paradox is due to the tendency, criticized above, to find the self invariably on a higher volitional level.

8. The term is Raz's (1986: 308).

9. Frankfurt makes a sharp distinction between attitudes and decisions. An attitude I take toward a desire may be internal or external, depending on the

sorts of considerations I have described. But a *decision* that I do not want to have a desire is sufficient for expulsion. My criticisms pertain to the claims made about the latter sort of mental occurrence.

10. A similar point of view is expressed by Thalberg (1989: 133–5).

11. Freud (1937) appears to withdraw the claim that the ego originates in the id in "Analysis Terminable and Interminable."

6. Autonomy and rationality

1. It is a mistake to suppose that a person with self-control inevitably exhibits this trait when he *opposes* his appetitive nature, his passions and impulses. A person may be under the sway of a passion he begins to entertain reservations about. Critical reflection may result in the formation of an opposing tendency which begins to dominate. He finds himself increasingly disposed to suppress action on behalf of his passion. The reflection may or may not have a moral character, but in the end, he may come to *reject* these powerful misgivings in one of two very different ways. The more familiar manner is that of becoming overwhelmed by passion. In spite of what may appear to be the conclusive nature of the reasons opposing passion, the strength of the latter is just too much and he succumbs. (There is, of course, a rich literature on the issue of weakness of will which addresses issues I am not directly concerned with.) The less obvious manner through which passion emerges victorious involves the exercise of self-control. Himmler does not simply ask the sadistic members of his staff to let their feelings direct their actions. For he realizes that they, too, can fall prey to certain human "weaknesses" and might be led to suppress their sadistic impulses through reflections upon the excruciating suffering of their victims. So he lectures them on the importance, at these moments of potential weakness, of discipline and strength of will. He asks them to keep their minds set on the goal, to remember their destiny, and not to be swayed by their doubts. They are being asked, not to *submit* to their sadistic impulses, but to act on them as an exercise of deliberateness, as a display of self-control. Even though, in the end, reason sides with passion – the Nazi concludes that a purified Europe is the supremely noble goal – there is enough humanity left in his bones to make it necessary to muster his willpower to continue his murderous ways.

2. Wolf (1990) does concede the possibility that reason fails to discern the Right should there be no Right to discern.

3. Both Haworth (1986: 20–1) and Gerald Dworkin (1988: 18) distinguish, along similar lines, substantive from procedural independence.

4. Nozick describes an ideally autonomous agent in *Philosophical Explanations* (1981: 352–62). And libertarians would like to think that ordinary human beings occasionally transcend naturally based limits and achieve the status of (temporary) ideally autonomous beings. One libertarian who wisely resists the temptations of this line of thought is Robert Kane (1985).

5. Nozick (1981: 354) worries that a rational agent would be bound by his rationality and could not, therefore, be perfectly autonomous.

6. During the last several decades, more and more researchers have uncovered the enormous variety of ways decision makers can behave irrationally. (See Abelson 1975.)

7. It does not follow that IAA would not choose to reserve for herself the power to reject rationality. IAA would not choose a character that is so inherently unstable; but she might still wish to preserve the power to reject rationality in ways that do not lead to self-disintegration.

8. I, thus, agree with Benn (1988: 196) that the ability of Jehovah's Witnesses to preserve their identity or integrity is not, as Young (1986: 16) argues, sufficient grounds to count them autonomous.

9. Thus, Swanton (1992: 133) observes: "The 'vantage point' from which one views motivations may be in thrall to the very oppressive forces which determine the underlying motivations."

10. See Chapter 2.

11. See Carl Hempel (1965: 463).

12. I borrow the term from Shapiro (1981).

13. A desirable result of this loosening of the connection between rationality and autonomy is that it more readily permits autonomous agents to perform acts of supererogation. For an autonomous agent who chooses the moral life may wish to do more than is morally required of him by sacrificing a core self-interest for the sake of others and it *may* be difficult for our best theory of rational choice to sanction the act as rational.

14. As Levi does in (1986: 64).

15. Levi would also have to suppose that a regulative ideal even for an irrational agent would be complete self-knowledge or, at least, knowledge of all relevant facts and values he needs to plug into his principles. If he decides on the basis of a crystal ball gazer's recommendation, he must at least know what the recommendation is and perhaps what information was provided the crystal ball gazer.

7. **Rationality, values, and integrity**

1. Nietzsche's actual doctrines are quite complex and a matter of scholarly dispute. There is always the possibility that no coherent doctrine can be extracted from the writings. For example, although Nietzsche speaks of the overcoming of morality by the Übermensch, he also speaks of the *right* of the Übermensch to exert authority over, even to destroy, the decadent and the weak. Recognizing that the latter conception embodies a new morality rather than the elimination of morality, some scholars (for example, Schutte, 1984) claim that Nietzsche distinguished the higher or superior man, under whom a superior morality would prevail, from the real Übermensch, in whose era there would be a genuine transvaluation of value. But the description of the "character" of the Übermensch or of life in this ideal world is perforce cryptic; we are told that he will embody the will to truth and will speak for life. It is also not clear that Nietzsche is a strict antiobjectivist in ethics. For example, there is something about the superior man which *confers* a right to impose his will on the masses. My remarks are, of course, only inspired by, not an accurate reflection of, Nietzsche's views.

2. MacIntyre (1981: 239–41), in demanding that we choose between Nietzsche and Aristotle, appears to deny the intermediate conception of autonomy I am advancing.

3. As St. Augustine says:

> But whenas I rose up proudly against thee, and when I ran upon my Lord with the thick neck of my buckler; then were these inferior things made my overmatches, and kept me under, nor could I get either releasement or space of breathing. They ran on all sides by heaps and troops upon me, broad-looking on them; but when I thought, these corporeal images waylaid me as I turned back, as if they should say unto me; Whither goest thou, O thou unworthy and base creature (St. Augustine 1912: 363).

4. This view of desires is compatible with the position taken in Chapter 2 according to which desires are one species of motivation. We are here insisting that motives that explain intentional action, even when they are not desires, have affective content. If I visit my mother because "I believe I ought to," the state to which I am referring is not simply a cognitive one. It incorporates, among other things, a disposition to feel guilt and a tendency to dwell uncomfortably on the thought of my lonely mother.

5. A similar identification model has been used to explain directly the phenomenon of personal evaluation or self-criticism. For example, the affect associated with parental approval or disapproval can move a child to engage in self-criticism in which the parent's principles, regardless of content, are the standard for the child's self-approval or -disapproval.

6. Aristotelian courage is more than plain courage according to Nerlich.

> Courage . . . is not mere steadfastness, but a course of action taken under threat to a range of one's values; it lies in a properly considered ordering of them and of the best means of preserving them from threat. . . . Aristotelian courage is a virtue only of persons already quite far-advanced in complex self-appraisal. (1989: 103)

In fact, Aristotelian courage is two steps removed from ordinary courage. For, not only does it presuppose the Evaluation Theory; it also presupposes the correctness of the evaluation.

> The man, then, who faces and who fears the right things and from the right motive, in the right way and at the right time, and who feels confidence under the corresponding conditions, is brave; for the brave man feels and acts according to the merits of the case and in whatever way the rule directs. (Aristotle 1931: 976)

7. Benn (1988) advances this criticism.
8. See Chapter 5.
9. Ibid.
10. See the discussion in Chapter 6.

8. The liberation theory of autonomy: Objectivity

1. I am grateful to John Christman for pointing out difficulties to which the above remarks are an effort to respond.
2. If we suppose that the person automatically makes a transition from the frightening character of the object to the belief that it is reasonable to fear or that it is dangerous, then we would have to deny that such a person *could* know that spiders are not dangerous. But that one afflicted with arachnaphobia behaves as if spiders are dangerous does not imply that he believes that they are – his avowals and betting behavior, for example, show this.

9. **The liberation theory of autonomy: The place of self**

1. Christman defends such an account. See Christman (1991, 1993) and the critique by A. R. Mele (1993). He concedes the objection being made here through the example of one who might "love being able to play the piano but hate the techniques my crotchety old teacher subjected me to" (1993: 289).
2. I have Christman's version in mind. He requires that the person's acquiescence to the process not come about under the influence of factors that inhibit self-reflection which is rational and free of self-deception.
3. Summerhill is a school in Sussex, England, that practices an extraordinarily high level of permissiveness.
4. Recall Watson's (1975) concern that Frankfurt, who places higher-order evaluations at the heart of his conception of autonomy, fails to construe them as evaluations. In noting the importance of higher-order evaluation, Frankfurt sees them as simple desires rather than pronouncements of worth.
5. I am grateful to Robert Kane, who brought to my attention deficiencies in an earlier account of the relation between autonomy and second-order evaluation.
6. Some theorists dispute the viability of this distinction. Hayden White, for example, contends that historical narratives are true only in the sense that metaphors are. He says that "there is no such thing as a 'real' story" and that "*all* stories are fictions which means, of course, that they can be 'true' in a metaphorical sense" (as quoted in Noel Carroll 1990: 135).
7. I have no right to assume that questions regarding personal identity or survival are invariably straightforward factual ones. There may be no theoretical resolution to the many puzzle cases found in the literature (e.g., teletransportation). We may have to embrace White's metapsychological relativism (1991: 160–1) according to which our conflicting intuitions on these matters are explained by variations in social practice which do not themselves admit of rational adjudication. To a certain extent, our views on autonomy would be affected by this doctrine insofar as the capacity for long-range planning would be in part a function of social practice. Thus, although societies A and B sustain equally extensive teletransportation practices, it could turn out that society A has more autonomy than society B just because only the persons in society A regard themselves as persisting through these dramatic alterations and are, therefore, capable of projects which transcend the changes.
8. This is not to say that the determination of wide sense is clear. Disputes about personal identity or unity will bear on this question.

10. **The value of autonomy**

1. I reject Haworth's arguments directed against the contrary thesis (1986: 183–216).
2. See, for example, Christopher Lasch's (1979) discussion.

Bibliography

Abelson, R. P. (1976). "Social Psychology's Rational Man." In Benn, S. I., and Martineau, G. W., eds. (1976). *Rationality and the Social Sciences*. London: Routledge & Kegan Paul, pp. 58–89.

Allais, M. (1979). "Criticism of the Postulates and Axioms of the American School." In Allais, M., and Hagen, O., eds. (1979). *Expected Utility Hypotheses and the Allais Paradox*. Dordrecht: Reidel, pp. 67–95. Reprinted in Moser (1990), pp. 113–39.

Alston, W. P. (1977). "Self-Intervention and the Structure of Motivation." In Mischel (1977), pp. 65–192.

Aristotle (1931). *Nicomachean Ethics*. Trans. by W. D. Ross. In McKeon, R., ed. (1941). *The Basic Works of Aristotle*. New York: Random House.

Audi, R. (1974). "Moral Responsibility, Freedom, and Compulsion." *American Philosophical Quarterly* 11: 1–14.

(1985). "Rationality and Valuation." In Seebass, G., and Tuomela, R., eds. (1985). *Social Action*. Dordrecht: Reidel, pp. 243–77. Reprinted in Moser (1990), pp. 416–46.

(1991). "Autonomy, Reason, and Desire." *Pacific Philosophical Quarterly* 72: 247–71.

Augustine. (1912). *Confessions*, vol. 1, book 7. Trans. by W. Watts. London: William Heinemann.

Aune, B. (1967). "Hypotheticals and Can: Another Look." *Analysis* 27: 191–5.

(1970). "Free Will, 'Can', and Ethics: A Reply to Lehrer." *Analysis* 30: 77–83.

Austin, J. L. (1961a). "A Plea for Excuses." In Urmson, J. O., and Warnock, G. J., eds. (1961). *Philosophical Papers*. 3rd Edition. Oxford: Oxford University Press, pp. 175–204.

(1961b). "Ifs and Cans." In Austin (1961a), pp. 205–32.

Baier, K. (1958). *The Moral Point of View*. Ithaca: Cornell University Press.

Beck, A. T. (1976). *Cognitive Therapy and the Emotional Disorders*. New York: Meridian.

Benhabib, S., and Dallmayr, F., eds. (1990). *The Communicative Ethics Controversy*. Cambridge: MIT Press.

Benn, S. I. (1976). "Freedom, Autonomy, and the Concept of a Person." *Proceedings of the Aristotelian Society* 12: 109–30.

(1988). *A Theory of Freedom*. Cambridge University Press.

Bennett, J. (1980). "Accountability." In van Straaten, Z., ed. *Philosophical Subjects: Essays Presented to P. F. Strawson*. Oxford: Clarendon Press.

Benson, P. (1987a). "Ordinary Ability and Free Action." *Canadian Journal of Philosophy* 17: 307–35.

(1987b). "Freedom and Value." *The Journal of Philosophy* 84: 465–86.

(1990). "The Moral Importance of Free Action." *The Southern Journal of Philosophy* 28: 1–18.

258

Bergmann, F. (1977). *On Being Free.* Notre Dame: University of Notre Dame Press.

Berlin, I. (1958). *Two Concepts of Liberty.* Oxford: Clarendon Press.

(1969). *Four Essays on Liberty.* Oxford: Oxford University Press.

Berofsky, B. (1964). "Determinism and the Concept of a Person." *The Journal of Philosophy* 61: 461–75.

(1970). "Purposive Action." *American Philosophical Quarterly* 7: 311–20.

(1980). "The Irrelevance of Morality to Freedom." In Department of Philosophy, Bowling Green State University, ed. *Action and Responsibility.* Bowling Green: Bowling Green State University.

(1983). "Autonomy." In Cauman, L. S., Levi, I., Parsons, C. D., and Schwartz, R., eds. (1983). *How Many Questions? Essays in Honor of Sidney Morgenbesser.* Indianapolis: Hackett.

(1987). *Freedom from Necessity: The Metaphysical Basis of Responsibility.* New York: Routledge & Kegan Paul.

(1992). "On the Absolute Freedom of the Will." *American Philosophical Quarterly* 29: 279–89.

Bettelheim, B. (1960). *The Informed Heart.* New York: Avon.

Brandt, R. B. (1978). *A Theory of the Good and the Right.* New York: Oxford University Press.

(1990). "The Concept of Rational Action." In Moser (1990), pp. 398–415.

Cameron, N. (1963). *Personality Development and Psychopathology: A Dynamic Approach.* Boston: Houghton Mifflin.

Campbell, C. A. (1940). "The Psychology of Effort of Will." *Proceedings of the Aristotelian Society* 40: 50–69.

(1951). "Is 'Freewill' a Pseudo-Problem?" *Mind* 40: 446–65.

Campbell, R. (1988). "Moral Justification and Freedom." *The Journal of Philosophy* 85: 192–213.

Carroll, N. (1990). "Interpretation, History and Narrative." *The Monist* 73: 134–66.

Chisholm, R. M. (1964). "J. L. Austin's Philosophical Papers." *Mind* 73: 20–25.

Christman, J. (1987). "Autonomy: A Defense of the Split-Level Self." *The Southern Journal of Philosophy* 25: 281–93.

(1989). *The Inner Citadel.* New York: Oxford University Press.

(1991). "Autonomy and Personal History." *Canadian Journal of Philosophy* 21: 1–24.

(1993). "Defending Historical Autonomy: A Reply to Professor Mele." *Canadian Journal of Philosophy* 23: 281–90.

Claridge, G. (1985). *Origins of Mental Illness.* Oxford: Basil Blackwell.

Crocker, L. (1980). *Positive Liberty.* The Hague: Martinus Nijhoff.

Darwall, S. (1983). *Impartial Reason.* Ithaca: Cornell University Press.

Davidson, D. (1982). "Paradoxes of Irrationality." In Wollheim, R. A., and Hopkins, J., eds. (1982). *Philosophical Essays on Freud.* Cambridge University Press, pp. 289–305. Reprinted in Moser (1990), pp. 449–64.

Dennett, D. (1989). "The Origins of Selves." *Cogito* 1: 163–73.

Dworkin, G. (1988). *The Theory and Practice of Autonomy.* Cambridge University Press.

Elster, J., ed. (1986). *The Multiple Self.* Cambridge University Press.

(1989). "Sour Grapes – Utilitarianism and the Genesis of Wants." In Christman (1989), pp. 170–88.

Eysenck, H. J. (1957). *Dynamics of Anxiety and Hysteria*. London: Routledge & Kegan Paul.

(1967). *The Biological Basis of Personality*. Springfield: Charles C. Thomas.

Feinberg, J. (1970). "What Is So Special About Mental Illness?" In *Doing and Deserving*. Princeton: Princeton University Press, pp. 272–92.

(1980). "The Interest in Liberty on the Scales." In *Rights, Justice, and the Bounds of Liberty*. Princeton: Princeton University Press, pp. 30–44.

(1989). "Autonomy." In Christman (1989), pp. 27–53.

Fischer, J. M., ed. (1986). *Moral Responsibility*. Ithaca: Cornell University Press.

Foot, P. (1972). "Reasons for Action and Desires." *Proceedings of the Aristotelian Society:* Suppl. vol. 46: 203–10.

Frank, A. (1952). *The Diary of a Young Girl*. Trans. by Mooyard-Doubleday, B. M. In *The Works of Anne Frank*. Garden City: Doubleday.

Frankfurt, H. (1971). "Freedom of the Will and the Concept of a Person." *The Journal of Philosophy* 68: 5–20. Reprinted in Watson (1982), pp. 81–95, and Fischer (1986), pp. 65–80.

(1973). "Coercion and Moral Responsibility." In Honderich, T., ed. (1973). *Essays on Freedom of Action*. London: Routledge & Kegan Paul, pp. 65–86.

(1975). "Three Concepts of Free Action: II." *Proceedings of the Aristotelian Society:* Suppl. vol. 49: 113–25.

(1976). "Identification and Externality." In Rorty, A. O., ed. (1976). *The Identities of Persons*. Berkeley: University of California Press, pp. 239–51.

(1992). "The Faintest Passion." *Proceedings and Addresses of the American Philosophical Association* 66: 5–16.

Freud, S. (1923). *The Ego and the Id*. Standard Edition, Vol. 19. London: Hogarth Press, pp. 3–68.

(1937). *Analysis Terminable and Interminable*. Standard Edition, Vol. 23. London: Hogarth Press, pp. 209–54.

Friedman, M. A. (1985). "Moral Integrity and the Deferential Wife." *Philosophical Studies* 47: 141–50.

(1986). "Autonomy and the Split-Level Self." *The Southern Journal of Philosophy* 24: 19–35.

Fromm, E. (1941). *Escape from Freedom*. New York: Rinehart.

Gauthier, D. (1986). *Morals by Agreement*. Oxford: Clarendon Press.

Gergen, K. (1991). *The Saturated Self*. New York: Basic Books.

Gewirth, A. (1978). *Reason and Morality*. Chicago: University of Chicago.

Gibbard, A. (1983). "A Noncognitivistic Analysis of Rationality in Action." *Social Theory and Practice* 9: 199–221.

Gill, M., ed. (1967). *The Collected Papers of David Rapaport*. New York: Basic Books.

Gilligan, C. (1982). *In a Different Voice*. Cambridge: Harvard University Press.

(1987). "Moral Orientation and Moral Development." In Kittay, E. F., and Meyers, D. T., eds. *Women and Moral Theory*. Savage, Md.: Rowman & Littlefield, 19–33.

Ginet, C. (1962). "Can the Will Be Caused?" *Philosophical Review*, 71: 49–55.

Goffman, E. (1959). *The Presentation of Self in Everyday Life*. New York: Doubleday.

Gray, J. A. (1971). *The Psychology of Fear and Stress*. New York: McGraw-Hill.

Green, T. H. (1885–8). "The Senses of 'Freedom'." In Nettleship, R. L., ed. (1885–8). *Philosophical Works*, vol. 2. London.

Greenspan, P. S. (1978). "Behavior Control and Freedom of Action." *Philosophical Review* 87: 225–40. Reprinted in Fischer (1986), pp. 191–204.

(1987). "Unfreedom and Responsibility." In Schoeman (1987), pp. 63–80.

Habermas, J. (1984). *The Theory of Communicative Action*, vol. 1. Trans. by T. McCarthy. Boston: Beacon Press.

(1987). *The Theory of Communicative Action*, vol. 2. Trans. by T. McCarthy. Boston: Beacon Press.

(1991). *Moral Consciousness and Communicative Action*. Trans. by C. Lenhardt and S. W. Nicholsen. Cambridge: MIT Press.

(1993). *Justification and Application: Remarks on Discourse Ethics*. Trans. by C. P. Cronin. Cambridge: MIT Press.

Haksar, V. (1965). "The Responsibility of Psychopaths." *Philosophical Quarterly* 15: 135–45.

Hartmann, H. (1939). *Ego Psychology and the Problem of Adaptation*. New York: International Universities Press.

Haworth, L. (1986). *Autonomy: An Essay in Philosophical Psychology and Ethics*. New Haven: Yale University Press.

Hegel, G. W. F. (1969). *Science of Logic*. Trans. by A. V. Miller. New York: Humanities Press.

(1971). "The Spirit of Christianity and its Fate." In *Early Theological Writings*. Trans. by T. M. Knox. Philadelphia: University of Pennsylvania Press.

(1977). *Hegel's Phenomenology of Spirit*. Trans. by A. V. Miller. Oxford: Clarendon Press.

Hempel, C. G. (1965). *Aspects of Scientific Explanation and Other Essays in the Philosophy of Science*. New York: Free Press.

Hill, T. E. (1991). *Autonomy and Self-Respect*. Cambridge University Press.

Jeffrey, R. C. (1965). *The Logic of Decision*. New York: McGraw-Hill.

(1977). "A Note on the Kinematics of Preference." *Erkenntnis* 11: 135–41.

Johnston, M. (1988). "Self-Deception and the Nature of Mind." In McLaughlin, B., and Rorty, A., eds. (1988). *Perspectives on Self-Deception*. Berkeley: University of California Press, pp. 63–91.

Kahneman, D., and Tversky, A. (1990). "Prospect Theory: An Analysis of Decision under Risk." In Moser (1990), pp. 140–70.

Kane, Robert. (1985). *Free Will and Values*. Albany: SUNY Press.

Kaufman, A. S. (1962). "Moral Responsibility and the Use of 'Could Have'." *Philosophical Quarterly* 12: 120–8.

Klein, M. (1990). *Determinism, Blameworthiness, and Deprivation*. Oxford: Clarendon Press.

Kohlberg, L. (1981). *Essays on Moral Development*, vol. 1. San Francisco: Harper & Row.

(1984). *Essays on Moral Development*, vol. 2. San Francisco: Harper & Row.

Kohut, H. (1971). *The Analysis of the Self*. New York: International Universities Press.

(1977). *The Restoration of the Self*. New York: International Universities Press.

Kolak, D., and Martin, R., eds. (1991). *Self and Identity: Contemporary Philosophical Issues*. New York: Macmillan.

Kraut, R. (1994). "Desire and the Human Good." *Proceedings and Addresses of the American Philosophical Association* 68: 39–54.

Kundera, M. (1974). "The Hitchhiking Game." In *Laughable Loves*. Trans. by S. Rappaport. New York: Knopf.

Laing, R. D. (1969). *The Divided Self.* New York: Pantheon Books.

Lasch, C. (1979). *The Culture of Narcissism.* New York: Norton.

Lehrer, K. (1968). "Cans Without Ifs." *Analysis* 29: 29–32.

Levi, I. (1986). *Hard Choices.* Cambridge University Press.

   (1994). "Rationality, Prediction and Autonomous Choice." *Canadian Journal of Philosophy:* Suppl. vol. 19: 339–63.

Lifton, R. J. (1987). *The Future of Immortality.* New York: Basic Books.

Lindley, R. (1986). *Autonomy.* Atlantic Highlands, N.J.: Humanities Press International.

MacCallum, G. (1967). "Negative and Positive Freedom." *Philosophical Review* 76: 312–34.

MacIntyre, A. (1981). *After Virtue.* Notre Dame: University of Notre Dame Press.

Masterson, J. F. (1985). *The Real Self: A Developmental, Self, and Object Relations Approach.* New York: Brunner/Mazel.

Mausner, J. (1990). *Towards a Psychoanalytic Theory of Will.* Unpublished doctoral dissertation. New York: City University of New York.

McBride, W. L. (1990). " 'Two Concepts of Liberty' Thirty Years Later: A Sartre-Inspired Critique." *Social Theory and Practice* 16: 297–322.

McCarthy, T. (1991). *Ideals and Illusions: On Reconstruction and Deconstruction in Contemporary Theory.* Cambridge: MIT Press.

McDowell, J. (1978). "Are Moral Requirements Hypothetical Imperatives?" *Proceedings of the Aristotelian Society:* Suppl. vol. 52: 13–29.

Mele, A. R. (1987). *Irrationality.* New York: Oxford University Press.

   (1993). "History and Personal Autonomy." *Canadian Journal of Philosophy* 23: 271–80.

Meyers, D. T. (1987). "Personal Autonomy and the Paradox of Feminine Socialization." *The Journal of Philosophy* 84: 619–28.

Miller, D. (1974). *The New Polytheism.* New York: Harper & Row.

Mischel, T., ed. (1977). *The Self: Philosophical and Psychological Issues.* Totowa, N.J.: Rowman & Littlefield.

Moser, P. K., ed. (1990). *Rationality in Action.* Cambridge University Press.

Nagel, T. (1970). *The Possibility of Altruism.* Oxford: Oxford University Press.

Nerlich, G. (1989). *Values and Valuing.* Oxford: Clarendon Press.

Nietzsche, F. (1964). *The Will to Power.* Trans. by A. M. Ludovici. New York: Russell and Russell.

Nowell-Smith, P. H. (1960). "Ifs and Cans." *Theoria,* 26: 85–101.

Nozick, R. (1969). "Coercion." In Morgenbesser, S., Suppes, P., and White, M., eds. (1969). *Philosophy, Science, and Method: Essays in Honor of Ernest Nagel.* New York: St. Martin's Press.

   (1974). *Anarchy, State, and Utopia.* New York: Basic Books.

   (1981). *Philosophical Explanations.* Cambridge: Harvard University Press.

Philips, M. (1987). "Rationality, Responsibility and Blame." *Canadian Journal of Philosophy* 17: 141–54.

Piaget, J. (1965). *The Moral Judgment of the Child.* New York: Free Press.

Piper, A. (1985). "Two Conceptions of the Self." *Philosophical Studies* 48: 173–97.

Price, R. (1948). *A Review of the Principal Questions in Morals,* Raphael, D. D., ed. Oxford: Clarendon Press.

Raleigh, J. H., ed. (1968). *Twentieth Century Interpretations of THE ICEMAN COMETH.* Englewood Cliffs, N.J.: Prentice-Hall.

Rapaport, D. (1951). "The Autonomy of the Ego." *Bulletin of the Menninger Clinic* 15. Reprinted in Gill (1967), ch. 31.

(1953). "Some Metapsychological Considerations Concerning Activity and Passivity." In Gill (1967), ch. 44.

(1958). "The Theory of Ego Autonomy." *Bulletin of the Menninger Clinic* 22. Reprinted in Gill (1967), ch. 57.

Rawls, J. (1971). *A Theory of Justice.* Cambridge: Harvard University Press.

(1980). "Kantian Constructivism in Moral Theory." *The Journal of Philosophy* 77. 515–72.

Raz, J. (1986). *The Morality of Freedom.* Oxford: Clarendon Press.

Renick, T. M. (1990). "Response to Berlin and McBride." *Social Theory and Practice* 16: 323–35.

Rescher, N. (1988). *Rationality.* Oxford: Clarendon Press.

Richman, R. J. (1969). "Responsibility and the Causation of Actions." *American Philosophical Quarterly* 6: 186–97.

Rodman, J., ed. (1964). *The Political Theory of T. H. Green.* New York: Appleton-Century-Crofts.

Ross, D. (1954). *Kant's Ethical Theory.* Oxford: Clarendon Press.

Sacks, O. (1993). "To See and Not See." *The New Yorker,* May 10: 59–73.

Sartre, J-P. (1956). "Being and Doing: Freedom." In *Being and Nothingness.* Trans. by H. E. Barnes. New York: Philosophical Library.

Schick, F. (1979). "Self-Knowledge, Uncertainty, and Choice." *The British Journal for the Philosophy of Science* 30: 235–52.

Schlick, M. (1939). "When Is a Man Responsible?" In *Problems of Ethics.* Trans. by D. Rynin. New York: Prentice-Hall.

Schoeman, F. (1987). *Responsibility, Character, and the Emotions.* Cambridge: Cambridge University Press.

Schutte, O. (1984). *Beyond Nihilism: Nietzsche Without Masks.* Chicago: University of Chicago.

Shackle, G. L. S. (1958). *Time in Economics.* Amsterdam: North Holland.

(1969). *Decision, Order and Time in Human Affairs.* Cambridge University Press.

Shapiro, D. (1965). *Neurotic Styles.* New York: Basic Books.

(1970). "Motivation and Action in Psychoanalytic Psychiatry." *Psychiatry* 33: 329–43.

(1981). *Autonomy and Rigid Character.* New York: Basic Books.

Shatz, D. (1985). "Free Will and the Structure of Motivation." In French. P. A., Uehling, Jr., T. E., and Wettstein, H. K., eds. (1985). *Midwest Studies in Philosophy* 10. Minneapolis: University of Minnesota, pp. 451–82.

Sher, G. (1987). "Other Voices, Other Rooms? Women's Psychology and Moral Theory." In Kittay, E. F., and Meyers, D. T., eds. *Women and Moral Theory.* Savage, Md.: Rowman & Littlefield, 178–89.

Stocker, M. (1979). "Desiring the Bad: An Essay in Moral Psychology." *The Journal of Philosophy* 76: 738–53.

Strawson, P. (1962). "Freedom and Resentment." *Proceedings of the British Academy* 48: 1–25. Reprinted in Watson (1982), pp. 59–80.

Stump, E. (1988). "Sanctification, Hardening of the Heart, and Frankfurt's Concept of Free Will." *The Journal of Philosophy* 85: 395–420.

Suls, J., and Greenwald, A. G., eds. (1983). *Psychological Perspectives on the Self,* vol. 2. Hillsdale, N.J.: Lawrence Erlbaum Associates.

Swann, W. B. (1983). "Self-Verification: Bringing Social Reality into Harmony with the Self." In Suls and Greenwald, pp. 33–66.

Swanton, C. (1992). *Freedom: A Coherence Theory*. Indianapolis: Hackett Publishing.

Szasz, T. (1970). "The Myth of Mental Illness." In *Ideology and Insanity*. Garden City: Anchor Books.

Taylor, C. (1976). "Responsibility for Self." In Watson (1982), pp. 111–26.

(1977). "What Is Human Agency?" In Mischel (1977), pp. 103–35.

(1979). "What's Wrong with Negative Liberty?" In Ryan, A. ed. (1979). *The Idea of Freedom: Essays in Honor of Isaiah Berlin*. Oxford: Oxford University Press, pp. 175–93.

(1989). *Sources of the Self*. Cambridge: Harvard University Press.

(1991). *The Ethics of Authenticity*. Cambridge: Harvard University Press.

Thalberg, I. (1978). "Hierarchical Analyses of Unfree Action." In Christman (1989), pp. 123–36.

(1983). *Misconceptions of Mind and Freedom*. Lanham: University Press of America.

Tversky, A., and Kahnemann, D. (1990). "Judgment under Uncertainty: Heuristics and Biases." In Moser (1990), pp. 171–88.

Walker, L. J. (1984). "Sex Differences in the Development of Moral Reasoning: A Critical Review." *Child Development* 55: 677–91.

Walker, L. J., DeVries, B., and Trevethan, S. D. (1987). "Moral Stages and Moral Orientations in Real-Life and Hypothetical Dilemmas." *Child Development* 55: 842–58.

Watson, G. (1975). "Free Agency." *The Journal of Philosophy* 72: 205–20. Reprinted in Watson (1982), pp. 96–110, and Fischer (1986), pp. 81–96.

(1977). "Scepticism About Weakness of Will." *Philosophical Review* 86: 316–39.

Ed., (1982). *Free Will*. Oxford: Oxford University Press.

(1987a). "Free Action and Free Will." *Mind* 96: 145–72.

(1987b). "Responsibility and the Limits of Evil: Variations on a Strawsonian Theme." In Schoeman (1987), pp. 256–86.

White, S. L. (1991). *The Unity of the Self*. Cambridge: MIT Press.

Williams, B. (1985). *Ethics and the Limits of Philosophy*. Cambridge: Harvard University Press.

(1990). "Internal and External Reasons." In Moser (1990), pp. 387–97.

Wolf, E. S. (1977). "Irrationality in a Psychoanalytic Psychology of the Self." In Mischel (1977), pp. 203–23.

Wolf, S. (1980). "Asymmetrical Freedom." *The Journal of Philosophy* 77, pp. 151–66. Reprinted in Fischer (1986), pp. 225–40.

(1987). "Sanity and the Metaphysics of Responsibility." In Schoeman (1987), pp. 46–62.

(1990). *Freedom Within Reason*. New York: Oxford University Press.

Wolpe, J. (1969). *The Practice of Behavior Therapy*. New York: Pergamon Press.

Young, R. (1980). "Autonomy and the 'Inner Self'." *American Philosophical Quarterly* 17: 35–43. Reprinted in Christman (1989), pp. 77–90.

(1986). *Personal Autonomy: Beyond Negative and Positive Liberty*. New York: St. Martin's Press.

Zimmerman, M. J. (1989). *An Essay on Moral Responsibility*. Lanham, Md.: Rowman & Littlefield.

Zurcher, Jr., L. A. (1977). *The Mutable Self*. Beverly Hills: Sage.

Index